FISHING ON THE RIGHT SIDE OF THE BOAT

FISHING ON THE RIGHT SIDE OF THE BOAT

STORIES, SYMBOLS & THE HISTORY OF MARY MAGDALENE

ALICIA ASSAD
AND
KELLY INGRAHAM

LA SUVERA PRESS

FISHING ON THE RIGHT SIDE OF THE BOAT
Stories, Symbols & the History of Mary Magdalene

Published by La Suvera Press
Bedford, New York
lasuvera.org

ISBN (paperback): 979-8-9989518-5-5
ISBN (hardcover): 979-8-9989518-7-9
ISBN (ebook): 979-8-9989518-6-2
ISBN (audiobook): 979-8-9989518-8-6
Library of Congress Control Number: 2026916227

Cover art and design by Gearbox Studio
Interior design and typeset by Katherine Lloyd, The DESK

For Mary.

CONTENTS

Prologue

THE TENTH HOUR OF NIGHT

Dendera, 5 BCE

It is said that color does not rest only on stone.

That what the eye traces, the body keeps.

That when you follow the lines of a zigzag cut into the sign of water, the river—steadied into its symbol—passes first through sight and then into bone.

Always, it is the blue that meets her first, flowing around the shapes that speak their stories. Like the water itself, blue carries the memory of origin. It is the current from which every form is drawn and to which all returns.

It is the color not only of distance, but of the depths from which we emerge.

*

She was born of these waters in the twenty-second year of the last Pharaoh, after a woman who had stood crowned in the sanctuaries, sovereign in her own right, passed into the West.

Mourning moved along the riverbanks, and with it came a fear of what would not return. She drew her first breath then, while the sound of lament was still carried on the current.

Her mother always insisted this did not soften her joy. She received her daughter as a sign the river would not fall silent and kept the old rites within her own walls, even as Rome took the count of days for itself.

She made certain her daughter knew that measure had once been held by a woman and could be again; that flood and field answered to a rhythm older than kings. Raised inside that certainty, she came of age as the calendar shifted and the way of reading changed, yet she did not surrender what had shaped her.

Though others turned toward a new order, the Iteru continued its rise and withdrawal, and the silt line marked her before any decree could.

She has never mistaken what the carvings hold or what the water carries.

She has always known that one does not merely read the walls of the temple—one is written by them.

Kneeling at her work, with a sheet of papyrus held across her lap, she lifts her eyes to the ceiling. Above her, the sky is a body where She Who Bears the Sun is stretched across the lapis expanse, thick with stars. The golden disk rests at her mouth and again near her womb, its course drawn through her as green springs forth from watery depths. Beneath the long shelter that has known her, she holds the image a moment, then lets her gaze fall.

The reed rests between her fingers, frayed and darkened at its tip. This hour has always belonged to ink and breath—when order is set in stroke and held in the shape of a mark. Within her chamber, silence gathers before the world stirs, and since the flood of her thirteenth year, she has kept this vigil in the early morning dark. Through twelve seasons she has returned, tracing what must remain unbroken.

Here she has copied hymns, festival tallies, flood heights, and star risings, learning the discipline of repetition and the humility of exactness. Writing becomes continuity held in form, and a line laid true keeps the voice whole while bearing what it was first given.

The ceilings remain blue. The stars stand fixed. But the naos no longer opens to her or the women of her order. The old signs are now followed by letters entered beside them in a more constricted script, sounding the name but unable to bear its fullness, reducing layered signs to single meanings. The law and the ledgers now move in another tongue and require all else to follow.

The star that calls the river to swell was once invoked in her rising: Sopdet, Lady of the Inundation. Now she is named Sothis, called Sirius, reduced to Dog Star, and set among the hunter's hounds in the sky. The alignment has long circulated; now it is enforced.

But the star is not a dog. She will not write it.

She was given to these inner chambers and trained within them, entrusted with what they guarded. Today, she will not remain where she has risen.

The roll lies open in the lamplight, its edges curling toward one another. Ink sits raised along the fibers, still dark, still alive. Through her work, what is written keeps time in its true proportion, holding the pattern through which sky, flood, and womb answer one another.

Only when the writing has settled does she set her fingers at the edge and furl the sheet inward in a steady spiral, the papyrus tightening into a clean roll. From the inside edge of her linen wrap, she frees a narrow strip and winds it once around the scroll, fastening it securely.

It is her hand that seals the sacred writings and restores them to their place. Not one is set without her. This scroll she binds and does not leave among the others, those who answer to her authority would never imagine her carrying it away. She slides it into the fold at her waist and cinches the sash firmly, certain that life lifts from what the water leaves behind.

Her steps do not falter as the inner floor gives way to the outer passage.

*

The sanctum recedes behind her as the corridor narrows, and walls press close enough to hold her shadow in flame. Offerings advance in carved procession along the walls toward her name—Hathor, Lady of the Sky, in whose keeping the roof rests; Golden One, by whose bearing the sun moves; Mistress of Turquoise, at whose command even the desert gives up blue. Her likeness saturates the shafts as her titles multiply across stone.

At her feet the priests stand in raised relief, hands lifted in worship, their names and titles set beside her own. Lower along the walls the chantresses and sistrum-bearers move in smaller registers, carved nearer the ground, while the men stand closest to her image.

Once, women were rendered in fuller scale, their figures rising nearer to the goddess they served. Now they remain, though diminished. And within the inner sanctuary, those who lift Hathor's image do not bleed for what they raise.

Despite the fear long trained to stifle it, the question rises within her. If her house denies its daughters, what god remains within it?

She slows beside the relief nearest the end of the passage, a face she has traced since she was small. Not the enthroned image within the sealed chamber, but the crescent-crowned visage along the western wall, worn smooth where hands have rested before hers.

Her fingers follow the curve of horn and disk—the calm, unblinking Mother who has watched the river rise and recede, who has crowned the sun above this roof of stone. The form presses forward from the wall with the same watchful strength it held when she stood here as a child and knew herself sheltered by the one who bends close to earth and receives the newborn and the dying alike.

Here she learned the rhythm of return, not as abstraction but as flood that recedes without vanishing, as breath that falls and rises again—even as the air around her has changed. The Lady has not withdrawn. No. She remains where the heart does not divide and the eye does not waver.

For a moment she lays her palm against the cheek, and in that touch remembers what was set in her before she could name it, the current she was born into and the charge carried from mother to daughter. She was not raised to kneel at a distance.

She crosses to the sandals she left before entering sacred ground and knots them with practiced economy. From a shallow recess in the wall, she takes the heavier linen wrap folded there and settles it around her shoulders, fastening it close against the pre-dawn air.

Only then does she reach for the torch and free it from its bracket, already moving toward the passage.

Light answers the corridor's dark, and as she moves, the cloak slips back along her shoulder. Fire finds the gold at her upper arm, where a serpent coils tight against her skin, its head raised, garnet eyes alive with knowing.

The metal is warm, pressing into her flesh as if answering the oath that fixed it there, the mark of her authority. It was laid upon her in the Tenth Hour under witness and flame, the hour when what is written binds what is lived, when night holds its deepest tension and what is given cannot be taken back.

Its weight moves with her stride, and she does not try to loosen it. Some bindings endure beyond refusal. The coil does not divide or reconcile but circles, holding venom and protection, restraint and power, fire and flesh in one unbroken line.

The Tenth Hour is the crossing before dawn. She walks it now while the sun waits below the horizon and the passage continues in darkness, carrying the seal without knowing whether she is keeping it or whether it is keeping her.

The cloak slides back into place, and the serpent disappears from view, though the pressure remains.

Ahead, the corridor widens, and the roof lifts as the air shifts toward morning. She steps from the inner block of chapels into the great hall, where the ordered sky keeps its course across the ceiling, unbroken for now. Columns rise around her, each crowned with the forward gaze of the goddess, while above them the sacred vultures stretch across the vault, the winged disk returning in endless procession.

The torch flares as she turns and the reliefs sharpen: sistrums lift, menats sway, figures advance in procession. Night is held here in sandstone, where time is not counted but carried. Decans rise and fall, and the sun is borne from wall to wall in solar barques, so that return is never lost.

Beyond these walls, time is being recalculated, aligned to other constellations, and fixed to tables that do not remember the river. She knows that pressure will eventually make its way inside. For now, around her, the boats move on in their steady passage.

She does not leave because the sky has failed but because she will not lend her hand to its diminishment.

Her eyes remain forward as her pace steadies into the step of one who has decided.

*

Passing beneath the lintel, she feels the temple give way to air as the carved sky falls back and the open night receives her.

The torch burns small in her hand, trembling in the wind as she steps into the enclosure court.

She lowers the torch and presses the smoldering end into earth; it hisses and disappears as darkness thickens until the court is emptied of flame. Only then do the stars take hold—first one, then another, until the sky resumes its own authority. They require no scribe.

Among them, one rises clean and certain: Sopdet. Bright on the ascent she is not entered beside another name, not confined to omen, not made servant to another sky.

Pharaohs lifted and were laid down. Dynasties rose and broke apart. Through it all, the river kept its season and the sky kept its count. Those were turnings of flood and recession, descent and return.

This is not that.

They may bind her to the hunter's path, call her hound, and chart her against foreign figures cut into another sky. Still, she rises in her place, bright at the edge of darkness, opening the year and calling the waters forward.

What is constant does not become a beast by their naming. Why defend what burns so plainly above her?

As Sopdet climbs, she steps forward beneath an uncarved sky.

Still, the waters come. Still, life answers.

The night opens around her, unroofed, and what was held in stone now moves freely overhead—river and light, horizon and birth answering one another without mediation.

Her breath catches, then steadies. The sky holds its alignment, with wandering stars tracing their long paths, others set deep and steady, and between them the great bodies that govern the day and return the night.

She lifts her gaze northward, searching for the Imperishables. Then she feels it: not a snap, not a break, but only a subtle easing, as though a cord long held taut has finally given way. The weight at her throat shifts. She reaches, too late. The fracture moves through her before she hears it, a sound too small for what it carries.

Turquoise strikes the earth. The teardrop curl shatters. The eye, not of sight but of wholeness restored, lies broken at her feet.

She does not move.

Her mother fastened it at her throat and told her it would keep her until it was time to let her go. But neither of them had known that time would come like this.

The stone was lifted from desert sand and carried by water. It belonged to this land before it belonged to her, before her mother, before those whose names are no longer spoken, held now only in the north that does not set.

She bends, fingers hovering over the broken curve. She could gather it. She could try to set it back into the shape it had been asked to hold. Her hand lingers over the fracture, as something lingers in her, too.

Grief rises in her throat, heavy and unhidden. A tear slips free, and she lets it. She straightens and leaves the turquoise where it fell, the shards catching starlight against a night that does not withdraw.

Her hand slips inside the fold of her cloak to the bound edge at her waist. It rests firmly against her side, held close beside the coil of gold at her arm, exactly where she placed it. She presses it once to steady herself, then lets her hand fall.

She continues on under the watching stars.

Behind her, the temple stands silent, its disciplined flames contained within its walls. Ahead, the lesser gate opens toward the cultivated land. She steps through.

The fields unfold in low, dark bands, irrigation channels holding thin veins of silver. Beyond them, the river moves unseen.

She turns first northward, then angles west in the direction of endings, of burial, of descent below the horizon. The river waits as night begins to thin at the edge of the sky. Dawn is close.

She moves forward as the world widens, carrying what could not remain within those walls—not because it was forbidden, but because it could not breathe there.

Beyond the green band of cultivation, the desert lifts pale and waiting. Somewhere ahead, there will be a boat.

She walks west into the dark that gives way to light, where what endures the night is permitted to rise.

Introduction

ANCIENT FUTURE HEART

ⲡ̣[ⲉⲩ]ⲁⲅⲅⲉⲗⲓⲟⲛ
ⲕⲁⲧⲁ
ⲙⲁ̣ⲣⲓϩⲁⲙⲙ

These three lines conclude a text copied on a papyrus leaf within a Coptic codex from late antiquity. The page is weathered and torn, split down the center by time, handling, or perhaps deliberate tampering—the cause cannot be known.

What can be said is this: the leaf is not a stray survival. It once belonged to a work of breadth, likely nineteen pages in total. Only nine remain. This is the final page—the place where ancient codices often carried their titles and authorial attributions, not merely to identify a text but to seal it. A name at the close did more than label what preceded it; it secured what had been entrusted to the page, as if the act of naming held what had once been spoken.

Rendered in Coptic script, though carrying inherited Greek terms, the closing inscription comes to rest in something immediately recognizable: *euangelion*, "message" or "proclamation"; *kata*, "according to." In the canonical tradition, that cadence resolves in the names of men: Matthew, Mark, Luke, and John. Here, "a Gospel according to" does what it has never done before, yielding instead to the name of a woman.[1]

ⲙⲁⲣⲓϩⲁⲙⲙ

The letters of this ancient word are shaped by Egyptian phonetic habit. The ϩ remains intact and the final consonant is doubled, giving ⲙⲁⲣⲓϩⲁⲙⲙ weight at its close. What this reveals is a name spoken close to breath and held inward, articulated with reverence.[2]

Its form resonates with Semitic variants: Miryam in Hebrew, Mariam in Aramaic, Maryam in Arabic, each retaining the closing -m. That -m persists in Greek Μαριάμ but is dropped in Μαρία, the form carried into Latin Maria and on into English Mary. The ending opens, and something of its weight falls away. ⲙⲁⲣⲓϩⲁⲙⲙ remains denser, less assimilated, unsoftened by imperial smoothing. And it does not summon the "Virgin" Mother later enthroned in doctrine and secured in icon and creed.

Instead, the name in this inscription invokes a figure history has struggled to contain. It calls forth Mary Magdalene, the woman who stands at decisive moments in the Gospel narratives: at the cross, at the tomb, and in the garden of recognition. Her name has been conflated with the unnamed sinner, collapsed into the penitent, tethered to the one from whom seven demons were cast, her memory pulled downward into sexualized shame even as it was lifted into witness. Exalted as apostola apostolorum—apostle *to* the apostles—yet persistently framed as secondary, if worthy at all, and always spoken of in relation to others. Honored. Diminished.

But here, in Coptic, a sacred text is sealed in her name. In these surviving pages, bound in leather, reportedly wrapped in feathers, and hidden as Christianity became empire, Mary Magdalene appears as teacher and interpreter, unwavering where fear fractures the room. Her presence passes into papyrus, where ink traced in fiber fixes her words and preserves the figure they reveal, carrying Mary beyond the reach of those who would later mute her voice and subordinate her authority.

It remains the only known gospel attributed to a woman.

Hidden long enough to be forgotten . . . but not lost.

Before 1896, no one in the modern world had ever heard of the Gospel of Mary.

It surfaced on the antiquities market in Cairo, purchased by a German Egyptologist under circumstances typical of the era: private, undocumented, and difficult to reconstruct. Its origins remain unclear, and its publication history was marked by delay and interruption. Early translators died. Two world wars stalled progress. In 1912, a prepared edition was destroyed when a water pipe burst just before printing. Decades passed before a scholarly edition appeared. English readers waited longer still.

Such a manuscript does not arrive already established. Its very appearance raises immediate questions. How old is it? Where did it come from? To answer them requires patient work studying the handwriting, examining the dialect, considering the material, setting its theology beside other early Christian literature, and weighing its language against related traditions. Gradually, through such cumulative labor, a text finds its historical footing. The Gospel of Mary withstood that scrutiny and is now widely recognized as an early Christian writing.

The manuscript purchased in 1896 is now known as the Coptic Berlin Codex. Copied in the early fifth century, this bound papyrus book preserves the most complete surviving version of the text. Its language, handwriting, and construction reflect an Egyptian scribal culture, a world in which Greek thought moved through Coptic speech and Christian texts were still being collected, copied, and debated. Within its covers, the Gospel of Mary appears alongside other sacred writings, kept by deliberate hands.

That Berlin Codex is not the only witness to the text's early circulation. Portions of the same work survive in Greek fragments dated to the third century, revealing that the text moved across cultural and intellectual boundaries within the early Mediterranean world. They surfaced at Oxyrhynchus, a city whose desert refuse mounds yielded thousands of papyri: private letters, tax receipts, contracts, fragments of Homer, and early Christian writings. Among them were worn copies of the canonical scriptures alongside fragments of other works once copied and read with the same regularity.

What Oxyrhynchus reveals is a Christian world in motion. Texts passed through many hands as they were read aloud, worn thin, and eventually replaced. Some were carried forward and multiplied. Others were condemned, prohibited, and often destroyed.

An estimated eighty-five percent of the early Christian literature we know about has been lost, a figure that does not begin to account for what disappeared without record.[3] Survival depended less on origin than on which voices secured protection, and which were pushed out by the increasing pressure of ecclesiastical authority. Once excluded, a text had little defense. Written words persisted because someone chose to copy them again—sometimes in defiance of suppression.

The Gospel of Mary was copied because, for a time, it circulated within early Christian communities before imperial consolidation. The surviving Coptic manuscript bears features associated with the monastic literary culture of late antique Egypt, suggesting that the text remained in circulation even as the boundaries of Christian authority hardened. Held together in codex form, it survives, fragmented but unmistakable.

Yes, enough remains to show that Mary was read alongside the texts that later came to define Christian tradition. In these pages, she appears as a woman who teaches, interprets, and steadies those who falter. Over time, she slipped from the center of Christian memory. That is how a voice grew unfamiliar, how what had flourished grew rare. Absence, too, leaves a trace, for what was displaced belongs to the story. What, then, did Christianity preserve, and what was set aside in the process?

Canon is not only a collection; it is a decision. Who made it, by what measure was sacred language determined, and why were some texts declared authorized scripture while others were excluded? These questions are not often asked by those who confess "one holy catholic and apostolic Church."[4] Creeds draw lines, and lines, once drawn, divide what had been whole.

The familiar names, Matthew, Mark, Luke, and John, now move almost automatically, spoken before reflection and fixed in memory. What happens when Mary is placed in that same breath, not as devotion or legend, but as gospel? The assumption of inevitability falters, and what now appears seamless is revealed as something once contested and carefully assembled.

The woman who speaks in the Gospel of Mary was not alone. Beyond the canon, women appear as interpreters and exemplars of spiritual wisdom across several early Christian texts. Many of these writings were lost for centuries, until the extraordinary discovery of the Nag Hammadi library in Egypt in 1945. The thirteen leather-bound Coptic codices, copied in the fourth century, remain the largest single cache of early Christian writings ever found. The recovery brought unknown gospels and theological works into view, reshaping modern understandings of early Christianity and altering how scholars approached texts already known, including the Gospel of Mary.[5]

In the Dialogue of the Savior and the Gospel of Philip from the Nag Hammadi collection, as well as earlier-known texts like the Gospel of Mary and the Pistis Sophia, Mary Magdalene appears among women who question, teach, and are praised for understanding. Their insight often provokes resistance from male counterparts unsettled by female authority. These works differ in theology and tone, yet they share a recognizable feature: women speak, receive revelation, and are commended for insight.

Beyond the texts themselves, inscriptions, reliefs, and recurring iconographic patterns likewise depict women in positions of speaking and instruction. The wider record reveals a terrain of debate, divergence, and gradual selection, in which women are constitutive participants in shaping meaning and proclaiming good news.[6]

To understand the imaginative world that made such authority in speech possible, we must attend to the language that sustained it. In the same Coptic milieu, a text known as The Thunder, Perfect Mind gives voice to a feminine essence that emerges in fullness and multiplicity. It unfolds through paradox, giving shape to contradiction:

> For I am the first and the last.
> I am the honored and the scorned.
> I am the whore and the holy.
> I am the wife and the virgin.
> I am <the mother> and the daughter.[7]

This is a form that holds opposing truths without collapse—one to which Mary also belongs. She exceeds any single frame. Her presence draws these tensions into coherence, and her logic follows the circle, moving from past to future and returning, tracing continuity rather than division.

She rises like the thirteenth moon, defying solar arithmetic, revealing the unevenness of time. She spirals like irrational numbers, threading through creation in asymmetrical motion, expanding beyond closure or final explanation. She pulses with the Venusian rhythm traced in Fibonacci growth, both generative and real, yet incompatible with tidy proportion.

These images point to a way of knowing that moves through tension and multiplicity, allowing meaning to unfurl rather than close. When such truth is bound, buried, or set aside, it settles into the ground of memory and waits. What has been forced below the surface does not vanish; it remains there, accumulating weight in silence.

What returns, then, is the uncontained. Beside the version that declared itself complete, the story strains, revealing where it tightens and where it opens. Mary, the one called Magdalene, is the ground from which the story first rose—and rises still.

*

That the voices and memories of women have been suppressed or recast across history is no revelation. But silence has never told the whole story. Women have continued to speak within the conditions available to them—as mystics and rulers, teachers and visionaries, artists and authors. Some have spoken aloud; others have guarded stories quietly, often at great cost. In recent decades, scholarship and creative labor have returned to these traces with care, though the work remains unfinished.

Recovering these voices also brings its own distortions. Erasure reshapes the record, but so does idealization: goddesses without fracture, mothers without exhaustion, saints without contradiction. These figures inspire, but they also lift women out of the human field where authority is lived rather than admired. Against such impossible perfection, women continue to measure themselves. What many women need is to be known within the texture of human life. The desire extends beyond representation toward stories that sustain the soul, stories capacious enough to hold strength and vulnerability, confidence and uncertainty, creation and loss at once.

Clarissa Pinkola Estés gave language to this hunger in *Women Who Run with the Wolves*, naming the figure of the Wild Woman—not as fantasy, but as an expression for what survives outside confinement, carried in the body and the bones. Her language echoes a primordial pattern in which what is dismembered is not gone; it waits for its scattered parts to be restored.

> Bone by bone, hair by hair, Wild Woman comes back. Through night dreams, through events half understood and half remembered, Wild Woman comes back. She comes back through story.[8]

That logic feels familiar now: something is lost, something is feared, something is buried or dismissed. And then, slowly, it reappears—not whole, not untouched, but alive.

To lean toward Mary is to listen with the whole self, soul forward and expectant, stepping beyond the safety of inherited answers and into terrain where certainty thins. It is to turn toward the wilderness places of memory, where stories are stripped to what endures. Recognition comes through fragments and forms that refuse to disappear because they answer a need that has never been stilled. This is the necessity of the heart, that inner place that knows when something essential is missing.

Women share a longing to return to the center, to live from meaning rather than measurement, with worthiness no longer negotiated but rooted in a motherland of love older than judgment. Fierce, ordinary, eternal, the feminine does not demand rescue. She asks only to be remembered. Orientation must be chosen, and choosing requires awareness. Sometimes, as Estés suggests, song is what initiates regeneration. Word by word, note by note, piece by piece, what was scattered begins to find life again.

To follow Mary in this way, attending to what takes shape around her and what moves through her, is to feel the current shift. If Magdalene marks the threshold, *Fishing on the Right Side of the Boat* becomes a vessel, carrying us between text and symbol, history and imagination.

At first there is wonder and recognition. Over time, attention steadies and rhythm replaces novelty. We trace the ebb and return as symbols surface and recede, as patterns withdraw and recur. We drift and breathe in what the light touches. Awakening occurs without drama. Slowly, we find ourselves at home in another landscape, one that was never absent, only uninhabited. What once seemed like mud obscuring clear water is now recognized as fertile silt nourishing new growth.

A woman who lived two thousand years ago remains both ancient and immediate. Her voice speaks into an era once again in motion, when the waters rise and we must decide whether to be carried by surface current or to attune ourselves to a deeper interior force. Her presence insists that her witness be reckoned with, that her stories contain a wisdom not confined to the past, but formative of what is yet to come. Such listening demands patience and the discernment needed to parse abiding truth from fleeting illusion.

When what was sealed as final begins to crack, courage answers. In time, the heart steadies into clarity. What at first appeared as disturbance reveals its purpose. What was once felt to be unraveling becomes the alchemy of renewal.

Often, the way in begins where something has already broken open. Scars become passage. Old stories become doors. Longing becomes a compass, drawing attention toward what still waits to be known. And sometimes, what remains must be gathered and tended long enough for song to pass over it, voice hovering over memory as breath once hovered over bone—until what seemed silent begins, slowly, to stir.

Chapter 1

LA GROTTE DE MARIE-MADELEINE

The trailhead of the Sainte-Baume mountain range is marked by a sign typical of any national park or preserve. Above the map and text, the French phrase *Forêt Domaniale* frames the landscape as protected land set aside for nature, culture, and public enjoyment. At first, nothing about its official presentation feels unusual. Even the limestone massif rising above the dense forest gives little hint of what lies ahead.

But as you read on, the language begins to shift. The sign first notes that the beech, oak, and holly trees ahead are remnants of the primeval woodland that once covered much of southern France. From there, it turns toward cultural memory, explaining that the Provençal word *baumo*, from which the mountain takes its name, means "cave." Almost at once, Mary Magdalene appears as an essential presence, tied to the local tradition that the grotto halfway up the sheer northern face is where she sought refuge and lived out her life as a hermit. By the final lines, the description has moved well beyond the register of a typical park sign. The grotto is presented as a destination "filled with a strong, singular, and often palpable sense of the sacred."

If you have arrived at Sainte-Baume following Mary, you might not be surprised that one of the most venerated sites devoted to her has such pronounced spiritual magnetism. It is as though the very air remembers the centuries of prayer and contemplation she is said to anchor here. You might also be mindful that what surrounds Magdalene is most often not truly about her, but about how her story invites us to search for something within ourselves. For centuries, that longing has drawn pilgrims here to connect with the land once walked by Mary herself, from kings and queens with their royal brigades to the humble faithful alike.

Such is the complexity of searching for Mary on the fringes of tradition and in the quiet depths of the everyday. A woman. A saint. Or a siren's call that reverberates against Provençal limestone like thunder, lingering as a silent echo on the face of a mountain we must climb to find her.

What you cannot see from below, as you begin to walk the golden sandy path toward the forest-fringed heights ahead, is the shape of the Jurassic sediment carved over millions of years. From a bird's-eye view, the mountain snakes through the landscape in a silhouette that has long inspired local legends. Its curves are said to trace the body of a dragon, and from that outline a lineage of meaning unfolds.

Stories of this scaled beast appear throughout antiquity, rising from Mesopotamian primordial goddesses and carried forward through time, eventually reaching the woman some believe to be the sister of Mary Magdalene. In later retellings, it is the biblical Martha who tames a dragon not with a sword, but with prayers, holy water, and her girdle.

Such tales are woven into these lands and help explain why countless followers of Mary have been drawn to Sainte-Baume, whether in person or through the myth and folklore that surround her. Where these stories began is difficult to trace, but they were first written down in the medieval era by a monk named Jacobus de Voragine. Mary's account was one among many saints' legends he compiled, and his text became one of the most influential in shaping her Provençal tradition.[1]

In *The Golden Legend*, the story begins with Mary and her companions cast adrift in a rudderless boat with no sails before landing on the French coast. Should you be fortunate enough to secure a wise guide native to the region, or to linger over a story from an elder in a café with a glass of Côtes du Rhône, you'll come to understand that Magdalene's life here is not considered myth but historical fact. Locals also believe that Christianity quietly took root in France through Mary from the first century onward, a truth obscured both by the passage of time and the persecution of early Christian communities in this region.

Deciding to see what remains of these stories for yourself, you draw nearer to the forest you must cross to reach the mountain. As you do, a desire stirs to see beyond the ordinary. It is then that the field of wheat and springtime poppies along your path begins to shimmer with significance.

In the blur of red, gold, and green, you begin to see her. Gold, the color of royal bearing, of a woman named in scripture as one who supported the ministry of Jesus from her own means. Red, primal and unambiguous: Magdalene as she appears across centuries of art, clinging in fierce devotion at the foot of the cross. Further along, flecks of pale sage stems come into view, their note of green crescendoing against the forested edge as if to harmonize a message of fecundity.

Yes, "fertility" is a word inseparable from Mary and the land charged with her memory. In reality, it speaks to the power of feminine creativity and to hope. Magdalene is both witness to the resurrection and, in some tellings, the Holy Grail.

The cup, vessel, and womb are among the symbols of divine receptivity that swirl around Mary, even though no direct lines can be drawn and no conclusions are easily reached when attuning to her presence. Instead, we encounter the Magdalene through the colors, shapes, and symbols that bring her to life—within the blank spaces of history left unpainted by the full generative force of the feminine. In doing so, we follow her on a trail infused with fragrant resins, herbs, and flowers ground into holy oils, and inhale the sacred scent of a mysterious woman known by her alabaster jar.

When searching for her in art, we attend to what can be discerned in symbols and portrayals. She is not always named, yet she remains recognizable. A jar may rest beside a skull she gazes upon, so we imagine her as a midwife of transformation, keeping vigil for what has been and what is to come. When pearls surround her, they mark the worldly things she renounced to turn toward Christ. So deep was her grief that her name gave rise to maudlin, a Middle English word derived from "Magdalene," shaped by sorrowful depictions across the ages, like a sacred mirror she is often shown gazing into. Look closely, and Mary's tears shift before your eyes, from weakness to alchemy, as grief dissolves into a sea where divine and natural worlds converge in renewal.

As the forest nears, you wonder what it means that a cave devoted to Mary rests high within a mountain set deep within an ancient fertility forest. How should we read the paradox of ascent and descent, womb and summit? Could holiness be sought not above, but within the same earth once worshipped for fertility, now sheltering the memory of the woman you seek? Are the names of lost babies etched in a damp corner of her shrine a continuation of a memorial that has always existed? And what of the lesser cave on this mountain, not far from Mary's but seldom spoken of, a hollow filled with the earth's own eggs, molded by water and time?

With these questions, you draw closer to the shadowed grove, along a path where a tide of crimson petals rolls through fields of gold, carrying a whisper of forgotten truths that invite you into the unseen terrain of your soul. Mary exists in the space between the material and the spiritual, and so does faith—rising where the known meets the unknown, like a wooded labyrinth whose turns may lead you astray before guiding you home.

But first, you must walk the small bridge crossing the threshold into the forest.

*

Even the air shifts with each tentative step beneath the trees. Cradled under a canopy that closes above, the light softens as you draw inward to a space where self and nature become one breath. Awareness heightens as the senses widen to meet the patterns of an untamed forest where the fern unfurls its spiral and moss breathes moisture into stillness formed into a heart on an ancient maple. The trees are vast, with mighty oaks rising like cathedral pillars, flanked by smooth-barked beeches and evergreen yews. Some have stood for centuries in a forest whose origins reach back nearly ten thousand years.

Wandering across the earthen ground where dirt, rock, and roots weave the floor beneath your feet, you are overcome by the tones and sensation of all that is green: lichen, ivy, the lighter olives of spring's first growth unfolding in patterns across wood and stone. Walking with reverence, you begin to notice the tiniest bugs. The black beetles call to mind the sacred scarab of Egypt, known for rolling detritus toward regeneration, life drawn from what has been cast off. You pause to count the spots on the ladybug crossing your path and find yourself wondering whether the number seven carries a hidden message.

Each step trod with an open heart and mind brings you closer to your destination, and the signs that appear along the way suggest that Mary has been with you all along. Yet within the verdant walls, is it Magdalene you sense, or the greater feminine? The forms here curve and fold in the way of what yields and holds, gesturing in openness and return, preparing you for a threshold hidden and inward. A cave is often considered a deeply feminine archetype because of its association with receptivity and containment, a sheltering space that protects like the generative darkness from which life emerges.

Nature has universally been regarded since prehistory as "mother," and as you survey the landscape around you, you feel how "Magdalene" resonates with the sacred feminine within the fabric of human spirituality. Tradition holds that this forest was protected by Artemis, and in some retellings by Druantia, the Celtic goddess-queen, placing Mary in a lineage in which the feminine has long guarded the boundary between wilderness and divinity, keeping the fertile mysteries of the land.

The meandering route offers a sure way through the tapestry of browns and greens, save for the golden yellow buttercup lifting its petaled chalice to reflect the sun. What catches your attention is the flower's fivefold symmetry and improbable shine, the mirror-like play of light, alchemizing its base yellow into the gold of sovereignty.

Arriving full circle in thoughts returning to gold, you catch a glimmer of white rock and lift your gaze to the mountain rising above, where a carpet of treetops gives way to bare stone cliffs.

*

And there you are, quite literally, in the deepest part of an ancient forest, when a turn in the path reveals a sign marked Trois Chênes, "Three Oaks." This crossroads was named for a cluster of old trees where monarchs, mystics, and pilgrims once knelt before beginning their ascent along the Chemin des Rois, the "Path of Kings."

You reflect on how rare it is to find a place of such magnitude devoted to Mary Magdalene rather than Mother Mary or any other saint. Attuned to her story, you begin to notice familiar symbols arranging themselves around her, and a fleur-de-lis catches your eye, white against a blue metal plate fixed to the tree. How charged it feels to find it here, this emblem of French royalty, associated with the lily, a feminine mark of purity in Christian imagination. In First Kings 7:22, the capitals atop the pillars of the First Temple of Jerusalem are described as being "in the shape of lilies," a motif often present in carved cathedral façades, designed to bring that ancient sacred space into the present.

Yet the emblem contrasts sharply with another ancient flower: the lotus. While the lotus is likewise a sign of spiritual enlightenment, its radiance is understood to emerge from darkness, petals rising from murky waters and the mud that roots them. And just as the lotus belongs most visibly to Eastern sacred traditions, the royal lily has become ubiquitous—even commercialized—in the West.

What now seems mundane still carries a trace of enchantment, reaching back to at least the sixth to ninth centuries. Triple-petaled motifs on Merovingian coins, seals, and scepters show the symbol as an early mark of sovereignty and sacred authority. Though fleur-de-lis in French literally means "flower of the lily," its form more closely resembles the iris flower. In symbolism, lily, iris, and lotus converge, sharing a visual lineage, each linked to resurrection, abundance, and divinity.

Why does this royal insignia greet you, the pilgrim, on the path to Magdalene's cave, weaving itself through her story? The stories you have heard about her linger as you navigate the changing path where dirt gives way to laid stone. As the ground turns beneath your feet, the fleur-de-lis seems to whisper of royal secrets. Such is the mystery of the medieval era, when long-buried stories began to attach themselves to Mary Magdalene.

Moving from what was organic to what became cultivated, you begin to see that the confusion surrounding Mary is the narrative she's been clothed in. The fleur-de-lis is both blessing and boundary, a container into which her contemplative image fits securely. Rather than releasing her from the role of the fallen woman, the white flower seems to draw her more deeply into the struggle between light and shadow, good and evil.

The primary legend associated with the cave centers on the most extreme account of Magdalene's asceticism. In *The Golden Legend*, she is said to have lived here for thirty years without food, sustained only by "spiritual nourishment." So the gilded version tells it: "Every day at the seven canonical hours she was carried aloft by angels and with her bodily ears heard the glorious chants of the celestial hosts."[2] Her seclusion is framed as expiation for former sins, making her the perfect mystic precisely through repentance—a broken woman transformed.

These words fill your mind now as the path shifts into uneven, moss-covered steps worn by centuries of Hail Marys. The way rises gently through a corridor of trees, a place where nature and history walk side by side.

*

The canopy of yew and beech loosens, and light seeps through widening branches. With every rise in elevation, the air sharpens as the earthen ground shifts to stone. You remember it was not only kings who climbed this path, but queens, though history records them less eagerly. It is easy to imagine the women who once came seeking the intercession of a saint who reflected something of themselves—one of the few spaces where their devotion could be seen.

In 1516, Queen Claude of France, accompanied by her mother-in-law Louise of Savoy and her sister-in-law Marguerite d'Angoulême, later Marguerite de Navarre, made this pilgrimage to Sainte-Baume. Traveling south to greet King Francis I on his return from the Italian campaign, they detoured to visit relics and sacred sites linked to Magdalene, including this ascent. Not named among them, yet almost certainly present, was another future royal: Anne Boleyn. She was then a young lady-in-waiting to Queen Claude.[3]

Whether documented or imagined, the story endures: a young Englishwoman on the path toward Magdalene's grotto long before her own name would reshape faith and history. How might the image of Mary as pure mystic have influenced these royal women's spiritual imaginations? Did they carry this version of Mary Magdalene with them while seeking the same integrity and perfection they had been taught to see in Mother Mary?

With each lift of the path, the illusions of royalty and striving fall behind you. Kingdoms, politics, hierarchies—all belong to another order entirely. As the trail steepens, you wonder what kingdom is truly being sought.

The pilgrimage grows deliberate as Christian imagery appears with increasing insistence: you notice crucifixes, statues, Dominican seals, symbols accumulating upon one another. Gradually, wilderness gives way to what is ordered and ordained. Before the friars took charge in the medieval era, this mountainside was simply an untamed sanctuary, where contemplatives and local women sought the divine in ways that exceeded Magdalene herself.

Resting on a stone landing, you recall the signs marking this as Dominican territory, and it occurs to you that Voragine, compiler of *The Golden Legend*, belonged to this same order. Because it was the Dominicans who codified her story and who still tend the path to her cave, you begin to wonder who they were and what it means that they have shaped not only this mountain but Magdalene's narrative. As you climb higher, passing crosses and iron gates tipped with spikes, another question arises. What was this place like before it was built up, before devotion hardened into architecture?

The tradition here maintains that Magdalene truly did live, teach, and pray in these lands in the first century. But folk memory does not rise through recorded history, and much of what you encounter here was shaped in the medieval era, its sacredness transposed long after her lifetime. For centuries, the cave was tended by local custodians, the Benedictine monks of Saint-Victor in Marseille, an ancient abbey with deep regional roots.

Following a vision by the king of Naples and count of Provence, the bones of Mary were excavated, verified, and reassembled into reliquaries in 1279. After this "discovery" of Magdalene's relics in a moment laced with political intention, everything shifted. The pope moved the care of these sites of Mary Magdalene out of Benedictine hands, giving "her" over to the Dominicans.[4]

Reaching back through centuries of story and record, you see that this sudden "establishment" at Sainte-Baume came only after Provence and neighboring Languedoc had suffered nearly a century of brutal suppression of a particular Christian sect, the Cathars. The Dominicans were the very order founded in 1216 to preach against them. Now they were the guardians of Magdalene's story. Whether that was accidental or intentional, the stone does not say. But the question, once seen, is difficult to unsee.

The cave comes into view almost before you realize it, sensed first as a quiet alertness. Once a hidden sanctuary for mystics deep within the forest, its spontaneity was pressed into the orderly frame of orthodoxy under the Dominicans. You feel the change in your body as the stone remembers. Its rough-hewn walls breathe an older holiness as you climb the steps carved by those same friars, following the path of pilgrims once urged to walk barefoot, to enter in humility and contrition, just as the reimagined Magdalene was made to do. What had centered on contemplative stillness was reconstructed and reinterpreted around a single theme: penance, the ceaseless longing for forgiveness and release from sin.

As you trace this history, another feeling surfaces. Magdalene seems to point to something more, something as unlikely as believing any human could survive long in a damp cave clinging to a cliffside. Despite the beauty of her meditation, this austerity feels like invention—more crafted than witnessed, more believed than known.

Higher now, the air is thinner and clearer, and you pause, letting your breath catch up.

*

At the top, you exhale, the earth steady beneath you, the dense forest hushed behind you like a world you've stepped out of. Only then do you notice a Pietà—not Michelangelo's marble lament from Saint Peter's, but a leaner vision, waiting like a guardian of the cave's deeper meaning.

Here, Mother Mary does not mourn alone; Magdalene is there, too, at the feet of Jesus, her posture heavy with grief. You feel a flicker of gladness to see her included, yet the image stirs a familiar tension. In art, she is so often on her knees, at the anointing beneath a room of men, or in *Noli Me Tangere* reaching yet denied touch. Always eyes down, tears glistening, sorrow made manifest. But is this how we want to remember her? Was this really who she was?

A new awareness stirs: the forest that held you, the intensity of these Dominican spaces, the weight of stone and silence—all feel like a signal. A quiet insistence that meaning is not inherited but chosen, and that such choice requires reconsidering everything. As that last thought settles, your gaze moves beyond the Pietà to the sweep of Provence, where light and distance feel impossibly alive. Fields unroll in gold and green, stitched with olive groves and a faint blue horizon; the wind carries resin and thyme. Over the hills, clouds build and move, the air thick with the promise of rain.

You are already there, not at the peak, but at the level of the cave you've been climbing toward, where Mary Magdalene was said to have once lived. Turning, you see that the church-like façade built over the cave's opening is not what you expected. In fact, it was Queen Claude who funded the "portal for the cave," shaping the meeting place between raw stone and the Christian structure built against.[5]

Standing here, you see that the story is never cleanly divided between those who color inside the lines and those who don't. Truth lives in the middle, where intention, invention, piety, and power blur. Parsing devotion from design is no simple thing.

If you were to step inside, you would find that what was once a natural hollow has been remade into a church with altars and niches where pilgrims confessed sins and received communion in exchange for indulgences. But for now, you stay, the wind moving softly around you. A small pink wildflower grows from a crack in the rock, opening in a star. You count the petals—five again, like the yellow buttercup below, the pattern returning here in a color long claimed by the feminine. Beauty persists.

You've made the journey, though no one will see that you are changed by it. Looking out across the landscape, you watch the weather form and dissolve. Every climb reaches this threshold, when effort eclipses wonder and you begin to question whether you can, or even want to, go on. Is it right for you? What are you even doing here?

There is no medal, no award, no crown. Is the kingdom without, or within? What did Mary Magdalene believe, or teach? What remains when titles, relics, and stories fall away?

Perhaps her faith was not in power but in witness—in seeing the divine even in what was broken, in knowing that resurrection begins within.

Chapter 2

THE MISSING MOTHER

Beneath an apple tree, a maiden once held a unicorn in her lap. But when the mysterious late-medieval Franco-Flemish tapestry was torn apart, she almost vanished, leaving only part of her arm and a few fingers behind. The two tattered fragments that remain now hang with the Unicorn Tapestries at the Cloisters, the Metropolitan Museum of Art's museum of medieval Europe, housed within a building assembled from architectural elements of French monasteries and surrounded by quiet gardens overlooking the Hudson River.

No one knows who commissioned the Unicorn Tapestries, though theories abound about the "A & E" initials woven throughout all seven panels, including the one with the missing maiden. Do these letters mark the name of a royal patron, the signature of a brilliant artist, or something deeper still? A silken cord tied between the two letters forms a knot eerily similar to the shape of the ankh, an Egyptian character that represents life's essence. This is one of many curious elements within these intricately composed works where each stitch is deliberate, every flower, gesture, and animal placed with extraordinary care. Something seems to move through these woven scenes, something sacred and secret, carried forward in the thread.

Based on their wool, silk, and metallic fibers, as well as the weaving techniques and artistic style of the compositions, scholars have dated the tapestries to between 1495 and 1505, placing them at the threshold between the late Gothic world and Renaissance naturalism. Beyond that glimpse of clarity, certainty gives way to mystery. Neither the designer nor the workshop has been conclusively identified, though most scholars believe they were woven in or near Brussels from designs likely created in France. More elusive still is why the Unicorn tapestries were made, what story they were intended to hold. These questions have animated scholarship for generations, particularly since the masterpieces entered public view at the Cloisters in 1938, after John D. Rockefeller Jr. purchased the six complete panels in 1922 and donated them to the Met in 1937.

The first curator of the Cloisters, James Rorimer, believed the Unicorn tapestries concealed a political and dynastic code revealed through symbols. Rorimer proposed that intertwined letters, the knotted cord, a pair of striped hose, and even a squirrel represented a constellation of clues that together commemorated the marriage of Anne of Brittany to Louis XII in 1499.[1]

Theirs was not a union of love, but the outcome of dynastic obligation—and Anne was no ordinary queen. Duchess of Brittany in her own right, Anne married two successive kings of France to preserve her duchy's autonomy, becoming the only woman crowned Queen of France twice. She was also one of the great artistic patrons of her age, commissioning magnificent Books of Hours, collecting tapestries, and fostering a court steeped in devotion to Mary, the mother of Jesus. Her celebrated *Grandes Heures*, with its exquisitely rendered flowers, birds, insects, and herbs, reveals the same delight in the natural world that animates the Unicorn Tapestries.

Anne's devotion did not end with her. Her daughter, Queen Claude, inherited not only the duchy of Brittany but also her mother's religious imagination, a faith that would later lead her on pilgrimage to Mary Magdalene's grotto at Sainte-Baume. In Claude's world, monumental tapestries such as this set were not simply decoration. These vast textiles were part of everyday life, shaping the spaces in which princes, queens, ladies-in-waiting, and nobles were educated, entertained, and formed. It is tempting to imagine Queen Claude, and perhaps even her young lady-in-waiting Anne Boleyn, standing before these very shimmering scenes, reading the intricate patterns held in their fine fibers.

Yet Rorimer's theory regarding Anne of Brittany has since been largely abandoned by scholars who point to insufficient evidence. As time has passed and the patron of the works has remained evasive, curators have largely shifted their attention toward the tapestries' narrative and symbolism. The unicorn does not yield a single meaning. Across rendered scenes, courtly love, aristocratic identity, the cultivation of virtue, and elements of Christian storytelling all converge. Following the narrative through the panels, the unicorn's suffering and death culminate in the final, and most famous, tapestry, where he appears whole again, enclosed within a circular garden and chained to a tree—a scene long understood as an image of resurrection.

Among the seven, the missing maiden has proved the cycle's most enduring puzzle. While the other six tapestries were purchased by Rockefeller in 1922 and donated to the Met in 1937, the surviving fragments of her hanging were acquired by The Cloisters separately in 1938. Even so, they have always been displayed in their traditional place within the sequence, and *The Unicorn Surrenders to a Maiden* remains the title listed by the Metropolitan Museum of Art. But not all scholars are convinced the fragments belong there. Adolfo Salvatore Cavallo argued that they may instead derive from a different composition altogether, which he reconstructed under the title *The Mystic Hunt of the Unicorn*, noting stylistic differences as well as the unusual dimensions of the surviving pieces.[2]

Whatever its original place, the maiden's tapestry remains unique for another reason—it is the only one of the seven to have suffered significant damage, though the implications of that loss are often overlooked. Curators suggest the panel was damaged during the looting of the French Revolution, when it was removed from the home of the noble La Rochefoucauld family, the earliest owners to whom the weavings can be traced with certainty. Nearly fifty years later, the tapestries were rediscovered in a barn, where they had supposedly been used for decades as agricultural tarps, covering potatoes or protecting fruit trees through the winter. Yet this panel now survives as two halves, the maiden herself almost cleanly excised from between them—her face and body gone. The absence begs the question: was this merely the slow work of time, or something more deliberate?

The remaining large strips reveal a wooden fence entwined with red and white roses, suggesting the maiden and unicorn once sat together in a *hortus conclusus*, an enclosed garden. Within this rose-strewn space lingers a single female figure, possibly identified as a courtier who was attending the missing maiden. This woman's expression is wary, and her eyes are angled toward the horn-blower outside the fence, as though communicating something unspoken. One hound looks upward, poised, while the other sinks its teeth into the unicorn's flank. Despite his wounds, the unicorn sits in rapt attention.

And there she is, only a small section of the maiden's right sleeve is visible beside the unicorn's throat, clearly encircling his neck. Her delicate fingers continue to stroke his mane as he beholds the space where her face must once have been. His hooves likely rested in her lap, and she may have held an object in her left hand. What might that missing detail have revealed?

Perhaps it was a mirror, like the one held by the maiden in *The Lady and the Unicorn* at the Musée de Cluny in Paris. Or maybe she grasped the unicorn's horn, a phallic gesture seen in another unicorn tapestry from Switzerland of the same era. But with so much lost, anything drawn from these tattered threads remains conjecture.[3]

To an aristocratic audience around 1500, the imagery would not have seemed foreign. These tapestries emerged from a culture steeped in the ideals of courtly love—the refined language of longing, desire, and noble devotion celebrated for centuries by troubadours and poets. And the eyes that first gazed upon them would have recognized in this scene the cadences of the Song of Songs, the Hebrew love poem that medieval Christians read at once as earthly love and sacred allegory: "My beloved is mine and I am his; he browses among the lilies."[4]

The double reading of love as both human and divine was old long before the Song of Songs was written. Across the ancient Near East, the bond between the feminine and the masculine was imagined as more than romantic, it was cosmic, a pattern the Greeks would later name *hieros gamos*, the sacred marriage. In its oldest forms it was told of a goddess and her consort, Inanna and Dumuzi in Sumer among the earliest examples, their union standing for the renewal of the land, the turning of the seasons, the very order of the world. The joining of feminine and masculine was how the ancient imagination pictured wholeness, the generative meeting of the great opposites, heaven and earth, life and death, out of which all living things came. Without the goddess, there was no union. Without the mother, there was no life.

The Song of Songs carries this older pattern, and so, faintly, does this panel—the maiden and the unicorn bound in an embrace that is tender and total, each incomplete without the other. But when Christianity inherited the language of sacred marriage, it kept the grammar and changed the bride. Christ became the Bridegroom; the Church, an institution, not a goddess, became the Bride. The divine feminine that had once stood as an equal half of the sacred union was written out of the godhead and handed down to human women instead, to Mother Mary and to Mary Magdalene, who would carry the role of the beloved without the divinity that had once come with it.

In the tapestry, love is what binds the union. It is love that draws the unicorn to the maiden, her presence alone enchanting him into surrender. Even if only her pale fingers remain, tangled in the white of his mane, the language of the Song of Songs and of the sacred marriage fills the space her body left, revealing how indispensable she is to the scene. She is the half without which there is no whole.

The unicorn is largely intact, his eyes gazing up at her softly, even as chaos and violence press in around them. He may have evaded the hunters in the fourth panel, but in the sixth two hunters drive lances into his neck and chest. A great holly tree rises behind him, and at the lower edge a lord and lady receive his body at their castle; his horn, a symbol of power and fertility, is removed. And in the seventh and final panel, the unicorn is miraculously restored, resting gently, horn aloft, his white coat bearing no wound, save for a stain of pomegranate juice.

If the tapestry with the missing maiden was indeed meant to hang between these scenes, its placement illuminates her role—her embrace marks the turning point. She is not only a witness to the unicorn's transformation, but the figure through whom the story changes, moving from surrender to death, and from death to new life. Across the ancient Mediterranean, the Near East, and Europe, the feminine often stood at the seam of life and death: the womb from which life first comes, and the presence that waits at the threshold where death gives way to what follows.

What the maiden's body carries is the shape of a story older than the tapestry itself, a symbolic inheritance that still moved beneath the surface of the late medieval imagination, where the old ways had not entirely loosened their hold.[5] Her mode of meaning was entertained much less easily in stricter ages, when the feminine, embodied in this way, came to be perceived as dangerous—temptation, seduction, suspicion. But when these tapestries were woven, courtly love still flourished in the songs of the troubadours, where love served as the emblem of devotion, fidelity, and faith.

And read from a tighter Christian frame, the missing maiden's role acquires a force that exceeds her being simply the Church, or even Mother Mary. A son and his mother do not embrace in this way, nor is Mother Mary a witness to the resurrection in the Gospels. If the unicorn is Christ—as readers have long understood him to be—then who is the maiden? Who is the woman whose embrace marks the passage from surrender to death, and from death to new life? There is one figure in the Christian story who stands exactly there—a woman in a garden, at the threshold of death and resurrection.

Mary Magdalene.

The tapestry need not have named her, or even fashioned the maiden in her image, to echo her. The pattern is woven too deeply into the sacred imagination to be undone. Mary and the missing maiden mirror one another—women of mystery at the seam between worlds, whose centrality was stripped from the very stories of divinity in which they once stood. And in that mirror something larger comes into view. Each comes to embody the feminine herself, torn from the sacred where she had once stood as primal, creative, and indispensable, leaving behind only the faintest trace of a presence that had once ordered the world.

When the maiden was lifted from the weave, when Mary Magdalene was edited, recast, and diminished within the Christian story, the loss reached far beyond either woman, because neither ever existed alone. The maiden was not removed by herself—she was taken together with her world: the trees, the flowers, the fence, her garments, her gestures, the object once held in her hand. What vanished was not a single female figure but an entire symbolic landscape, every element intertwined, each lending meaning to the others, inseparable as nature itself. And so Mary Magdalene cannot be restored alone either, because neither her meaning nor her authority ever existed apart from the world that gave them shape.

To recover Magdalene is to recover the fullness around her—to widen the view until the whole scene returns. To see the rose-strewn fence: the

Virgin Mary. The branches heavy with fruit: Eve. The forest beyond: Asherah. The flashes of bright blue sky: the many goddesses who came before. And, at the center, the face that emerges through them all: the mother. This is the work the chapters ahead will undertake—not to mourn what was cut away, but to learn again how to see it.

MARY CALLED MAGDALENE

To know the historical Mary Magdalene may be a dream forever suspended in longing, permanently beyond reach. She arrives through blurred and layered narratives, her life refracted rather than recorded. Questions about the life she lived, where she was raised, what she knew, who she was, and what she meant to the message of Jesus Christ remain unanswered. Disentangling innuendo and correcting what is simply wrong have been tasks taken up by many scholars, especially women, over the last several decades. But even with these immense strides toward a renewed understanding of Mary Magdalene, confusion still clings to her image, as though she were almost designed to shift with the times in which she is revisited.

And yet, miraculously, Mary Magdalene has continually evaded the net of interpretation cast around her. As the woman most frequently mentioned across all four canonical Gospels, Mary is remembered, above all, as the primary witness to the resurrection of Jesus Christ. Aside from Easter, and perhaps her feast day on July 22, "Magdalene" is rarely spoken from Christian altars or pulpits. Still, her presence in the Christian story is so pivotal that she appears in the finest art of every century, rendered by master hands. Sometimes she stands where the Bible names her—at the foot of the cross. At other times, she inhabits the scene tradition has long given her as the woman anointing Jesus with sacred oil.

It is well-established that the long arc of Mary Magdalene's diminishment reached its formal ecclesiastical expression in Gregory the Great's Homily 33, delivered in September 591. Preaching in Rome, Gregory declared, "It is very evident, my brethren, that this woman, formerly addicted to forbidden deeds, had used perfume to give her flesh a pleasant odor."[6] By weaving the ambiguities of multiple women into a single reputation, he branded Mary Magdalene as a prostitute. While his sermon likely solidified what had previously circulated as rumor, it marked the moment when a sexualized shadow of shame and sin took lasting hold, lingering even as the Catholic Church has, in more recent centuries, quietly acknowledged the error and elevated her saintly status.

For all Gregory espoused, however, the primacy of Mary Magdalene's role in the story of Jesus Christ could not be fully concealed. Christian tradition relied on her testimony as the first witness to ground the proclamation of a fully embodied, divine resurrection. Over time, Church leaders and writers, especially those later remembered as the "Church Fathers," learned to walk a careful line between acknowledgment and affirmation. Mary had to be named, but not too fully, because the evidence surrounding her pointed to immense authority. And so, dressed in submission and alliteration, the image of Magdalene as the "penitent prostitute" was cultivated across centuries, a construction driven by politics more than piety.

Meanwhile, in the Eastern Orthodox tradition, Mary Magdalene was never identified as a prostitute. Instead, she was honored as an *Isapóstolos*, or "Equal to the Apostles," a title reserved for those who announced the good news with steadfast faith. Nor did the stigma introduced by Western Christian interpretation succeed in diminishing her hold on the public imagination.

For centuries, Mary has captured hearts, her name gracing countless churches, hospitals, chapels, and houses for the poor. Even burdened with negative connotations, Magdalene-as-prostitute became a source of consolation for those bearing the weight of life's adversity. At her lowest, Mary emerged as a figure of mercy, a testament to the belief that no one stands beyond forgiveness. Goodness was always inextricable from her name, it seems, recognized despite the weight of distortion placed upon her.

Even so, the wounds of women's suppression in Western Christian history cannot be disentangled from the story told about Mary Magdalene. These complexities surrounding her image have been explored extensively by scholars, including Jane Schaberg in *The Resurrection of Mary Magdalene*, Susan Haskins in *Mary Magdalen: Myth and Metaphor*, Karen King in *The Gospel of Mary of Magdala*, Ann Graham Brock in *Mary Magdalene, The First Apostle*, Elisabeth Schüssler Fiorenza's *In Memory of Her*, and many more.[7]

The Gospels present a Jesus who consistently moves toward women, speaking with them in public, listening, teaching, and receiving them as full participants in a world that often restricted their voices and presence. More radical still was the trust he placed in women as figures of faith and revelation, with Mary Magdalene among the most prominent. But that Gospel vision of female authority would later be divided.

While one Mary was intentionally diminished, another was lifted into prominence. Mary, mother of Jesus, came to occupy the center of feminine devotion, preserving within Christianity a reverence for the feminine that theology both honored and contained. She held that presence in a carefully framed form. Exalted, but obedient. Venerated, while held secure. Not fully divine, yet no ordinary mother either.

THE MOTHER OF GOD

Ave Maria. Regina Caeli. Blessed Mother. Our Lady. By any of these names, the girl who gave birth to Jesus Christ was likely no more than fourteen years old when she became a mother. Such details are largely lost amid the familiar pageantry of Christmas, where Mary becomes one figure in a story layered with many texts and traditions.

A donkey carries the Holy Family. The innkeepers shut their doors. A star is followed. A boy is born. The baby in a manger is nestled among gentle barn animals, his doting parents bent over him. Humble shepherds lean on staffs as they guide their fluffy flocks to see the tiny king. Mysterious wise men draw near to honor him, bearing gifts charged with meaning: gold for kingship, frankincense for divinity, myrrh for death. A dove, an ancient sign of peace across the Mediterranean, hovers above the gables. Watching, waiting. For all its joy, Mary's role in the Christmas story tends to be overshadowed by these supporting characters. Her role, her labor, in the miracle of birth is rarely centered. The narrative, replete with layered symbols, foreshadows how Christianity would come to shape Mary and the feminine—visible, venerated, and carefully contained.

The richest and most detailed storytelling surrounding the birth of Jesus, particularly Mary's role in it, is found in the Gospel of Luke. In a scene known as the Annunciation, God sends the angel Gabriel to Mary in Nazareth with an astonishing message. "Greetings, you who are highly favored," the angel declares with gentle praise. "The Lord is with you."[8] Initially, she is troubled by his words, prompting Gabriel to calm her before announcing the impossible: she will conceive and bear a son, a king whose reign will have no end. Mary lingers in uncertainty. "How will this be," she asks, "since I am a virgin?"[9] The angel answers that the Holy Spirit will come upon her, and that the child conceived will be holy. It is then that Mary softens into acceptance, replying, "I am the Lord's servant. May your word to me be fulfilled."[10] With this, Gabriel departs.

Traditionally, the Annunciation has been the most pivotal of Mother Mary's appearances across the Gospels. It is certainly the longest and most detailed. Mary's response to Gabriel has been upheld as a model of attentive listening and faithful service, a willingness to enter into divine will no matter the difficulty ahead. However, in *Choosing the Better Part*, Barbara E. Reid probes the delicacy of this story from a woman's perspective.

Given Mary's tender age and the limited agency available to her within divine command, the boundaries of willing consent begin to waver and the language presses the point further. Reid points out that the word translated in the Annunciation as "servant" is not *diakonos*, the Greek term for a voluntary minister or attendant. Luke uses *doulos*, a word that can signify bondage or enslavement. Reid suggests that, alongside its portrayal as a model of openness and receptivity to God, the narrative can also prove difficult for women who struggle to assert themselves or make choices for their own good within a male-dominated world. Where does devotion end and vulnerability begin? And what becomes of women's agency in the space between?[11]

The humanness of young Mother Mary's situation is often obscured by the effort to define her in singular terms. She is, after all, most widely remembered as the "Virgin" Mary, with a capital "V," a title that became her defining attribute in Christianity. Yet only two Gospels, Matthew and Luke, address Mary's conception and virginity at all. Both describe her as legally betrothed to Joseph and conceiving Jesus before they lived together. Betrothal was binding in first-century Judaism, and Mary's young age would not have been unusual for the time and place.

These same two Gospels are also the only ones to include genealogies, and they use them differently. Luke connects Jesus' human ancestry and divine promise more closely to Mary, while Matthew secures his legitimacy through Joseph's line. It is a quiet but consequential divergence. Luke preserves Mary's virginity and Matthew anchors Jesus within patrilineal descent. The claim of her virginity, however, belongs to a more complicated origin.

The story of a young woman conceiving a child both human and divine—not by her husband but by God—may sound strange to modern readers. In antiquity it was not without precedent. Though the details would be debated for centuries before hardening into doctrine, the basic grammar of a god begetting a son with a mortal woman was legible to a first-century audience, Jewish or pagan, even if it was never ordinary.

The Greeks told such stories endlessly—Zeus came to mortal women across a vast number of tales. Danaë bore Perseus after he came to her in a shower of gold, an image Christian artists and apologists would later draw upon. Semele bore Dionysus, the "twice-born" god of wine and ecstasy. Apollo fathered Asclepius, god of healing, on the mortal Coronis, then snatched the infant from his mother's funeral pyre. Some of these children were heroes, half-divine while others were full gods. Either way, the pattern was familiar: the god comes to the woman, and what she bears is more than human.

Beyond these tales of a distant, legendary age, the claim of divine paternity moved from myth to politics. Augustus, ruler of Rome at the time of Jesus's birth, was surrounded by divine-birth traditions. Suetonius preserves the story that his mother, Atia, fell asleep in the temple of Apollo and conceived after the god came to her in the form of a serpent—ten months later she bore the boy who would become emperor.[12] Augustus was called *divi filius*, "son of the deified one," and in Greek, *theou huios,* son of God.

The idea reached back further still, and further south. In Egypt, Amun-Ra was said to visit the queen in the form of the reigning pharaoh to beget the next king, his presence signaled by an overpowering fragrance. The story was carved on temple walls, and claimed even for a woman who ruled as king: at Deir el-Bahri, Amun takes the shape of Hatshepsut's father to father his own daughter, the pharaoh Hatshepsut.

Against this crowded backdrop, Israel had its own tradition of miraculous birth: Sarah, Rebekah, Rachel, Hannah, the mother of Samson, and, in Luke, Elizabeth, who bore John the Baptist. But in these stories, God opens a barren womb within a marriage. He makes conception possible, but he does not replace the father. That was where Mary's story departed from Israel's inherited pattern and entered more difficult theological ground.

In ancient stories of divine motherhood, it was common for the mortal woman to be a virgin when the god arrived. But the way Christian tradition came to value physical virginity, insisting within a century that Mary remained virginal not only before but through and after giving birth, is genuinely rare in religious narrative.

"Virgin" is the defining word attached to Mary, absorbing her persona, forming the foundation of Marian theology. It follows her, hauntingly, overshadowing the fullness of a woman more complex than any single word can hold—a misunderstood word, shaped by a disputed prophetic translation and inextricable from older ideas about feminine divinity, purity, and fertility.

THE VIRGIN

Of the two Gospels that address Mary's virginity, Matthew is particularly insistent. Scholars widely agree that this Gospel reflects the most overtly Jewish perspective, consistently grounding its narrative in Israel's sacred writings, the texts later received by Christians as the Old Testament. Matthew connects her virginity directly to a prophecy in Isaiah: "Therefore the Lord himself will give you a sign: The virgin will conceive and give birth to a son, and will call him Immanuel."[13] At first glance the passage appears straightforward. But it may not say what it seems to, not within its original Jewish context, and not in the original Hebrew.

Written in the eighth century BCE during a political crisis in Judah, Isaiah offers King Ahaz a sign: "Behold, the *'almāh* shall conceive and bear a son."[14] Within the story, this was an immediate prophecy, something to come to pass in Ahaz's lifetime. It promised that before the child reached the age of moral reasoning, the threat pressing on Judah would dissipate. Its concern was eighth-century Judah, not a distant messianic future, and the child it announced was a child of that moment.

There is no surviving evidence that Isaiah 7:14 was understood messianically during the Second Temple period, roughly 500 BCE to 70 CE, let alone as the prophecy of a virgin-born savior.[15] The community at Qumran who produced and preserved the Dead Sea Scrolls and quoted Isaiah copiously never turned this verse toward a coming messiah. Matthew's use of the passage is therefore retrospective, a Christian rereading shaped by the conviction that Jesus' birth had fulfilled Israel's scriptures.

The word Isaiah used was *ʿalmāh*, Hebrew for a young woman of marriageable age. It marks a stage of life, not a sexual condition. When virginity was specifically in view, Hebrew more often reached for *bĕtûlāh*, and even then frequently reinforced it with an explicit clause defining bodily virginity. Isaiah used neither, leaving the intention of *ʿalmāh* open. Yet when the Hebrew scriptures were rendered into Greek in the Septuagint, produced across the third and second centuries BCE, *ʿalmāh* became *parthenos*.

Even in Greek, *parthenos* held a range—maiden, young woman, or virgin. This was the register Matthew worked from, a Gospel written in Greek, reading from the Septuagint rather than the original Hebrew. The narrowing of the word, the turn toward physical virginity, came with Latin. The earliest versions had already rendered *parthenos* as *virgo* by the time Jerome, the ascetic scholar commissioned by Pope Damasus I to standardize the Latin Bible for the newly Christian empire, made the choice deliberate and durable.

Translating the Old Testament, Jerome returned to the Hebrew, the Hebraica veritas, which meant that Jerome was not inheriting the Septuagint's parthenos or the Old Latin virgo without question. He addressed the Hebrew beneath those translations. Moreover, Jerome was well aware that Isaiah had used *ʿalmāh*, not the more explicit *bĕtûlāh* and he knew Jewish readers had long used that distinction to challenge the Christian reading of the verse. Yet he chose to keep *virgo*, doubling down on bodily virginity through translation, and from *virgo* eventually came the English "virgin."

With each transmission, the word drifted farther from youth, vocation, and sacred status, and closer to a verdict on the body. And yet something older still lingered with it, an ancient register in which virgin signaled not sexuality alone, but sacred potency.

Parthenos carried another meaning in Greek—autonomy and inviolability. It was used of goddesses who belonged wholly to themselves, like Artemis: untouchable, complete, answerable to no consort. In this register, virginity was not literal and it had nothing to do with the mechanics of sex and procreation. It named something else entirely—the intuition that the feminine divine did not always require a male counterpart to create. And just as a mortal woman impregnated by a god was far from an original idea in this land and era, the notion of an independently creative divine feminine was ancient, tracing back to carved and molded figures of fertile female bodies, to goddesses who generated life by their own power, to the creativity of the earth, and to the everyday miracle of birth.

Still, virginity could move even beyond the feminine, because in the context of divinity it signaled not only creativity but spiritual purity. Across the ancient Mediterranean, sexual abstinence was understood as a condition of ritual cleanness, a clearing of the channel between the human and the divine. In temples across Rome, Greece, and beyond, those who served the gods most closely were often required to set ordinary bonds of marriage and childbearing aside, as though sacred service demanded a body set apart from the claims of domestic life. Virginity was not moral, it was consecration, a life withheld from ordinary use and given over to the divine.

So when Mary came to be called a miraculous "virgin" and the "Mother of God," her portrayal emerged within a world already fluent in the symbolic language of feminine creativity. Christianity did not invent the sacred *parthenos*, it inherited the image and radically redefined it. What had once signified feminine autonomy and self-generating divine power became, in Mary, a statement about sexual purity. She was exalted beyond all women and at the same time severed from the older lineage of goddesses whose creative authority had belonged to them by nature.

Mary could carry the divine into the world, but the source of creation was no longer imagined as feminine. Her motherhood was declared divine even as her humanity was steadily abstracted away, her virginity elevated until little room remained for the ordinary, embodied realities of motherhood at all.

THEOTOKOS

Eyes lifted, hands raised, frontal, even bearing objects of ritual and respect—this is how female figures, including Mother Mary, appear in the earliest surviving Christian art. In *Mary and Early Christian Women: Hidden Leadership*, Ally Kateusz traces this recurring visual grammar of authority: Mary at the center, sometimes draped in a pallium-like garment later associated with episcopal office. The language was not reserved for Mary alone. Kateusz finds women marked with the same signs of authority in art from the heart of Old Saint Peter's Basilica to churches and objects across the Mediterranean—one fourth-century plaque showing a female figure with uplifted hands, inscribed "Virgin Mary, Minister of the Jerusalem Temple."[16]

Kateusz reads these images through what she calls female bio-power: the way a culture's rules about the body—whether a woman may raise her arms in prayer or must lower them, whether she may stand or must kneel, whether she may speak at all, whether she may meet another's eyes or must drop her gaze—are mapped onto the female form to govern it. Iconography, in this reading, is not decoration but instruction. And across the centuries, the instruction changed. Kateusz follows the gestures of these women as they shift, showing how the figures who once stood upright, gaze steady, hands lifted in sacred authority, are gradually drawn downward—head bowed, hands folded, eyes lowered.

As she puts it, when scribes and artists remade Mary "from an arms-raised liturgical leader to a silent woman who physically expressed her submission by looking at the floor,"[17] something dramatic had changed in the cultural ideal held up to women themselves. The posture changed because the theology did—art and literature moving in step with consolidating doctrine. The commanding Mary gave way to the Mary of Luke's Annunciation, defined above all by consent, her shaping inextricable from another woman, one marked instead by dissent—Eve.

The Mary-and-Eve counterpart was the work of the second-century Fathers, who extended the typology to the two women with one bound to fracture, the other to repair. Justin Martyr drew it first, in the *Dialogue with Trypho*: "Eve, who was a virgin and undefiled, having conceived the word of the serpent, brought forth disobedience and death. But the Virgin Mary received faith and joy . . . and she replied, 'Be it unto me according to thy word.'"[18] A generation later, Irenaeus of Lyons, one of the principal architects of orthodoxy, gave the parallel its full theological force, naming Mary the new Eve. In *Against Heresies*, he wrote that as Eve, "having indeed a husband, Adam, but being nevertheless as yet a virgin . . . was made the cause of death, both to herself and to the entire human race; so also did Mary . . . by yielding obedience, become the cause of salvation, both to herself and the whole human race."[19]

The cause of death to the whole human race, or obedience unto salvation—this was the starkness with which feminine roles were being drawn. Increasingly, the Church Fathers extolled perpetual virginity and moral purity, holding up Mary as the exemplar and model for Christian womanhood. And in this process of dogmatic development, Mary's motherhood became central to Christianity's most destabilizing question: how could Jesus be both fully human and fully divine?

If divinity took form in Mary's womb, defining the Son required defining the mother. As the debate moved from letters into imperial councils, Mary acquired technical vocabulary. Was she Theotokos, "God-bearer," or merely Christotokos, "Christ-bearer"? The first affirmed that the one she conceived was fully divine from the beginning. The second implied a division between Christ's humanity and divinity. Beneath the words stirred imperial anxieties and the ambitions of bishops.

Early in the fifth century, Nestorius, newly made Patriarch of Constantinople, resisted Theotokos and collided with Cyril of Alexandria, a combative bishop who defended his authority with relentless force. Their fight was no refinement of nuance but a war of denunciations and forged alliances. By now the Mary under contest bore little resemblance to the woman who mothered Jesus as her title had become a battleground for the future of the faith. At the Council of Ephesus in 431, Cyril moved first, opening proceedings before Nestorius's allies arrived and securing his condemnation. Mary was declared Theotokos, and the full divinity of Christ became the Church's official position.[20]

For centuries, Ephesus had been one of the great sacred cities of the ancient world, home to the Temple of Artemis, counted among the Seven

Wonders. Pilgrims came from across the Mediterranean to honor Artemis Ephesia, a goddess far larger and stranger than the Greek huntress alone. Many-breasted, many-named, and rooted in older Anatolian mother traditions, she carried echoes of Cybele and the great mother goddesses of the region. Her temple was not a local shrine but a vast religious, civic, and economic center, the heart around which the city's identity had long been formed. So to enthrone Mother Mary seems less likely to be coincidence than continuity, or even challenge. The ancient archetype of the mother carried quietly into a new name, one divine mother written over another.

As Christianity grew, Mother Mary merged with the divine feminine wherever she traveled, absorbing local myths and titles woven into the land since time immemorial. Organic devotion buoyed her even as ecclesiastical authority controlled her image. Crowned with stars and haloed in gold, she accumulated the symbols of heavenly glory through the medieval and Renaissance centuries. The Reformation then recoiled, curtailing her veneration in the name of Christ alone, and with it faded the most visible female face of the sacred.

A FORGOTTEN MOTHERHOOD

It is very likely that Mother Mary carried and raised more than one child—a possibility that could ground her identity in the ordinary rhythms of motherhood, in all their inherent sacredness. Pregnancy, labor, nursing, nurture, joy, loss, discipline, and resilience, all of this could be carried by her image, if she were acknowledged for the humanity of her motherhood. Yet she is not, even while the scriptures themselves suggest she had more children, that Jesus had siblings.

References to Jesus' "brothers" appear across all three Synoptic Gospels of Matthew, Mark, and Luke. Paul the Apostle, the early Jewish follower of Jesus whose letters comprise a weighty portion of the New Testament, likewise wrote that he "saw none of the other apostles except James, the Lord's brother."[21] The Greek term *adelphoi* can mean brothers, but it can extend to kin, cousins, or close relatives. These references are neither obscure nor isolated within the text, yet they have often been minimized or reinterpreted, though the historical question remains open.

While modern Christianity has largely set aside the texture of Mary's human motherhood, early Christian imagination sought to fill the silences left by the Gospels surrounding Jesus' childhood. A second-century text, the Protoevangelium of James, describes how Mary's pregnancy was marked by tension. Joseph feared scandal, a midwife was summoned, and Mary's labor was vulnerable, the narrative lingering over her body and the risks of childbirth. Another second-century work, the Infancy Gospel of Thomas, portrayed Jesus as a miraculous yet mischievous child tended by Mother Mary. While Jesus fashions birds from clay, unsettling the neighbors and confounding teachers, Mary is present and protective. She questions him, corrects him, and worries over the consequences of his power, her interior life recognizable to any mother.

In first-century Jewish households, mothers carried the faith—teaching the prayers, reciting the psalms, guarding the stories. Jesus' earliest memories of God would have come through Mary's voice, an essential and formative part of her role in his life and ministry, and one far too often unseen. Their bond surfaces even at the end, in the Gospel of John, where among his final words on the cross Jesus entrusts his mother's care to the disciple whom he loved. The moment is brief, but it preserves something the doctrine would later bury. Before Mary was a symbol, she was a mother watching her child suffer.

That grief is what Michelangelo's Pietà renders so unbearably—not the serenity of a queen of heaven, but the oldest human sorrow, a mother holding the body of her son. She cradles him as she must once have cradled him as an infant, and the marble insists on what the councils had abstracted away. She was not sinless statuary but a woman who had borne this child, and now held him in death. Her motherhood, elevated out of reach by Theotokos, returns here in stone—not her perfection, but her loss.

And then, in the traditions surrounding her own death, called the Dormition, told in narrative and painted in icon, it was her son who came for his mother. Christ descended to receive her soul, and the images rendered her as a swaddled infant, wrapped and held in his arms. The Madonna and Child was reversed—the one who was now carrying, the mother who gave him life now gathered like a newborn into his arms. Mary's death was imagined not as an ending but as a birth, a tender answer the early

Christian imagination gave to a life doctrine had lifted into abstraction. At last, mother and son were embracing, reunited in heaven together.

When Mary's influence on Jesus is fully considered, more questions naturally arise about the value of women as mothers to both sons and daughters, about the immensity of the impact a mother has on her child's life. How did Mary come to shape Jesus—who he became, what he taught, who he was? Did the wisdom of the woman who raised him extend throughout his ministry? Was he formed by heaven alone—or also by her?

The tenderness he showed the sick. The respect he extended to women. The gentleness and compassion he shared with people of all walks of life. Are these the marks of Jesus' own divinity? Or are these the signatures of a human mother, found present in his attitudes, his gestures, his stories, his beliefs, his teachings? Beyond royal lineage, or sanctified purity, what in Jesus was formed in the vastness of his mother's love?

As her aura of flawlessness expanded, Mary carried the burden of an impossible contradiction. She was to be entirely humble and wholly ordinary, yet stripped of the emotional depth, contradiction, and vulnerability such a life entails. Proclaimed the "Mother of God," she was not herself divine, but strangely suspended between humanity and God. This pressure, cultivated through Mary, continues to shape the lives of women, not only within Christianity but across Western culture, even as she remains a source of comfort and divine support.

And yet Mary is only the latest mother to be narrowed and contained. The same diminishment runs backward through the tradition, older than Bethlehem, older than the Gospels—reaching to the first mother, and beyond her, to a feminine divinity the tradition would labor to forget.

MOTHER OF LIFE

Mothers create, and creation stories bear the marks of what a culture has gestated, the ways it has conceived, carried, and struggled to understand human life. Within Judaism and Christianity, the primary account of humanity's first making comes through Genesis, the opening book of the Tanakh, received by Christians as the Old Testament. With the first ideas of humans come the first ideas of the feminine, and here the scriptures themselves differ sharply from the interpretations later cast upon them. These stories were never created in isolation. They were imbued with symbols carried from the farthest reaches of antiquity.

Genesis is preserved among the Dead Sea Scrolls in some of its earliest known manuscript witnesses, with fragments copied in the third and second centuries BCE. Yet scholars widely regard the text as the culmination of many centuries of oral tradition, its present form likely taking shape during the sixth or fifth centuries BCE. That places its composition within the Babylonian Exile and its aftermath, when Israel was forced into sustained contact with Mesopotamian civilizations whose myths reached back millennia.

The modern insistence that Genesis be read as documentary history, a literal record of how the world began, would have puzzled its earliest hearers. Waters, gardens, serpents, sacred fruit, and floods were creative materials that transcended Israel, appearing across the literature and art of the wider world. The Babylonian *Enuma Elish* and the flood epic of Gilgamesh were already ancient when Israel's scribes set down their own account of beginnings, and the parallels are unmistakable: watery chaos, the ordering of the world, the deluge and the saved remnant. Older still is the visual vocabulary. On Mesopotamian cylinder seals carved centuries before Genesis, the same charged elements appear repeatedly—a seated figure reaching toward a fruit-bearing tree, another figure opposite, a serpent rising behind.[22]

The communities that shaped Genesis were not inventing from nothing. They were composing memory, meaning, and theology in dialogue with this older world, sometimes echoing it, sometimes answering it. And it is precisely when Genesis is read against that world, and followed closely in its own Hebrew, that a different feminine emerges. The subordination later built upon these chapters rests, again and again, on the translation and interpretation of a single word.

After the days of creation and the seventh of rest, moisture rises from the earth and God forms a being: "The Lord God formed *ha-'ādām* from the dust of the ground and breathed into his nostrils the breath of life, and *ha-'ādām* became a living being."[23] Later readers heard this first creature as "man," a male individual. But *ha-'ādām* is the human drawn from *adamah*, the soil, the earth-creature, bound to the ground from which it came, its sex not yet the point. Genesis had already said as much in its own account, making humanity "male and female" together and at once. An entire theology of female subordination has been built on a sequence the text does not clearly give.

Eden follows—rivers shaped through the land, abundance named, the boundary set between the tree of life and the tree of the knowledge of good and evil. Only after this does the divine voice declare: "It is not good for the man to be alone. I will make an *ezer kĕnegdô*."[24] This phrase has carried immense consequences, most often translated as "helper," a word worn by centuries of domestic expectation. But *ezer* is not a servant-word. Elsewhere in Hebrew scripture it names God's own saving strength, the aid that rescues and sustains. Paired with *kĕnegdô*, the phrase suggests not an assistant beneath the man but a strength corresponding to him, a power standing face to face. Yet as with *ʿalmāh* in Isaiah, the passage from Hebrew into Latin changed a woman's fate. In the Vulgate, *ezer* became *adiutorium*, "assistant."

Then there is the infamous rib: "Then the Lord God made a woman from the rib he had taken out of the man, and he brought her to the man."[25] But the Hebrew rendered "rib" is *ṣēlāʿ*, a word that, as Lizzie Berne DeGear observes, almost everywhere else in Hebrew scripture means "side," often the side of sacred architecture, the chambers of the tabernacle that houses the divine presence. It is not the ordinary word for a small anatomical bone. It carries structure, support, consecrated space. And in the ancient imagination, DeGear notes, inner sanctuaries of temples were described in womb-like terms. Read within that resonance, *ṣēlāʿ* begins to make sense not as a spare bone but as the side, chamber, the generative interior from which life emerges.[26]

The body itself confirms the strangeness of the literal reading. Men and women possess the same number of ribs, and ancient people knew this. What distinguishes the female body is not a missing bone but the capacity to bear life. And the line that follows, "the two shall become one flesh," deepens the symbolism. What is taken from the first human and given to the woman enables union, embodiment, and the bringing-forth of life. Read in this light, the logic coheres far more closely with womb than with rib.

To replace the organ of female creativity with an expendable bone is no small choice. It makes the woman derivative, secondary, fashioned from a man's spare parts rather than drawn from the same original mystery and made for a creative power uniquely her own. And because the substitution arrives clothed as sacred scripture, her subordination begins to look divinely ordained. With one word, the Hebrew's stranger vision of divided humanity seeking reunion gives way to a portrait of the feminine as God's afterthought.

This change in language prepares the ground for what comes next: the garden, the fruit, and the fall. It is there, at the threshold of that story, that the woman finally receives her name as Ḥawwāh, the mother of all living. Yet as it passed from Hebrew into Greek, Latin, and English, that living meaning was lost, the name still familiar to the ear but severed from its root, until the mother of all living would be remembered for something else entirely.

MOTHER OF SIN

With Eve, the story returns to the garden, the place where the fracture is said to have occurred, at least in Christian imagination. But that was not necessarily the intention of ancient Israelite people and scribes who shaped this story. This narrative functions as what scholars call an etiology, a form of creation story crafted to explain why the world is the way it is. Why do bad things happen? Why do suffering and hardship persist? Why are violence and death woven into the fabric of human existence?

Jewish theologians have long interpreted Eve, the serpent, and the fruit not as the beginning of permanent corruption, but as a story of choice, consequence, and the long arc of repair. The Hebrew word *ḥaṭa'*, translated as "sin," literally means to miss the mark, to go astray, to err, to make a mistake. Not a trivial one, but a human one. Eve's act was disobedient, yes, but within the narrative it has often been read as a moral awakening as much as a transgression, opening the way to consequence and repair. In Judaism, this work of repair is called *teshuvah*: return, restoration, the disciplined turning back to God. Eve was generally understood in Jewish tradition as a figure of folly rather than of cosmic fall, and she largely remains so.

Only one surviving pre-Christian Hebrew text approaches the notion that Eve's mistake carried consequences for humanity. In the Wisdom of

Ben Sira, also known as Ecclesiasticus or Sirach, composed around 180 BCE in Jerusalem, the sage writes, "From a woman sin had its beginning, and because of her we all die."[27] The line is severe, but even there the broader passage concerns wives and household order, not inherited guilt. Scholars even dispute whether "a woman" refers to Eve at all rather than to a bad wife.

In the Gospels, Jesus never addresses Eve, not as the origin of sin, not as the reason for his mission. When he turns to Genesis, he assigns no blame. He recalls instead that "from the beginning" male and female were created together and joined as one. The reinterpretation of Eve begins with Paul.

Facing a question the Church too would struggle to answer, why Jesus had come, and how his death could be read within Israel's story of God, Paul reached for Genesis and set in motion the metaphor that would become central to Christian theology, Christ as the "last Adam." But it is Adam, not Eve, who carries death in Paul's argument. In Romans and First Corinthians, sin and death enter the world through the man; Eve appears only briefly, as a warning about deception. Elsewhere Paul's letters gesture toward an openness the later tradition would forget: "There is neither Jew nor Gentile, neither slave nor free, nor is there male and female, for you are all one in Christ Jesus."[28]

Then there is First Timothy: "Let a woman learn in silence with full submission.... For Adam was formed first, then Eve; and Adam was not deceived, but the woman was deceived and became a transgressor."[29] For centuries these words would sanctify the silencing of women. But Paul did not write them. Broad scholarly consensus identifies First Timothy as pseudonymous, a later writer attributing his work to an authoritative name, less as forgery than as a way of anchoring new instruction in respected weight. Of the thirteen letters bearing Paul's name, only seven are undisputed; the rest are contested or considered pseudonymous.[30]

The language of First Timothy is pointed, polemical, written not in anticipation of female authority but in reaction against its visible presence. It is commonly dated to the late first or second century, an era when women were patrons, prophets, teachers, and leaders. Notably, this is also the period to which the Gospel of Mary is often dated, with its preservation of Mary Magdalene's female authority. By placing Paul's name on this letter, the author gave the text a power it might never have commanded on its own, and from there it would shape centuries of doctrine about Eve, Mary, and all Christian women.

For a time, gentler readings prevailed. Origen of Alexandria read Adam and Eve allegorically, as figures of the human soul. A century later, Ephrem the Syrian still described Eve with a tenderness that would grow rare, not as the source of corruption but as wounded innocence longing for restoration, blessed as the mother of the lineage through whom redemption would come. These were the roads not taken.[31]

Tertullian, writing at the turn of the second century into the third, extended Eve's act to all women with biting force: "Do you not know that you are each an Eve? . . . You are the devil's gateway."[32] A century on, John Chrysostom turned Eve into household law, teaching that women's obedience ran from pew to home, wives to yield, daughters to be disciplined.[33] And Jerome, the same scholar who rendered *ʿalmāh* as *virgo*, ranked marriage and motherhood far below virginity, each tainted by its nearness to the body: "I praise wedlock, I praise marriage," he wrote, "but only because they give me virgins."[34]

Eve was no longer a character in Genesis but a mandate. Each Father systematized the suspicion of those before him, until the inheritance reached the one who would fix it permanently in the foundations of Western Christianity: Augustine of Hippo.

MOTHER OF DEATH

There are moments in a life that ordinarily stay private, and among the most private are a person's earliest sexual experiences. This was especially true in antiquity, long before the memoir (or social media) had become a way of speaking openly about oneself. But some people are ahead of their time, or simply more forthcoming than others, and the Church Father Augustine of Hippo was one such man. In an autobiographical work of startling candor, the Confessions, he laid bare the intimate experiences of his youth, inadvertently offering a psychological backdrop for the theology he would later make foundational to Christian thought.

In his essay, "How St. Augustine Invented Sex," Stephen Greenblatt has explored how one such experience, remembered across decades, worked its way into that architecture. In the year 370, in the provincial town of Thagaste in Roman North Africa, a sixteen-year-old Augustine went with his father to the public baths. His father, Patricius, noticed the signs of his son's puberty—a stirring of the body, an involuntary arousal—and was, in Sarah Ruden's translation, "over the moon" at the prospect of grandchildren.[35] It was an unremarkable moment between a father and an adolescent son, the kind that usually stays buried in private memory. But Augustine would not only remember it for the rest of his life—he would set it down for the world.

To trace this moment and the others he confessed, and to hold them against the theology he built, is to see how central his own sexuality would be to his worldview—one that would not remain personal, but became universal. From such moments—the body moving on its own, without the consent of the will—Augustine constructed a theology that bequeathed to the West, in Greenblatt's words, "the conviction that there is something fundamentally damaged about the entire human species."[36] A boy's involuntary arousal, witnessed in a bathhouse, would become the cornerstone of a doctrine that subordinated women for a thousand years.

That worldview was shaped, first, by women, and by his fraught relations with them. One stands at the center of the *Confessions*: Monica, his fiercely Christian mother, who wept for his conversion, pursued him across cities, and pressed relentlessly upon his conscience. Her influence reached even into his intimate life. For fourteen years Augustine lived with a woman he never names, the mother of his son. At Monica's urging, he dismissed her so that a more advantageous marriage could be arranged. But the intended bride was too young to wed, and by then Augustine had begun turning toward renunciation altogether. He described the turmoil as being torn within, and staged it in the Confessions as a contest between lust and a radiant figure he called Lady Continence, beckoning him toward celibacy. It was to her, a woman of purity who lived only in his imagination, that he credited his deliverance from the appetites of the flesh.[37]

Augustine would become a bishop, and one of the principal architects of Western Christian theology, building his ideas of sin, grace, and sexuality on a foundation laid by these women and his recoil from them. His suspicion of the body had philosophical roots as well. For nearly a decade before his conversion he had belonged to Manichaeism, a third-century Persian religion that cast the cosmos as a war between light and darkness, with sexual reproduction an entanglement of the soul in matter. Though he rejected its cosmology, the dualism lingered, reinforced by his formation in Platonism and Neoplatonism—frameworks that likewise raised spirit above matter.

What fixed Augustine's attention, Greenblatt argues, was not sexual maturity itself but its involuntary character—the aroused body moving without the will's consent, genitals rising unbidden or failing when summoned. To Augustine this was not a curiosity but a wound, one he read into the creation story. Earlier Christians had interpreted Genesis many ways, but Augustine fixed it in place. It was Augustine who lifted the story of Adam and Eve out of the embarrassed neglect into which it had fallen and made it central—carrying, in Greenblatt's phrase, "principal responsibility for its prominence" in Western thought.[38]

Reading in Latin, through the language of female subordination Jerome had penned, Augustine approached Adam and Eve not as archetypes but as historical figures, the literal first parents of humanity, whose disobedience altered the human condition. The garden ceased to be a symbol and became an event. He went further still, asking in what sense a woman could be a "helper" to a man at all. Not for labor, he reasoned, since a male helper would serve better and not for companionship, since two male friends could "enjoy companionship and conversation in a life shared together" more agreeably than a man and a woman. Only one purpose remained: "I do not see in what sense the woman was made as a helper for the man if not for the sake of bearing children."[39]

Beneath it lay a hierarchy drawn from Platonic thought—men aligned with mind and reason, women with body and emotion, the rational mind ordained to govern the flesh. Because women were bound more closely to the body, they were judged more vulnerable to the passions that escaped reason's command, and so to temptation. The logic was circular but internally coherent, resting on an unspoken premise that control belongs to the masculine, disorder to the feminine. And so one man's private war with his own desire—his shame at a body that would not obey him—was lifted out of his biography and installed as the structure of reality.

For Augustine, the moment Eve took the fruit and Adam followed carried the whole weight of what came after. Eve, bound in his mind to body and desire, was the gateway—the one through whom temptation entered. But it was through Adam, father of the whole human race, that the consequence passed down. Every person born afterward would inherit his guilt. This was the wound Augustine called "the Fall," and the condition it left behind he named "original sin." It was a sharp departure from the Jewish reading. In Augustine's vision, the guilt was inherited, present already in newborn infants who had done nothing at all—transmitted, with grim precision, through the act of sexual reproduction.[40]

Though Adam's seed was the mechanism, Augustine's theology fixed on lust, on the body, on desire—which he bound to the feminine, to Eve. Here his own history became doctrine. Before the Fall, he believed, the sexual organs would have obeyed the will as readily as a hand or a foot, in perfect calm. Their rebellion now was a punishment that fit the crime—as the first humans had defied God, so their own bodies defied them. He even imagined how sinless intercourse in the garden would have unfolded, governed wholly by reason, untouched by passion. It was a vision found nowhere in Genesis.

Like Paul, Augustine meant the doctrine to serve a redemptive end—to explain why Christ had to come. But the burden of that explanation fell heavily on Eve, and through her on every woman after. If the feminine was bound to the body, to desire, to the gateway of sin, then a woman of power and devotion could not simply remain powerful and devoted. She had to be drawn back into the only role the framework allowed her: fallen, sexual, in need of correction.

Two centuries later, when Gregory the Great named Mary Magdalene a repentant prostitute, he did not need to cite original sin because the groundwork was already laid. Augustine had made Eve's guilt foundational and placed female sexuality near the center of the Christian story of sin and forgiveness. Gregory's Magdalene emerged from a world already trained to understand women through Eve.

What began as one bishop's inability to make peace with his own body became, under the authority of scripture, a justification for the judgment, restriction, and silencing of women—not only across Christianity, but across the Western world and the lands its empires would reach. The woman first named for life had become, in the Church's telling, its undoing. Ḥawwāh, mother of all living, turned into the mother of all dying, the one through whom death entered the world and passed to every child after her.

THE GODDESS

Before Eve could be made the mother of sin, the goddess had already been driven from the center. Earth, sky, water, wind, and breath. Seed, sprout, bloom, and decay. Across the oldest layers of sacred imagination, the powers of life, death, and return belonged again and again to the goddess. The earliest cultures that shaped the world around Israel, Egypt, Mesopotamia, the Levant, Anatolia, Greece, and Rome, imagined the feminine divine as central, creative, and near. Life was a mystery, after all, and its first visible threshold was the body of a woman.

For early people, this was not metaphor but revelation. The womb held creation: life emerging from darkness, nourishment from within, blood and milk sustaining fragile bodies. Motherhood was not sentimental. It was survival. It was miracle. The mother bound communities together, embodying love as visceral and sacred. Her holiness was mirrored in the stories, symbols, and identities of the goddesses.

Long before the names Mother of God, Queen of Heaven, Virgin, and Lady of the Sea were carried by Mother Mary, long before the roles of protector, intercessor, and comfort attached to her, they belonged to goddesses. And behind those goddesses stands something older still: a recurring figure that scholars gather, not without dispute, under the name of the Mother Goddess. The Venus of Laussel with her raised horn, the Minoan women with serpents lifted in each hand, and countless carved and molded forms across unconnected cultures and thousands of years share a single insistence: the divine given the body of a woman.

What any one of these figures meant to the hands that made it cannot be recovered, and the boldest reading of them, Marija Gimbutas's vision, with Merlin Stone's, of a coherent prehistoric religion of the Goddess, remains contested among archaeologists. But the recurrence is not in question, only its meaning. Across the ancient world, the sacred kept taking female form.

Fertility was what she proclaimed, central to the rhythms of daily life in agricultural societies ordered around planting and harvesting. Growth, decay, and renewal were lived realities, mirrored in earth, soil, and season. "She" was the terrain itself. The feminine was imagined as earth and sky, as water and wind, singular and paired, mother and daughter. Her facets proliferated as human civilization expanded, her manifestations widening with the growth of culture itself.

As human societies grew larger, more stratified, and more organized around kingship and war, their pantheons changed with them. Distinct goddesses of love, war, wisdom, and harvest emerged, even as male deities rose in prominence, their authority mirroring the new structures of human rule. The feminine divine was changing register, no longer only the terrain and its fertility but something more cosmic and complex, her image lifted from earth into the heavens—Nut arching across the Egyptian sky, Sopdet heralding the Nile's flood.

In Sumer and Babylon, flood and drought were read as expressions of divine will, mediated through sky and storm gods who commanded thunder, lightning, and rain. Here the twelve constellations of the zodiac were first systematized, tracing the sun's path through the heavens. In storm-centered pantheons, where survival hung on the violence of weather rather than the steady rhythm of soil, the feminine did not disappear, but she was increasingly cast as wife or counterpart. The West Semitic world from which Israel emerged shared this vocabulary. Yahweh—the God of Israel, the deity who would become the God of the Bible—thunders over the waters, wrapped in wind and cloud and fire, in the imagery of Near Eastern sky-gods, even of Baal, the Canaanite storm deity the scriptures condemn.

Still, the great goddesses did not vanish. Hera, Athena, and Artemis held their place in Greece; Isis in Egypt and far beyond it; Asherah across the Semitic world. But through the upheavals at the end of the Bronze Age, migration, conquest, collapse, the volcanic catastrophe on Thera that shook the Aegean and the Minoan world whose imagery had been so vividly feminine, the old order strained and shifted. The goddess did not fall in a day. Her eclipse unfolded slowly, through transformations too diffuse to fix to a single moment. But by the close of that age, the feminine divine had begun its long retreat from the center of the sacred, reconfigured, subordinated, and in one corner of the Near East, soon to be actively erased.

GOD'S WIFE

In 1975, at a remote desert way station called Kuntillet Ajrud in the Sinai, excavators found inscriptions painted on storage jars and plaster, written by Israelites in the eighth century BCE. The blessings invoke Yahweh, the God of Israel—and someone standing beside him. They ask for blessing "by Yahweh of Samaria and his Asherah," and "by Yahweh of Teman and his Asherah." A second inscription, from a tomb at Khirbet el-Qom, blesses the dead "by Yahweh and by his Asherah."[41] The words are ordinary devotion, written by believers in the formula of everyday faith. Yahweh and his Asherah. For at least some of ancient Israel, God had a wife.

Asherah's presence reaches back centuries. In the older Ugaritic texts she appears as Athirat, consort of El the high god, called "mother of the gods," a figure of fertility, vitality, and sacred authority woven through West Semitic worship. From the eighth to the sixth centuries BCE, small terra-cotta female figurines, hands cupping their breasts, appear in Israelite homes across the land, a maternal presence kept close in ordinary life: protective, sustaining, near. The goddess was not a foreign intrusion at the edges of Israel's faith, she belonged to hearth and home.

As Israel's religion consolidated around one God, imagined in emphatically masculine terms, the goddess who had stood beside him became first a rival, then forbidden. In *The Invention of God*, Thomas Römer traces this as a broad cultural redefinition over centuries. As kingdoms stabilized and political tensions intensified, Israel's leaders pressed for religious uniformity as cultural cohesion. In a region where divine plurality was assumed, exclusive monotheism was an extraordinary innovation, one that would define a nation and reshape belief for millennia.[42]

As devotion narrowed to one God, the older patterns of divinity did not simply fade. They were displaced. The mother goddess, the consort, the feminine slipped from public devotion and into prohibition. Against this backdrop, the biblical commands took shape: "You shall tear down their altars, break their pillars, and cut down their Asherah poles." A figure once imagined as a divine partner was gradually redefined as illicit, and then intolerable—an "abomination." What began as contested theological distinction rippled outward over centuries, shaping Judaism, Christianity, and later the monotheistic imagination inherited by Islam.

While the name "Asherah" has largely faded from popular memory, especially among Christian audiences, "Jezebel" remains potent. To call a woman a Jezebel is to call her scheming, brazen, sexually corrupt, a seductress who destroys the men around her. The word has been preached from pulpits and hurled across centuries, though most who use it could not say where it came from. It came from a queen.

Jezebel was a Phoenician princess, married to Ahab, king of Israel, in the ninth century BCE. She was a foreigner who kept faith with the gods of her homeland, Baal and Asherah among them, in a court increasingly pressed toward exclusive devotion to Yahweh.[43] In the book of Kings, shaped in its final form centuries after her lifetime, she was cast as manipulative, idolatrous, and dangerous, the archetype of the woman who must not be obeyed. But read against the grain of the text's hostility, Jezebel can also be seen as a politically formidable queen who maintained the gods of her homeland, standing her ground even before the prophets who opposed her.

The story told about her gathers its suspicion around every sign of her power. Her authority became manipulation; her foreignness, corruption; her fidelity to her gods, rebellion. In the account of her death, as her enemy rode in to kill her, Jezebel painted her eyes, dressed her head, and went to the window to meet him. Tradition made this final act another proof of seduction, as if even at the edge of death her danger lay in her allure. Yet a queen adorning herself to face her murderers may have been performing the dignity of her office, meeting death as a sovereign rather than a victim. From that single image came the "painted Jezebel," and with it the durable suspicion that a woman's beauty was a form of corruption. She was thrown from the window, trampled, and left for the dogs, her death staged as the triumph of God.

Her name was carried into the last book of the Christian New Testament, the book of Revelation, penned around the end of the first century. There, Jezebel was no longer a queen of history but a label, fixed upon a woman in the church at Thyatira, a prophet and teacher whose influence the author meant to destroy by branding her a seductress and purveyor of false teaching. From there the name passed into the vocabulary of the Church Fathers, into preaching, and into the mouths of people who have never read the book of Kings. A slur for women who were too potent, too beautiful, too powerful.

A figure from Judaism who became entwined with this ancient feminine lineage, and with Eve in particular, was Lilith. Modern retellings often present her as the suppressed woman before Eve, Adam's first wife erased by patriarchy. But that version of Lilith came centuries later, in medieval texts such as the Alphabet of Ben Sira and the Zohar. Her name, however, reaches further back. It appears in Isaiah 34:14, where a figure called *lilit*, often rendered "night creature" or "screech owl," appears amid a landscape of judgment and ruin. The word itself is usually linked to Mesopotamian traditions, where *lilītu* and related spirits were associated with wind, night, illness, and desolate places. What Lilith reveals, then, is not a hidden biblical woman before Eve, but the modern impulse to return to these female figures and ask what was said, what was suppressed, and what was lost.

In ancient Israel, Jezebel helped make loyalty to older gods shameful by embodying it in a woman portrayed as seductive, defiant, and corrupt. In Christianity, her name served another purpose: silencing women who taught and led by recasting authority as seduction. Eve's downfall through Augustine did not emerge from nowhere. It drew on older patterns of suspicion around women, bodies, beauty, and forbidden worship, patterns Christianity inherited, intensified, and made doctrinal. The sacred feminine did not vanish by accident or time. Across centuries, and through the interwoven aims of theology, politics, and power, she was diminished, vilified, and renamed, until a goddess, a queen, and the first woman all came to mean the same thing—danger.

THE HOLY SPIRIT

Even after the goddess was made an abomination and divinity rendered singularly masculine, the feminine persisted, hidden in plain sight, within the sacred scripture of Judaism, and therefore of Christianity. But what doctrine could expel from worship, it could not fully expel from language. The mother was not entirely absent. She endured as Spirit.

In the first lines of Genesis, the Spirit moves over the primordial waters. Breath above the deep, presence above darkness, life not yet formed but already stirring. Across Mesopotamian, Egyptian, Greek, and Near Eastern traditions, life rises from watery chaos through divine breath, wind, voice, or hovering presence. And in Hebrew, the grammar of that Spirit is feminine. *Ruach*, breath, wind, spirit, is a feminine noun, and the verb describing the Spirit "hovering" over the waters, *merachefet*, is feminine as well.

In the Dead Sea Scrolls, *ruach* remained feminine whether it names the spirit of God or the spirit within a human being. Later rabbinic and mystical traditions carried the thread forward in related concepts: *shekhinah*, the indwelling presence of God among the people, especially in exile and suffering, and *bat kol*, literally "daughter of the voice," the lingering echo of divine communication after the age of the great prophets had passed. Most striking of all is Wisdom, Ḥokhmah in Hebrew, Sophia in Greek, a feminine figure who appears in Proverbs as present with God at the creation of the world, and who would take on a life of her own in later Jewish and Christian thought.[44]

These were not identical ideas, but together they formed a shared field of meaning—breath, presence, voice, wisdom, each preserving an imagination in which the nearness of God could still be understood in feminine terms. What language held in grammar and figure, symbol held in image.

Long before the dove became Christian shorthand for the Holy Spirit, the small white bird had belonged to the goddess—linked to the Sumerian Inanna, the Phoenician Tanit, the Greco-Roman Aphrodite, and likely to Asherah within older Hebrew traditions as well. Across temples, shrines, and carvings, the dove carried the feminine sacred for millennia. So when it descends in the Gospels over the waters of Jesus's baptism, it carries her still—the feminine divine flying almost unnoticed from the old world into the new.

This feminine Spirit lived openly in the faith's first centuries, before orthodoxy pressed it to the margins, a survival traced by scholars such as Elaine Pagels, Susan Ashbrook Harvey, and Ally Kateusz, who have followed the feminine through early Christian communities whose scriptures were excluded from the canon and whose beliefs were suppressed.

Fragments remained even in the writings of the men who meant to discredit them. In the second century, bishops like Irenaeus attacked the systems they found too plural, too mythic, too open to the feminine, and in attacking them, preserved them. Irenaeus complained that the Valentinians paired the divine as male and female, "Christ (male) and the Holy Spirit (female)."[45] Hippolytus condemned the Elcesaites for teaching that the Son of God was accompanied by "his sister, the Holy Spirit."[46] And Jerome too preserved a fragment of the noncanonical Gospel of the Hebrews in which Jesus says plainly, "My mother, the Holy Spirit."[47]

When the Nag Hammadi library was recovered in the twentieth century, this older imagination came back into view. In the Apocryphon of John, the divine voice declares, "I am the Father. I am the Mother. I am the Son."[48] The Gospel of Philip goes further, reasoning that because the Spirit is herself female, the familiar formula cannot mean what the Church says it means: "Some say Mary conceived by the Holy Spirit. They are in error . . . When did a woman ever conceive by a woman?"[49]

By the fourth century, the debates over Father and Son had widened to take in the Spirit, coalescing into the doctrine of the Trinity, formalized at the First Council of Constantinople in 381. The very next year, in 382, Jerome began the work that would become the Latin Vulgate. He knew the Spirit in Genesis, *ruach*, was grammatically feminine. He knew the Greek had already softened it to the neuter *pneuma*. In Latin, it became masculine as *spiritus*. The choice was partly the structure of the language, but it ran with the current of an increasingly masculine Trinity, and the same hand that had turned *ʿalmāh* into *virgo* now closed the feminine out of the Spirit.

In the East, the feminine Holy Spirit held on longer. Syriac Christianity, whose language stayed close to the Aramaic Jesus spoke, went on speaking of the Spirit as Mother without strain or scandal. As Sebastian Brock has shown, it was only after the late fourth century that "Mother" began to recede from the Syriac manuscripts, as the standardization of a masculine Spirit spread across the Christian world.[50]

And it is in this Syriac-adjacent tradition that the feminine Spirit meets a familiar figure. In the Acts of Philip, reconstructed by François Bovon from scattered Byzantine manuscripts, a disciple named Mariamne,

Philip's sister, appears as a leader, teacher, baptizer, and miracle worker, learned in sacred teaching and acting with what later ages would call priestly authority. In one passage she teaches a noblewoman named Nicanora what Bovon renders as: "You are guilty of having forgotten your origins, your Father in heaven, and your spiritual Mother. If you wake up, however, you will receive illumination."

Bovon argued that Mariamne may preserve a memory of Mary Magdalene, and that across the later manuscripts of the Acts of Philip, her prominence is steadily reduced, her authority diminished by deliberate hands, copy after copy.[51] If he is right, then here is Magdalene as a teacher of the feminine divine, speaking of the Mother as a reality Christians had been taught to forget. And here, in the manuscript tradition itself, the shrinking of her authority becomes visible.

Still, the mother lingered. Kateusz describes a medieval Bavarian fresco of a Trinity centered on a female figure; the Cathars ordained women and appear in inquisitorial records invoking the Holy Spirit as "Our Lady"; the same current ran on through mystics, visionaries, and local devotions long after official theology had hardened around a masculine Trinity. The memory of the feminine sacred was never erased entirely.[52]

Mary and Mother, Magdalene and Holy Spirit. Each carried traces of a feminine presence that had once moved more openly through Christian tradition. Across centuries of doctrine, translation, and consolidation, those presences were not destroyed but diminished, pushed toward the edges. Still they remained, hovering over water, hidden in language, waiting to be heard again.

SEEKING THE MOTHER

Religion has always been an effort to orient human life within mystery. Every society creates its sacred framework in the shadow of its fears and its needs, and no religion evolves apart from the reality of governance. As civilizations grew and empires rose, sacred language narrowed to mirror the structures that sustain power. Monotheism flourished within this environment because it reflected and reinforced authority that was singular, vertical, and unquestioned—the ideal organization for hierarchy and obedience.

As political authority centralized, divine sovereignty followed. Empire consolidated power on earth while monotheism claimed it in heaven. Within that paradigm, the liminal, the cyclical, and the mysterious were not just inconvenient, it threatened order. What had once been complex, adaptive, and symbolically dense was recast as error. This was not the design of one religion alone. It is a recurring story where power and belief entwine, of divine order fashioned in the image of those who ruled beneath it.

As doctrine tightened, complexity thinned and ambiguity gave way to definition. Certainty steadies people in unsettled eras. Clear lines promise order. But when lines harden, the world they attempt to contain grows smaller. What cannot be absorbed is expelled. What resists simplification is renamed. The unknown does not vanish; it slips from view—present still, but dimmed, because the myths that once named it are now suspect.

In that shift, the mother went missing. The feminine divine was pared back wherever it threatened to speak too clearly of older truths. Traditions that once spoke in the language of balance, including Egyptian Ma'at, Platonic harmony, and the reciprocity of yin and yang, yielded, especially in the West, to sharper moral partitions: saved and damned, pure and corrupt, orthodox and heretical. The cosmos flattened into verdict, a chasm opening between these widening divisions.

Mary Magdalene emerges from this abyss, from the darkness left in the absence of the feminine. What was drawn apart left her oscillating between extremes—apostle and prostitute, sinner and saint, witness and hysterical woman. Her complexity did not translate cleanly into the language forming through the institutionalization of Christianity.

"Heretic," from the Greek *hairesis*, once meant simply "one who chooses." Choice was revised as unbelief because freethinking agitated those who sought stability from above. "Pagan," from the Latin *paganus*, meant "country dweller," a civilian beyond the center of imperial power. Attachment to land and outsider status were quietly reframed as deviance, labels deployed as instruments of confinement and separation. How fitting, then, that the land itself—once revered as the source of sustenance, as mother, as goddess—should lend its name to a term of derision for those who did not fall fully within the boundaries of organized Christianity.

Like Persephone rising from the underworld, a metaphor for the scarcity of winter and the return of spring, of sun and warm wind, of bloom and vegetation that feed and nourish—Mary Magdalene embodies this ancient register of verdant potential.

If Mary is the maiden of the tapestries, then the history of the feminine in Christianity, even the heritage of the goddess, forms the green foliage of the forest, the roses climbing along the fence, the colors of her garment, and the scallop shells on the hounds' collars. By attending to these remaining details, the elements not torn out or erased but rendered peripheral or ornamental, the portrait of the missing woman begins to come into view.

Each detail, when seen in relation to the others, yields deeper insight, even revelation, showing that what was unraveled can be rewoven. Threads once pulled apart, even damaged, can still be traced, if not fully recovered then at least reimagined. With every story, every symbol, every return to what was once set aside, the image of Magdalene—and with her, the feminine at the heart of what is sacred—is not recreated, but remembered.

To see her again in her fullness is to let the whole scene return. The rose-strewn fence, the branches heavy with berries, the thick green trees beyond, the flashes of vivid azure sky.

Chapter 3

CAMPAGNE PROVENÇALE

Sunlight filters through the glass, warming your skin as you drive through a countryside where time slows into pastoral ease. The road relaxes beneath the tires, as if the land were teaching you how to move in its rhythm. Lavender fields appear in low, silver-green rows, still early in the season. Their buds are small yet, just hinting at the color to come, with more promise than bloom.

Olive trees stand gnarled and patient, their leaves turning to catch the midday sun, flashing pewter notes of peace. Rows of cypress rise like sentinels, framing the vision with dark, vertical grace. Then it becomes unmistakably Provençal when the stone houses appear, their walls mellowed to the color of soft sand and their shutters a dusty blue-green that lands somewhere between sage and turquoise painted on surfaces chalked by years of weather and salt air.

Here, the landscape is illuminated in a way artists have cherished for centuries. Light dissolves shadow and turns stone, olive leaf, and lavender into living color. Paul Cézanne found it in the shifting planes of Mont Sainte-Victoire; Pierre-Auguste Renoir in the flesh tones of Cagnes-sur-Mer; Henri Matisse and Pablo Picasso in the saturated coastal air of Antibes and the Riviera. Each was changed by the brilliance of Provence—a light that does not simply reveal but transforms, inviting experiments with form that render the world as if newly made.

As you move through Provence carrying Mary Magdalene in your thoughts, the sea-kissed countryside alters again. The brightness softens;

the hills seem to listen. What was merely beautiful grows luminous with meaning, as every olive tree offers a measure of sacred oil and every drift of herb-scented air is warmed by the memory of her presence. Traces of her story are scattered across this land—in chapels that bear her name, small shrines tucked into vineyard walls, and pilgrim paths that wind toward caves high above the plain.

Though the north once claimed her relics at Vézelay, and the Cathar hills further east hold whispers of a hidden Christianity, Provence insists on her footsteps. Whatever roads Mary walked or wherever devotion later placed her, all paths return to a single source, an origin.

*

In Provençal tradition, the story begins at the edge of the Camargue, in the fishing village of Les Saintes-Maries-de-la-Mer. The Rhône rushes here from the Alps through Arles, where Vincent Van Gogh painted its waters streaked with lamplight and stars beneath a night sky, before emptying at last into the Mediterranean. Drawn south, he found himself in a place long linked with Mary Magdalene, writing to his brother Theo: "the Mediterranean—has a colour like mackerel, in other words, changing—you don't always know if it's green or purple—you don't always know if it's blue—because a second later, its changing reflection has taken on a pink or grey hue."[1] In *Fishing Boats on the Beach at Saintes-Maries*, the color is less the subject than the sensation, as the air softens the edges, dissolving sea and sky until everything trembles.

Still, this shoreline is remembered less for his canvases than for a faith far older than paint—one that tells how Mary Magdalene, the other Marys, and a company of disciples were cast adrift together in a boat without sail or oar. Medieval chronicles, later compiled in *The Golden Legend*, said the authorities meant for them to vanish at sea. But a miracle intervened. Guided by the hand of God, their vessel crossed the breadth of the sea and came to rest at last on the Provençal shore.

In the centuries that followed, the legend opened to another presence: Sara. Sometimes remembered as a servant of the Marys, sometimes as a woman of the region who welcomed them ashore, she remains the most mysterious—her image dark against the southern sun, like the moon to its light, holding the hidden half. Each May she journeys to the sea, carried from her crypt in Saintes-Maries-de-la-Mer, draped in bright silks, voices rising as the waves touch her skirts in a procession as ancient as tide or birth, whispering of arrivals long awaited.[3]

Did Mary pull her boat up among others, as Van Gogh once painted, hulls resting in the bright air of Saintes-Maries? Did she fall to her knees in gratitude, pressing her hands into the sand before crossing this land to bear good news? Was she a leader in the assemblies of Marseille and Aix, bringing converts by the thousands? Or did she withdraw into the forested heights, a solitary soul in the cave at Sainte-Baume, taking her final communion in the care of Saint-Maximin?

Even the simplest customs seem to bear her imprint, such as the *navette*, a golden biscuit molded into a small boat. It keeps the tale of that landing alive in the hands of local bakers, her presence folded quietly into the dough. Each February, for Candlemas, the ovens of Marseille fill with these boat-shaped offerings recalling an ancient arrival: women on the waves, belief carrying hope across the sea. In this way, following Mary becomes a journey of trust in its most unconventional form—a path that asks us to lean into what we cannot yet perceive. To look beyond in order to see beyond.

With each turn of the road, you start to notice what might once have escaped you, like a bakery sign whose painted loaf suddenly resembles a tiny boat, or a mandorla behind a saint. Then the faint trace of anise and citrus seems to lift in the air just as you slow for the roundabout. It isn't that anything has changed—only that you're paying attention now. The story rises through scent, memory through taste, until one becomes the door to another.

Your mind might leap—from this Provençal landscape to *une madeleine de Proust*, that famous shorthand for a sensory spark that summons memory back to life. Perhaps it begins with the word itself: *Madeleine*, a name French women have carried for generations, written into everyday life across café awnings and street signs, its very letters echoing *Magdalene*. She who was strong and steadfast took on so many forms, from a Parisian heroine of a children's book to a small scalloped cake—the very one Marcel Proust dipped into tea. It is a shape that speaks to a deeper current—where the scallop and the sea both point back to Magdalene, the feminine presence who holds interiority, devotion, and the desire to recover what has been lost.

Not *lost time*, as Proust would have it, but lost meaning. Lost stories. Lost women.

And from here, another form rises to the surface, that of Sandro Botticelli's Venus, emerging from the sea with hair like a radiant red veil—a vision of beauty and birth that echoes Magdalene in her naked penitence, covered only by her own cascading flame. In Greek myth she is Aphrodite, born from the sea foam itself; the Romans later called her Venus. This story traveled far, carried across the water into Italy and France, where its imagery intertwined with that of Mary. To follow it farther back is to find the same current running deeper still. In the ancient Levant, goddesses moved within a world of sea and star. Some were associated with the bright morning and evening star, the planet later called Venus by the Romans, while others were invoked in language that bound divinity to the waters. Much later, Marian devotion would give the Virgin Mother the title Stella Maris, "Star of the Sea." The names differ. The imagery persists.

Greek myth locates the sea-birth of Aphrodite at Cyprus and Cythera, her scallop shell drifting toward land where the Horae stood ready to clothe and crown her. Like so many sacred arrivals, she comes by water, unnamed until received. Archeology gives material form to what the story preserves symbolically; these Aegean islands belonged to a world deeply attuned to the feminine form. Shrines, seals, frescoes, and figurines return to that image—radiant, serpentine, enthroned.

"What's in a name? That which we call a rose / By any other name would smell as sweet."[2] William Shakespeare's line drifts through your mind, reminding you that these women and goddesses are not separate, but reflections of a single essence older than time. Symbols expressing the same wholeness. Venus or Diana, Mother Mary or Mary Magdalene, she becomes the most familiar face of that eternal feminine, her greatest archetype and emblem: Love.

As you move down the road, you feel the same sense of floating, carrying these stories within you—whether you're rounding a bend or pausing where the land asks you to look again. Sometimes it is as simple as beholding a goddess in a half shell rising from fifteenth-century brush strokes. Other times it is the quiet recognition that the sacred does not need grandeur to be felt; it arrives through whatever the moment offers. Even in a glass of Provençal wine, the land is already speaking.

Here, the vineyard carries its own sacred story, where grapes, branches, fruit, and soil become something more than themselves. Wine, after all, is one of the oldest forms of purposeful alchemy in Europe—reminding us that transformation has long been the work of earth and spirit. And that sense of shifting doesn't remain on the tongue; it moves through you, perhaps when you stand before a painting whose blue shutters return you to clay and lavender, salt and sun. Or when you listen to *Clair de lune*, letting Claude Debussy's melody, answering Paul Verlaine's verse, speak to the soul like an impressionist dream.

In that music, as in moonlight, the visible world gives way to the felt one. Verlaine captured its mood in language, Debussy in tone, each translating the same ineffable ache into a different form of brilliance. Within this silver haze the feminine we seek begins to appear—a softer radiance that reveals what noon conceals. Beauty is a vessel; it carries what history forgets, what we set out to remember. And, *la lune est le rêve du soleil*—the moon is the sun's dream, a gentle reflection of a truth too bright to face directly.

Still, the inward dream is only half the story. The world reaches back through place, through body, through memory. A painting in moonlight, a biscuit in tea, the shoreline where a story once arrived, and the road still unwinding before you. The real shift comes through encounters that might appear ordinary, whether in pilgrimage or in daily life, yet they take on a greater potency when you are on a journey. The eye awakened by a blend of pigments, the skin brushed by wind, the tongue tasting salt and honey, the ear listening for waves under stars. Mary, Venus, love—in whatever form she appears—feels suddenly near, permeating the senses.

This is where the painters of Provence understood something essential, for the landscape participates in revelation. Van Gogh's swirling skies and fields trembling with light show perception in the very act of changing. To follow Mary Magdalene is to live that way, too—moving with senses open, vision deepening, seeing until what is hidden finally comes into view.

And so you keep going.

*

Because not every place shaped by Magdalene's memory bears her name, you look for traces of her in the land. At Château Bas, good vines dig into limestone, and excavation has revealed an ancient sanctity set deep in the earth, older than wine. You pull in, the car rolling over sand-colored French gravel, and step out—not for a typical wine tasting, but to stand where centuries of worship layered themselves into one potent place.

It looks, at first, like any Provençal estate, with rows of vines stretching toward the sun, a modern tasting room open to those who want it, the soft churn of work still happening somewhere out of sight. But even within these walls, the past surfaces when you happen upon a marble goddess unearthed from the soil and placed in an alcove, her face eroded but her form still sacred. You smile, becoming ever more aware that "she" is almost always present, even when silent. This statue is Diana—Artemis in Greek—whose presence followed the currents of Greek settlement and Roman rule into Provence. She recalls that long before Christianity, this land was already in harmony with a feminine divinity.

As you stand transfixed by this stone figure of a woman, you remember what *The Golden Legend* recorded: that when Mary landed on these shores and began to preach, she spoke out against the very images through which such divinity had once been honored. But something in you hesitates, sensing in the tale, a subtle turning meant to draw her away from the women who came before her. On the steps of a temple within Marseille, the story goes, Magdalene "saw the people gathering at the shrine to offer sacrifice to the idols," and stepped forward. With her "serene face" and "calm manner," she inspired and disarmed the indigenous people with "well-chosen words," calling them to Christ:

> All who heard her were in admiration at her beauty, her eloquence, and the sweetness of her message . . . and no wonder, that the mouth which had pressed such pious and beautiful kisses on the Savior's feet should breathe forth the perfume of the word of God more profusely than others could.[4]

You let the received words settle. For a moment, there is still the thrill of Mary's authority, her voice moving through public space. But the hesitation remains. The story allows her to speak, only by severing her from the women who came before.

You step away from the tale and begin to wander, letting your eyes adjust to what the legend cannot contain. Château Bas is a vineyard today, but its roots run deeper than the limestone, once a Roman settlement built beside a freshwater spring in the Crau plain. Stone and soil, water and wine all partake in the same conversion. Devotion never stops flowing here. It simply changes form, much like the way the painters watch the light move and remake the world before them.[5]

Walking the land in quiet contemplation, your gaze begins to settle into its surroundings. Morning glories spread low across the open ground as you follow a field-edge forward. Wild roses appear, their five petals expressing a geometry rooted in the feminine and whispering of the planet Venus drawing her rose in the sky, the five-pointed path traced over eight years from earth's view, thirteen in Venus's count.

Step by step, the same pattern returns along the tide-line and altar. After Venus shapes her star, the shore answers with a shell, a gift from the sea whose ribs carry a measured rhythm. The fan of lines radiating from its hinge sets out the oldest pattern of becoming, a point unfolding into being and source widening into expansion—a mandala of creation. The spiral deepens in the sea's own architecture, the golden ratio hidden in the nautilus, a proportion the world keeps repeating, one artists have long carried into stone and canvas.

Even Botticelli, in *The Birth of Venus*, has long been read as following those same harmonies as he staged her rising. Such forms remind us that beauty follows a rhythm older than language. The sea-born goddess rides this vessel of desire and remembrance; Magdalene keeps hush at the center. The living world is our first sanctuary, and artists are simply those who pause long enough to honor it, knowing that whatever grows freely knows its kinship with the divine.

The path narrows into shade, and then through a gate of ancient stone. Two serpent-carved columns flank either side, their sinuous lines climbing skyward, marking the boundary between the ordinary and the once holy. It feels like passing through a story older than the one you were told—when the serpent was still wisdom and renewal, long before a single interpretation hardened around it, tethering Eve, and all women, to a blame that never belonged to them.

What was hidden begins to reveal itself as you continue toward the temple site. Moss-covered altars mark each threshold, guiding the body forward, asking you to loosen what you carry so you can cross into what remains of the sacred. Renovation revealed the remains of a first-century BCE temple beneath a later Christian church. Its columns still rise among the rows, evidence that this land has been consecrated long before Christian memory claimed it. Little can be known for certain, but archeologists believe it may have been a temple of water and fertility, perhaps honoring Diana or a local goddess, reminding you that the earth was considered sacred long before the Church built its own holiness upon it.

Is the legacy of Mary Magdalene in Provence not a Christian ornament added later, but a continuation of a much older truth? Are the retellings in *The Golden Legend* that placed her against the indigenous rites factual? Would she have conflicted with, or been in quiet continuity to, the feminine threading through the land where vine takes root and ripens?

The body remembers what the mind forgets. What was held in darkness returns to light. Devotion, like water, keeps moving, changing form as needed, filling hollows, carving further into banks and stone. Magdalene's story is like this—fluid and ever-reshaping. Yet beneath each turning, something faithful endures, like the planet Venus descending into shadow only to rise again as morning's first glow.

Beyond the serpent-carved columns, the path continues beneath the wooded canopy. It is a gentler passage than Sainte-Baume, where light filters easily through leaves instead of shadow. The air thickens as you follow the trail until, almost without warning, the trees part. The path ends. The land opens and you have arrived at the temple. There it is, half-veiled in green, pale stone catching the sun. An ancient exhale.

The ancient sanctuary sits atop a rise where the fabric of time lies exposed in its layers. From one side you see the Roman ashlar masonry squared into blocks; above it, fluted columns remain from the temple's classical façade. The ruin speaks of eras built one upon another, stones reused, faiths shifting even as the architecture remains. Your mind traces the persistent female face of the divine, her symbols reweaving across time.

Daughters of the mother goddess, Diana, Venus, even Magdalene arrive in different vessels, the sacred altering its name and shore yet rising from the same current. Diana of the forest and springs; Venus of the ocean and islands. Diana, the guardian of the hunt, an emblem of independence, courage, wildness; Venus, of fertility, beauty, and creative abundance. Spring water or ocean waves. Moon or morning star. Untamed or connective.

You climb toward the ruin, the ground sloping gently beneath your feet. On either side, massive Roman blocks rise like the bones of a long-buried structure, still marking out the original perimeter. It stands plain and exposed, its edges speaking their old precision. Grass threads up through the gaps, green insisting softly through joints once held tight. And even with so much missing, the mind reconstructs what stood here: a courtyard open to the sky, columns in procession, a spring-fed center that drew worshippers upward. With each step, your own body completes what time has removed, walking the old lines of devotion back into being.

Roman temples rose where water rose, places ancients understood as the navel of life. So it is at Château Bas: the temple's foundation, and later the small Romanesque chapel built against it, both mark a living spring that is a symbol of renewal, purification, and the passage from death into life. You follow the seam where medieval stone presses against the older blocks beneath it, as the architecture leads you toward the only remaining passage.

As you turn to move inside the chapel, you see a door painted that unmistakable Provençal blue, the same weathered shade you've watched flash across shutters throughout these hills. Here, too, the paint has been sunstruck and salt-worn, peeling where hands have pushed to pray for centuries. You touch that color as you pass, noting how it deepens up close as light from the open door floods the space ahead, where three Marys keep watch. The smallest is a devotional statue in a niche, her hands lowered in the gesture of Our Lady of Grace, offering silent blessing to the room.

The older stone sculpture, the clear focal point of the chapel, shows a mother seated with Jesus and John the Baptist: two barefoot children leaning into her with the ease of brothers before the story divides them. The Christ child lifts a goldfinch in his small hand, recalling Raphael's *Madonna del Cardellino*. A few steps away stands the third Mary, a newer figure, bright and smooth as if carved from moonlight. She cradles the Christ child close, her head bowed in a gesture of contemplation and protection. Dried sprigs of bay and wild leaves rest at her feet, offerings left by those who came seeking comfort.

Her shadow stretches across the ancient stone, and for a moment the two larger statues seem to mirror one another, mother as shelter and mother as shrine, two masks of one faith. But with the smallest icon and her outstretched blessings, you wonder, standing amid this trinity of "Mother Marys," how the vast expressions of the sacred feminine have been distilled into a single image in Christianity—how she alone was permitted to remain, carrying the weight of all others forgotten.

Perhaps that is why their gaze, folded now into hers, feels both tender and unyielding, as though she knows all that she holds, from compassion and silence, to loss and endurance. In those depths, something older stirs in the memory of other names spoken, other faces remembered. Diana in her moonlit grace and Venus rising among the multitude of goddesses once honored in Rome and beyond.

Lost meaning. Lost stories. Lost women.

Time does not erase; it only hides. They wait—ready to be resurrected and rewritten, seen anew through a lens capable of perceiving them.

The moon, after all, is the sun's dream: unseen yet pulling on the tides and the hidden waters of the world and our bodies. It reminds us that what seems to withdraw still shapes the rhythm of creation. And creation, too, begins in reflection—in the stillness before the dawn.

To make it sacred again, to redefine the shadows as form and color, as artists have always done, is the act of taking up the pen, of writing a new beginning from the inside out, unfurling truth into form, light into matter. And it is here that hope floats, or rises, like a goddess from the depths, born of the same light she carries back into the world.

If hope is a rainbow of color, and the expression ours to choose, then creation is a spectrum—fractals and emanations passing through a single prism, each vibration revealing another tone of luminosity. Maybe then we have always needed many expressions of the divine feminine, each one a different way of naming what cannot be contained in a single form, just as the painter's eye finds color dancing differently on every surface of the same water.

And so, what are we creating? What are we depicting, seeing, and offering before the saints and the sea, our own small tokens laid at the edge of mystery?

It is the season when poppies burst through the fields, crimson as the flame that once rose from the sea, the hue that follows Magdalene in legend through sea salt, unbound hair, and tears turned into pearls. It is the season when lavender is poised to bloom, its scent already on the wind, a promise of sacred oil, balm for what love has opened.

And with the stories rising in the spring air, you feel the pull to move again, to lean into the same current that once carried the Marys across the water as you turn and walk back through the open door—past the turquoise paint, sea-colored and deep with memory—into the sun once more.

This current you've surrendered to—could it be the same that shapes all things, the inner tide Verlaine once called the soul?

"Your soul is a chosen landscape," he wrote in *Clair de lune*.[6]

You stand within it now, light moving through you as through the hills, changing you quietly, from the inside out.

So, it seems, the light of Provence is no longer something to behold, but everything to become.

Chapter 4

TOWER OF FAITH

Midnight thickened in the dormitory when a small luminous child roused the young novice sister from sleep and asked her to follow. Barefoot, she moved through the corridor behind him until they reached the chapel, shut for the night yet inexplicably lit by candles that should have been extinguished.

There, in the stillness before the altar, she heard it—the unmistakable swish of silk, though no footstep had crossed the floor. Only then did the figure appear, one the sister would later say she recognized instantly as Mother Mary, present not as a symbol but embodied, almost human. Months later, in a second vision, Mary appeared again, silently displaying an image and instructing that it be impressed onto a medal, exactly as shown.

On the "Miraculous Medal," Mother Mary stands in a flowing robe, her head gently bowed. Twelve stars arc around her as if swirling in motion, while her eyes are cast downward in quiet grace. Her arms extend loose and open, rays pouring from her fingertips. Beneath the pooled fabric of her dress a snake lies under her feet, resting upon a half-globe.

Though such elements recur in Marian art, their precise configuration on the Miraculous Medal derives from the 1830 visions of Catherine Labouré, then a sister in formation with the Daughters of Charity at their Convent on Rue du Bac in Paris. Catherine confided the experience only to her confessor, but the image did not remain cloistered. It was pressed into a faith that could be carried while the visionary herself receded into obscurity.

Catherine's biography surfaced much later and through many layers of mediation: to her confessor, Father Jean-Marie Aladel; the Vincentian community to which she belonged; and the nineteenth-century Catholic Church. Her original accounts passed through these channels, and so did the details of her life. Her origins, her family, her temperament, each facet was carefully arranged for public reception, constructing a woman fit to stand at the center of a divine event. A close reading of the narrative built around her reveals the distinction between what is illuminated and what is allowed to recede, which traits are amplified, and which are muted.[1]

Catherine Labouré, born in 1806, was one of eleven children. When she was nine years old, her mother died, and she was sent to live with her uncle and aunt in Saint-Rémy—a village within a day or two's journey of the Romanesque basilica at Vézelay. For centuries, Vézelay had been a major pilgrimage site, revered as the resting place of Mary Magdalene's relics since the Middle Ages. During Catherine's childhood, the abbey remained a commanding presence in regional devotion. While her biographies draw no explicit link between Catherine and Magdalene, she grew up in a terrain already saturated with Mary's memory. Even her mother's name, Madeleine, echoed that legacy.

Catherine's childhood is presented as rustic and simple, though she was born into a relatively prosperous farming family in their village. Her father was an educated man who once studied for the priesthood and her mother had worked as a village teacher before marriage. Several of Catherine's older siblings received formal schooling and pursued professional paths. Catherine, however, is described as having been excluded from formal education, remaining functionally illiterate until late adolescence.

One biographer remarks, "It's hard not to see here the design of heaven to keep Catherine ignorant, so that the divine origin of her visions, with their accurate delineation of deep doctrine, might be the more apparent."[2] The implication is that her innocence was supernaturally fashioned to secure later credibility. Catherine is described as solemn and devout as a child, serious beyond her years. She walked six miles to Mass in the predawn dark. She prayed constantly, kneeling before a weathered image of the Annunciation. Pious, disciplined, and unremarkable—except, of course, for her visions.

Accounts suggest Catherine was inclined toward mystical experience from a young age, though only one early episode is preserved. At eighteen, she dreamt of assisting an elderly priest at Mass. In the dream, she was seized by what biographers call a "wild fright" and attempted to flee, though the reason for her fear is never explained. Before she could escape, the priest addressed her: "You flee from me now, but one day you will be glad to come to me. God has plans for you: do not forget it."[3]

This episode surfaces only in later biographies, and its symmetry with her eventual vocation is difficult to miss. The priest is identified as Vincent de Paul, founder of the community she would one day enter—the very setting in which her Marian visions would occur. Whether interpreted as foreshadowing or careful narrative framing, the result is the same: Catherine's earliest mystical experience secures her to male ecclesial authority before she even dons the habit.

Her youth is presented as moving inevitably toward religious vocation, though surviving details complicate that account. Catherine declined three marriage proposals. Her father, once trained as a priest, opposed her desire to enter the convent. His resistance was not mild, because he initially withheld the dowry required for admission. In nineteenth-century France, families typically financed a daughter's vocation; convent dowries formed part of the financial structure sustaining religious houses, and without one, entrance could be delayed or refused altogether. Her entrance into the sisterhood, then, was neither seamless nor foreordained.

Once she arrived in Paris, the visions began. She entered the Daughters of Charity on January 22, 1830. Six months later, on the evening of July 18th, the night before the feast day of Saint Vincent de Paul, Catherine placed on her tongue a small piece of linen, a preserved relic of Saint Vincent de Paul, before going to sleep. Relic devotion was deeply embedded in nineteenth-century Catholic practice: sacred objects were kissed, touched, worn, and believed to mediate grace. Even so, ingesting a fragment of textile was not customary. This act stood at the outer edge of extreme piety—unusual enough to register yet recorded without comment. The strange detail of Catherine ingesting the relic served to invoke the male saint by name and body, anchoring her vision to the institution she had only just entered.

It was only then that the child, later identified as an angel, appeared and led her to the chapel where Catherine encountered "the Holy Virgin" in an apparition that lasted through the pre-dawn hours of July 19th. The figure she witnessed was visibly and spatially present—she spoke as if tangible, not imagined. In the account recorded by her confessor, Father Aladel, the Virgin addressed Catherine regarding a current national crisis: "The times are very evil. Sorrows will befall France; the throne will be overturned."[4] This was the midst of the July Revolution, when the Bourbon monarchy collapsed and Charles X was forced to abdicate amid mass uprisings in Paris. The Virgin's discourse moved restlessly between intimate direction, national catastrophe, communal regulation, and visions of blood in the streets. The fate of the monarchy, the discipline of the Vincentian houses, and Catherine's personal obedience were expressed in one seamless prophetic arc. Catherine reported this account to Aladel soon after the event, at least according to his testimony, in which he portrays himself as measured, even cautious.

Whereas the first vision unfolded in extended speech, the second arrived in silence. On November 27, 1830, the Virgin appeared again while Catherine was absorbed in evening meditation in the very same chapel. This time the drama was sparse. The Virgin stood above the altar, hands extended, light issuing from her fingers and the rings she wore.

Some stones blazed with light while others remained dim, understood to signify the graces given in response to prayer, and those left unclaimed because they are never asked for. The figure Catherine beheld was to be struck into metal and worn around the neck. Even the inscription appeared as though the words were somehow present without sound: "O Mary, conceived without sin, pray for us who have recourse to thee."[5] The reverse was equally specified: a large "M" surmounted by a cross, two hearts below—one encircled with thorns, the other pierced by a sword—enclosed by twelve stars.

After Catherine relayed these details to Aladel, he sought counsel from Church authorities and eventually brought the matter to the Archbishop of Paris. Two years later, amid a devastating cholera outbreak, permission was granted to create the medal. Within months, the "Medal of the Immaculate Conception" entered wide circulation. In the shadow of epidemic fear, it moved through the city with the quiet urgency of contagion: worn against the throat, pressed into palms, and stitched into garments in hope of protection. Stories of miraculous healings and conversions traveled with it.

Within a decade, millions had been distributed and over time that figure has climbed easily to hundreds of millions.[6] By mid-century this specific icon of Mother Mary had crossed borders and traveled oceans, its small oval form settling into the devotional vocabulary of global Catholicism. Its success was extraordinary—Marian doctrine in material form, shared amid a time of crisis, carried through the daily adversity of life.

Meanwhile, Catherine herself lived in obscurity. She washed linens and scrubbed floors, remembered by her superiors as ordinary and obedient, guarding what she apparently called her "great secret." Only six months before her death in 1876 did she speak publicly of the apparitions, though not as a personal claim, but as a quiet confirmation of what had already been disseminated and approved. By then, the medal's circulation and reputation were secure. The devotion began with her, but the image carried her vision without carrying her name. As revenue accumulated and Marian theology advanced, the woman whose experience set it in motion remained unseen.

What *did* Catherine behold those evenings?

No account of the apparitions survives in her own hand from 1830. Is it plausible that a woman described as mystically inclined experienced only those visions, and nothing more? How fully do the preserved narratives capture that night, from the words attributed to the Virgin, the silence of the second apparition, the serpent at her feet, and the twelve stars above her head? Which elements stem from Catherine's own perspective, and which reflect scriptural expectation or later theological framing? When read through the layers of clerical mediation that shaped her testimony, the record suggests that more occurred than can now be recovered. This filtering—interpretive, institutional, controlled—was not unique to Catherine. It reflects a recurring pattern in the making of sacred history, especially around women.

In vastly different centuries and circumstances, both Catherine and Mary Magdalene witnessed something that would carry far beyond their own voices. In each case, a woman's interior encounter did not remain singular. What she saw, how she saw it—what was literal and what was symbolic—does not reach forward in her own words. It was stabilized, interpreted, and circulated by communities that derived coherence, and at times material strength, from its transmission. Yet, somehow, these mediated accounts still retain something authentic, something true, something miraculous, even if only in traces.

Mary Magdalene's witness, though not cast in metal, was inscribed into proclamation: her encounter with the risen Christ became foundational to resurrection theology and to the authority of the Church that declared it. However distant the canonical Gospels may be from Mary Magdalene's own voice, they still bear the imprint of her presence. Details remain, ones that when read with care, can reveal glimpses into who she was, what she saw, and all that remains unspoken. In that process of discernment, attention turns to language, sequence, emphasis, and omission—to the places where later interpretation has overlaid earlier memory, and to the moments where the text has resisted erasure. The aim is not invention, but proximity, an effort to approach, as nearly as the sources permit, the historical and theological contours of Mary Magdalene's identity.

THE WITNESS

Mary Magdalene's most recognized presence and role within the Gospel accounts arrives at the most crucial moment of Jesus's life and death: his resurrection. While women appear at remarkably powerful and pivotal moments across these scriptures, especially in the Gospel of John, the placement of Magdalene as the key witness to the resurrection in the Christian story remains astonishing. Though the details diverge, her presence holds; she is named first—the witness through whom recognition begins.

For a woman to stand as witness to the event on which an entire religion would come to rest was no small thing in antiquity. In the first century, women were presumed emotional, unstable, and easily deceived. A woman's word carried less legal and social weight than a man's; she could be excluded from formal testimony or dismissed when the stakes were highest. Early critics of Christianity recognized this vulnerability in the resurrection story and exploited it. The second-century philosopher Celsus dismissed the resurrection by attacking its source. He called her *paroistros*, "frenzied" or "stung to madness," reducing her testimony to delusion.[7] If a claim rested on a woman's word, it could be dismissed.

But tradition did not correct for the liability: it preserved Mary Magdalene as the witness. Evangelists and scribes could have eclipsed her, removing her name or diminishing her role in this moment, changes that would have made the resurrection claim more acceptable within a culture structured around male authority. For the most part, Mary remained the woman named first at the tomb in Mark and Matthew, a detail Luke preserved but softened while the Fourth Gospel elevated her dramatically, giving her one of the most crucial recognition scenes in the New Testament.

The staying power of Magdalene at the tomb is one of the strongest arguments for memory. Her presence was likely embedded in the story from its earliest telling, making her name resistant to removal even in a culture that would have had every reason to prefer a male witness. If the resurrection narrative were a later fabrication, it would likely have taken another shape. Magdalene remained in her role because it was where she stood from the beginning.

There were rare acknowledgments of Magdalene's authority, but more often Christian writers and interpreters found ways to contain the radical implications of her role. Jerome, for one, called Mary a "tower of faith," rising above what he names as the weakness of her sex.[8] Meanwhile, Augustine of Hippo, John Chrysostom, Ambrose of Milan, and Gregory the Great position her in relation to Eve: because a woman was the herald of the first fall, a woman becomes the first witness of its reversal.[9] When Magdalene's witness could not be erased, it was converted into symbol. No longer treated as a historical figure, she became a motif—and a curiously paradoxical one.

Some early Christian writers read her as a continuation of Eve: another fallen woman, whose tears and repentance mirrored humanity's own descent and return. Others read her in exactly the opposite direction. Origen and Ambrose treated Magdalene at the empty tomb as a figure of the Church itself—the Bride of Christ, the faithful soul longing for and recognizing the risen Lord. Penitent sinner in one reading, faithful Bride in the other; the two operated in opposite directions yet produced the same effect. The historical woman dissolved into whatever the interpreter required: repentant humanity restored, the receiving community, or the institution of male clergy that absorbed her authority. The named woman at the tomb gave way to a metaphor. Modern readings repeat the move, recasting her as a function of gender, evidence of Jesus's inclusivity of women, rather than reckoning with Magdalene herself and the authority of her witness. In every form, interpretation displaced presence—and Magdalene was overlooked. None of these frameworks accounts for the intimacy and precision of the encounter recorded in the twentieth chapter of John.

AT THE TOMB

The chapter opens: "Early on the first day of the week, while it was still dark, Mary Magdalene went to the tomb and saw that the stone had been removed." Even this line invites questioning. Why was a woman outside the city walls before dawn? Was the darkness chronological, or did it signal a change in state—the hour when night gave way and something not visible began to take form? His body is missing.

Mary ran to Simon Peter and the disciple Jesus loved, called out, breathlessly, "They have taken the Lord out of the tomb, and we don't know where they have put him!" A race ensued, the men sprint in tandem till the Beloved Disciple outpaces, arriving first. The Beloved Disciple stood back as Peter burst forward into the tomb, trying to make out what happened from the linen cloths that remained. The Beloved Disciple "saw and believed," before the men departed the scene. Mary remained behind, weeping.

Absorbed in grief, she looked into the darkness and discovered two angels in white, seated where the body had lain—one at the head, one at the feet. "Woman, why are you crying?" they ask. "They have taken my Lord away," she said, "and I do not know where they have put him." This exchange reads as restrained, almost intimate. Then Mary "turns." The Greek *strapheisa* can describe a simple movement, but in John, what is implied is recognition—a marker of spiritual realization. Jesus repeated the question: "Woman, why are you crying?" He asked again, more pointedly: "Who is it you are looking for?"

In this Gospel, complete recognition consistently occurred through extended dialogue, and this scene fit that pattern. That Mary Magdalene needed a moment to realize exactly what was unfolding was also practically understandable, given the miraculous nature of the moment. The narrative recorded she mistook the risen Christ for a gardener, a detail later read as a moment of female obliviousness. But in John, it was not a mistake, but a symbol, part of her process of recognition. The appearance of a gardener also served to ground the risen Jesus in multiple ways: it marked him with the humility and nurturance of one who tends the earth; it connected him to Eden making this a new creation story; and it implied that he seemed literally embodied.

Believing him ordinary, Mary spoke without hesitation: "Sir, if you have carried him away, tell me where you have put him, and I will get him." The offer was practical—even daring. And before explanation, before proof, he replied with her name: "*Mary*." The sound of her name initiated a transformative spark of recognition. Her excitement was conveyed by her motion: *turning*, she cried out, "*Rabboni!*" The text glosses it as "Teacher," a term that implied familiarity.[10]

Then came the line that would influence centuries of interpretation: "Do not hold on to me, for I have not yet ascended to the Father." Later rendered into Latin as *Noli me tangere*, "do not touch me," the phrase came to be interpreted by Church fathers and clergy as though Mary had grasped at Jesus in confusion or desperation. Yet in context, the passage reflects not confusion, but the ongoing process of spiritual awakening, charged with longing that is relational as much as physical.

Jesus qualified the status of his resurrection: "I have not yet ascended to the Father." His risen body had not completed ascent; something remained in motion. He then did something decisive—so consequential it would strain the consolidation of ecclesial power: he commissioned Mary to spread the message of his ascension. "Go to my brothers and tell them, 'I am ascending to my Father and your Father, to my God and your God.'"[11]

Before doctrine settled, before office was defined, a woman was sent to speak what had happened by the risen Jesus Christ. But the commission extended further than announcement. It lay in the language itself, in the precision of the pronouns: "my Father and your Father. My God and your

God." If unity alone were intended, "our Father" would have sufficed. It did not appear. The distinction remained: *my* Father and *your* Father; *my* God and *your* God.

Throughout John, Jesus's relationship to the Father is singular. It is articulated with a depth and exclusivity that exceeds standard Jewish communal address, where God is invoked collectively as "our Father." In this Gospel, the Son's intimacy with the Father is uniquely his. And here, that intimacy is extended. What Jesus asked Mary to declare reaches beyond the announcement of his rising. She was entrusted with sharing this new relationship with God, and she stands within that first "your."

So, Magdalene was not only the first to witness the resurrection. She was the first addressed within this new relationship to God, and the one sent to speak it. Later tradition did not sustain the weight of this moment, nor did it explain why a woman, why Mary Magdalene received it. Instead, men were elevated: Peter, Paul, the male names on the Gospels. The woman who saw, recognized, and was sent to announce the resurrection was remembered, in the West, as a penitent prostitute.[12]

AT THE CROSS

Tomb and cross—these are the two places where Magdalene takes her most concrete form, a continuity reflected in scripture and carried across centuries of art, from gilded triptychs to fresco cycles. One of the most iconic renditions is Giotto di Bondone's rendering upon the indigo walls of the Scrovegni Chapel in Padua. There, Magdalene clings to the cross, her hand at Jesus's feet, lips parted in grief, long golden hair falling over a rose-colored garment edged in gold and lined with green. Giotto's version became a template for Renaissance crucifixions, its colors and iconography repeated and reworked by artists who mimicked the intimacy and grief he captured.

What distinguished the Gospel accounts of the crucifixion was less identity than distance. Magdalene was consistently named first. In the Matthew and Mark, the women watched "from a distance," named alongside Mary the mother of James and Joseph and either Salome or the mother of the sons of Zebedee. Notably, Magdalene was not described as a mother, a sister, or a wife. Another detail stands out. Matthew and Mark defined the women's role clearly, the texts say they had "followed him from Galilee to care for his needs."[13] The Greek *diakonousai* indicated the women were in active service.

Then, in John, the scene shifted in scope and tone. It zoomed in, quite literally, the women gathering at the very foot of the cross while Jesus suffers. This time Jesus's mother is described as being present, alongside the Beloved Disciple. This was the intimate arrangement later favored in art.

In Luke, the women at the cross are present but unnamed. This Gospel first refers broadly to those who knew Jesus, then clarifies that this included the women who had followed him from Galilee. Not only did the language of the women's service disappear, Luke's author only mentioned them after the crucifixion at the tomb, naming Mary Magdalene, Joanna, Mary the mother of James, and others. It seems the author of Luke was intentionally placing the women at a distance in an act of diminishment. Rather than elevate the women as witnesses, Luke's author emphasized their fright, their confusion, their "bowed" faces, and that the men did not believe them.[14]

Across these variations, one feature remained constant: Mary Magdalene. Where fear and grief might have inspired retreat, she stayed. She witnessed the depths of Jesus's pain, through to his last breath, embodying a rare resilience in the capacity to remain with suffering.

THE PATRONESS

Mary Magdalene appeared only once in the Gospels prior to the passion narratives, within a brief passage that would prove instrumental in coloring her memory. At the start of chapter 8, Luke's author introduced Magdalene first among a group of women the author described as having traveled with Jesus and the Twelve disciples. Yet again, Mary's name did not bear qualifiers of a husband, father, or brother. She was simply Mary, called Magdalene:

> Soon afterward he went on through cities and villages, proclaiming and bringing the good news of the kingdom of God. And the twelve were with him, and also some women who had been healed of evil spirits and infirmities: Mary, called Magdalene, from

> whom seven demons had gone out, and Joanna, the wife of Chuza, Herod's household manager, and Susanna, and many others, who provided for them out of their means.[15]

The final clause of the passage drew little sustained attention until female scholars began to examine its implications. What they realized was that these lines qualified the women, including Mary Magdalene, as having financially sustained Jesus's ministry.

Scholars like Barbara E. Reid have pointed out that the verb *diēkonoun* translated as "were ministering" or "were serving" shares its root with the later term "deacon." The phrasing placed these women within the practical infrastructure of Jesus's ministry—its travel, its sustenance, its continuation. The words at the close of the passage, "out of their own means," made plain that these women provided resources, wealth, within their own control. No mention of families, husbands, or fathers—these women may have had a level of financial independence.

Reid and others like Elisabeth Schüssler Fiorenza and Jane Schaberg have demonstrated that in first century Judea, the patronage of women was uncommon but feasible. Moreover, these scholars argue that Luke depicts Mary and the other women as structural actors in Jesus's ministry—a detail long overlooked. Perhaps a woman's eye was necessary to identify what was always present in the text: prominent women providing material support in Jesus's community, with Magdalene listed first among them.[16]

FULLY HEALED

Even before their names were listed, Luke mentioned a detail that would become salacious, that the women "had been healed of evil spirits and infirmities." The phrase arrives charged by centuries of interpretation and imagery—bodies contorted, priests invoking power over chaos, the female body made legible through disorder. But beneath those projections, the words carry another possibility tradition did not allow. Here, the Greek vocabulary is essential.

In the Gospel narrative, the ailments from which the women were collectively healed are described as *pneumatōn ponērōn*, "evil spirits." *Pneuma* is a capacious term in Greek: it can cover breath, wind, soul, spirit—human or divine, even the Holy Spirit. Paired with *ponēros*, meaning harmful or wicked, the phrase takes on moral force. It appeared elsewhere in the Gospels, for example, in a warning from Jesus that an unclean spirit may return with seven others even more destructive. So in Luke's passage, this designation carried an explicit force, because evil spirits were understood on typical terms. But that term described the women as a group.

When Mary Magdalene was addressed, the vocabulary shifted. There were not "seven" *pneumatōn ponērōn*, "evil spirits." She is described as "Magdalene, from whom seven *daimonia* had gone out."[17]

To a modern reader, "demon" sounds inherently sinister, and easily merges into evil spirits. However, in classical Greek thought, *daimonion* encompassed a wide range of meanings: a spirit, a divine presence, an unseen intermediary. Homer and Hesiod at times described *daimones* as guiding forces woven into the fabric of life. In philosophy. Plato described love itself as a "great *daimōn*," mediating between mortal and divine. Each soul, he suggested, was accompanied by a guiding *daimōn* that shaped its earthly course. Aristotle's *eudaimonia*, often translated "happiness" literally "having a good *daimōn*," from *eu*, meaning "good," and *daimōn*, suggesting a life rightly aligned. Later Greco-Roman writers imagined them as presences inhabiting the air between earth and moon, mobile, influential, permeable to human experience. By the first century, Middle Platonists considered *daimonia* to be intermediary powers: forces operating between gods and humans that mediated inspiration, dreams, guidance, and enabled communication between visible and invisible realms.[18]

Luke was composed by a highly educated man, indicated by the polished Koine Greek, and tradition named him as a "physician."[19] Luke's author did not need medical knowledge to be well aware that *daimonia* carried a diverse register of meaning. Whatever nuance was intended, *daimonia* did not automatically imply moral failure. The explicit charge of "evil spirits" was not repeated. The shift from *pneumatōn ponērōn* to *daimonia* does not deny affliction; but it reframes what it possibly meant. It is possible that *daimonia* inferred a healing event, physical or spiritual. Additional language in the passage reinforces the possibility it was a physical healing: the women were described as having been healed not only from "evil spirits" but also from *astheneiōn*, "infirmities." The term denotes illness, frailty, and lack of strength; its tone is clinical, not moral.

In the ancient Mediterranean world, the mind and body were often attributed to spiritual forces; medical and religious frameworks did not sharply divide the two. The verb applied to Mary's seven *daimonia* offers more clarity. The verb usually used exorcism scenes, *ekballō*, "to cast out," did not appear at all in Luke 8:1–3. Instead, the verb used for these women is *tetherapeumenai*—"having been healed," or more precisely, "restored," a standard term for physical illness. The verb used in reference to Magdalene's seven *daimonia* is *exelēlythei*, "had gone out." Not as cast out, or even removed, but simply as having completed their departure.

In the earliest surviving reflections on this passage, no major Christian writer emphasized Mary's seven *daimonia*. Even Tertullian, despite his often misogynistic posture, did not dwell on the detail. Hippolytus of Rome, who wrote extensively on Magdalene's encounter at the tomb, likewise passed over it, honoring her instead as the "apostle to the apostles." The silence is striking, especially given that Luke is commonly dated to the late first century. Not until the third century did Origen of Alexandria become the first surviving writer to comment directly on Mary's seven *daimonia*, interpreting them symbolically as spiritual disorder or ignorance before illumination. Ambrose of Milan, likewise, framed her condition in terms of transformation rather than disgrace.[20]

The fixation on this phrase—and its assumption as being "demonic"—did not arise until Gregory the Great, in the same homily that cast her as a "penitent prostitute." Only after Gregory did *daimonia* become an accusation. The timing and singularity make it far more likely that *daimonia* were never intended as demons but reflect a later manipulation.

One detail in the passage remains barely examined, and it is one that would not have escaped an ancient ear. A clue not of possession, but of elevation: the number itself. Seven.

THE MASTER

Numbers counted more than time and accumulation in antiquity. They reflected meaning, giving form to structure, proportion, and an intelligible order of the world. For centuries, seven held a specific signal, and was considered universally among the most divine—the completion of a cycle, the point at which nothing further needed to be added.

Seven drew its significance from sky and earth. Seven celestial bodies moved against the fixed stars—the sun, the moon, and five wandering lights. The lunar month unfolded in roughly four seven-day phases; the seven-day week followed its rhythm. In the night sky, clusters like the Pleiades, the Seven Sisters, and the Great Bear sparkled with clarity. Music moved through seven tones before resolving to the octave. Even the head held seven points of perception: two eyes, two ears, two nostrils, and a mouth. Seven was not an abstraction imposed upon reality, but a pattern observed within it. One so constant, so recurrent, that seven came to feel like a signature of cosmic coherence.

Mathematically, seven resists division. As a prime number, it cannot be formed by multiplying smaller integers. Ancient thinkers, such as the followers of the Greek sage Pythagoras, called it "virgin," because neither born from other numbers nor giving birth to them, it stands alone. In geometry, the regular heptagon resists simple construction with compass and straightedge—its proportions slip into irrational relations.

What mathematics expressed in abstraction, myth conveyed in narrative. In Greece, wisdom gathered in the Seven Sophoi, wisemen whose sayings shaped philosophical memory. Mesopotamians spoke of the Apkallū, seven primordial teachers emerging from the sea to instruct humanity. In India, the *ṛṣis*, the Saptarishi, were ancestral seers, custodians of sacred knowledge traced to the beginning remembered as seven.

Seven marked passage and transformation. In one of the earliest written narratives, the Sumerian goddess Inanna descended through seven gates before rising again. In Egypt, the Seven Hathors appeared at birth to pronounce destiny. Buddhists remembered Siddhartha taking seven steps immediately after birth. In Hellenistic cosmology, the soul ascended through seven planetary spheres. In Hindu thought, seven chakras traced a vertical path through the body toward enlightenment.

In Judaism, seven structured sacred time: the seven days of creation, the seventh-day Sabbath, the seven-branched menorah, the sabbatical cycle of seven years, seven times seven culminating in Jubilee. The number marked divine intervention—seven circuits around Jericho, sevenfold rites of purification.

Across these traditions, seven marked stages traversed and thresholds crossed. It represented the completion of a process, wholeness reached only after every gate had been passed. The author of Luke would have been aware of these patterns when he attached the integer to Mary Magdalene. What seven carries would align not with demonic forces, but with healing, fullness, mastery.

The significance of seven dovetails with another detail—the action implied by the phrase itself. In Magdalene's case, the *daimonia* are described as having "gone out." No dramatic expulsion is narrated, no external agent explicitly named; the movement is already complete. Grammatically, the action remains centered on her. In a symbolic world where seven signified completion, that phrasing carries particular weight. If Mary, herself, had released or transcended seven *daimonia*, what did that act reveal?

Middle Platonic thought offers one possible horizon for understanding the language. Knowledge was imagined as a movement through ascending states: from *doxa*, opinion, to *gnōsis* or *epistēmē*, knowledge, and ultimately to *sophia,* the integration of learning into wisdom.[21] For some, the process culminated in *teleiōsis*, a state of completion or spiritual maturity. Such ideas circulated widely through the educated Mediterranean world in which Luke was composed, shaping the intellectual atmosphere even beyond explicitly philosophical circles.

Through this lens, the seven *daimonia* may signify not corruption, but completion—a passage already traversed. The *daimonia* could represent forces involved in the ordering of the soul within the cosmos, stages through which one passes rather than stains permanently carried. Attached to Magdalene, the phrase could suggest elevation: someone who had moved through disorder and arrived at a state of understanding, even deep realization. Perhaps the sort of understanding that might qualify her to witness a miraculous resurrection.

This Middle Platonic lens on the significance of seven *daimonia* tracks astonishingly closely with the mysterious final passages of the Gospel of Mary. Often called the "Ascent of the Soul" by scholars, the text begins mid-narrative as just after this many pages have been torn out. The soul is described as moving through three powers when it arrives at a fourth power that has seven forms.[22]

It is possible the appearance of seven in Luke and seven in the Gospel of Mary is coincidental. It is possible the Gospel of Mary, dated to the second century, somehow borrowed from Luke—though the texts are vastly different. It is also possible the seven connected to Magdalene reflects memory, an association between her and this sacred number that points some level of transformation, attainment, spiritual mastery.

Yet, seven in the modern Christian imagination would take on another texture, a negative one. And again, perhaps it's just a coincidence, but the prevailing interpretation of Magdalene's seven demons and a framework of seven sins originate with the same individual: Gregory the Great.

THE SEVEN

In his famous homily, Gregory opened by affirming that seven signifies universality; the whole of time held in seven days. Then he pivoted. Leaning on demons, he declared that Mary was full of all vices, elaborating on her stains and her shame. No list of sins—let alone seven—materialized in his sermon.[23]

That list, the Seven Deadly Sins, emerged elsewhere: *Moralia in Job*, Book XXXI. Gregory began composing it in the late 570s or early 580s while serving as papal envoy in Constantinople. He became pope on September 3, 590. Homily 33 followed a year later, in September 591.[24]

Scholars date Gregory's reduction of Evagrius Ponticus's eight *logismoi*—patterns of destructive thought identified for ascetic discipline—to the mid-590s. Evagrius, a fourth-century monk writing within the ascetic culture of the Egyptian desert, described eight recurring disturbances of the mind: gluttony, lust, avarice, sadness, anger, acedia, vainglory, and pride.[25] These were not ethical failures but recurring movements of thought, impulses arising within the mind that required discernment and mastery through spiritual practice. In this way, *logismoi* and *daimonia* occupied related ground: both named forces moving within the inner life, whether understood psychologically or spiritually. But there were eight, not seven. What Gregory created was distinct in structure.

Gregory's system took on a new purpose and tone, transforming what had belonged to psychological observation into a moral structure. Writing for a pastoral church—not for desert ascetics like Evagrius—Gregory condensed the eightfold *logismoi* into seven capital vices inspired, in large part, by Augustine of Hippo. For Gregory, pride was the root, or what he called the "queen," while the seven were vainglory, envy, anger, sadness or sloth, avarice, gluttony and lust. From these all moral disorder flowed: faults to be confessed, corrected, and preached against through the authority of the priest and the Church.[26]

Gregory's indictment of Magdalene in 591 coincided with the period in which he was consolidating this framework. These were not distant developments, but adjacent acts of interpretation, undertaken by the same hand. Gregory never stated that Mary's seven *daimonia* corresponded to his seven vices—he did not need to. He made the assertion of Magdalene's sinfulness, entangling Luke's anointing woman with Mary's seven *daimonia*. And subsequently published a list of seven sins. The convergence was implied, and at the very least, what his framework did was obscure the ancient, positive, sacred resonance of the number seven.

Seven's older sacral gravity gradually receded from memory. It briefly resurfaced in medieval intellectual culture—in the seven liberal arts, in the ladders of Lady Philosophy, in scholastic cosmologies—but those stayed within learned traditions. Gregory's seven, by contrast, entered popular imagination. To this day, when the number is heard, it is heard as sin.

Language is the key to Mary Magdalene's portrayal, and it's what can still exonerate and elevate her. Just as the meaning of the seven *daimonia* can be reconsidered, her name carries more than place.

THE MAGDALENE

Mary. She shares this name with Jesus's mother, with Mary of Clopas, with the indistinct "other Mary." The recurrence of "Mary" in the Gospels reflects what historical research into first-century Judea confirms: Miriam was common. As Tal Ilan's study of Jewish names in late antiquity shows, Miriam appears with notable consistency across the surviving record.[27]

Scholars have proposed that the popularity of Miriam in this period may have been inspired by Mariamne, wife of Herod the Great. Mariamne was a princess of the Hasmonean line, the priestly royal dynasty that emerged from the Maccabean revolt and ruled Judea in the second and first centuries BCE. When Herod murdered Mariamne, Jewish families may have answered by naming their daughters in her honor.[28] Earlier still was Moses's sister, Miriam the prophetess, who anchored the name in Israel's memory. After the crossing of the Red Sea, Egyptian-born Miriam took a tambourine and led the women of Israel in song and dance. Her memory came to be overshadowed by her brothers. Ultimately, she was remembered less for her vision and song than for when she spoke against Moses and was struck with leprosy by Yahweh.

"Mary" retains an element of mystery, in part through the phonetic resonance between Miriam and the Egyptian *mry*, "beloved."[29] Still, it is not "Mary" that distinguishes her among the women of the Gospels. It is Magdalene.

Many English Bibles render her name as "Mary of Magdala," and medieval legends do the same. At this layer of construction, Magdalene becomes simply a matter of geography—a woman from a town, a pilgrim's stop on the northwestern shore of the Sea of Galilee. Tradition treats it as a settled fact: Magdalene was a place, reflected broadly in Christian culture and any basic information about her.

Across the Gospels, she appears as Μαρία ἡ Μαγδαληνή, Μαρία ἡ ἀπὸ Μαγδαλά, or Μαρία Μαγδαληνή. At times the article ἡ is present, at times absent. Occasionally ἀπὸ marks origin—"from" or "out of," a straightforward locative construction. But in Luke chapter 8—the same passage as the seven *daimonia*—the phrasing changes. There she is Μαρία ἡ καλουμένη Μαγδαληνή, "Mary, the one called Magdalene." The participle καλουμένη—from καλέω, "to call" or "to name"—does not reflect place. It marks designation. She is not just "from" somewhere, she is *called* something. Grammatically, it reads as an epithet.

Μαγδαληνή has no independent meaning in Greek. It is widely believed to reflect a Semitic root *mgdl*; "tower." Tower could signify place—settlements in Judea often incorporated *migdal* into their names. But the morphology itself does not compel a geographic reading. The construction leaves open another possibility: not origin, but name.

As biblical studies moved beyond ecclesiastical control in the twentieth century, long-held assumptions came under scrutiny with "Magdalene" among them. Raymond E. Brown acknowledged the uncertainty without pressing it. Jane Schaberg noted its narrative weight. Susan Haskins traced the associations that accumulated around her name. The question was recognized but rarely pursued. It resurfaced in modern discussion through Margaret Starbird.

In *The Woman with the Alabaster Jar*, she argued that "Magdalene" was not a place name, but a title derived from *migdal*, "tower." Drawing on "tower of the flock," the Hebrew Migdal-Eder in Micah 4:8, she read the passage as prophecy and applied it to Mary.[30] From this point she advanced a far more controversial claim: that Mary had been the wife of Jesus and part of a concealed royal lineage. Those conclusions were widely disputed, but Starbird reopened the linguistic question of "Magdalene."

In 2021, Elizabeth Schrader and Joan Taylor conducted the first comprehensive reassessment of "Magdalene," evaluating whether the term functioned as a place name or a title. In their joint article, "The Meaning of "Magdalene:" A Review of Literary Evidence," the authors meticulously surveyed the earliest textual and geographical evidence.[31]

As Schrader and Taylor show, the Magdalene-as-city theory has substantial holes. Flavius Josephus, writing in the late first century, referred to a major Galilean settlement called Taricheae, a Greek-named center of the fish-salting trade, destroyed during the Roman-Jewish War. He did not call this town Magdala. That designation appears later in rabbinic literature as Migdal Nuniyya, "Tower of Fish"—alongside a parallel name, Migdal Tsebayya, "Tower of Dyers." Schrader and Taylor argue that the rabbinic 'Migdal-' places cannot be securely identified with Tarichaea, and that there is no evidence anyone ever called Tarichaea "Magdala." What remains problematic is the timeline, because there is no evidence the town was called "Magdala" in Mary's lifetime, or even by the time the Gospels were composed.

Early Christian writers, as Schrader and Taylor note, offered no clarity. Origen of Alexandria and Eusebius of Caesarea, both familiar with the region, referred to Mary Magdalene but did not anchor her to a town or place. A fifth- or sixth-century Coptic encomium falsely attributed to Cyril of Jerusalem situates Mary "from Magdala" through her grandfather's provenance—the first source to anchor the name to a specific city.

Macarius Magnes, defending Christianity against pagan critics, preserved the opponents' charge that Mary came from "some very miserable little village," a phrase Schrader and Taylor note may well have referred to Bethany rather than a Galilean Magdala. A confident identification did not appear until the sixth century, when Theodosius, a German archdeacon, recorded "Magdale" on the Galilee shore as the place where Mary was born—the earliest surviving attestation of Mary Magdalene as actually from this location. From that point forward, pilgrim itineraries attached her memory to a Galilean site simply called "Magdale," though its identity with any earlier attested city remained unclear.

Schrader and Taylor circled the earliest testimonies. Writing in the third century, Origen took "Magdala" to be a place name but never linked it to a Galilean city. For him, what mattered was its meaning: "magnification." He turned to the Aramaic root *g-d-l*, "to make great" or "magnify," reading the name as a title of magnification rather than a place. Jerome followed suit, interpreting the designation as strength rather than place: "Mary, properly 'the Magdalene'—who, because of diligence and ardent faith, received the name 'of the tower'—deserved to see the risen Christ first before the apostles." Rather than designating a city, Jerome's use of "deserved" conveys that "Magdalene" reflects the reason why she was qualified to witness the resurrection.

Symbolic naming was embedded in early Christian practice. Simon became Peter, Petros meaning "rock" in Greek, a designation interpreted to mark role and characterization. If "Magdalene" functioned similarly, as a nickname, a title, not a place, then the question followed: what did "tower" signify?

A tower was fortified architecture, built to withstand siege, intended to endure when cities fell. Its walls contained not only soldiers but townspeople, markets, and the ordinary life of a community seeking refuge. Its defining faculty was vision: rising above the horizon, a tower extended sight into distances otherwise unseen, keeping watch where danger or promise. For this reason, vertical structures carried sacred resonance in antiquity. Height signified contact between realms. Towers, poles, trees, mountains, all marked a point of exchange between earth and sky and became subjects of ritual and worship. Mircea Eliade described this pattern as the *axis mundi*: the point where heaven and humanity meet. But these structures extended vision not only outward, but inward too. Meeting places inherently imply thresholds between the visible and the invisible.[32]

The syntax of "Magdalene" carries not only the Hebrew *migdal* for tower, but the Hebrew *gādal*, "to be great," and the Greek *megalynō*, "to magnify," recognized by Origen and Jerome. Together what registers is a distinct sense of elevation, stature, and distinction. In myths, the number seven is explicitly linked to ascent and elevation, from the ancient poems of Inanna to even the Gospel of Mary. Movement toward the divine was imagined not as a single leap or moment, but as a sequence, laddered, tiered, often sevenfold. It belongs to the same symbolic field as towers—a shared language of height and passage, between beginning and completion, seen and unseen, earth and heaven. If "Magdalene" does not fix a place, then it leaves her unbound to one. With that, her identity opens, along with the possibility that she has been read as two where she may have been one.

THE ANOINTING WOMAN

In Christian art, saints are often known by the symbols they are depicted with. Saint George astride a white horse slaying the dragon; Saint Catherine crowned, the wheel at her side; Saint Peter holding the keys. Iconography condensed complex narratives into a single image, allowing a figure to be recognized across centuries. Mary Magdalene carried her own signature: the jar.

Sometimes the vessel shown with her is small and simple, smoothed by use, resting gently in her embrace, close against her breast. Other containers are ornate: gilded, cylindrical, sometimes raised on a pedestal, capped with a long, pointed lid. They can be so elaborate that they resemble a miniature tower, a Eucharistic tabernacle, or a chalice. Whatever its form, the jar remains constant, and its meaning unmistakable. The jar she is portrayed with designates Mary Magdalene as the anointing woman of the Gospels.

Some works render the scene in full drama, as in *The Feast in the House of Simon the Pharisee* by Peter Paul Rubens. There, a crowded table of male authority surrounds a single woman at their feet. She bends low, her hair is loosened, tears visible, and the jar catches the light. The identification of this woman supplied by painters and curators is consistent: Mary Magdalene. This is an assumption that extends far beyond art too. Pastors, priests, and even well-read Christians often refer to Mary Magdalene as the anointing woman. Yet there is a glaring problem. Her name never appears in *any* of the four Gospels accounts of this pivotal moment.

The anointing is one of the few stories found across all four Gospels. While the versions in Matthew and Mark are closely aligned while the versions in Luke and John diverge in essential ways. These distinctions tend to be obscured by the way the Gospels have long been read together, a tendency initiated by Irenaeus when he first named the four Gospels.[33] From that practice, a single, continuous Christian narrative took hold, a style of reading scripture that would shape interpretation for centuries. It was through this intentional style of harmonization that the four women of four stories became blended into one and ultimately connected to Mary Magdalene.

When narratives are read together, their edges begin to soften and their details overlap. Unity can blur distinction, smoothing away nuances that give each account its particular meaning. The anointing stories illustrate this clearly. They differ in setting, timing, characters, and theological emphasis. In three, the woman remains anonymous; in one, she is named. Within each telling, there are details that carry weight, subtle clues that may illuminate how Magdalene came to "hold" the jar.

In the parallel accounts of Matthew and Mark, the scene unfolded in Bethany, in the house of Simon the Leper: "While Jesus was in Bethany . . . a woman came to him with an alabaster jar of very expensive perfume, which she poured on his head as he reclined at the table." She was unnamed and unmarked, defined only by the criticism her act provoked. Mark recorded the value of the perfume as "three hundred denarii." The disciples protested in unison, condemning the anointing as wasteful, to which Jesus responded decisively in her defense: "Leave her alone," he said. "Why are you bothering her? She has done a beautiful thing to me." He then made an extraordinary declaration: "Truly I tell you, wherever the gospel is preached throughout the world, what she has done will also be told, in memory of her." The memory of an unnamed woman was promised worldwide acclaim by Jesus.[34]

Luke reshaped the narrative decisively, grounding the moment in an entirely different setting. While the other three Gospels located it in Bethany, Luke situated the anointing in Capernaum at Simon the Pharisee's home. This placement, in a religious teacher's personal space, charged the room with male authority. A woman is described as appearing seemingly out of nowhere, though marked by reputation: "a woman in the town who lived a sinful life." She carried an alabaster jar as she approached him from behind. This is the only Gospel that noted she was weeping. As her tears fell onto Jesus's feet, she wiped them with her hair, kissed them, and poured the oil. On his *feet*, not his head—a crucial difference to Mark and Matthew. As in every account, male objection followed.

Simon the Pharisee remarked: "If this man were a prophet, he would know who is touching him." He reduced her to a category: "what kind of woman she is—that she is a sinner." The label is repeated, clearly it defined her according to Luke's author. But Jesus refused the reduction and he answered with a parable: two debts, two pardons, pride and grace set in contrast. Then, turning toward the anointing woman, Jesus measured her devotion against the host's neglect: "You did not give me water . . . you did not give me a kiss . . . you did not anoint my head." The repetition created force as Jesus honored her: "Her many sins have been forgiven—for she loved much." Before the assembled table, the unnamed woman—described only as a sinner—was declared to have surpassed the Pharisee in faith.[35]

John set the event in Bethany, like Matthew and Mark, and described anointing to be of the feet, as in Luke. But the household changed, and with it, the tone shifted. What in Luke was described as a tense gathering edged with scrutiny, becomes in John a meal shared among familiar companions. The woman was named, Mary. "Mary took about a pint of pure nard, an expensive perfume; she poured it on Jesus's feet and wiped his feet with her hair. And the house was filled with the fragrance of the perfume." But this is Mary of Bethany, as the text records, with no "Magdalene" marked present.

The common thread of male complaint followed, this time from Judas Iscariot, the disciple who would soon betray Jesus. In John, no parable was offered, nor any declaration of love or memory. Jesus's commentary tied the act to his impending death. "Leave her alone," he said. "It was intended that she should save this perfume for the day of my burial. You will always have the poor among you, but you will not always have me."[36]

Matthew and Mark reflected the same connection between anointing act and burial. In a practical sense, a jar of oil or ointment once opened could no longer be preserved; it could not have been kept for later use. Jesus's statement can be interpreted to mean that the anointing woman, Mary of Bethany, may have had an anticipatory sense that Jesus was going to be killed. This would have implied that Mary of Bethany had awareness or knowledge the disciples lacked, at least in that moment.

However, the connection between anointing and burial remains suggestive and interpretive rather than explicit. Nowhere do the Gospels reflect that same oil was used at the burial. Nor is it clear whether this anointing act might have been a part of later burial preparations, in a literal rather than a symbolic sense. The connection exists, nonetheless, stated by Jesus across three of the Gospels.

If the narratives are compared, the women at the tomb varied in name and function. However, neither Mary of Bethany nor the unnamed sinner appeared at the tomb, not in any account. But Mary Magdalene did. In John she arrived alone at dawn, not to anoint, but to witness. In John, Jesus's body had already been prepared by Joseph of Arimathea and Nicodemus. In Matthew, Magdalene was mentioned simply as witness. In Mark and Luke, Magdalene was named first among the women who arrived carrying spices for a funerary anointing.

The tension lies in one of the most persistent mysteries around Mary Magdalene. Is she the same woman as Mary of Bethany?

MARY OF . . .

In the Orthodox East, the Marys always remained distinct in tradition. Mary Magdalene was set apart from Mary of Bethany, each honored in her own right. However, over time, Mary of Bethany came to be counted among the Orthodox tradition of the "Myrrhbearers," the women remembered as bringing burial spices to the tomb even though the text did not place her at the tomb. This same mixing of Marys has been even more pronounced across the Christian West, conflations found across interpretation, art, and popular culture.

A third century resurrection homily attributed to Hippolytus of Rome described Mary Magdalene at the tomb alongside Martha of Bethany—a strange pairing that departs from the Gospels.[37] Whether critical, metaphor, or simply wrong, Hippolytus's account suggests that these women's identities were fluid and not fixed in memory. Other writers continued to treat the Marys separately, including Origen of Alexandria, John Chrysostom, and Jerome, but by the fourth and fifth centuries, commentators increasingly read the anointing accounts as one. Ambrose of Milan treated the scenes as variations on a single moral drama, while Augustine of Hippo acknowledged the differences while allowing their figures to echo one another. The Marys' identities had not formally fused quite yet, but the distinctions between Magdalene and "Bethany" had begun to soften.[38]

When Gregory the Great preached in Rome in 591, he spoke with a certainty earlier authority figures had left unresolved. His Homily 33 exists as the earliest known explicit identification of Mary Magdalene with Mary of Bethany and the unnamed sinful woman in Luke. Gregory's reasoning was circular: Magdalene must be the sinner because she had seven demons, and those demons must signify sexual sin because she was the sinner. From that point forward, Mary Magdalene was fixed not only as the anointing woman, but as a figure marked by sexual disgrace.[39] She and Mary of Bethany were fused so completely that in medieval saintly legends, especially the popular stories from the South of France, the siblings from Bethany, Martha and Lazarus, are recorded as traveling with her.

Magdalene's portrayal and the layers of confusion surrounding her exemplify how scriptural interpretation was filtered through ecclesiastical authority. Literacy in antiquity and into the medieval period remained extremely low, generally below 10 percent of the population, rising modestly only after the Renaissance.[40] Those who could read were wealthy. For the vast majority, the Bible was not read but received, delivered through the local priest or pastor—and his opinions, personal and doctrinal. In the West, Jerome's Latin Vulgate held a near-total monopoly for more than a millennium. Vernacular translations were extremely limited and, when they did emerge, they were restricted and actively suppressed. The invention of the printing press and the upheavals of the Reformation widened access, but independent reading remained uncommon for generations. Church Fathers, preachers, artists, and clergy determined what was taught and what was withheld, what counted as truth and what was condemned as heresy.

Mediation was only one mechanism that hardened Magdalene's characterization. More decisive was Christianity's insistence that sacred narrative function as history. The Gospel accounts were treated by Christian authorities as objective records of events, not dissimilar to the way that Augustine of Hippo had concretized Adam and Eve into literal human beings who walked the earth. This historicizing impulse set a veil of obscurity and contradiction over the history of Christianity, establishing rigid intellectual boundaries and excluding voices beyond accepted perspectives.

Only in recent decades have scholars, armed with historical-critical, feminist, and sociocultural tools, returned to Christian texts with sustained scrutiny. By re-situating early Christianity within its social, economic, and religious realities, they have begun to recover the agency and significance of women in the earliest communities whose voices were long obscured or erased.

Among these scholars, Elizabeth Schrader Polczer turned to the earliest copy of John with forensic attention to detail and exacting ingenuity. She has identified compelling evidence of scribal interventio—edits that center on Mary of Bethany, and may, in turn, obscure Magdalene.

ONE IOTA

Composition dates and surviving manuscripts for ancient works rarely align—a gap of a millennium is not unusual. Flavius Josephus composed *Antiquities of the Jews* around 93–94, though the earliest substantial Greek copies survive from the eleventh century. Homer's *Odyssey* is generally dated to the late eighth century BCE, while the earliest complete manuscripts are medieval.[41] The same pattern appears with Eusebius of Caesarea, whose *Ecclesiastical History* was completed in the fourth century but survives primarily through medieval Greek manuscripts.[42]

The Bible is no exception. The Gospels were composed between roughly 65 and 110 CE. The earliest complete copies survive in fourth-century codices such as Codex Sinaiticus and Codex Vaticanus, where the four accounts are bound together. Even conservatively, this leaves a gap of nearly three centuries between composition and the earliest complete manuscripts. In relative terms, this is not unusual. It is, however, long enough for texts to pass through generations of scribes. It is long enough for errors to enter and revisions to take hold.

A field of scholarship known as textual criticism addresses these discrepancies by comparing manuscripts and identifying points of divergence. Medieval copies of Josephus and Eusebius, for instance, contain passages widely believed to have been revised to align more closely with the Christian narrative.[43] Similar examples appear within the Gospels, well known in academic circles yet rarely addressed from the pulpit. The story of the adulterous woman is absent from the earliest manuscripts of John, including Jesus's famous declaration, "Let anyone among you who is without sin be the first to throw a stone." Mark offers another clear case: its earliest manuscripts end at 16:8, with later copies appending endings that include references to Mary Magdalene's seven *daimonia*.[44]

Since the Nag Hammadi discovery, additional pieces have surfaced through excavations, rubbish heaps, private collections, and antiquities markets allowing scholars to trace this process in motion. Each fragment of papyrus offers a glimpse into the past, revealing how much of early Christianity still remains unknown. No surviving manuscript of the New Testament dates to the first century. The earliest fragment, Papyrus 52, is scarcely larger than a credit card. It contains a passage from John. Pieces of the Synoptics date slightly later. The earliest near-complete manuscript of any Gospel is again John: Papyrus 66, discovered in 1952 near Dishna in Upper Egypt and dated as early as 200 and as late as 250. It remains the oldest surviving, near-complete copy of a canonical Gospel.[45] Even the smallest scrap illuminates the literary process: how texts were copied, transmitted, corrected, harmonized, and reshaped. What once lay buried or unnoticed is now examined through journals, conferences, and books, making visible the layered and evolving formation of the Christianity.

Papyrus 66 is fragile, its edges frayed with small gaps interrupting the lines. It rests at the Bibliotheca Bodmeriana in Cologny, Switzerland, but it is digitized and accessible, allowing scholars to examine every stroke and correction. In the spaces between letters, Schrader Polczer noticed something others had overlooked. Scholars call it "textual instability."[46]

That instability centers on Martha, the sister of Mary of Bethany and Lazarus. Martha appeared in two chapters of John. In chapter 12, while Mary of Bethany anointed Jesus, Martha served a meal. In the famous miracle of chapter 11, where Jesus raises Lazarus from the dead, Martha appeared alongside Mary. At the opening of that scene, Martha greeted Jesus upon his arrival. It is here, in the opening lines of Papyrus 66 chapter 11, that Schrader Polczer identified unusual disruptions: erasures, corrections, and irregularities clustered around the women's names.

The distinction was subtle. Other evaluators of the text had noticed it but looked no further. Schrader Polczer focused on the first five verses and noticed that a scribe had altered the name "Mary" to "Martha" and changed the singular "sister" to the plural "sisters." In Greek, the shifts were simple, easy enough to dismiss as scribal confusion at first glance. Yet by attending closely to the movement of the pen and the form of the script, Schrader Polczer determined this was no accident. The scribe had made an intentional adjustment, changing "Mary" to "Martha" through the alteration of a single letter: an *iota* replaced with a *theta*.

As she traced the changes in Papyrus 66, Schrader Polczer surveyed the earliest mentions of this scene in other manuscripts and patristic commentary. Some early writers alluded to the scene while making Martha absent. A brief mention by Tertullian is particularly revealing. In his account, Mary is the woman who utters the confession that Jesus is the Son of God. Later in the same chapter, just before Jesus raises Lazarus, Martha made the key theological declaration: "I believe that you are the Messiah, the Son of God, who is to come into the world." This revelatory recognition comes in Martha's voice in modern Bibles—but Tertullian described it in *Mary of Bethany's* voice.[47] Schrader Polczer followed the pattern further, suggesting that John Chrysostom occasionally attributed to Mary actions usually assigned to Martha.[48] Egeria, a fourth-century female pilgrim, recounted visiting Bethany and noted that Mary—not Martha—greeted

Jesus.[49] Early printed Bibles, including Tyndale's 1526 New Testament, the 1591 Bishops' Bible, and the first printing of the 1611 King James Version, render John 11:3 with a single sister, "And his sister sent unto him . . . ," preserving the older singular reading rather than the later plural "sisters."[50] Small changes—single letters and altered plurals—clustered precisely where Martha entered the narrative.

Even the canonical text as it stands contains strange elements. Both Mary and Martha address Jesus with identical words: "Lord, if you had been here, my brother would not have died." Scholars note this duplication likely reflects later editorial shaping.[51] It is divergence, not consistency, that is reflected through centuries of manuscripts. These incongruences suggest that the Bethany sisters weren't fixed from the beginning but standardized gradually.

All these attestations support what Schrader Polczer has proposed: there may have been an earlier version of the story in which Martha was absent, not only from the opening lines, but from the entire narrative. And if Mary of Bethany both anointed Jesus and made this confession, she would have been an extraordinarily significant figure in John. Mary of Bethany would have been more theologically prominent than any male disciple and arguably as essential as Mary Magdalene.

What if one woman became three, her stature and significance diffused across multiple characters? Placing Magdalene and the sisters of Bethany together draws together extremely powerful roles and attributes: discipleship, financial support, anointing, recognizing, meal preparation, presence at the cross, witness of the resurrection, and commissioning by Jesus to spread the good news. On their own, the women are extremely potent, their actions create powerful examples for Christian women seeking to participate in faith. But together, they become a powerful argument for Mary as the preeminent apostle.

As written in the Bible, Mary Magdalene is witness and patron, possibly master of sevenfold wisdom. Yes, before turning to the Nag Hammadi texts, the Gospel of Mary, or deeper questions about her origins and relationship with Jesus, Mary Magdalene begins to come into view. What obscures her is not absence, but perspective.

THE TOWER

Mary's own account did not survive. She embodied a form of authority rooted not in institution or hierarchy, but in support, in witness, and possibly much more. Of all her roles in scripture, the most potent one remains her exchange with the risen Christ in the garden in John. We do not have her words, her version of what she saw, or how she understood the man before her. What remains is memory transmitted through others, shaped, changed, made to fit what was needed of her.

Magdalene's testimony was crucial in anchoring the belief that Jesus had ascended not merely in spirit, but in body. This shift from metaphor to literal, from immaterial to physical, was a concept that carried profound weight in a religious world already familiar with myths of dying and returning divinities: Osiris, Dionysus, Attis, and Adonis, among others. Jewish texts like the book of Daniel and Second Maccabees imagined the dead rising bodily at the end of time. Greek philosophy proposed that spirit was privileged above matter, with salvation often understood as the ascent of the soul beyond the material world.

The resurrection of Jesus therefore had to be narrated carefully in the Gospels and clarified through doctrine in order to distinguish it from surrounding religious and philosophical ideas. Paul described a transformed or "spiritual body,"[52] while the later Gospel accounts increasingly emphasized the materiality of the risen Christ: wounds touched, bread broken, fish eaten. By contrast, texts discovered at Nag Hammadi often portray the resurrection event less as the revival of a corpse than as a transformation of consciousness or soul.

In the Gospel of Mary, the Savior's communication with Magdalene is described as an interior vision. He even told her, "Where the *nous* is, there is the treasure."[53] *Nous*, often translated simply as "mind," was complex. It could be used for spiritual perception or the inner faculty of divine understanding—more akin to the spiritual heart.

The Church Fathers worked through arguments written, exchanged, and debated to define resurrection as fully embodied. Writing against "heretics" who interpreted the event more spiritually or metaphorically, Irenaeus insisted that Jesus truly took flesh, suffered, died, and rose. Tertullian, too, made the body a battleground of salvation. Augustine later folded flesh, sin, grace, and resurrection into the architecture of Western Christianity. Doctrine made Mary Magdalene's encounter with Jesus in the garden increasingly useful because John's narrative is carefully grounded in physicality—the mistaken identity, the "clinging," the exchange of names. These gestures reinforced the bodily reality of the risen Christ, even as Mary's own perspective disappeared behind the proof her encounter could provide.

One of the most unusual elements of Catherine Labouré's visions centuries later carried this same emphasis on embodiment regarding her received Marian apparition. When "the Blessed Mother" appeared to her, the encounter was described not as a mystical vision, but as something tangible and physical. This quality distinguishes Labouré's account from many Marian apparitions described in more ethereal terms. But it is not entirely unique. Nearly two centuries later, another vision would occur, a public phenomenon witnessed by millions of people.

On the night of April 2, 1968, two Muslim mechanics working across the street from the Coptic Orthodox Church of Saint Mary in Zeitoun, Egypt—just outside Cairo—noticed an apparition atop the church. Looking up, the men saw what they thought was a young woman standing on the roof. She appeared real to them; solid, vulnerable, and dangerously close to the edge. Fearing she was about to jump, they shouted warnings and a crowd gathered. But as people stared upward, panic gave way to silence. The figure was luminous, robed in white, and resembled the mother of Jesus.

Egypt is home to one of the oldest continuous Christian traditions in the world: the Coptic Orthodox Church, even though the country has been predominantly Muslim for centuries. The Coptic Orthodox Church of Saint Mary in Zeitoun had long been associated in local tradition with the route taken by the Holy Family on their flight into Egypt, referenced in Matthew's Gospel. In 1968, Egypt was still reeling from its devastating defeat by Israel in the Six-Day War. So although the apparition was a Christian miracle, it was received by Egyptians of many faiths as a sign of consolation, unity, and hope.

The Marian figure disappeared that first night—but then returned, and returned again. Over the months and years that followed, she appeared repeatedly, at times before crowds numbering in the thousands: Christians and Muslims, skeptics and believers alike. Often surrounded by light and accompanied by birdlike forms described as doves or pigeons, she offered no messages and spoke no words. Witnesses nevertheless insisted the figure was not ghostlike, but tangible—floating, yet fully formed.[54]

In Roman Catholicism, reported apparitions typically enter an apparatus of discernment in which testimony is questioned, recorded, shaped, approved, resisted, or absorbed into devotion. The Marian apparitions at Rue du Bac, Guadalupe, La Salette, Lourdes, Pontmain, Knock, Fátima, Beauraing, Banneux, Akita, and Kibeho each passed through some version of this process.[55] Once approved or encouraged, apparition sites became powerful economies of pilgrimage, where shrines, medals, candles, books, hotels, tours, donations, and devotional objects gathered around the vision until revelation, empire, and commerce became inextricable. Unlike Catherine's vision, unlike Magdalene's encounter, Zeitoun was not confined to one woman's testimony or preserved only through institutional retelling. It was collective, and therefore harder to edit.

Zeitoun was received and affirmed not by the Roman Catholic Church, but by the Coptic Orthodox Church, whose ancient tradition already held the site within sacred memory. No single visionary carried a message back to authority. No secret was entrusted to children. No medal was requested. No doctrine was spoken. Witnesses described light, beauty, awe, tears, unworthiness, and a presence that seemed at once bodily and impossible. She remained silent, yet the absence of words did not empty the experience of meaning; instead, it created space for each witness—Christian or Muslim—to receive her according to their own longing: as peace, healing, or a call toward freedom.[56]

Sight is personal, whether exterior or interior. Embodied encounters and mystical revelation are not always easily separated. Within the subjectivity of human experience, the boundary between them collapses. Color, memory, words, and impressions all blur as they pass through the individual filters each person carries, moving through eye, ear, mind, and heart.

This truth renders claims of absolute authority tenuous at best, because belief itself cannot be fully controlled. In the same way, the stories of God,

Jesus, Mother Mary, and Mary Magdalene communicate not only through what is written, but through silence, symbol, and the space between certainty and faith. No one will ever know exactly what Catherine, what Mary, what any witness saw—it is impossible to see exactly what the eyes of another beholds. One can witness another, but between self and other, body and soul, exterior and interior, known and unknown, a space opens. A space like the *nous*, where a sovereign sort of sight emerges.

Chapter 5

WELLS CATHEDRAL

You hear the rain first, insistent and close. The curtains give way, then the painted shutters, damp and faintly resistant. When they open, the world arrives in a single sweep—Somerset revealed in its pure elements, green and wet. The fields stretch outward, almost unnaturally vivid in their saturation, bordered by a low and very weathered rock wall whose lichen and moss have been revived by the downpour. Beyond it, hedgerows dissolve into soft mist.

Only then do you notice him, the lion set against the wall, his sculpted body holding the garden's edge with a composed authority that pulls you back to last night's arrival at your refuge in the English countryside. Now, in daylight, looking out from your room in the charming bed-and-breakfast, the memory of walking the long, pebbled drive remains unblurred: damp leaves underfoot, the bite of an autumn night, the faint outline of a Victorian Gothic façade, and the two lions flanking the entrance with their unspoken welcome and watch.

You pull back from the window, collecting your things and preparing to go down to breakfast as the rain holds steady outside. The room, carefully restored in the late twentieth century, carries that Gothic impulse inward, softened to domestic life. What cathedrals once declared at monumental scale is translated here into detail: ornamental stonework runs into wallpaper, rose windows resolve into stained-glass rosettes, choir screens thin into carved panels, and sacred geometry follows them underfoot in the eight-point rhythm of the parlor floor you remember crossing as you passed between the lions.

Your hand finds the banister as you begin to descend the staircase. It is only then that the motif fully registers. The lions, quietly stationed, repeating, appear again within, less as guardians than as reminders. Across cultures, the lion carries a consistent register of rulership and force, tied to the high-summer power of Leo, when the constellation dominates the northern sky and its brightest star, Regulus, is bound to authority and ascent.

In Egypt, the lion signaled not only kingship but cosmic timing: light, return, and the hinge between what ends and what begins. In Sanskrit, Magha, "the Mighty One," carries associations of height and exaltation that are resonant, if not technically linguistically related, with the Aramaic Magdala, which gives Magdalene her name. Her feast day, aligned in Hellenistic reckoning with the Sun's entry into Leo, overlays the lion's season with her own. In Christian iconography, these symbols converge around Christ, regal and watchful at the turning point of the human story.

The sole explicit identification of Jesus with the lion appears in the book of Revelation, a visionary text sharply divergent from the Gospels. Naming him the "Lion of Judah," its author anchored Jesus in royal lineage and scriptural authority, casting him as a conquering ruler.[1] This contrasts starkly with the Jesus of the Gospels, who identifies instead with humility and love, and gentler motifs: the shepherd, the bridegroom, the true vine, the lamb, the son, the servant.

Wandering through a home layered with antiques, you move through sitting rooms arranged for the rhythm of entertaining, opening one after another with blue-and-white porcelain on lacquered shelves, ochre damask walls warming the space like candlelight, draped chintz framing the gardens beyond with views clear to the Tor, and gilt sconces holding their steady glow. But it is the scent of coffee blooming in the air, warm pastry and butter, and the English promise of sausage, eggs, beans, and tomatoes that finally draws you onward, toward the table where the day's pilgrimage begins.

Known as the breakfast room, the space is gracious and restrained. The meal is served with silver and china, its old formality intact even in morning light. Lingering there, you notice the room's subtler order. Your gaze lifts to the border running along the walls, where a bold, carved fleur-de-lis pattern repeats, its petals divided by small rectangles.

This design comes into view quietly, simply present, as though it has been waiting to be noticed, much like the lions. It's hardly surprising to find the fleur-de-lis here, a mark of sacrality and royalty so ubiquitous it appears far beyond France.

When it is time to leave, you run through the rain to your car. Gravel shifts underfoot, wet leaves turning and slipping as the storybook inn dissolves behind you into mist and rain. What follows feels less like an ending than a passage, as though you have crossed a threshold whose meaning has not yet come into focus.

*

Hidden in one of the quietest and most picturesque medieval towns in England, Wells is less renowned than others of its stature, from Chartres to Canterbury. Yet its nearness to Glastonbury makes it a natural stop for anyone following the layered history of Christianity, and of cathedrals as places where wisdom and magic were deliberately encoded, leaving clues behind. You have come searching, as you always are, for Christianity in the earliest forms you can find: the symbols, the art, the essence, encountered before they are explained. Magdalene is never absent from the search, but here she has not yet stepped forward by name.

The broad lawn, edged by Georgian and Tudor façades, is enclosed by ancient walls, moats, and cobbled streets, anchoring you at its center. Rising nearly 220 feet and stretching half the length of a football field across its west front, Wells Cathedral occupies the square with calm, balanced authority. The space feels suspended in another age, inviting your mind to wander to a time when it rang with the rumble of carts, the tolling of bells, and the murmur of traders and pilgrims. It was a world shaped by faith and war, where countless lives were spent in pursuit of glory.[2]

And then the illusion sharpens. A group of young choristers crosses the green in long, dark robes, their white collars bright against the cathedral walls. They are on their way to rehearsal, and for a moment they look like figures out of a *Harry Potter* film, as if time were not linear here but layered: one century briefly visible through another.

It is in that overlap that the order of the place becomes perceptible, quietly but insistently. "As above, so below," you remember, the old conviction that heaven could be mirrored in earthly form, that harmony could be built. The symmetry doesn't stop at the façade. It reaches you, stilling your breath, loosening your jaw, holding you in silence until all that remains is the sound of your heartbeat.

Reverence, of course, was always the aim. For the master masons, bishops, and patrons who conceived such spaces, architecture was not simply construction but devotion—a way of giving form to what could not otherwise be seen. Wells, conceived wholly in the Early English Gothic style, was among the first to give that vision full expression, beginning to rise in 1175.

Built of honey-colored Doulting limestone, the cathedral seems to carry a light of its own. Even beneath the grey veil of an English sky, its surface remains warm and alive, with arches and niches folding into one another like the contours of land shaped slowly by time. From a distance, the west front reads as sheer mass and balance. But as you draw closer, the intricacies clarify into a tapestry of stone. Up close, more than three hundred medieval figures rise across the façade, each fixed in gesture and stance, arranged into an ordered vision of sanctity and authority. Kings and queens, prophets and saints, angels and ancestors stand in tiers where holiness is rendered legible and hierarchy is given form.

The west front speaks fluently in the language of lineage and dominion. Sculpted portals and tracery weave Old Testament themes. The design follows a cosmic ascent—from the spring-fed earth of Somerset through human struggle and upward toward the heavens. Like all cathedrals, Wells echoes the symmetry of Jerusalem's First Temple, but with a particular insistence, for its western doors and hidden proportions draw you inward.

What is it that calls us toward the divine, no matter the age we live in? And what of Mary? How does she appear within such a structure of masculine order, all height, precision, and reason reaching ever upward?

It is here that the thought attributed to Bernard of Clairvaux, the twelfth-century Burgundian Cistercian abbot, comes forward: "What is God? Length, breadth, height, and depth." The phrase reflects a conviction that the divine could be approached through measure—that proportion, balance, and restraint might carry meaning where language fails. This intuition aligns with a much older claim attributed to Pythagoras: "All is number." Even the infinite, Pythagoreans believed, could be apprehended through pattern. In cathedrals, that belief was given material life, with ratios set into walls and vaults, and measurements inscribed into masonry.[3]

What, then, is written here? Not theology alone, nor beauty for its own sake, but a kind of poetry: faith translated into proportion, restraint transformed into radiance, spirit made tangible. The way such symmetry is expressed in architecture is much like a melody by Wolfgang Amadeus Mozart or Johann Sebastian Bach, eliciting the same sense of calm as morning birdsong or evening crickets. It speaks directly to the body as much as to the mind, registering before it is understood.

What can be formed in architecture or composed into harmony is ultimately an impression of patterns already present in nature, reflected in the simplest forms of growth. In certain plants, seeds, and flowers, this spiraling order takes visible shape. Its geometry can be traced through the Fibonacci sequence: 0, 1, 1, 2, 3, 5, 8, 13, where each number arises from the two before it, continuing outward without end.

Step nearer still, and the storytelling deepens.

*

Unlike the medieval pilgrim who approached from the west through sculpted portals dense with biblical story, modern visitors meet the cathedral differently. You move instead to the right of the building, entering through a glass-walled contemporary passage. You buy a ticket. You pass the gift shop.

The shift from sunlight to shadow brings its own small revelation, a pause of adjustment as your eyes recalibrate while you walk through long, austere corridors that feel built for clergy rather than townspeople. This redirected path brings you along a quieter axis until the space opens and you are standing before an extraordinarily massive pointed arch spanning the nave, crowned by a mirrored arch above it, together forming the shape of a figure eight.

This structure balances tension and thrust so precisely that it seems to breathe, spirit and technology meeting in architecture. Its beauty derived from necessity, born of a crisis when the foundations began to fail in 1313, a dramatic reminder that Gothic cathedrals were feats of engineering before they were works of art. The Scissor Arches, sometimes called St. Andrew's Cross arches, take their name from the X-shaped saltire of the cathedral's patron saint, their form becoming both structural solution and symbol of continuity.

You notice the interior is unusually pale; its surfaces are whitewashed and spare. Simplicity soothes the nerves, drawing your eye to the geometry of ribs and arches, the rhythm of line and light. Now, color remains only in faint traces, as in the Persian-style blue and red vines visible on the soaring ceiling, a remnant of what once enveloped this place in sacred bloom. This delicate floral palette reflects Islamic artistic influence on Gothic architecture. Innovations in geometry, light, and structure—where mathematics expressed *tawḥīd*, divine unity—moved westward into Europe and were transformed by Christian builders into a luminous expression of ascent.

In medieval times, the walls were alive with painting, but much of it was lost during England's break with papal authority. Wells survived the Dissolution of the Monasteries largely because it was not a house bound to Rome, and its clergy were already embedded within royal and episcopal structures. Even so, income was stripped, sacred objects confiscated, and Marian imagery likely removed. The greatest damage came later, during the English Civil War, when Parliamentarian forces destroyed much of the medieval stained glass, later reordered and partially replaced.

As you gaze at the kaleidoscopic windows where light refracts through saintly figures, you try to distinguish what is original from what came later. Even the structure resists clarity, because when one master builder set down his tools, another took them up, and design unfolded over time. Meanings shift as symbols are repeated or altered. What emerges is not a single finished vision, but a living structure—an accumulation of devotion, rupture, repair, and reinterpretation—where time itself becomes architecture.

You arrive at the north transept, where you find the astronomical clock. It is a marvel that tracks cosmic cycles: the phases of the Moon, the days since the New Moon, and the Moon's position within the twelve constellations of the zodiac. The Earth rests at its center while the luminaries revolve, four winds blowing from the mouths of angels at each corner. Faith and measurement together express an older sense of universal order, recalling a world in which astronomy, theology, and daily rhythms once aligned.

Playfully, two small, armored figures appear from the bottom of the clock. It is the quarter hour, and these tiny knights begin to strike the bells. Much softer than a great tower peal, their chiming bounces gently off the vaulted walls as you continue along the left aisle before turning sharply again, leaving the cathedral's main body and approaching perhaps the most famous place within Wells.

*

Just beyond the entryway, a stone stairway awaits, its treads and risers worn into soft waves by centuries of passing feet. Builders intentionally used soft local limestone for this staircase. The curve feels organic, as if shaped less by design than by repetition, like stone slowly learning the flow of water. As your stride settles into the hollowed steps carved by generations past, you can almost feel the men and women who climbed here following faith, their movement preserved in the very material beneath you.

Bernard of Clairvaux famously praised Mother Mary as Stella Maris, "Star of the Sea," a title that, like "Queen of Heaven," carries echoes of something far older: the primordial mother goddess resurfacing through the seams of Christian form. This undulating stairway feels born of that same rhythm, an intermediary space carved of gravity and grace.

You are ascending toward the Chapter House, set just beyond the cathedral, along stairs once used solely by clergy convening for daily meetings within this unusually designed space. As you climb, to your left, sunlight streams in through some of the most ancient stained glass in the building: sepia-toned, six-petaled flowers set within a hexagram, with central concentric rings of indigo, garnet, and emerald. A passing guide remarks that these panes survived simply because they were beyond reach when the glass smashers came through.

You pause here, noticing how the stairs continue onward to a narrower rise—yet, taken together, this long ascent is believed to be structured with intention. When every step is counted, lunar cycles come to life. The seventeenth step separates the two staircases, drawing both eye and imagination into motion through this deeply sacred integer—a prime number of wholeness that cannot be divided.

The water-like flow sweeps you into the Chapter House, and suddenly you are enveloped in the wonder of this grand vaulted room. A central pillar rises like an ancient tree in a forest, its stone ribs branching outward in perfect harmony. The carved foliage across the ceiling—stylized oak leaves and acorns—recalls the oak as an ancient, indigenous symbol of the divine masculine, long before this cathedral was ever conceived. Even the story of the room's practical use by clergy seems to fall short of the magnificence revealed in its octagonal form.

Eight is often overlooked in favor of the celebrated seven, yet sevenfold patterns frequently carry a silent eighth—a moment of completion that opens into renewal. What seven concludes, eight initiates, much like an octave resolves through seven distinct notes before returning to the first, transposed. Octagonal forms were favored in sacred architecture because they mediate between worlds, bridging the grounded square of the earth's four directions and the infinite circle of the heavens.

As you move back toward the stairs, an inscription at the entrance to the Chapter House catches your eye: *Sub Rosa*, "Under the Rose." In the medieval world, this phrase signaled secrecy, a vow that whatever passed beneath the rose would remain hidden. What this communicates to you is that here, in this house of light and order, something of mystery abides, undiscovered.

Back on the staircase, you find yourself almost starstruck, marveling at the rhythms and patterns of sacred geometry. You feel slightly dizzy as you move through a place designed not only to be seen but felt. Past the seventeenth tread, you continue onto the narrower staircase, one less traveled by everyday visitors. Ahead lies the Vicars' Close, once home to the priests who sang daily in the cathedral. Now your footsteps follow a more specific route, where holy men moved daily between prayer, communion, and home. Realizing you have gone too far beyond the cathedral's domain, you turn and begin to descend.

Then you stop, mid-step. A female figure etched in stained glass has suddenly commanded your attention.

You behold a young woman with long hair flowing over robes patterned with circles marked by a central dot. She makes you look twice as your eyes move between the icons she holds: in her right hand, a tower with three carefully rendered windows, and in her left, a golden circle you immediately recognize as a Eucharistic host.

In this moment, you attend only to what is actually before you: the symbols themselves and the way your mind moves toward meaning. Her flowing hair. The tower-like object in one hand. The authority of the circular host in the other. You simply know, in a way that transcends reason or validation, that she is Mary Magdalene.

She lives in this hidden corner of the cathedral, unassuming, yet splendid. The yellow tone edging her halo and dress, tinting her hair and both symbols, is the work of age, not design. But it reads as illumination, as though the years have been quietly working to reveal her in yellow light. Your eye follows the roundels patterned across her cloak, each marked by a central point that feels primordial, echoing sacred geometry's circumpunct: the point of origin from which creation unfolds. Circle after circle, point after point, the pattern seems to train your gaze until it returns to the golden disk in her hand. There, the circular form is no longer ornament alone. It becomes sacramental. A host, too, is a circle with a center, bread transformed into presence, matter made radiant with meaning.

A woman holding a host is not unthinkable. Scholars have identified early images of Mary the mother of Jesus, draped in the white cloths of Eucharistic officiants, especially in regions shaped more by Orthodox traditions than by Rome.[4] What, after all, is communion in an ancient landscape where ritual consumption was common?

Still focused on the golden circle, your mind keeps widening the symbol. The host becomes not only bread, but sun and source. Your thoughts return to the lion, to Regulus, the royal star in the constellation of Leo, whose threshold begins on July 22. A golden disk, like the one in her hands, may be a holy wafer, you muse, or it may also recall an Egyptian sun disk, a mark of origin and authority.

Slowly, you resume your descent, numbering each tread. When you reach the bottom, you have counted forty-four steps from the place where you encountered your Mary Magdalene, illuminated in gold, to the threshold below. Leaving behind your stained-glass heroine, you move back to the ordinary world, among believers and tourists now beginning to wander through the space that, for a time, had been your own.

As you return to the main body of the cathedral, you spot an official passing through the aisle. Before you can overthink it, you step toward him and ask about the woman in the glass up the stairs beyond the Chapter House.

"Could she be Mary Magdalene?"

After all, Magdalene is often more present by suggestion than by name, recognized through images that accumulate around her.

He answers easily, almost without pause: "Saint Barbara." The name lands strangely. *Barbara*.

Standing off to the side of the aisle, with your phone in hand, you begin to search. Barbara, you learn, belongs more fully to legend than to early Christian record. Her story tells of a third-century woman imprisoned by her wealthy pagan father, Dioscorus, who locks her in a tower to prevent her conversion to Christianity. But confinement does not keep her from faith. Inside the tower, she secretly converts. She marks her belief on the building itself by having three windows made in honor of the Holy Trinity.[5]

Now the tower in the stained glass makes sense. So do the three carefully rendered windows. Aside from her long hair and her enclosure, Barbara seems to have little in common with Magdalene.

Another detail catches you: 1969. In the wake of the reforms initiated by the Second Vatican Council, Saint Barbara was removed from the General Roman Calendar, not because her story had lost its symbolic power, but because it could not be firmly established as history. In that same atmosphere of reevaluation, Magdalene's image was also being reconsidered, subtly disentangled from the long-standing conflation with the unnamed sinner. Barbara was quietly lowered from the calendar. Magdalene was quietly clarified. Decades later, in 2016, Mary Magdalene's memorial was elevated to a feast.[6]

How interesting, you think, that the question is not simply who these women were, but how they move through time: named and renamed, lowered and lifted, confused, corrected, absorbed into one another. Saints become part history, part devotional vessel, carrying myth, memory, theology, and longing at once. Barbara may not lead you away from Magdalene after all, but toward a deeper understanding of how sacred meaning survives even when historical certainty does not.

By now, you want to make your way toward the Lady Chapel, where the eastern end of the cathedral seems to be calling. But you feel the pull to know more about this glass. About Barbara. About why this small figure, tucked away beyond the Chapter House, has unsettled you so completely.

You wander back toward the gift shop near the entrance, where shelves of cathedral books wait amid the morning bustle. Delighted, you pick up a heavy volume on sacred geometry, *The Cosmos in Stone: Sacred Geometry of a Master Mason* by Tom Bree, then a slimmer companion, *Wells Cathedral: An Architectural & Historical Guide* by Elsa Van Der Zee. You leave with both, along with a small gold Wells ornament, a token for something that feels important before you can explain why.

Just outside, you open the smaller guide and begin to flip through its pages until the figure in the glass appears before you again. The text confirms that the etching dates to the 1460s and is one of the oldest intact pieces in the entire building. Then you read something stranger still. Van Der Zee writes that the glass "had found its way into private hands but was returned to the cathedral by the owner, on the condition that it could be seen and enjoyed by visitors."[7] You pause over this sentence: *returned on the condition that it could be seen.*

You feel the dissonance immediately, because this invaluable piece of stained glass is not in plain sight. You found her tucked into a quiet corner beyond the main flow of visitors, easy to miss unless you wandered far enough and happened to look at the right moment. One of the oldest pieces of glass in Wells now waits almost hidden from view. How strange, you think, that a figure meant to be seen should require discovery. Still carrying that thought, you tuck the guidebook beneath your arm and move back toward the eastern end of the cathedral.

As you move past the quire toward the Lady Chapel, you notice that a small daily service has begun near the front. Voices rise and fall, low and rhythmic—the space that earlier felt almost private now stirs with worship, movement, and sound. You do not want to interrupt, so you keep slightly to the side, letting the liturgy continue around you as you approach one of the open arches.

At the edge of the chapel, you pause. The Lady Chapel of Wells stands at the cathedral's easternmost end. Designed by the master geometrician Thomas of Witney and completed in 1326, it exists among the most breathtaking examples of Gothic England. Long before the Reformation curtailed Marian devotion, Mother Mary flourished in medieval Europe as an embodiment of compassion and mercy. It was within this climate that lady chapels emerged on the eastern ends of churches, drawing on an older impulse to align sacred space with the sun's movement and to set apart places for revering the feminine.

Standing just to the side, you do not yet understand the pattern. You only sense that the building holds a language of its own, so you look up. Through one of the three open arches that separate the Lady Chapel from the body of the church, its form begins to unfold. The walls and intricately vaulted ceiling resolve into an elongated octagon, its upward stretch drawing your gaze to the Persian tracery above, where an eight-pointed star bursts across the ceiling.

Here, eight meets five. At the center of the star-shaped dome appears Christ in glory, encircled by four angels, his hands, feet, and head marked with the five wounds of the passion. In Christian symbolism, five signifies the human dimension of Jesus—his embodied life and suffering. Yet, like the five great windows surrounding the space, glowing with largely nineteenth-century-stained glass, the number's meaning extends beyond doctrine into an older, cosmic sense of order.

In the Fibonacci sequence eight follows five, like the five-pointed star in an eight-year rhythm of the planet Venus. The Lady Chapel mirrors this dance of five and eight in the underlying geometry of its design. The eastern walls of the chapel imply a pentagram, while the five western walls create an octagon. Then, read axially, the Lady Chapel extends into a vast five-pointed star across the cathedral's east end, evoking another mathematical pattern: the golden ratio. Five plus eight yields thirteen, following Fibonacci, to land on another number associated with what is both feminine and unseen.

While modern Christianity often downplays or rejects sustained attention to the cycles of the stars, biblical texts suggest a continued engagement with the sky. In Revelation, Jesus names himself the "bright morning star," an image and title linked to the planet Venus.[8] Yet this space in Wells is not designed to evoke a Venusian Jesus of Revelation. As its name implies, the *Lady* Chapel is devoted to the feminine, to Mary.

As the sun rises in the east, so the light of God in Jesus was believed to enter the world through a woman's womb—an image akin to Egyptian goddesses crowned with sun disks and one that can still be found in the descriptions of the Holy Spirit in texts outside the canon. Sun to Venus to Earth: this cosmic exchange is set into the surrounding stone, an imagination that understood creation as interdependent. The vaulting lifts your body upward, releasing your form from its own weight, until a nearby voice arrests you.

"Sorceress," the female Anglican priest reads from Exodus 22:18. "Do not allow a sorceress to live."[9]

Written as part of an ancient legal code intended to stabilize a fragile community, the passage would later be reinterpreted and wielded to justify centuries of violence against women. And while a five-pointed star may register as "witch" or carry negative connotations now, such associations arrived late, emerging only through nineteenth-century esoteric inversions of what had always been benevolent.

The pentagram, in its earliest forms, signified protection and divine order, appearing as early as 3500 BCE in Sumerian cuneiform. It later functioned as a symbol of harmony and health among the Pythagoreans and appeared on ancient coins as a mark of order, value, and cosmic balance. In Jewish tradition, the five-pointed star was used as a protective sign and decorative motif, appearing in synagogal art, seals, and amulets. The planet was imagined as the embodiment of the goddess as early as Sumerian Inanna, whose poetry read: "Inanna, the Lady Who Ascends into the Heavens, is radiant."[10]

Your eyes travel again up the five elongated windows to the trefoil ones above, each framing an angel, arranged in rows that become a triangle. Four angels, three angels, two angels—each gazes upward toward the highest window, marked with the face of a saint, or in the central one, the unmistakably European Jesus, pale-skinned with dark hair. His right hand is raised, two fingers extended to signify his dual nature. His left hand clutches a golden disk, a Eucharistic host, identical to the one held by Saint Barbara, your Mary Magdalene, in the stairwell.

You count these angelic windows: ten sets of five. The triangles form a Pythagorean *tetraktys*, a pattern a sacred geometer might marvel over, and one a devout Catholic might use to count the rhythms of Hail Marys on a rosary. It occurs to you, as you find yourself so immersed in this feminine space, that what we hold in common transcends all that divides us, if only we choose to awaken to it.

Your neck aches from looking up so long, but you cannot bring your gaze back down. You feel as though you have become a bridge between earth and heaven. Here in the Lady Chapel of Wells, the idea that cathedrals invoke *ascent* becomes visceral.

In medieval Christian symbolism, the Virgin Mary was sometimes described as Rosa Sine Spina—the "thornless rose" of Eden, an image of spiritual perfection. Roses and women are far older than Tudor monarchs or Christian iconography. The flower was always feminine, and long before its petals came to signify purity, their unfolding layers were understood as revelations of the true self. As the cosmic encoding of the stone around you settles into your body, it becomes clear that Mother Mary did not always need to stand as a figure of obedience alone, but as a woman entwined with the enduring presence of the feminine.

Roses, too, have long been associated with Mary Magdalene, especially within mystical and esoteric traditions. Yet you realize it is not ultimately about one flower or one woman alone—not only the rose or the lily, not only Magdalene or Saint Barbara. Or even whether the lion, or the morning star, belongs to Jesus, his mother, or even Magdalene herself. All that has so often been divided, separated, or set against itself need not remain so. What rises in you instead is awe.

Was that stained glass woman Mary Magdalene? And do you now sense her presence beneath this eight-pointed, vaulted star? Are you imagining it all? Or is this what it feels like to encounter the divine—without artifice, without technique, without anything but wonder? Perhaps this is what such soaring heights were always meant to invite: a communion beyond the ordinary.

Chapter 6

WISDOM AND HER SERPENT

Her caravan advanced north from Marib along the established incense route, a formation whose order and protection signaled sovereignty as much as commerce. Camels moved deliberately under the watch of appointed guards, bearing containers of frankincense and myrrh.

This was wealth meant to burn. The resins filled temples, courts, and burial chambers across the Near East, giving ritual its breath as offerings rose in smoke and the consecrated was made present. The perfume in her possession carried proof of power, a commodity that governed treaties as readily as devotion. It moved through sanctuary and court without distinction, a fragrant currency upon which diplomacy and recognition were built.

Nothing in the procession suggested tribute or subservience. It carried the confidence of command, of royalty crossing borders to be received as an equal. And it was led not by a king, but by a queen: the queen of Sheba. Her arrival was more than a display of opulence. She came already secure in her authority, requiring no king beside her to make it complete.

Moving fluidly between history and symbol, the queen of Sheba remains vivid in the collective imagination well beyond what her brief scriptural account preserves. Her counterpart in Jerusalem inhabits this same register, not simply a monarch bound to a throne, but a mind whose legacy became architecture and sacred narrative: King Solomon.

Of the rulers named in the Hebrew scriptures, Solomon occupies a singular place, remembered for the joining of power and insight, a man who carried knowledge into governance and vision into stone. Just as

Sheba's caravans carried the wealth that perfumed altars, Solomon's hands were said to shape the space where that smoke would rise: the First Temple in Jerusalem.

No physical trace of the First Temple has been definitively identified, and no contemporary inscription independently confirms the biblical account that Solomon built it. Its existence rests on biblical memory and later tradition rather than secure archaeological finds. Questions remain about the Temple's material reality, but its legendary afterlife was immense. The Temple's tripartite design, its gold-clad inner sanctuary, and its massive bronze pillars shaped a sacred vision of order and divine presence. This vision would travel across centuries, finding architectural expression in the vaulted cathedrals of medieval Europe. Interpreters would see in these features a language of proportion and sacred geometry, wisdom conferred in stone. Whatever its historical footprint, the structure described in First Kings was destroyed in 586 BCE, when Babylonian forces under Nebuchadnezzar II razed Jerusalem.

Likewise, the meeting between the queen of Sheba and King Solomon survives in narrative, but not in material proof. No inscription, royal archive, or archaeological artifact corroborates their encounter. And just as Solomon's historical footprint remains debated, the queen of Sheba too eludes definitive identification. Scholars have often linked "Sheba" with the Sabaean kingdom of South Arabia, later Yemen, documented from at least the eighth century BCE onward as a politically complex center of the incense trade. Its commerce centered on aromatic resins used in medicine, healing, and religious ritual across the Near East. The biblical story is plausible as a memory of diplomatic exchange, even if the encounter itself remains unconfirmed.

According to the scriptural account, this was not an exchange of trade, nor was it a visit romantic in nature, despite later insinuations. The queen of Sheba had traversed deserts and rivers for an intellectual meeting, as First Kings states explicitly: "She came to test him with hard questions."[1] The phrasing places her in the position of evaluation, measuring the famed wisdom of Israel's king. This is extraordinary for a female sovereign, in a historical era when few women ruled, let alone held the standing to enter this patriarchal culture. If historical, this queen must have come bearing an esteemed reputation. Even if she were only literary, Sheba stood not beneath Solomon, but opposite him—a woman of formidable intelligence, curiosity, and discernment.

"Solomon answered all her questions; nothing was too hard for the king to explain to her," the narrative records. This assertion of the king's mastery simultaneously confirms the depth of the queen's inquiry and receptivity. As she listened, she observed the order of his court before she delivered her judgment with clarity. The queen of Sheba confirmed, "In wisdom and prosperity you far surpass the report I had heard." Her affirmation does not diminish her authority; it establishes it. Her word is awarded weight and gravity, as is the gift she chooses to bestow upon the king in recognition: "Never again did spices come in such quantity as that which the queen of Sheba gave to King Solomon."[2] The narrative in First Kings lingers over the abundance, her offering read as confirmation of Solomon's renown.

The questions around the queen extend far beyond the historical potential of her kingdom and this meeting, even if she was symbol alone. Why was a woman granted such prominence within a tradition largely shaped by masculine authority? Is the queen of Sheba merely a narrative flourish, a foreign monarch inserted to magnify a king, her gender a bit of intrigue and nothing more? Or did her presence signal something more lasting, something about feminine power that extends beyond the narrative that contains her?

Much like the magnificence of the First Temple, later Jewish and Christian tradition gathered a vast body of sacred literature under Solomon's name. Proverbs, Song of Songs, and Ecclesiastes bear his attribution; several psalms are linked to him; later works such as the Wisdom of Solomon and the Psalms of Solomon invoke his authority. Modern scholarship does not regard Solomon as the literal author of these texts, but tradition continues to cast him as the fountainhead of wisdom. Within these scriptures, Wisdom herself speaks—not as abstraction, but as a woman.

Chokhmah, the Hebrew word for "wisdom," a feminine noun carrying meanings of skill, artistry, and insight, appears not only as a quality to be possessed but as a living presence. She speaks in the first person. She calls from the gates of the city. She stands beside God at creation. She is described as master worker, companion, and delight. Public teacher and cosmic architect, Wisdom precedes kings and instructs nations, guiding humanity toward life. And she is *feminine*. In the Wisdom of Solomon, she comes fully into view in chapter 7, beginning at verse 22:

> . . . for wisdom, the fashioner of all things, taught me. There is in her a spirit that is intelligent, holy, unique, manifold, subtle, mobile, clear, unpolluted, distinct, invulnerable, loving the good, keen, irresistible, beneficent, humane, steadfast, sure, free from anxiety, all-powerful, overseeing all, and penetrating through all spirits that are intelligent, pure, and altogether subtle.[3]

If Solomonic tradition gives Wisdom a woman's voice, the arrival of the queen of Sheba can be interpreted as its embodiment. She becomes Wisdom stepping from poetry into narrative form, from ideal to woman. Why else would a queen, not a king, have come to judge Israel's wisest monarch?

The Hebrew Wisdom was far from alone. All across the ancient world, creative intelligence was imagined in feminine terms, radiant and preexistent. Wisdom and Spirit moved together in concept and form, each reflecting an intuition that women are naturally inclined to a specific form of intelligence. The kind of knowledge needed to give birth, to heal a wound, to create a meal, to nurture plants and animals, to tend to the young, the ill, the dying. This is the same impulse that recognizes the feminine as the source of life, death, and rebirth, reflected in all goddess-centered religious cultures. It is the sort of wisdom that comes from the unknown, the unseen, the spiritual, the creative, and makes it manifest through what might appear, at times, as magic.

That Wisdom preserved feminine pronouns in the Hebrew scriptures was remarkable, given a priesthood that remained firmly male and excluded women from ritual office and most public religious life. As Christianity took shape, feminine Wisdom survived only in increasingly abstract symbolic forms. In the medieval era, Mother Mary was enthroned as Sedes Sapientiae, the "Seat of Wisdom," but the throne attached to her role rather than to her: Wisdom was transposed into Church. What was etheric and divine became community and clergy. Even when Mother Mary resonated in some way with Wisdom, her doctrinal identity rested firmly on her purity and obedience, not her intelligence. Theotokos, Mother of God, still did not place her close to the source of creation, where the Hebrew scriptures described Wisdom, and Spirit too. Faint already in the masculine cast of Judaism, Wisdom, as feminine and creative and a source of knowing, all but disappeared in Christianity. That is, if the non-canonical sources are not considered.

When the Nag Hammadi texts were discovered, scholars found within them a prominent mythical figure who was present at creation, a kind of deity, given the name Sophia, wisdom in Greek. The stories around Sophia vary widely across texts and the communities that shaped them. Sometimes she carries traits of Hebrew Wisdom, sometimes of Eve. In Valentinian texts, Sophia's longing for the unknowable God leads to a fall that sets the material world in motion, and her restoration becomes the long arc of salvation. In Sethian texts, she is closer to a primordial mother, the source from which lesser beings descend and toward which they are called back. From the highest perspective, Sophia is a revealer, the figure who turns the seeker toward what lies behind appearances.

The parallels between Mary Magdalene and Sophia have been difficult for scholars to set aside, even if the resonance is amorphous. In these non-canonical sources, both Sophia and Mary bring forth hidden wisdom, each is described in proximity to a male savior, and both are diminished in the narratives that surround them: Sophia into matter and error, Magdalene into legend and accusation. Most of all, each figure is a female responsible for revelation. Sophia draws the seeker toward *gnosis.* Mary Magdalene is the first at the tomb and the first to be told in the Gospels, she offers spiritual instruction in the Gospel of Mary, and she is described as a wise student asking questions in the Dialogue of the Savior and the Pistis Sophia.

Rather than one figure informing the other, or either standing as a literal continuation of Hebrew Wisdom, each of these women seems to express, in her own register, an older sense of what feminine intelligence does, working at the edge of the unseen and carrying what it finds back into the world. Like dawn, the movement from night into day.

Wisdom in antiquity was never accidental; it was cultivated through discipline and sacred learning. To be wise was to transform information into knowledge, an alchemy of the mind that was prized as the highest currency in intellectual and philosophical circles. Wisdom had to be earned, whether through an external system of progression or through an interior process like *gnosis,* a Greek word for direct, inward knowing of spiritual truth. For a figure like the queen of Sheba to be qualified to evaluate Solomon could not have come out of nowhere; she would have been highly educated, her intellect well-proven. For a woman like Mary Magdalene to have been the first witness to the resurrection, there must have been a reason she was remembered with such authority. This becomes even more compelling if Mary was the anointing woman, and if she lived out her portrayal as inquisitive and authoritative in the non-canonical texts.

Like Jesus, whose life record emerges suddenly at the beginning of his public ministry around the age of thirty, Mary Magdalene has no clear background described in any scripture. Beyond the text lies mostly imagination, conjecture, and fringe speculation. Mary was trained, somehow; she was formed. She did not simply appear out of nowhere, a woman of means who became a patron alongside others. Certain details preserved in the Gospel accounts, however, offer clues to the historically plausible identity of Magdalene. So how did she become a woman of wisdom, long before she followed the teacher from Galilee? Who *was* Mary?

THE ACT OF ANOINTING

As the image of Mary Magdalene the repentant sinner has receded, the uncertainty surrounding her identity has opened new space for interpretation even beyond academic conversations. Within Christian circles, Mary has become a focal point in debates about women's roles in the Church. The question has become more intimate. People want to know Mary, and that hunger has produced an entire literature of Magdalene novels and spiritual texts. In the passion of those imaginings, the line between fact and fiction blurs. But one possibility, persistent enough to keep returning, may carry a historical thread worth taking seriously, and it concerns spiritual authority. In fiction and feminist spiritual communities, the suggestion is no longer whispered: did Mary Magdalene train in sacred rites? Was she, at some point in her life, a formally initiated priestess?

The image is powerful: red robes, alabaster jars, circles of women reclaiming intuition and sacred authority. The priestess archetype answers a deep longing to find the divine feminine in something more tangible than myth or symbol, in practices women may once have lived and carried. But longing, however meaningful, cannot carry the argument. Words and rituals taken out of context cannot provide a sound basis for any thesis that Mary Magdalene was a trained priestess. If this portrait of Mary is to be taken seriously, the question must be asked plainly. Is it historically feasible?

From a strictly traditional Christian framework, the suggestion sounds inconceivable. Viewed within the wider religious landscape of the ancient world in which Mary lived, however, it becomes harder to dismiss. Certain details recur throughout the Gospel accounts: the number seven, the public and deliberate act of anointing, and the later accusation of sexual impropriety. Taken together, these elements invite closer attention. Across the Mediterranean world, women who held recognized religious roles—whether Jewish, Greco-Roman, or Near Eastern—were frequently associated with similar signs of ritual authority.[4]

A priestess was a public religious figure serving within structured systems of worship. She participated in communal rites that bound heaven and city together. In the ancient Mediterranean, religion and public life moved as a single body, temple and state intertwined. Priestesses, often born in elite or ruling families, were entrusted with maintaining divine favor and civic harmony, even agricultural prosperity. Their work was tactile and embodied: preparing sacred space, tending altars, handling incense and costly oils. Anointing, in certain cultures and contexts, was a central ritual act.

It is tempting to assume that the nature of the anointing of Jesus would have required formal priestess training. The Gospel accounts are not so clear-cut. The question of whether Mary Magdalene was Mary of Bethany remains unresolved, let alone what that means for the Synoptic anointing accounts. The significance of the anointing itself is also uncertain, given the varied details across the four accounts. Each uncertainty overlaps with the next. What is historical, what is symbolic, or both at once? There are no easy answers; these are open issues that remain subjects of continuing debate in both scholarship and Christian tradition.

In the Hebrew scriptures, anointing marks divine appointment. The earliest instance is not of a person but of a place: Jacob pours oil over a stone at Bethel, consecrating the ground where he encountered God. Later, the gesture inaugurates institutions. Moses anoints Aaron and his sons to establish the priesthood. Samuel anoints Saul and David to establish kingship. Oil becomes the visible sign that authority has been set apart by divine command.

That structure did not survive the exile. When the Babylonians destroyed the First Temple in 586 BCE, the Davidic monarchy fell with it. Later Jewish tradition remembered the sacred anointing oil as lost, never recreated. So when the Temple was rebuilt in 516 BCE under Persian rule, the sanctuary returned without the older structure of kingship. No Davidic ruler was restored, and the ritual world that had once crowned kings through anointing receded with it. Rabbinic tradition would later maintain that the priests of the Second Temple were invested through sacred vestments rather than oil.[5]

By the first century, anointing remained common but was used in ordinary ways: to soothe skin, to honor guests, and to prepare bodies for burial. The act survived, but the old royal and priestly functions tied to anointing had largely vanished. Yet beyond the historical function of anointing in Judaism, there is a serious stumbling block to any suggestion of Mary Magdalene as a Jewish priestess. Despite fictional renderings, there is no precedent for a Jewish woman serving as priestess or performing ritual anointing. The agreement within academic Judaism, Second Temple studies, and biblical scholarship is unequivocal: no first-century Jewish woman would have been formally trained as a priestess or as a ritual anointer.

Across the surviving sources—Philo of Alexandria, Flavius Josephus, the Dead Sea Scrolls, and the Hebrew scriptures themselves—the boundaries hold. Women could be prophets, poets, patrons, and judges. They could sing victory songs and pronounce judgment. But they did not serve at the altar, enter the inner sanctuary, or perform priestly consecrations. Oil might pass through a woman's hands in the rhythms of domestic life, at weddings and festivals, in acts of hospitality, or burial preparation, but such practices belonged to household devotion, not to religious formality.

If Mary Magdalene was formed solely within the Jewish world, the category of "priestess" closes before it opens. The evidence does not allow such a role inside the Temple system. Any exploration of the possibility that Magdalene engaged in formal sacred arts must therefore look beyond the boundaries of Judea to the wider world in which she may have moved.

ANCIENT DIASPORA

Jewish communities flourished across the Mediterranean basin, especially in cosmopolitan cities where cultures overlapped and religious traditions traveled along trade routes. Between the conquests of Alexander the Great in the late fourth century BCE and the First Jewish-Roman War, the relative stability of Hellenistic kingdoms and the Roman Empire fostered a Diaspora shaped by exile, voluntary migration, commerce, and settlement. As Paula Fredriksen observes in *Ancient Christianities*, Jewish life unfolded within a vast religious landscape where temples, priesthoods, and sacred traditions from many cultures existed side by side.[6]

The label "pagan" did not emerge until the fourth century, when Christians adopted it to mark those outside the Church. In Jewish terms, the more common distinction was simply "Gentile," indicating non-Jewish peoples in a world where religion and ethnicity were deeply interconnected. These were rhetorical dividing lines that rarely shaped daily life. Across the Roman Mediterranean, and long before, cultural exchange ran in both directions. Fredriksen describes how Jews and their neighbors shared ritual practices, sacred instruments, symbolic language, and assumptions about communication between divine and human realms. Ancient religious cultures, beliefs, and rituals held much more in common in ordinary practice than is readily acknowledged. The starkness of the Bible's rhetoric against non-Jews and "pagans" was, in part, in reaction to this fluid cultural exchange.

In major urban centers, this proximity was even more pronounced. Jewish communities existed alongside Greek, Egyptian, and Roman traditions within shared streets, markets, associations, and sometimes households. Archaeological and literary evidence shows Jews participating in civic institutions, educational systems, foreign armies, theaters, and athletic culture. Even Galilee, in Jesus's own lifetime, sat within this current of exchange.

John Dominic Crossan and Jonathan L. Reed have argued that Jesus and his father likely worked the construction sites of Sepphoris, a Hellenistic city north of Nazareth. There, Jesus would have heard Greek alongside Aramaic, seen Hellenistic architecture and trade up close, and lived within the cross-cultural exchange of a Roman-administered city. Galilee, in other words, sat inside the same Hellenistic world that ran through every urban center of the Roman East—and nowhere did that movement concentrate more fully than in Alexandria, the Queen of Cities founded by Alexander just west of the Nile Delta.[7]

Alexandria became one of the largest centers of Jewish life outside Judea—at times comprising a substantial portion of the population, with estimates ranging between one fourth and one third. Jewish communities built synagogues, held civic roles, and participated fully in the city's intellectual and economic life. Jewish, Greek, and Egyptian traditions met not as abstractions but as people meeting, trading, practicing and debating. This synthesis is epitomized by Philo, who read the Hebrew scriptures through Greek philosophy. It is reflected in the remark attributed to Numenius of Apamea: "What is Plato, if not Moses speaking Attic [Greek]?"[8] Even the Septuagint demonstrated how fully Jewish thought had entered the currents of the Hellenistic world. Later, Alexandria was an early site of Christian thought, where philosophical, symbolic and mystical traditions gave shape to a uniquely diverse religious imagination.

The exchange of cultures in antiquity, in Alexandria and beyond, occurred not only on a public stage, but within households, patronage networks and communal gatherings. What happened in homes, of course, involved the labor and input of women. And in Egypt, this dynamic was even more prevalent, because there women held more rights, status, and wealth than anywhere else in the ancient Mediterranean world. In Egypt, women could contract their own marriages, inherit equally, own and manage property independently, and initiate divorce. Law often favored mothers and children; marriage tended to occur later, extending a woman's period of autonomy. Women could lend money, operate businesses, manage estates, and serve in temple roles. They owned vineyards and workshops, ships and trade goods, as well as perfume, agricultural, and transport enterprises. In Ptolemaic Egypt, as much as a third of the land may have been held by women within a generation of Cleopatra VII. Within elite circles, this autonomy extended into education. Women could receive training in philosophy, rhetoric, and mathematics, participating, directly or indirectly, in the same intellectual culture that shaped Alexandrian thought.[9]

Ancient sources register the permeability of these environments. Josephus noted the observance of Jewish customs among non-Jewish populations, particularly women. Roman authors including Epictetus, Juvenal, and Tacitus commented, often critically, on the attraction Jewish practices held for women across the Roman world. What appears to be true is that women were at the center of this cross-cultural exchange of ideas and practices, theological ones included. In certain cities like Alexandria, women held unusual influence, power, and access to philosophical and spiritual life. And among them, Jewish women had their own visible roles.[10]

Fredriksen notes that Jewish women frequently served as patrons of religious life. Alexandria preserves especially strong evidence: inscriptions and documentary texts attest to women who funded communities and held public titles within civic and religious life. Epigraphic research by Bernadette Brooten has identified women bearing synagogue titles across the Diaspora, reflecting the high standing of women in patronage, not priesthood. Tal Ilan has shown how dramatically women's religious authority and participation could vary between Jewish communities. Influence did not always declare itself through office; it circulated through financial support, education, and access.[11]

This cultural permeability extended beyond intellectual life into family structures. As early as the fifth century BCE, documents from the Jewish military colony at Elephantine attest to marriages between Jews and Egyptians or Persians. Papyri from Alexandria and Oxyrhynchus preserve contracts and archives revealing mixed households.[12] Some voices resisted such unions—Philo explicitly discouraged them.[13] Even the need to warn against intermarriage reflects that it was social reality, one difficult to regulate. Texts such as Joseph and Aseneth, likely composed in Egypt in the first or second century, resolved this tension narratively. The novella expanded the brief biblical mention of Joseph's marriage to Aseneth, daughter of an Egyptian priest, into an elaborate conversion narrative in which she underwent a mystical transformation and embraced the God of Israel before the wedding.[14]

In fact, the connections between Jewish sacred history and Egypt run deep. The earliest layers of the story, Israel's slavery and exodus under Moses, described years of immersion in Egyptian land and culture. The Babylonian exile of the sixth century BCE moved the same drama eastward, dispersing Judah into another foreign empire whose beliefs contrasted with their own. Centuries later, the Maccabean Revolt fractured the Jerusalem priesthood, and Onias IV, son of the high priest Onias III, fled to Egypt and established a temple at Leontopolis under Ptolemy VI Philometor, allowing the Zadokite line to continue for two centuries beyond its displacement from Jerusalem.[15] Even the Gospel of Matthew preserved this Egyptian thread, framing the return of the infant Jesus from refuge there with the words of Hosea: "Out of Egypt I called my son."[16]

As a Jewish woman in the first century, Mary Magdalene would have been less culturally isolated than is usually assumed—even in a thoroughly Jewish locale like Jerusalem or Bethany. But it is also entirely plausible that she came from a different city altogether, one whose culture would offer a compelling explanation for her ability to support Jesus's ministry from her own means. That city is Alexandria, where Platonic philosophy was potent and present enough to offer another reading on Mary's seven *daimonia*, and even possibly shaped the Gospel of Mary's philosophical elements. If Mary was from Alexandria, she could have been raised and educated in a city of mixed cultures, possibly of Jewish and Egyptian heritage herself. In that world, she would have grown up within sight of the priestess traditions that were still flourishing in her lifetime.

THE PRIESTESSES

Priestess is a word that arrives shimmering, charged with intrigue and suspicion; it can stir fascination just as quickly as skepticism. Priest, by contrast, feels ordinary, an office made familiar by centuries of patriarchal religious structure. A haze hovers around ancient priestesses, mystic or romantic, easily projected upon—becoming liberating or dangerous, a source of hope, unease, or judgment. But across the ancient world, priestesses were simply part of daily life: established religious figures just like their male counterparts, women trained, appointed, and publicly recognized as guardians of sacred life.

Numinous as their role was, priestesses were public officials, and so their temples were tied to governance. The priestess's rituals were intended to create order. Offerings, processions, songs, prayers, sacrifice, even scribal work—all aimed at drawing favor from the gods and goddesses: for abundant harvests, for social harmony, for royal authority, for victory in war. The function of the priestess was not esoteric; it was communal. Her actions provided protection, ensured survival, and held civilization whole. While priestesses across the Mediterranean shared many aspects, the roles, deities, and identities of these women varied from region to region.[17]

In ancient Mesopotamia, women composed hymns and prayers, performed ritual processions, and managed temple estates through formal temple offices such as the *entu* and *nadītu*. Enheduanna, daughter of Sargon of Akkad and *entu* of the moon god Nanna at Ur, was the earliest named author in literary history: she was the first person, woman or man, to sign her name to a work of literature. On Minoan Crete a millennium later, frescoes from the palace at Knossos placed female officiants at the center of processions, altar rites, and the bull-leaping ceremonies that lay at the heart of the island's sacred life. In Greece, the priestess of Athena Polias held a lifelong office passed for generations within a single Athenian family. The priestesses of Demeter at Eleusis and Hera at Argos served as figures of state religion in their cities. At Ephesus the temple of Artemis—one of the Seven Wonders of the ancient world—maintained a continuous female priesthood from the seventh century BCE until the temple's destruction in 268.[18]

Rome in the first century presents a comparable picture, though priestesses there operated within more tightly regulated structures. Six Vestal Virgins at a time, chosen as young girls from elite families, served the goddess Vesta for thirty years. A decade as novice, a decade as serving officiant, a decade as teacher of new initiates was spent tending the sacred flame that symbolized the continuity of the Roman state. Their office granted unusual privileges: independence from male guardianship, property ownership, and even the authority to intervene on behalf of condemned individuals. Priestesses also officiated in the cults of Ceres, Cybele, and other deities embedded in the religious life of Rome.[19]

No ancient culture left behind more evidence of women's religious authority than Egypt. The record extends over more than two thousand years, manifest in every form imaginable: titles, funerary monuments, statues, dedicatory inscriptions, ritual instruments, and autobiographical traces that name women as chantresses, musicians, temple attendants, and at times scribes. Barbara Lesko's survey of the material evidence shows how profoundly women were woven into Egyptian religious structures for centuries upon centuries. Egypt's priestesses were markedly powerful, their temple institutions generated income, archived sacred scripture, displayed public performances, and even served as treasuries.[20]

The divine was never abstract in Egypt; it was "the temple of the whole world" as Hermetic treatise *Asclepius* would later call it.[21] The gods and goddesses were palpable in a culture that rendered all things sacred, and priestesses played an essential role in communicating with them. Statues and images of gods and goddesses were awakened at dawn, bathed and robed, perfumed, carried in procession, and ceremonially restored at the day's end. These practices engaged with materials that evoked all the senses: resin, flame, linen, water, oils, perfumes. In *Sacred Luxuries*, Lise Manniche describes anointing in Egyptian ritual life as a daily devotion, not ornament. Here, oil marked reverence, distinction, and recognition.[22]

Anointing was a medium of consecration, a gesture through which sacred presence was acknowledged, honored, and renewed. Oils were bestowed upon divine statues and on the priests, rulers, and initiates authorized to approach them. Reliefs show priestesses wearing perfumed oils and cones of scented fat that slowly melted during ceremonies, releasing fragrance as an act of purification and sanctification. Egyptian ritual texts highlight seven sacred oils, used in burials and offerings, their names inscribed on jars and labels, but their exact substances are not securely identified.

Among the ancient temples that still rise from the Egyptian landscape is Dendera, known to the Egyptians who built it as Iunet, or Iunet-tantore, and to the Greeks who came after as Tentyris. Napoleon's expedition through Egypt of 1798–1801 found it half-swallowed by sand, but subsequent excavations revealed one of the most spectacular and complete temples to survive from antiquity. The land was home to sacred space for millennia, but the present temple began construction in 54 BCE under Ptolemy XII Auletes and continued under his daughter Cleopatra VII. Across the south wall, Cleopatra and her son Caesarion stand opposite the goddess presenting offerings; the queen wears the horn-and-sun-disk of Hathor with the double plumes of the pharaoh, claiming a shared register of feminine sovereignty.[23]

Dendera is famous for its color, a blue that moves from cobalt to aquamarine, alive on walls and ceiling, a color that seems to echo Hathor's title Lady of Turquoise. Far away, at Sinai, turquoise was drawn from the desert stone under her protection. Beside the turquoise mines, where a temple to Hathor presided over the laborers, scribes, and expedition officials who came to the mountain, Semitic workers adapted Egyptian signs into Proto-Sinaitic. It remains among the earliest known alphabetic scripts, the distant predecessor of Phoenician, Greek, Hebrew, and Roman letters.[24] At Dendera, that same blue illuminates Hathor's face on the column capitals, the cosmic timetables of hours and decan stars across the ceilings, and the famous Dendera Zodiac, a rare Greco-Egyptian twelve-sign wheel removed from the temple complex in the nineteenth century and now housed at the Louvre in Paris.

At Dendera, Hathor was a cosmic goddess, universal and total, an embodiment of sky and river; mother and sovereign; she ruled music, sexuality, fertility, and renewal. Called Lady of Iunet, Mistress of the Sky, and the Golden One, at Dendera she was blended with the powerful goddesses of Egypt: with Isis, Nut, Nepthys, and even Ma'at, the feminine principle of cosmic order. Her priestesses are remembered in the temple's limestone walls and ceilings, where their titles endure in reliefs, inscriptions, and statues. The Hathor priestesses were known for their music, especially two instruments—the sistrum, a sacred rattle bearing Hathor's face, and the *menat*, a heavy beaded counterpoise worn as a necklace and used percussively.

Alongside Hathor at Dendera, the dominant goddess and priestess culture in Egypt centered on Isis. Isis, known in Egyptian as Aset, was mother of the falcon god Horus, sister-wife of Osiris, a goddess who would in time absorb the attributes of nearly every other female deity. She first appeared in the archaeological record in the Old Kingdom c. 2400 BCE and persisted into late antiquity, temples still active and carrying her name into the fourth and even fifth centuries. Although she came to be called Isis Panthea, "Goddess of All Things," her primary functions in Egyptian myth and religion were magic, protection, healing, motherhood, and fertility. The most famous story in all of Egyptian culture surrounds her: a drama of love and resurrection recorded in the funerary texts, hymns, temple inscriptions, and countless other sources.[25]

Despite variations, the shape of the legend is as follows: Osiris was a just and benevolent king who brought civilization to a world once wild, teaching humanity and overseeing harmony. But his brother Seth was restless and jealous of his light. Seth trapped Osiris in a coffin and threw him in the Nile. Isis recovered the body. Seth, finding it again, tore Osiris into pieces and scattered them across Egypt. Isis journeyed through every corner of the land to gather his remains, fourteen pieces in total. Guided by a faith deeper than despair, she grieved, sang, spoke, and breathed life back into the fragments of Osiris. In her arms, Osiris was resurrected into the hidden divine realm, becoming god of the underworld. Through their miraculous union, Isis gave birth to their son, Horus, and fiercely guarded him from Seth, hiding with her infant in the marsh grasses of the Nile Delta under the protection of the goddess Selket and her seven scorpions. Through her devotion, Horus eventually challenged Seth and ascended to the divine throne, restoring his father's cosmic order.[26]

By the first century, this Egyptian religious world remained intact under Roman administration. Hathor's chantresses still served at Dendera; the temple of Isis at Philae was still vigorous; and in Alexandria, Isis stood beside Serapis, the Greco-Egyptian god formed from Osiris and Apis. Female initiates, attendants, and sacred functionaries appeared in inscriptions and held ritual office in public view. But this world would not endure unchanged. Imperial rule had long pressed upon indigenous traditions, where temple hierarchies had already begun shifting toward male control. Even so, the religious cultures of the ancient Mediterranean continued through Persian, Greek, and Roman domination. During the lifetime of Mary Magdalene, temples, priestesses, and goddess traditions still formed part of the sacred landscape of the empire. The decisive rupture came later, with the advent of Christianity.

Without surviving biographical details, it is impossible to know for certain whether Mary Magdalene received any training as a priestess, formal or cultural. Of all the details preserved in the Gospels, the one that speaks most to that possibility is the anointing moment. The anointing provides the most direct point of comparison with the ritual world of priestesses, particularly in Egyptian temple traditions. Yet the difficulty of reconciling what it all meant goes well beyond the tangle of Magdalene and Mary of Bethany—it extends into the anointing act itself. Christian culture has long assumed, however loosely, that this was a sacred moment. But the exact intention and significance of the act remain unresolved in the Gospel accounts.

THE CROWN

While the anointing appears in all four Gospels, the accounts do not align neatly, and their differences resist collapse into a single explanation. Variations in setting, audience, and even the words attributed to Jesus leave several possibilities open. Was the act domestic, affectionate, funerary—or initiatory? The answer shifts on the subtlest detail, with interpretation coloring any conclusion that can be drawn. One aspect, however, carries a particular weight in an anointing: where the oil is placed. In Mark and Matthew, the woman anoints Jesus's head; in Luke and John, the oil is placed on his feet. The distinction is highly significant. Within the symbolic vocabulary of the ancient world, this variation would change the nature of the anointing act, entirely.

"She broke the jar and poured the perfume on his head," Mark records, aligned with Matthew in bodily placement and narrative emphasis.[27] In Israel's scriptures, prophets anoint kings by pouring oil upon their heads as a visible sign that God has chosen them. Samuel anoints Saul, then David—ordinary men transformed, through ritual gesture, into rulers. The act does not create kingship but publicly proclaims the power it holds. Priests were consecrated in a similar manner during the First Temple period, before the sacred anointing oil was lost in exile. Psalm 133 evokes the image vividly: oil poured upon Aaron's head, running down his beard and garments—a visual of sacred appointment flowing from crown to body.

Beyond Israel, rituals of enthronement sometimes included oil, though the practice was not widespread and its centrality varied. Egyptian royalty followed different ritual forms, crowning with the white and red crowns, performing ritual purifications and offerings. Greek and Roman traditions did not rely on cranial blessing in the same way. The Hebrew tradition appears unusually explicit in its emphasis on the head as the site of consecration.[28]

The Hebrew verb *māšaḥ* means "to anoint." From it comes *māšîaḥ*, "anointed one," rendered in Greek as *christos*, from which the title Christ derives. In its earliest usage, the term referred precisely to the ritual described in Israel's scriptures: a king or high priest set apart through oil. The title itself assumes anointing. By the late Second Temple period, the term had developed into a technical designation for the awaited royal or priestly deliverer of Israel. Yet the exact form of that expectation varied widely across Jewish groups; no scripture or surviving document attests to a specific anointing ceremony as part of the prophecy.[29]

Chronologically, scholars would say the title Christ first appears in the letters of Paul. Paul shifts between variations of "Jesus Christ" without pausing to explain, a detail that scholars interpret to mean that the title was well-known and used by the time he was writing, around the mid 50s CE. The earliest creedal formulas in Paul's letters tie the title to the resurrection: Jesus was declared or revealed as Christ through being raised from the dead. However, the Gospels present Jesus as claiming or accepting the title during his ministry. The term opens Mark and appears as part of Peter's christological confession: "You are the Christ." Meanwhile, the christological confession in John attributed to Martha of Bethany, but possibly, as Elizabeth Schrader Polczer's work suggests, originally belonging to Mary, uses the word "Messiah." Some scholars believe that Jesus may not have used the title Christ or Messiah even during his ministry. For instance, Mark strangely describes Jesus as repeatedly silencing those who proclaim him as Messiah.[30]

If the anointing moment was the resurrection, as Paul suggested, then the theological significance of the anointing woman's act changes. Yet even then, Mary Magdalene, first witness to the resurrection, would still figure as an actor in whatever Paul meant by a resurrection-as-anointing scenario.

Since at least the end of the second century, Christian tradition has treated the Gospels as historical documents that preserve a real account of what happened in Jesus's life and ministry. If anointing the head marks a divine man who comes to be called *christos*—the chosen messiah, king and priest in one—would not that single anointing be the most sacred moment of his ministry? It would make perfect sense, then, for the rite to be performed by a priest, or even to have taken place in the Temple—which John's Gospel depicted him visiting often. So, is it not astonishing that Mark and Matthew placed the anointing on his head, and entrusted that gesture to an unnamed, unidentified woman? A woman who by her gender alone would have had no possible path to performing such a sacred gesture within an entirely male priesthood.

If Mark and Matthew are correct, then this woman must have had some authority to do what she did. One theological explanation holds that the authority vested in Jesus by divine nature supersedes any authority required of the one performing the anointing. Another interpretation moves the gesture entirely into the realm of symbolism, treating it as devotion rather than ritual, the woman's gender simply a sign of Jesus's humility and his disregard for social rankings. Still, in a Christian culture that elevates the act of anointing, but overlooks the woman's identity and significance, she becomes a token, a novelty, something to be explained away or dismissed easily.

Yet in the Christian traditions that have followed, anointing the crown of the head has remained a deeply sacred rite, performed only by an ordained priest or pastor. European monarchs continue to be anointed by clergy during coronation, often shielded from public view because the moment is considered the most sacred point of the ceremony. In Catholic sacramental life, oil is placed upon the crown during baptism and confirmation by an authorized minister, marking the individual as consecrated and set apart. The underlying symbolism remains consistent: to anoint the head is to designate—and it must be done by someone with vested religious authority.

The context of this scene within Matthew and Mark heightens the significance of the scene. Immediately after the anointing, Judas went to the chief priests and agreed to betray Jesus for thirty pieces of silver. The narrative juxtaposes the costly oil poured out by the woman—Mark recorded its value as three hundred denarii, nearly a year's wages for a common laborer—against the thirty pieces of silver Judas accepted for the betrayal: the price the Torah set for a slave. But the sequence does more than create moral contrast. The anointing becomes a tragic turning point that precedes, and may have provoked, the decision that sets Jesus's death in motion. Richard Bauckham has read it precisely this way, pointing to Mark's "sandwich" placement of the anointing between the chief priests' plot and Judas's offer of betrayal. Is it possible the anointing itself was what pushed Judas over the edge; that the woman's gesture, outrageous in how it marked Jesus as *christos*, was what drove him to the chief priests?[31]

If the head was where Jesus's body was anointed, then the gesture would place the woman, and possibly Mary Magdalene, within the register of sacred commissioning, whether symbolic or literal. It would mean that either this woman was literally trained in sacred arts, possibly as a priestess, or that she carried some other high form of spiritual authority that qualified her. A king, a priest, a prophet, a divine man could not have been anointed on the crown by an unnamed woman. If anything, it makes it all the more probable that the anointing woman was Mary of Bethany, and that Mary of Bethany was Magdalene. Why else take her name away? If Jesus declared that her memory was to be proclaimed, how does one proclaim the memory of an unnamed woman? It is impossible. At some point, her name was held in this story, and at some point, it was erased.

THE FEET

The anointing woman in Luke is, inevitably, the "sinner" Gregory the Great would later identify directly as Mary Magdalene. She anointed Jesus's feet, not his head, a detail Luke's author lingered upon: "As she stood behind him at his feet weeping, she began to wet his feet with her tears. Then she wiped them with her hair, kissed them and poured perfume on them."

The description is so evocative that master painters returned to it throughout history, men gathered around a table, a woman bent low. The parallel scene in John offers far scanter detail, and certainly less provocative material. There, Mary of Bethany "poured it on Jesus's feet and wiped his feet with her hair."[32] From Luke to John, the detail of her loose hair remains; the tears and kissing disappear. The dividing line between deliberate omission and narrative flourish is impossible to determine from such a distance. But oil at the feet carries a very different meaning than oil on the head.

If the head signifies elevation, the feet describe contact with the ground. In a world of sandaled travel and unpaved roads, washing a guest's feet was not symbolic abstraction but practical necessity. Oil might soothe cracked skin, ease fatigue, or honor one received with reverence. The gesture could be affectionate, grateful, and even intimate. However, in Judaism and across the wider Mediterranean world, anointing the feet did not function as a rite of consecration. There would have been no need for a priest, or priestess, or any other qualified figure to perform such a gesture.

Jewish and Greco-Roman households alike treated foot-washing as an ordinary courtesy of welcome, performed by servants and sometimes by hosts themselves. It signaled deference rather than authority. In Egypt too, oils and perfumes were used in healing and ritual contexts, but there is little evidence that anointing the feet conferred status. More often, it marked care, purification, or preparation for burial, movements that belonged to domestic life and fell well within the sphere of women.

Hebrew scripture preserves stories where foot-washing is the centered gesture. Abraham hastened to wash the feet of three visitors beneath the oaks of Mamre. Lot offered the same hospitality to strangers in Sodom. Abigail declared herself willing to wash the feet of David's servants as a sign of humility and allegiance. In each case, the gesture conveys reverence and service, not authority. Across the Gospels, the only one to preserve a foot-washing moment is John, where it becomes one of the narrative's most beautiful and consequential moments.

At the Last Supper, only days after the anointing at Bethany, Jesus rose from the table, removed his outer garment, and tied a towel around his waist. He poured water into a basin and began to wash the disciples' feet, drying them with the cloth wrapped about him. Every movement was charged with symbolism. When he laid aside his outer garment, John uses the Greek *tithēsin ta himatia*, the same verb later used for Jesus laying down his life. The towel at his waist was the dress of a slave, the visible mark of one who served. And the water bound the moment to John's larger imagery of living water: the water of life Jesus had offered the Samaritan woman at the well, the rivers of living water he had promised would flow from within those who believed. The feet in this moment signified humility, which Jesus himself made plain: "Very truly I tell you, no servant is greater than his master, nor is a messenger greater than the one who sent him."[33]

Crown to feet, king to servant; the symbolism is intentionally reversed. This detail has been widely analyzed in scholarship, with many competing readings. Some hold that it belongs to John's later composition, a shift resonant of the wider theology of John where the foot-washing and its convergence with the commandment of anointing seem to tie the feet to love symbolically. But what reads as metaphor could just as easily be genuine, especially given that Luke's narrative opening insisted its author had surveyed all the accounts and set out to record what was most true. And again, love is the thread. There is no foot-washing in Luke, but Jesus did praise the unnamed sinner saying: "Therefore I tell you, her many sins have been forgiven, as her great love has shown."[34]

Luke brings sin into it; John leaves sin out of it. Luke links forgiveness with love; John links tender care with love. It could be said that the head would have served Luke's narrative better than the feet—so why remember feet? And why write the anointing woman as a sinner?

Perhaps a clue lies in the hair. Why is the unnamed sinner or Mary of Bethany using her hair, apparently, as a towel for Jesus's feet during the anointing? In *Jewish Women in Greco-Roman Palestine*, Tal Ilan describes how unusual it was for a Jewish woman of this era to wear her hair long and unbound in public. Hebrew scripture associated loose hair with suspected adultery and rabbinical literature listed going out with hair uncovered among the grounds for divorce.[35]

Luke perhaps drew upon this cultural norm, hair becoming proof of the woman's sinfulness; it could have been a deliberately transgressive choice. But none of that negativity is present in John. There, she is Mary of Bethany, a woman described just one scene prior as a dear, even a beloved, friend of Jesus. The narrative places the anointing in her home, a private space where—depending on the company—it may have been acceptable for her to loosen her hair. Another possibility would be that Mary's hair was down in mourning for Lazarus, who was raised from the dead by Jesus just one chapter prior.

In First Corinthians, Paul calls a woman's long hair her *doxa*, her glory, and some interpreters have connected this to the anointing woman's hair—though Paul did not explicitly do so, nor did he mention this scene at all. Then, there is the Song of Songs. The combination of the costly ointment, the long hair, Luke's detail of kissing, and the pouring of oil has long been interpreted as clearly echoing this ancient love poem. It is a connection that links this anointing directly to Mary Magdalene, because the same Song of Songs imagery runs through her resurrection witness in John.

There is one other strange detail with her hair. She uses her hair to wipe his feet. Even more odd, she wipes after anointing, a sequence that makes the gesture incoherent as a consecratory rite because it removes, in part, the holy oil. Some mystical readings have pondered whether the wiping transferred the sacred oil to her own body through her hair, joining them in a way, again echoing the Bride-and-Bridegroom imagery.

Even with all that remains uncertain, taken together the details begin to coalesce. The placement on the feet, the loose hair, the wiping with hair, and Jesus's own words in context, all describe a moment that was intimate and personal, an expression of love. These scenes do not feel priestly or ritual, in a formal sense. They do not relate a gesture that would have required the anointing woman to be trained in a temple necessarily. What might be most peculiar about the hair is that, like the jar, it became one of the most iconic symbols of Mary Magdalene across art, for centuries.

In *The Testimony of the Beloved Disciple*, Richard Bauckham has argued that the shift from head to feet was protective. The original anointing, on his reading, really was a sacred rite, one performed on the crown, like the anointing of a king or priest, but Mark and John each found a different way to shield the woman who performed it. Mark preserved the political implications of a royal anointing while keeping her anonymous. John named her, identifying her through her brother and sister, but moved the oil to her feet, hiding the messianic significance of the gesture. Bauckham anticipates the obvious objection—that it would be surprising for the Messiah to be anointed by a woman—and answers that she could have been acting as a prophet, like Samuel anointing David in First Samuel 16.[36]

But the Samuel parallel only sharpens the question. Samuel was named, his prophetic function known, his authority part of the scriptural record. The unnamed woman in Mark, and even the named Mary of Bethany in John, are given no comparable prophetic identification. If she was functioning as a prophet, why would the Gospels withhold that identification entirely? And what qualified her for the role?

No consensus has prevailed; each explanation resolves one tension only to introduce another. Yet there is one more detail, one that appears at both the head anointing in Mark and the foot anointing in John, that may offer the clearest clue to what this moment signified: the kind of oil she used. Nard, or spikenard.

SPIKENARD

Olive oil would have made the purpose of the anointing immediately obvious. It was the daily oil of the Mediterranean world, used in hospitality, cooking, lamps, and the everyday washing of a guest's feet. If the oil had been the sacred compound of Exodus 30—pure myrrh, sweet cinnamon, sweet calamus, and cassia in a base of olive oil—the gesture's priestly character would have been unmistakable. That was the formula reserved by Mosaic law for anointing the tabernacle, the priests, and the kings of Israel.

Or if oil had been one of seven sacred oils of Egyptian temple liturgy, the enchanting idea of an Egyptian priestess tradition would have become harder to dismiss.[37] But the oil the woman used was rarer, more valuable, and more unusual than any of these. Mark and John each set its value at around three hundred denarii; Mark said more than that figure, John named it exactly. While Matthew and Luke glossed it as *murou*, generic perfume, Mark described it as *nardou pistikēs*, and John recorded *murou nardou pistikēs*—pistic nard, the high-grade oil derived from *Nardostachys jatamansi*, a plant native to the Himalayan regions.[38]

Thick, musky, and intensely fragrant, spikenard traveled along long-distance trade routes and ranked among the most expensive scents in the ancient Mediterranean. However, it is not securely attested in pre-first-century ritual contexts. Across Jewish, Egyptian, and Greco-Roman sources, the evidence for nard among the standard oils used for formal religious anointing is difficult to locate, surprisingly so given the detailed records of temple resins, sacred compounds, and perfumery that survive from each tradition. Even in Egypt, where administrative inventories, medical papyri, and cosmetic recipes preserve precise knowledge of aromatics, spikenard has not been securely identified in temple lists.

Modern attempts to identify spikenard with the Egyptian term *šdḥ* remain conjectural, resting largely on phonetic resemblance and lacking firm linguistic or archaeological support. Plutarch, writing in the first century, described the ingredients of Egyptian temple incense *kyphi* without mentioning nard.[39] When nard does appear more clearly in the Egyptian record, it surfaces in the Greco-Roman magical papyri of the second to fourth centuries. Its use in private rites, healing formulas, domestic rituals, and erotic incantations sits at a distance from the formal temple practices of earlier centuries, and the surviving witnesses are later than the Gospel narratives.

The absence of references to nard in a temple setting does not prove the oil was never used ritually. Endless documents have been lost, and in antiquity the highest rituals were often not written down at all; what was most sacred was frequently reserved for oral tradition. The field of ancient Egyptian aromatic identification is still actively contested, but the absence is striking across the major catalogs. There are many well-attested ancient oils used for anointing in every culture this moment could plausibly have touched and spikenard is not among them. Within the limits of the surviving record, and the scope of what is publicly accessible for research, the lack of clear reference to spikenard in formal ritual shifts the balance of evidence away from a strictly priestly significance.

Further, the use of spikenard is difficult to reconcile with a simple gesture of hospitality. It was too rare, too costly, too charged with meaning. Nor does it fit easily with ordinary Jewish or Roman burial practice. Unlike myrrh or aloes, the aromatics commonly associated with burial and referenced in the accounts of Jesus's own, spikenard was not chiefly valued for covering the odor of a body. Even though Jesus did state this anointing prefigured his burial in every account except Luke, the nard must have carried a symbolic significance beyond practicality.

The one context in which spikenard does appear evidently in the literary record is an intimate one: as a healing or ornamental oil used by women. In *De materia medica*, the first-century physician Pedanius Dioscorides described Indian nard as a prized aromatic used in both perfumery and medicine.[40] It appeared in ointments meant to warm the body, soothe inflammation, treat digestive complaints, and perfume the skin. While no source links nard explicitly to wedding rites, perfumes were part of bridal preparation, and its extreme luxury suggests it may have been worn by wealthy brides. Archaeological evidence—trade records, perfume vessels, residue analyses—places nard firmly in the sphere of elite consumption and personal adornment rather than temple ritual.

This bridal element brings the relevance of the anointing moment back to the world of Song of Songs. Within the entire Hebrew Bible, nard appears in Song of Songs and there it is mentioned three times, each referring to the fragrance of the beloved woman. "While the king was on his couch, my nard gave forth its fragrance," the bride declared. The image is intimate and private; her own perfume, released in the presence of her beloved. Nard returns in the lover's later imagery of her body as a garden of spices: "henna with nard, nard and saffron, calamus and cinnamon, with all trees of frankincense, myrrh and aloes."[41] The nard in the Song is not the oil of a priest. It is the perfume of a woman in love.

The Gospel writers knew of the Song of Songs, as would many Jews formed by the scriptural world of the period. Whether the poem was already read liturgically at festivals is harder to establish. The later practice of reading the Song of Songs at Passover is attested in rabbinic tradition, but not in surviving Second Temple sources.[42] Even so, it belonged to a scriptural world Jesus and his followers likely inhabited, making its imagery recognizable both within the Gospel tradition and to many of its early readers.

Did the anointing woman use spikenard intentionally—was the reference to the poem her own? Or was nard included by the Gospel writers as a dramatic embellishment, one designed to connect the moment to Song of Songs? Neither possibility resolves the moment, because the ambiguity of the Song itself, its clear sensuality and even eroticism, makes the resonance all the more puzzling.

If Luke's anointing woman was meant to be read as a sinner, the spikenard might have served his negative portrayal of her, given the sexual register of the Song of Songs. But Luke omitted the nard. So did Matthew. And yet the Song of Songs connection was established firmly enough that even Gregory the Great, in Homily 33, reached for Song of Songs imagery to interpret Luke's scene and paint Magdalene as a prostitute.

There is one more detail: the jar. Jars carried not only oil, wine, grain, and perfume in antiquity; they were objects of symbolic resonance. A jar contained, transformed, released—qualities Hesiod's poetry epitomized in Pandora. Her container was not a box, or a *pyxis*, but a *pithos*, a large storage jar. When Pandora opened it, the universal and unavoidable conditions of life escaped into the world: struggle, suffering, illness, labor, and death. Much like Eve, Pandora gradually became associated with feminine transgression and the danger of opening what should remain closed.

Plato echoed this vessel symbolism in the *Gorgias* when he compared the well-ordered soul to a properly sealed container, in which what is good is preserved and what is harmful is kept in check. In "Women and Medicine," Holt Parker describes how ancient Greek texts at times explicitly compared the womb to a vessel or jar, situating that vessel in relationship to the female body.[43] So, in a Hellenistic symbolic frame, a poured-out vessel signaled release. In Greek and Jewish practice, pouring out was libation, an offering to the divine, which might signify loss or disorder, but also fulfillment, completion, or even revelation.

All three Synoptic Gospels qualified the material of the jar as alabaster; another name for Egyptian calcite, a warm translucent stone soft enough to be carved easily into vessels. Alabaster was used for jars, bowls, and containers across the Middle East. Archaeologists have found alabaster in elite Jewish places: Herodian palaces, high-status homes, and communities such as Qumran. However, it was far more commonly used in Egypt. In any region, alabaster was an ordinary material. It might signal wealth, but the material of the jar does not lend any formal ritual significance.

An alabaster jar of rich, fragrant, costly oil is poured out before a crowd, honoring Jesus in some way during the final period before his death. What is undeniable is that the mention of spikenard links the anointing to the Song of Songs. The nard, opened and touched to feet or head, presses the question of intimacy rather than resolving it. The nature of the relationship between Mary and Jesus becomes impossible not to ask.

THE WIFE

The woman in the Song of Songs is not a prostitute, nor a sexual sinner of any kind. The poem sings in the register of two lovers, with language of fragrance, searching, garden, and beloved that comes startlingly close to both the anointing moment and the resurrection encounter. Very early, this imagery began to coalesce around Mary Magdalene. In the third century, Origen was already reading Magdalene's search for the risen Christ through the bride's search for the beloved. By the Middle Ages, this symbolic vocabulary had become deeply powerful, drawing both bride and Magdalene into a world of devotion, longing, romance, and courtly love.

It is admittedly peculiar, at least from a modern view. Why would this lyrical, bridal imagery gather around Magdalene at all? In the resurrection garden, the alignment is unusually direct: two figures stand at the center of the scene, Jesus and Mary Magdalene. He appears as the one sought and found; she appears as the woman searching in grief and love. The convergence does more than draw Magdalene closer to Mary of Bethany. It opens the question of how early Christians understood her relationship with Jesus, and where symbol ended and memory began.

The resonance proved so potent that later interpreters displaced Magdalene into abstraction. In patristic theology, Mary Magdalene became a figure of the future Church. Jesus became the Bridegroom, with a capital B, and Mary became the Bride, not herself, but a term. Later, Bernard of Clairvaux often called "the last of the Fathers," gave this imagery poetic intensity, interpreting lines such as "Let him kiss me with the kisses of his mouth" as the soul's union with Christ.[44] The framework preserved the bridal symbolism while continuing to cut Magdalene out of it. Her own identity became secondary to the institution she was made to prefigure.

Even in the more mystical lineages, Mary's own identity was not centered. She remained a metaphor; Mary was eclipsed by a Church that did not yet exist in institutional form when the Gospel was written.

But metaphor became concrete in recent decades. The coupling of Magdalene and bride has been interpreted as historical fact hidden in plain sight. The wave began with *Holy Blood, Holy Grail* by Michael Baigent, Richard Leigh, and Henry Lincoln in 1982, was extended by Margaret Starbird in *The Woman with the Alabaster Jar* in 1993, and was catalyzed into popular culture by Dan Brown's *The Da Vinci Code* in 2003. From there it became standard fodder for novels and spiritual texts on Mary Magdalene. Yet in the fervor of excitement, explanations often leap beyond plausibility.[45]

The Gospels do not identify Mary Magdalene as Jesus's wife, though silence alone cannot settle the question. Unlike many women in the narratives, Magdalene is not defined through attachment to a husband or father, whether named as herself or as Mary of Bethany. Some have proposed that she may have been a widow, since widowhood could grant a woman a degree of financial independence. The texts themselves offer no evidence for this. Jesus's own unmarried status has likewise drawn attention. Marriage was common among Jewish men of his age, including those who occupied positions of religious authority, but it wasn't legally required. Exceptions existed: the Essenes at Qumran practiced celibacy and John the Baptist appears to have been unmarried.[46]

The burial narratives offer a possible thread of familial ties. In three of the four Gospels, Mary Magdalene is among the women who come to the tomb carrying spices to tend Jesus's body. In Jewish practice of the period, washing, anointing, wrapping the dead in burial preparation was typically undertaken by family members or close associates, often women. Other small details are picked up on, such as when Jesus addresses her at the tomb, "Woman, why are you crying?" and he uses the Greek *gynē*. The word ordinarily means woman, though in certain contexts it can refer to a wife. Yet elsewhere in John—at Cana and at the cross, addressing his own mother—Jesus uses the same word without implying marriage. Some speculators have even proposed that the wedding at Cana was Mary and Jesus's own, but that idea belongs to conjecture.[47]

When Mary Magdalene becomes one with Mary of Bethany, the possibility of intimacy becomes more compelling. The anointing's use of nard, the loose hair, the closeness of the gesture, each detail is astonishingly intimate. If Mary of Bethany was simply a follower of Jesus, the anointing would have been at the very least a lavish and insightful expression of her love for him. There are subtle clues, too, around the raising of Lazarus: how Jesus's love for the siblings at Bethany was highlighted, how Mary stayed in the house longer, how Jesus possibly joined their mourning in a way reserved for family. But none of these details necessitates marriage between husband and wife.

Symbols that enter myth and art tend to gather meanings across centuries. Even the later tradition that cast Mary as a prostitute was sometimes reinterpreted as a deliberate veil concealing the deeper truth of her marriage to Jesus. This is an appealing theory, but tragically, there are infinite reasons for the defamation of Magdalene's character. Sexual shame was a tactic deployed upon all women of power, prominence, and intellect.

The texts discovered at Nag Hammadi added new complexity and intrigue to the question of Magdalene's relationship with Jesus. The Gospel of Philip, a third-century Valentinian work preserved in Coptic, includes a passage that remembers Mary Magdalene as the companion of Jesus. It states: "There were three who always walked with the Lord: Mary his mother, and her sister, and Mary Magdalene, who was called his companion." The Greek *koinōnos*, translated as companion, can describe partners in work, participants in a mission, or those who share a spiritual bond. The same text preserves a fragmentary passage stating that Jesus loved Mary more than the other disciples and kissed her often. The damaged Coptic leaves the location of the kiss uncertain. Even apart from that uncertainty, a kiss in antiquity wasn't inherently erotic. In Jewish, Greek, and early Christian contexts, it could signify greeting, blessing, reconciliation, or the transmission of teaching.[48]

The dynastic-marriage and sacred-bloodline theories take specific clues even further—most notably *Holy Blood, Holy Grail*, and the writing of Starbird. These reconstructions build on the Gospel genealogies that trace Jesus to King David, suggesting that a marriage to Magdalene could have produced a royal lineage with both theological and political significance.

In this telling, knowledge of that bloodline was concealed by ecclesiastical elites, royal families, and encoded across centuries in art and legend.

For one brief moment in the twenty-first century, the question seemed to acquire new evidence. In 2012, the historian and expert on the Gospel of Mary Karen L. King announced a small Coptic fragment soon known as the Gospel of Jesus's Wife, its most explosive line appearing to contain the phrase "Jesus said to them, 'My wife . . . '" Poised to answer this forbidden question, putting the answer in Jesus's own mouth, the fragment gained worldwide attention. However, the excitement collapsed relatively quickly when the fragment was exposed as a modern forgery, albeit a convincing one, and the historical record settled back into silence.[49]

No clear evidence resolves the question of Magdalene's relationship with Jesus, but the texts preserve an unusual closeness between them that tradition has struggled to explain. What remains is a persistent fascination sustained by symbols and stories still not fully understood. Yet the fixation on Magdalene as wife may have distracted from a fuller reckoning with her identity and role within the Christian narrative. As Jane Schaberg put it bluntly: "I think the recent interest in making Mary Magdalene Mrs. Jesus or the lover of Jesus in part has more to do with Jesus than with Mary Magdalene . . . It's another way of using a woman to think about a man."[50]

UNION MISUNDERSTOOD

Asking only whether Mary Magdalene and Jesus were romantically involved may be to misread the way that symbols move and speak. Symbols resist easy translation to plain ideas or language. That is part of what made myth so powerful: its strangeness, what it said and what it withheld, the meaning it carried through an object, a landscape, an animal, a color, a number, in ways that cannot be rationally explained in a straight line. There are other ways to understand the intimacy between Mary and Jesus, ones that still speak to union, but through the older systems of sacred patterns.

In Song of Songs, there is no wedding. Its lovers remain suspended in search, their bond defined not by law or lineage but by recognition and desire. From the earliest traces, the poem was interpreted as an allegory of divine communion. Jewish and Christian tradition alike read it as divine love. Even when it is traced back to Mesopotamian and Egyptian love poetry, the same impulse holds. The poems of Inanna are famously erotic, and often sensationalized, but some scholars believe their sexual language was intended primarily to carry allegorical weight. Such poems function as *hieros gamos*, meaning symbols and stories that use marriage of man and wife as allegories of divine union. *Hieros gamos* expressed the joining of complementary forces, heaven and earth, divine and human, ruler and land, through myth, procession, song, and ritual drama.[51]

The same line of thinking around the Song of Songs, sexuality, and Mary Magdalene circles back to the possibility that Magdalene was a priestess. The logic is tempting: perhaps her later designation as a prostitute preserved, in distorted form, an older memory that she was a sacred woman. From there, modern assumptions about priestesses and ritual sex do much of the work. If priestesses are imagined as women who enacted *hieros gamos*, Magdalene's anointing of Jesus and the erotic charge around her story begin to look like clues. But the theory rests on a fragile premise: that priestesses in antiquity commonly functioned as sacred prostitutes, an idea modern historical scholarship has largely dismantled.

In *The Myth of Sacred Prostitution in Antiquity*, the historian Stephanie Lynn Budin argues that the concept rests largely on mistranslations and hostile polemic. The Greek terms once rendered as sacred prostitute—*hierodoulos, porne, hetaira*—referred to entirely different legal or social roles when restored to their original contexts: temple servants and slaves, common prostitutes, and elite courtesans, none of them institutionalized as cultic functionaries. Even the famous temples of Aphrodite at Corinth and Eryx were not houses of ritual sex, despite long-standing claims to the contrary. The most-cited ancient witnesses are Herodotus's report that every Babylonian woman was required once in her life to sit at the temple of Mylitta, and Strabo's figure of a thousand sacred prostitutes at Corinth. Budin reads both as Greek polemic against foreign or rival customs, not as ethnographic record. At most, Budin argues, some prostitutes dedicated earnings to the goddess as acts of personal piety, a practice attested in Athens and elsewhere, not evidence of institutionalized cultic prostitution.[52]

The same caution applies to claims of sacred-marriage ritual within the so-called mystery traditions. The Eleusinian rites were secret and dramatic, centered on the death-and-rebirth myth of Demeter and Persephone; Christian polemicists claimed they involved ritual intercourse, but those accounts are now widely read as hostile invention. The cult of Isis emphasized restoration and fidelity. And the Dionysian movements—portrayed by Roman critics, most famously by Livy in the aftermath of the Bacchanalia scandal of 186 BCE, as sexually chaotic—are now widely understood as instances of political anxiety and moral panic rather than as objective record.[53]

Pop culture often compresses these priestess theories into seductive fragments that travel easily online but shed the historical context that would make them intelligible. Magdalene becomes a *hierodule*, a priestess of Isis, a sexual initiatrix, a keeper of goddess mysteries, an initiate of Egypt, Tantra, or the older Near Eastern cults. Each version promises a hidden key. But *hierodoulos*—the Greek term meaning sacred slave or sacred servant—has no place in Jewish or Alexandrian-Jewish religious structure, where the priesthood was hereditary and male and no equivalent cultic-attendant category existed. And many of these readings still depend on assumptions about ancient female religious specialists that Budin and others have shown largely do not hold up.

What Budin's work reveals is that women in visible religious roles were repeatedly described through a sexualized lens by male authors: sometimes mocking, sometimes hostile, sometimes moralizing. Greek writers did it to foreign cults; Christian writers did it to pagan traditions. Over time, insinuation became accepted narrative.[54] Mary Magdalene's reduction to a prostitute follows that logic: it reveals less about her life than about the stories men tell about powerful women. She need not have been a prostitute, or even a secret wife, to draw such treatment. In antiquity, any woman who deviated from expectation—crossing boundaries, challenging norms, unsettling male authority—could be recast in a negative light within a historical record shaped by male, often misogynistic, voices.

Take Cleopatra VII, the last Ptolemy of Egypt, who ruled for two decades and managed the most consequential political alliances of her age. She spoke as many as nine languages, including the Egyptian her predecessors had never bothered to learn, and she presented herself to her people not as a foreign sovereign but as their pharaoh, as a goddess: Nea Isis, the

New Isis. Stacy Schiff's biography *Cleopatra: A Life* details her education among the greatest philosophers, mathematicians, astronomers, and physicians the Library and Mouseion of Alexandria had to offer. In antiquity, Cleopatra was credited with penning treatises on medicine, cosmetics, and systems of measurement. She expanded her kingdom's territory through skillful diplomacy and managed its economy through severe droughts and famine. She was the last independent ruler of a civilization three thousand years older than Rome.[55]

Yet the historical record left by her conquerors made her primarily a seductress. Octavian's propaganda machine reduced her brilliance to sexual manipulation, and the dominant memory that survived her was not the ruler but the lover, first of Caesar, then of Antony, a memory that has held for two thousand years. Schiff reads that record as a master class in how male propaganda transforms a brilliant female sovereign into a sexual caricature. Mary Magdalene was caught in the same machinery—reduced, like Cleopatra, from witness to seductress, from authority to sinner.

Ancient reports could not quite deny that Cleopatra loved Mark Antony, or that her bond with Julius Caesar may have been a genuine romance. Love need not have diminished her legacy. But in the hands of the men who told her story, romance became another instrument of diminishment. Mary Magdalene has borne a similar fate. The Song of Songs language that clung to her may, at first, seem to hint at marriage. But what the language symbolically suggests is divine union: the coming together of masculine and feminine, of opposites that reflect the one with greater power. It is possible Mary was married to Jesus. No one can know with certainty; the record is too sparse. What the evidence in the Gospels and beyond raises instead is the possibility of partnership and union at a level beyond marriage, a potential far more threatening to later authorities than either a priestess or a wife.

LINEAGE OF WISDOM

It is unquestionable that Mary Magdalene was perceived as a spiritual authority in certain early Christian circles. Pistis Sophia, a third- to fourth-century Coptic text, praises Mary's intelligence and heart through the voice of Jesus, ranking her above the male disciples in awareness: "Mary, thou blessed one, whom I will perfect in all the mysteries of those of the Height, discourse in openness, thou whose heart is uplifted to the Kingdom of Heaven more than all thy brethren."[56]

In the Dialogue of the Savior, a late-second-century text from Nag Hammadi, Mary is described in terms that reverberate in the same vocabulary used for goddesses: "She uttered this saying as a woman who knew the All."[57]

Mariamne appears in the Acts of Philip, usually dated to the fourth or fifth century, with striking ritual and apostolic authority. She prepares the bread and salt for the breaking of bread and is addressed by Jesus as "chosen among women." She receives reverence alongside the male apostles, heals a woman named Nicanora, and, at the climax of her martyrdom, becomes a luminous vessel, "like an ark of glass full of light and fire."[58]

In the Gospel of Philip, dated variously between the second and fourth centuries, Mary is named among the "three" Marys who walked alongside Jesus, with his sister and mother. There Magdalene is called *koinōnos,* a term used across antiquity for partners in work, in suffering, in divine participation. Paul calls Philemon his *koinōnos.* Peter, James, and John are *koinōnoi* in their fishing trade. Hebrews speaks of those who share Christ's afflictions as *koinōnoi.* The word does not specify marriage, it evokes sharing: the deep mutual participation that comes when two people are bound by a common calling. That is the term the Gospel of Philip chose for Mary's relationship with Jesus, rather than the Greek for wife, or friend, or disciple.[59]

There is also the puzzling final saying in the Gospel of Thomas, possibly the oldest of these texts, with some scholars dating it to the middle of the first century. There Peter tries to expel Mary from among the disciples, declaring that women are not worthy of life. Jesus answers that he will lead her himself, so that she too may become male and enter the kingdom of heaven. The saying sounds at first like exclusion but understood within the philosophical world of the ancient Mediterranean, it becomes nearly the opposite. Because "male" signified the rational and the spiritual, while "female" represented the material and the bodily, becoming "male" was an expression used for reaching the higher spiritual state. In plain terms, the logion says Mary can enter the kingdom, and Jesus himself will lead her there. And out of all hundred and fourteen sayings, the Gospel of Thomas chose to close on this exchange.[60]

In all of these texts, most scholars identify this Mary as Mary Magdalene, not in a literal sense but a symbolic one: a memory of who she may have been transposed into story and carried through communities who valued her as a figure of *wisdom*. Is it possible that Magdalene's prominence derives less from romance or ritual status than from intellect and intuition, from her capacity to grasp and articulate what others struggled to understand?

Scholars have long noted the parallels between Magdalene and Sophia in Valentinian and related texts.[61] Though Sophia carries a complex mythic history, she echoes the earlier tradition of Hebrew Wisdom: preexistent, creative, central to divine activity. What if the resemblance between Mary, Sophia, and Wisdom reflects Magdalene's education, philosophical training, and spiritual discipline?

Throughout the ancient Mediterranean world, philosophy was not just an academic pursuit; it was a way of life, an effort to live in accord with what was understood as the underlying order of existence. Philosophers sought to engage the divine source of reality and to discern the patterns that shaped the world: the movements of the heavens, the formation of character, the structures of nature, the subtleties of human wellbeing. Philosophy concerned the relationship between human and divine, individual and community, soul and body. Like the *gnōsis* described in some early Christian texts, philosophy in practice aimed at transformation through insight, discernment, and disciplined understanding.

Early Christianity, as many scholars have noted, functioned similarly to a philosophical school. Communities gathered around a teacher, cultivated disciplined ways of living, transmitted teachings orally and in writing, and aimed at the transformation of character. In its earliest generations, Christian teachers, *didaskaloi,* were lay instructors who traveled, taught, and led assemblies within homes. Jesus himself could be described as reminiscent of an ancient philosopher: he engaged with questions of ultimate reality, taught through dialogue and parable, called disciples into a shared way of life, and grounded insight in ethical practice.

Writers such as Justin Martyr, Clement of Alexandria, Athenagoras, and Origen described Christianity as the *true philosophy*. Roman critics including Celsus, Galen, and Emperor Julian likewise treated Christianity as a philosophical system. Stanley K. Stowers has shown that Pauline communities resembled Hellenistic philosophical movements in their intense focus on ethical formation and self-discipline. The Acts of the Apostles even depicts Paul debating Epicurean and Stoic philosophers in Athens, placing early Christian preaching within a shared intellectual terrain.[62]

Plato, Heraclitus, Plutarch, and the later Stoics all acknowledged that wisdom could be conveyed through a woman. The Pythia of Delphi was a priestess who delivered inspired pronouncements believed to come from Apollo. Her voice stood among the most respected sources of counsel in the Mediterranean world: kings, generals, and lawgivers traveled to Delphi to consult her judgment. And while her words were attributed to the male deity, she alone possessed the gift to hear and translate divine authority. The memory of Themistoclea—a woman who tradition says instructed Pythagoras himself—illustrates how easily the boundaries between priestess, prophetess, and philosopher could blur in antiquity.[63]

Women appeared within formal philosophical communities as well, though their presence varied across schools and centuries. The Pythagorean tradition was remembered for including women in its intellectual life. Later sources preserve the names of female Pythagoreans named Theano, Damo, Phintys, Melissa, as companions of great men and as contributors to discussions of ethics, cosmology, mathematics, and the ordering of nature. Aspasia of Miletus was a woman who presided over an influential Athenian circle, renowned for her rhetorical acuity. Plato's dialogues preserved the figure of Diotima as teacher of the ascent toward Beauty and Love. Hipparchia of Maroneia taught publicly as a Cynic, courting both admiration and scandal. Centuries later, Hypatia of Alexandria would stand among the most renowned philosophers of the late antique world.[64]

Alexandria, the great intellectual capital of the ancient world, was precisely the kind of city where these possibilities converged. If women participated in philosophical life anywhere in the first-century Mediterranean, a center as diverse as Alexandria, with its libraries, schools, and overlapping religious traditions, would have been among the most likely places for it. And there is a remarkable attestation to a Jewish philosophical community on the outskirts of Alexandria in the first century: one that included women.

Philo of Alexandria is the sole surviving witness to the Therapeutae, whom he described in *De vita contemplativa* as a Jewish community whose life blended scriptural devotion with contemplation and philosophical reflection. Some scholars have dismissed his portrait as idealized; others argue that it preserves the outline of a real group whose existence complicates assumptions about women and wisdom within first-century Judaism. Joan Taylor has carefully investigated Philo's account in *Jewish Women Philosophers of First-Century Alexandria*, arguing that the Therapeutae were neither a Jewish counterpart to the sectarian communities described by Josephus nor an Essene offshoot. The Essenes, as they are typically described, were marked by strict communal discipline, ascetic practice, and overwhelmingly male membership, shaped by traditions that often treated women as sources of distraction or impurity and excluded them from the highest forms of religious life. The Therapeutae, by contrast, cultivated a contemplative community in which women and men pursued study and devotion side by side.[65]

Taylor illuminates how Philo portrayed the lives of the female Therapeutae as centered on study and stillness. Six days each week were given to prayer, scriptural meditation, and allegorical interpretation, where sacred texts were approached as layered wisdom rather than literal law. Every fiftieth day, men and women gathered for an all-night vigil of song and dance modeled on the prophetess Miriam and her Song of the Sea. Celibate and economically independent, these women were not defined by marriage or domestic obligation. Philo's description of them is careful, even protective: he emphasizes their modesty, maturity, and restraint, language that made their authority legible within Jewish and Greco-Roman expectations. Taylor suggests that in a world quick to sexualize or dismiss women who taught or led, such framing was likely deliberate.

Examples of female philosophers and priestesses do not establish certainty around Mary Magdalene's background, but they do open possibilities worth imagining. These ancient worlds of sacred women offer compelling environments in which Mary might have developed the perception, resilience, recognition, and intelligence she demonstrates across canonical and noncanonical accounts. Especially in Alexandria, a first-century Jewish woman of means could have encountered Greek philosophy, mathematics, and astronomy; studied the scriptures of her own tradition and others; and moved within a wide exchange of ideas about the sacredness of life. In such a world, a woman could move between priestess and philosopher, between sacred intuition and disciplined thought. In such a world, a woman could be formed within more than one order at once—between measure and meaning.

SEVEN & SERPENT

Seven, that integer of wholeness, circles Mary Magdalene. It surfaces in the seven *daimonia*, the seven powers of wrath of the Gospel of Mary, even in her feast day: in July, the seventh month. Seven, conspicuously, belongs to feminine wisdom, finding a home in nearly every spiritual tradition that imagined her. Seven oils and Seven Hathors in Egypt. Seven pillars built by Wisdom in her house in Proverbs 9:1. Inanna-Ishtar descend through seven gates of underworld. The list of sacred sevens, drawn from stories and systems that signal the intelligence of cosmic order, are almost too many to count.

Seven counts what is complete through accumulation, work, and ordeal. Sometimes that effort is described as a movement down, other times it is an ascent, a rising, a climb. Up or down, it is a threshold—tower or gate—and it allows sight and knowledge beyond the ordinary. And wherever ancient traditions described this awakened perception, the same figure reappeared: the serpent. The creature with unblinking eyes and a body that sheds and renews, whose venom is medicine and whose medicine is venom. In nearly every culture that imagined wisdom, the snake was the one who knew.

The serpent marked transformation, a quality earned through simple observation: skin shed in cycles, a body that moved silently between landscapes, the power of a slender animal to heal and to kill. As far back as symbols go, the snake is present. The Minoan snake goddess figurines of Knossos on Crete, dated to roughly 1600 BCE, depict bare-breasted priestesses gripping serpents in each raised hand. In the Greek sanctuaries, the snake was attached to Asclepius and his daughter Hygeia. Egypt raised the snake onto the royal crown: the cobra goddess Wadjet became the *uraeus* at Pharaoh's brow. Serpents wound through Astarte and Anat in the Canaanite traditions that flowed into the Hebrew Asherah. In Anatolia the Great Mother Cybele was linked to serpents, a tradition that would later graft onto Artemis of Ephesus. Greek goddesses—Hecate, Demeter, Persephone—all drew serpents toward the cycles of death and rebirth they presided over. Athena raised the half-snake Erichthonios as her protected ward in the citadel of Athens. And in Rome, there was Salus, a goddess and protectress whose image was stamped on coins with a serpent eating from a bowl in her hand.[66]

Even in Genesis, the serpent is described as *ʿarum*, a Hebrew word that can mean subtle, perceptive, cunning in the older sense of knowing. A turn of a word raises a question long asked, if quietly and only in certain circles, a question still perceived as dangerous, even blasphemous.

What if Eve was not the first sinner, but a woman seeking Wisdom? What if, like Pandora and Sophia, her bite of the fruit, as irreversible as a jar of oil poured out, transformed humanity in a way that was not necessarily negative? At the very least, perhaps there is nothing malevolent in the pursuit of knowledge, in eating from the tree of the knowledge of good and evil. What if the two trees were once one, divided in the telling, like the rib in Genesis, like the splitting of one woman into many? What if wisdom and life grow from the same root?

To be intelligent and to be a woman, deity or human, has long been viewed from a masculine lens as frightening. A power that feels uncontainable. Euripides is said to have stated it cleanly: "A woman who is clever, this is a dangerous thing."[67] His ancient words betray a perspective that still moves through culture in modernity: intelligence tilts into transgression when it appears in a woman. A woman who speaks too much, knows too much, can do too much, is threatening or deceptive. Women are still rarely permitted to be like the snake: to move between worlds, to transform and change, to swing between extremes.

In Greco-Roman myth, the healing power of the serpent gathered around the Greek demigod Asclepius. The serpent-on-the-rod on medical logos is attributed to him, but the power of the serpent did not originate with him. In one story, Asclepius observed a serpent helping to heal another snake and used the same cure to revive the young prince Glaucos. In another, the power of Asclepius derived from the blood of the Gorgon Medusa, given to him by Athena after Perseus slew her. Of course, the snake-haired woman is read as a monster even now. But before that telling took hold, evidence from pre-Hellenic archaeology shows that the *gorgoneia* were emblazoned on temples, shields, and armor.[68]

In myth, Medusa's blood drawn from the right side was cure; from the left, poison. The serpent speaks to the duality of power, and to the question of how power is used. Isis belonged to the serpent's deepest mystery where venom, protection, magic, and renewal become difficult to separate. A surviving example resides at the Metropolitan Museum of Art in New York: the Metternich Stela, a smooth dark greywacke slab just over two feet high, dating to the reign of Nectanebo II in the fourth century BCE. Its surfaces are densely cut with hieroglyphic spells against snake and scorpion bites, and on the front the child Horus grips snakes and dangerous beasts in his hands. On one side, Isis stands upon a serpent and declares, in the spell's address to every serpent that bites: "I am Isis the goddess, mistress of magic, doer of magic, effective of recitations: every biting serpent-mouth listens to me."[69]

If the serpent could kill, the goddess could heal to the point of resurrection, reaching into the spiritual realm to bring what was dead back to the material domain of earthly life. Transformation, at its simplest, means to change from one state to another, a power that belongs to the snake and to women. To conceive and carry life, to pass through the trial of birth that brushes with death, to tend, nurse, heal, nurture children, as well as land, animals, spouses, communities, that is the work of women. Mystery lives at the edge of fear and devotion: this is the realm the feminine and the serpent both belong to.

This is what it means to communicate between worlds and bring something to life. But what is magic? The word is surrounded by fear and hope, wrapped in projections and illusions. For Isis, magic was not spectacle but sacred speech, the hidden force by which a name, a word, or a gesture could move through matter and spirit at once. At its simplest, magic is the belief that life is both material and spiritual, and that the two are intertwined, with a shared language between them.

The practice of magic, *kishuf*, is repeatedly condemned in the Hebrew Bible and in Second Temple texts. However, archaeology has recovered Aramaic incantation bowls inscribed with protective spells, invoking the God of Israel, named angels, and biblical verses. The same goes for talismans, phylacteries, and other ritual objects. These were magical tools used by ancient Jews, with similar objects traced to early Christians. Protective amulets, healing tokens, Christogram pendants, gospel passages folded and worn against the body have been found across the Roman empire. These practices were hope made manifest, prayer worn, protection invoked in ways that felt tangible and effective in a world marked by war, disease, violence, and hunger. A Miraculous Medal, a Sign of the Cross, a Kiss of Peace, even holy water, creeds recited in unison, crucifixes—these are objects and acts whose sacred power would have been recognized as magic in an ancient world.[70]

Magic, the serpent, the ascent to seven—each of these acts and symbols speaks to the transformation of the ordinary into the extraordinary. A miracle may be the outcome of magic, an event prayed for, not promised, but one that arrived anyway in a manner that can only be described through faith. Wisdom, then, is not magic itself—it is the fabric beneath the actions. It is the creative feminine source, the same one illuminated in the Wisdom of Solomon: "For she is a reflection of eternal light, a spotless mirror of the working of God, and an image of his goodness. Although she is but one, she can do all things, and while remaining in herself, she renews all things."[71]

Chapter 7

FIELDS OF SOMERSET

For centuries, people have said that when mist drifts across the fields of Somerset, Glastonbury Tor becomes something else entirely. The hedges disappear, the roads dissolve, and the hill rises like an island drawn out of the fog, its tower floating above it all like the mast of a ship. The image is so uncanny that it seems to have written itself into legend, carrying with it the names that endured: the "Isle of Apples," the "Isle of the Blessed," a paradise imagined in medieval tales, yet rooted in stories passed down by local people long before.

Here, the veil between things begins to feel unusually thin. Stories rise through soil and masonry alike, beckoning you toward a world only half hidden. Is this the hidden island of healing? Is it the hill of Saint Michael, the old Christian guardian set over more ancient ground? Is it a remnant of something even earlier, a place where myth kept changing its name but not its pull? And where, in all of this, does Mary Magdalene belong?

Mist has a way of making distinctions feel less certain. It thins the boundaries of this world, allowing legend, history, devotion, and imagination to move together beneath the surface. It is easy to understand why earlier generations believed this was Avalon, the island where the wounded king was carried to heal, withdrawn just beyond the reach of ordinary sight. But the condition that draws someone toward such a place is not reserved for kings. It belongs to anyone whose pain has been hidden, misnamed, or carried too long.

And so, sooner or later, that search takes shape in a place like this, where the hill rises before you, asking to be climbed.

*

Stepping through the gate, you feel the ground soften beneath your feet, still holding the rain. Puddles settle in the low places, catching the light like small mirrors scattered across the grass. The pasture opens around you, thick and wind-swept, while sheep graze along the hillside, heads bent low. Beyond them, the land lifts in long green folds toward the tower above, across a landscape where seekers have come for centuries, drawn by the promise that what was lost might still be waiting somewhere beyond ordinary sight.

You keep walking through the pasture as the field opens around you in every direction, thinking about the pull of a place like this, where so many have come looking for Mary, for Avalon, for healing, for some lost feminine face of the sacred, though none of it is overtly named on the hill. Officially, this is a Christian hill, crowned by Saint Michael's tower and marked by the language of pilgrimage, sanctity, and ascent. Yet the older longing remains palpable, moving beneath the surface like water under grass.

That's when a single buttercup catches your eye, still in bloom against the autumn air—one small, improbable flash of yellow in the endless green. It seems almost too delicate for the season, too bright for the weathered hillside, and for a moment it stops you completely.

Buttercups are resilient flowers, often dismissed as weeds, though botanists know them as *Ranunculus*, kin to the layered blooms cultivated in gardens and bouquets. Even in this wild form, growing low against the path, the flower might easily pass unnoticed. But once you see it, you cannot look away. Its yellow surface catches the sun until it gleams like metal, holding the light the way a chalice might hold wine.

That image is enough to change the hillside. A moment ago, the flower was only a flower. Now the chalice recalls the Holy Grail, one of Glastonbury's most enduring legends: the cup sought through stories of knights, adventure, and longing. But the Tor has already grounded the symbol in another language, through grass, grazing, milk, and the body as source. In older mythologies, life was often imagined through cups, bowls, cauldrons, udders, and wombs—symbols derived from the feminine body and its generative power. Yes, before the Grail became an object of pursuit, it belonged to a deeper memory of nourishment, abundance, and return.

In Celtic tradition, the goddess Brigid was connected with cattle, fertility, and abundance, her blessing said to multiply milk and grain. Another goddess who became a saint, Brigid of Kildare, carried traces of those older traditions forward: red-haired and radiant, she was linked to fire, healing, poetry, and sacred wells. Medieval legend later tied her to Glastonbury, claiming she came there and visited Saint Patrick at Beckery, "Little Ireland." A small relief of her is carved into the tower above. Like Mary Magdalene, Brigid became a woman suspended between sanctity and memory, with later imagination often linking both figures to red hair.

Red-haired saints fold into golden-haired maidens, and sacred women become the center of quests. Suddenly you find yourself thinking of Princess Buttercup in *The Princess Bride* and even Fiona, the tower-bound princess in *Shrek*. The connection feels ridiculous, until it doesn't. These films parody the old machinery of romance and rescue, but they also depend on it: the beloved hidden away, the quest set in motion, the sacred object or missing woman around whom the whole adventure turns. They belong to the same strange family of stories as Perceval, Galahad, Gawain, Monty Python, and Indiana Jones. But what keeps returning is not only the Grail. It is the longing arranged around it—the missing beloved, the guarded source, the lost promise of life. Magdalene hovers at the edge of it all, not because she belongs to any single story, or because long flowing hair, whether red or gold, can prove what history has blurred, but because the ache surrounding her is older and larger than any form it takes.

And if *Raiders of the Lost Ark* sends the imagination racing toward deserts, tombs, and Egypt, the connection is not only cinematic. Egypt is where the image of life-giving mystery reaches back into older forms. There, Hathor appeared with the face of a cow, nursing kings and bearing the sun between her horns, imagery later absorbed into the worship of Isis as divine mother and sustainer. Milk in these traditions was not just food but cosmic substance, life flowing between heaven and earth.

But you are not in Egypt, and you are not inside a film. You are walking on a wet hillside in Somerset, wondering what happens if the old search is seen through different eyes. What is the Grail when the seeker is not a knight, an archaeologist, or a prince, but a woman looking for what has been scattered, softened, or buried? Who is Magdalene then? And what changes when the quest is no longer arranged around finding her, but begins from the place where she stands?

Once the recognition settles in your mind, it does not ask to be explained. It repeats: goddesses, milk, fertility, healing, abundance, the maternal not as biology alone, but as the power to nourish, shelter, and bring life forth. By now, Magdalene seems to move through the mists of Avalon. She enters the Grail's mystery less through the language of quest than as a trace of what the quest may have covered over. And in Glastonbury, that buried memory does not remain inside old stories. It rises into the present, where women come not as maidens to be won, vessels to be guarded, or beloveds waiting at the center of someone else's adventure, but as seekers themselves. They follow whatever thread leads them back to a sacred inheritance they can recognize as their own, undertaking a search no less ancient because history has so rarely cast women as the heroes of such journeys.

Along High Street, shop windows display goddesses, crystals, herbs, spells, and old fragments of folklore and magic once pushed to the margins as dangerous or forbidden. The same longing appears again in pilgrimage posters and festival announcements across the town. A familiar scene unfolds in flower crowns, drums, ribbons, and small processions winding their way up the Tor. On certain days, the path fills with women dressed in flowing skirts, some in red, others in white, making their way toward the summit.

Is it a spectacle? Perhaps sometimes. But within that performance lies a deeper instinct, a desire to embody what has too often been denied expression, the sense that something in the feminine spirit was pressed into diminished shapes and is now trying to remember its older power. Women are still looking for ways to claim what was scattered, softened, renamed, or made suspect. What if the point is not to judge the form that remembering takes? And besides, does it really matter how we claim or remember, so long as we feel free enough to do so?

This impulse calls to mind the dancer Isadora Duncan, who more than a century ago cast aside the rigid choreography of classical ballet to move barefoot and outdoors, believing the body should move as freely as the wind and sea. It is said that she once urged, "You were once wild here," a recognition that opens into a warning: "Don't let them tame you."[1]

By now the pasture has begun to change. The open field narrows into a path, and the ground starts to lift below your feet, with grass rising on either side as the Tor swells into a slope. Wind moves across the hillside, brushing your face and hands as you walk, and you realize you do not need robes or ritual to feel what the others are searching for, any more than a knight needs shining armor and a battle to make his journey real.

Some arrive through ceremony, through color and procession. Others come simply, in the act of walking a hill, sitting quietly with a book, or pausing to look closely at a flower. Like the flowers and creatures woven into a medieval tapestry, the buttercup lingers within the design, easy to overlook and yet essential to the whole. However simple it may appear to one person, to another it becomes a clue, a small detail that carries the story forward.

The same flower you might lift to a child's chin to watch the light turn to gold still flickers in your thoughts, shining back.

As the climb becomes more deliberate, steps appear where countless feet have worn the hillside smooth, and the grass falls away from the path in uneven banks. The air opens around you now, moving more freely across the slope.

When you turn to look back, the town of Glastonbury spreads out below you in soft gray stone and slate roofs, the fields beyond divided into neat green patches by hedgerows and drainage canals. The Somerset Levels stretch outward in every direction, so flat they almost resemble water. Before geological shifts and centuries of drainage reshaped them, these lowlands were largely marsh and floodwater, leaving the Tor set apart above them. Even now, as you climb its slopes, it's easy to imagine the hill surrounded by shallow lakes and drifting fog, less a fantasy than a memory shaped by water and distance. Avalon begins to make sense that way, in the charged overlap between landscape and legend.

Still, hills like this follow a stranger logic. The higher you climb, the less the movement feels simply upward. In older Celtic imagination, certain hills were not solid masses but hollow places, openings into the Otherworld. Before faeries became the winged figures of children's books, they belonged to an untamed, more unsettling realm: beings who lived within the earth. Such crossings are rarely left unguarded, and at their edge, a feminine figure often appears—not always as ruler, not always as beloved, but as mediator, witness, lure, or guide. The old tales do not always preserve her clearly. Sometimes she comes as sovereign, sometimes as guardian, sometimes as the woman beside the well, the mound, or the hidden chamber. Sometimes she receives the visitor; sometimes she tests him. But the design remains: before the treasure, before the revelation, before the return, a woman is already there.

Long ago, Celtic traditions merged with older indigenous beliefs into a pantheon of deities known as the Tuatha Dé Danann, "the Tribes of the Goddess Danu." Danu, whose name may be linked to the Danube River, was a mother goddess associated with fertility, sovereignty, and life-giving water. Later Irish tradition remembered the Tuatha Dé Danann as an otherworldly people who withdrew beneath the hills when new peoples arrived, their presence unseen yet still held within the land. Across Ireland and Britain, ancient mounds and hollow hills became sites of burial, ritual, and ceremony, as at Newgrange. And here, at Glastonbury, local legend holds that under the Tor lay a cave leading into the otherworld realm of Annwn, ruled by Gwyn ap Nudd, lord of the underworld.

By the time the Grail attached itself to the Tor, the hill was already bound to stories of enchanted realms, powerful objects, and the guardians who protected them. It did not arrive in an empty landscape, anymore than Magdalene did. Both entered a hill already crowded with memories of entrances, treasures, and journeys into the Otherworld.

Held against these stories, the ascent begins to feel like more than just a walk up an ordinary hillside. With each step, you rise into open air while moving deeper into the hill's buried past.

*

The slope steepens, and the terraces reveal themselves. Long green ridges wrap around the Tor, carving the hillside into horizontal layers. From a distance, they appear as natural folds in the land, but once you are on the hill, their deliberate rows become clear to your eye. The modern path does not follow them, but cuts across the slope at an angle, so that the climb moves through the layers rather than along them.

Some say these terraces preserve the trace of an ancient labyrinth, a pilgrim's path winding toward the summit. Others interpret the marks as evidence of medieval stepped farming, sheep paths, or even military earthworks designed for defense. Their purpose remains unsettled. But by the time you notice them, the hill has already begun to work on you, not simply as ground underfoot, but as form, measure, and mystery. The terraces encircle the Tor in concentric green rings, enough that many visitors begin to count them, and often arrive at seven. Seven lands almost unconsciously, stirring associations that have long moved with Magdalene.

Though you are not following those seven bands of grass, you imagine what it might have felt like to ascend by labyrinth path from base to summit. You recall the faerie underworld believed to lie beneath the soil underfoot, and the Grail returns to mind. What began as a glimmer in the buttercup becomes harder to dismiss here, where the hill seems shaped by hidden approach and delayed revelation. In the growing world of Arthurian romance, the Grail entered literature as an enigmatic vessel moving through a landscape marked by injury, mystery, and suspended restoration. Long before it settled into the Holy Grail of Christian legend, its meanings remained unstable and difficult to claim.

Between 1180 and 1190, Chrétien de Troyes composed *Perceval, ou le Conte du Graal*, an Old French romance. In the story, a young knight arrives at a mysterious castle where an injured king, known as the Fisher King because Perceval first encounters him beside a hidden river, waits while a gleaming vessel passes silently through the torchlit hall. Chrétien called it simply *un graal*, a term that originally referred not to a sacred relic, but to a serving dish used to carry food to the table. Yet within the story, the object already possessed unusual significance: it sustained the Fisher King and became bound to the possibility of healing a fractured land.[2]

Of course, the restorative power of such a vessel reaches farther back than Chrétien's *graal*. Before it became a sacred cup of Christian legend, there was the Cauldron of Dagda carried to these islands by the Tuatha Dé Danann, a cauldron of abundance from which no one left unsatisfied. Further still lies the shape behind the symbol: the rounded form that holds, nourishes, contains, and restores. The womb, the woman, the passage of birth.

Walking the path beside the terraces, you can imagine how stories like this took root in landscapes such as these. Looking out across the Levels, you find yourself in the terrain of medieval romance for a moment: wandering knights, hidden castles, luminous vessels, and kingdoms afflicted by wounds no ordinary sword could heal. Or older still, a world inhabited by faeries, goddesses, and a sacred presence so alive it could almost be seen.

*

The climb narrows into a long, exposed approach. The ground falls away on either side of the path, while the wind moves across the ridge with nothing left to slow it. Ahead, the tower that had remained distant throughout the climb suddenly feels much closer, no longer fixed to a point on the horizon but the remnant of something larger.

Long before the solitary tower stood here, a full church crowned the summit of the Tor. Dedicated to Saint Michael the Archangel by at least the eleventh or twelfth century, it belonged to the powerful monastic community at Glastonbury Abbey below. Medieval pilgrims climbed this same hill to reach it, following paths not entirely unlike those that lead upward today. But by then, the stories embedded in this landscape were already beginning to change, as institutional authority and sacred geography began to be bound together.

Before de Troyes described the mysterious *graal*, Geoffrey of Monmouth composed the *Historia Regum Britanniae* by 1136, blending history, legend, and political imagination to shape Britain's cultural memory. It was in this text that Avalon first emerged as the enchanted island to which the wounded King Arthur was carried after battle. Geoffrey neither identified Avalon with Glastonbury nor mentioned a grail. Yet when

Perceval, ou le Conte du Graal appeared years later, Arthurian tradition began drawing these narratives together.

Soon after a fire devastated Glastonbury Abbey and the surrounding complex, the monks announced a startling discovery. In 1191, during repairs and excavations, they claimed to uncover the graves of King Arthur and Queen Guinevere deep within the cemetery, between two ancient stone pyramids whose meaning had long been forgotten. The burial reportedly contained the remains of a man and woman alongside a lead cross inscribed: *Hic iacet sepultus inclitus rex Arturius in insula Avalonia cum Wenneveria uxore sua secunda*—"Here lies buried the renowned King Arthur in the Isle of Avalon, with Guinevere, his second wife."[3] This was the moment Arthur, Guinevere, and Avalon became explicitly tied to Glastonbury.

Toward the end of the twelfth century, another writer began anchoring the Grail more firmly within Christian history: Robert de Boron. A few years after the Glastonbury discovery, he transformed the mysterious vessel of earlier Arthurian romance into a chalice that caught Christ's blood at the foot of the cross. In his telling, Joseph of Arimathea—the follower of Jesus who placed his body in the tomb—carried the vessel westward across the sea, and Avalon became the place where the Grail was hidden. From that point on, Avalon, the Grail, and Glastonbury became deeply linked in the medieval imagination.

Local traditions elaborated the story further. Some claimed Joseph of Arimathea buried the Grail beneath the Glastonbury Tor. Others described how upon arriving at nearby Wearyall Hill, Joseph planted his staff in the earth, where it miraculously took root as the famous Glastonbury Thorn. Through such stories, Avalon, the Grail, and the sacred authority of the Church became woven into a single mythic geography. More and more pilgrims arrived to climb the Tor and visit the abbey, journeying through a world where legend and devotion seemed to affirm one another.

For several centuries, the story held, until the English Reformation transformed the country. In 1539, during the Dissolution of the Monasteries under Henry VIII, the last abbot of Glastonbury Abbey, Richard Whiting, was arrested, accused of treason, and executed. Accounts describe how he was dragged to the summit of Glastonbury Tor and brutally killed—hanged, drawn, and quartered in full view of the surrounding countryside. The abbey below was stripped of its wealth and abandoned, while the church atop the hill was dismantled soon after, leaving only the tower that still stands today.

This is the ruin your gaze stays upon as the path rises again in a straight run of steps, the grass banked high on either side. After all that has passed through it—church, pilgrimage, legend, and violence—the tower no longer feels like a marker on the horizon, but the last surviving witness.

*

The final steps give way to level ground, and the Tor opens suddenly into a wide grassy plateau. As you scan the countryside, your eyes catch on the distant spires of Wells Cathedral, one of the great monuments of medieval England, rising beyond the trees. Seen from here, Wells and the Tor seem to answer each other across the landscape: one still whole and astonishing in its Gothic grandeur; the other open to wind, grass, and sky.

You walk around the tower, its gray stone walls roofless against the sky. Without the church that once surrounded it, the structure feels both monumental and small, its tall, hollow windows framing nothing but moving clouds. Air passes through the empty arches, unhindered by roof or altar, while grass grows where the nave once was. The authority that radiated from this place has long since dissolved into silence. What remains feels less like triumph than the remnant of a story that once tried to claim the hill and failed to hold it forever.

From the summit, the view stretches in every direction, and it becomes clear why places like this draw monuments upward. High ground lifts meaning into view. Yet towers belong not only to churches but to stories about women: maidens sealed away, daughters confined by fathers, queens held within stone walls in the name of purity, protection, or power. The image recurs across centuries in Rapunzel lowering her hair from her tower, Saint Barbara imprisoned by the father who feared her independence, and even Anne Boleyn passing through the gates of the Tower of London before her execution.

Such stories seem to gather inside the hollow shell of Saint Michael's. Saints, queens, and maidens begin to converge, all women made central to moments of crossing, then enclosed, renamed, feared, or torn away by the structures built around them. Standing here, you marvel at the way symbols refuse to remain isolated, until the line between conflation and continuation becomes almost impossible to see.

Over time, the Grail story became entangled with speculation about Mary Magdalene, as though the vessel pointed toward her body and her possible role as bearer of a hidden bloodline. The cup, the jar, the anointing woman with long flowing hair, and the beloved witness beside Jesus begin to merge into one symbolic field, where tower and container, ascent and descent, outer quest and inward movement all reflect the same mystery. Meggan Watterson, whose *Mary Magdalene Revealed* carries its own pilgrimage through Glastonbury, puts it this way: "Ascension according to the Gospel of Mary is more accurately a descent into the heart; so farther up is actually further in."[4] But if the movement turns inward, then Mary cannot simply be reduced to an object found at the end of a quest.

That reduction may be tempting, but it disguises the subtlety her symbolism is meant to preserve. The Grail is not simply a woman. A chalice is, first and foremost, a vessel, and a vessel does not merely hold fluid—wine, water, oil, or blood. Its meaning moves toward something more elemental: the circle as point of origin, capable of containing all things or any one thing.

Yet another ancient symbol transposed. The spring waters that always flowed from the base of this hill, nourishing people who lived or moved through here since time immemorial, came to be interpreted as manifestations of Jesus's blood—a sign the Holy Grail was, in fact, buried here. One spring runs deep red with iron, staining the stone channels a rust-hued crimson. White for purity, red for blood. While the White Spring moves through a Victorian well house, the Red Spring is curated in the gardens of the Chalice Well.

Red and white. The pairing is difficult to ignore. In medieval England, the red cross on a white field associated with Saint George gradually became a national emblem. Later, under the Tudor dynasty, the colors fused into an even more explicit emblem: the red rose of Lancaster joined to the white rose of York after the wars that reshaped England's throne.

As the pieces begin to gather together, another realization emerges. It was a Tudor king who ordered the destruction of the monastery below, the execution of its last abbot, and the dismantling of the church that once crowned this hill. The same religious reforms swept across England, destroying Marian shrines, sacred objects, monasteries, and countless works of art. That upheaval belonged to the wider Tudor fracture that had made Anne Boleyn queen and then sent her to the scaffold. Yet the violence embedded in these places often gives way to more beautiful narratives, the kind that draw pilgrims, and revenue, more easily than bloodshed.

As the institutional authority that once governed this place collapsed, the hill did not become empty. Instead, it grew increasingly open to projection. Stories accumulated where certainty had fractured, each generation adding new meanings to the landscape without fully erasing what came before. The fields of Somerset are now read through overlapping layers: medieval romance, Celtic mythology, Christian relic lore, Marian devotion, and modern esoteric imagination. Avalon, the Grail, Joseph of Arimathea, Magdalene, ancient goddesses, sacred geometry—each tradition offers another explanation for a terrain dense with meaning.

As the wind moves through the grass and whips cold around the tower, you find yourself stretching to hold all these paradoxes together, allowing the contradictions to stand and releasing the need to judge them. Here, you become less interested in resolving the questions than in experiencing the layers of history held in this place, as though a veil within you lifts gently.

And somewhere below, in the pasture, the small yellow buttercup still lifts its bright cup toward the sky—not buried, not hidden, simply catching the light.

*

The way down begins more awkwardly than the climb. The descent is slippery, the grass damp underfoot, mud gathering along the edges of the path. What moments ago seemed layered with myth now feels stubbornly physical through slick grass, wet earth, and the weight of each step landing hard through knees and ankles. You turn your feet sideways for traction, edging downward one careful step at a time, and the hill settles back into the ordinary. There is nothing buried here—no golden cup, no hidden chamber beneath the hill, no secret portal concealed under the grass. Only earth and water. Mud and stone. The stories and symbols remain, circling into one another, not as artifacts waiting to be unearthed so much as paths waiting to be followed.

A chalice holds wine. A jar carries oil. An ancient cauldron bears the sustaining broth of life. A mother's womb brings forth a child she cradles in her arms, her body straining to nourish through milk and tender care. Held in its full complexity, the Grail ceases to be merely an object lost inside the landscape and becomes instead a recurring symbol of nourishment, restoration, and longing.

Now your feet move over pavement again, as you return to the street below and walk toward the White Spring. A phrase catches you, painted in white block letters on a weathered gray stone wall: "LOVE ONE ANOTHER." Yes, from a Gospel, but also simply human, universal. Perhaps this has been the pattern behind the Grail all along, asking us not to possess, prove, or discover anything, but to believe what was wounded might still be met with love.

And maybe this is what Mary Magdalene has always carried: the hope that love can still make us whole.

Chapter 8

THE BELOVED DISCIPLE

The distant peaks of dusky blue mountains fade into soft green foothills seen through the high windows that illuminate the table from behind. Three open casements punctuate the rear plane of the room, framed by side walls hung with tapestries whose dark patterns recede beyond discernment. Their rectangles echo the squares of the coffered ceiling above and the long white surface of the table below. Geometry governs the room in *The Last Supper*, the masterwork of Leonardo da Vinci. Every line draws inward, directing the eye toward a single vanishing point that centers one figure: Jesus.

Dressed in a red tunic and blue mantle, he sits before the central window, slightly offset, yet clearly the compositional heart of the scene. His arms extend gently across the table, forming a concealed triangle that steadies the commotion around him. The disciples cluster in four animated groups of three, arranged symmetrically with six on each side of Jesus, their bodies leaning toward one another in charged reaction, every face distinct in expression. Earthy reds and warm ochres move through the garments, punctuated by indigo and mossy greens that catch the light. Gold and mustard tones lend the scene its underlying warmth, and all is muted by more than five centuries of fading tempera.

Around the table, expressions shift from consternation to disbelief to accusation. Heads turn sharply, hands rise in questioning gestures, bodies press forward as if the air in the room has shifted. Drapery falls in restless folds as the movement spreads from figure to figure. Beside Jesus, one among them mirrors his calm. Clothed in pale blue and soft rose, the figure appears serene, set apart from the turbulent atmosphere of the room. Eyes lowered, arms relaxed, this figure's posture mimics the stillness grounded by Jesus.

The painting does not present a blended or generalized version of Jesus's final meal with his disciples derived equally from all four Gospels. Instead, Leonardo staged a pivotal moment from the Gospel of John, suspended between treachery and devotion. The mysterious figure seated at the right hand of Jesus is not described in the Synoptics, yet in John, this unnamed disciple becomes the model of belief. This is the Beloved Disciple, known only through a cryptic phrase: "the disciple whom Jesus loved."

Leonardo painted the Beloved Disciple's face with sfumato, a technique that blends tones and softens edges to create features that seem to emanate from light rather than line. Hair falls in gentle waves around a face fairer than any other present—this individual is bright, contemplative, and strangely calm amid the surrounding tumult. To modern eyes, the figure reads as ambiguous to the point of androgyny, appearing youthful and delicate, poised somewhere between masculine and feminine form.

Encoded—the word has always seemed to swirl around Leonardo's masterpieces, and no two paintings have invited that language more persistently than *The Last Supper* and the *Mona Lisa*. Secrets, hidden meanings, and layered symbols cling to his art. Moving within papal and royal circles, where privileged knowledge was often carefully guarded, Leonardo developed a taste for indirection that found expression in his work. His compositions are deliberate, structured through symmetry and symbolism that gesture beyond straightforward Christian illustration. He created images meant to intrigue as much as instruct, allowing mystery to keep inviting interpretation.

Begun roughly five years after *The Last Supper*, the *Mona Lisa* carries the same sense of ambiguity. Now hanging in the Louvre Museum, the portrait resists definition in more ways than one. Her features are softened through sfumato, the contours of her mouth and eyes dissolving into shadow. Her expression shifts as the viewer looks, becoming at once serene, knowing, and elusive. Like the Beloved Disciple, her presence holds steady while generations of viewers murmur around her, searching her face for meaning.

All that Leonardo rendered in paint through technical mastery was grounded in a deeper philosophical vision. The Florentine world in which he trained was steeped in Renaissance Neoplatonism, which understood beauty as the outward expression of inner harmony. Leonardo described this pursuit in his notebooks as the *moti dell'animo*, the "motions of the mind," which he sought to reveal through subtle shifts in expression and form. This is why his figures seem alive with thought and feeling, however still. Masculine and feminine, intellect and emotion, activity and contemplation are cultivated into a delicate equilibrium. It is this sensibility that gives the figures of the Beloved Disciple and the Mona Lisa their lasting aura of mystery, the former seeming to anticipate the latter.

The Last Supper was commissioned by Ludovico Sforza and painted within the Dominican convent of Santa Maria delle Grazie in Milan. Monumental and communal, it is fixed and architectural, created for many eyes at once. The *Mona Lisa*, by contrast, turns inward, becoming small, portable, and sustained at the scale of a single viewer. It is generally believed to have been commissioned by the Florentine merchant Francesco del Giocondo as a portrait of his wife, Lisa Gherardini. But Leonardo seems never to have relinquished it. He continued to rework the painting, carrying it with him until his death.

When Leonardo departed for France at the invitation of his great admirer Francis I, King of France, the Mona Lisa went with him. Francis was married to Claude of France, daughter of Anne of Brittany. During Leonardo's final years at Clos Lucé, he lived only a short distance from Claude's court, where Anne Boleyn resided for a time. Their paths may never have physically crossed, but their proximity within the same world deepens the intrigue that surrounds both Leonardo and Boleyn.

Leonardo's intimate attachment to the *Mona Lisa* contrasts sharply with the fate of *The Last Supper*, which languished for centuries in the dining hall of Santa Maria delle Grazie. The mural deteriorated rapidly, damaged both by Leonardo's experimental technique and the passage of time. It fell into severe disrepair, narrowly survived wartime bombing, and underwent repeated restorations, including the major modern phase completed in 1999. At one point, a practical doorway was cut directly through the lower center of the composition—necessity intruding into one of the most valuable works of art in the world.

Damage notwithstanding, *The Last Supper* was designed for its place, painted into the ordinary rhythm of monastic life, where it presided over the monks' dining room at Santa Maria delle Grazie. These were men immersed in scripture daily, trained to recognize the theological gravity of the moment Leonardo depicted. While they ate their own suppers, passages from the Gospels were read aloud in Latin, the cadence of sacred text accompanied by the clinking of dishes and cutlery. Meals became acts of contemplation beneath the immense image stretching across the north wall, confronting the monks with the tension of the scene. Gazing upon it, perhaps they asked themselves: Am I Judas? Am I Peter? Am I the Beloved Disciple?

Jesus's farewell discourse in the thirteenth chapter of John, shared over a meal just before Passover, begins with one of the most pivotal theological gestures in any Gospel: the washing of the feet. Kneeling to bathe the disciples' feet one by one, the act is widely understood as an embodiment of the humility at the center of his message. "Very truly I tell you," he says, "no servant is greater than his master, nor is a messenger greater than the one who sent him." And so, the meal begins in tenderness, a mood soon to be broken by the jarring statement Jesus makes, the moment that Leonardo depicted.

Discussing how the foot washing set an example for the disciples, Jesus shares a shocking declaration: "One of you is going to betray me." His words send a wave of disbelief through the room as the disciples glance uneasily among themselves, "at a loss to know which of them he meant." Leonardo gave each figure a varied expression: alarm, confusion, suspicion, or grief. Amid this chaos, the Beloved Disciple stands out visually, their countenance reflecting the Gospel's description: "One of them, the disciple whom Jesus loved, was *reclining* next to him."[1]

In other translations, the closeness between Jesus and the Beloved Disciple is expressed even more vividly, described as leaning "on Jesus' bosom" or "close to his breast." This privileged position becomes central to the scene. The Gospel records that Peter "motioned" toward the Disciple, saying "Ask him," meaning Jesus, "which one he means." Leonardo portrays this gesture by painting Peter with a sharply angled posture, his fingers pointed directly toward the Beloved Disciple's throat. Meanwhile, the Disciple's own hands remain softly folded. Between them, Judas reaches toward the same dish as Jesus, enacting the prophecy that the betrayer "is the one to whom I will give this piece of bread when I have dipped it in the dish."[2]

Such carefully orchestrated details, combined with the mystique surrounding Leonardo's own life, have helped propel the painting to the center of modern theories about hidden meanings and esoteric design. *The Da Vinci Code* may have popularized the idea that Leonardo's Beloved Disciple veiled Mary Magdalene in plain sight, but the theory circulated earlier in *The Templar Revelation* by Lynn Picknett and Clive Prince. Likewise, *Holy Blood, Holy Grail* and Margaret Starbird's work argued a similar concept of encoded traditions and sacred-marriage possibilities connected to Magdalene, themes woven together and amplified through Dan Brown's bestselling novel and film adaptation.[3]

Even as fascination with the possibility of Mary Magdalene as Leonardo's painted Beloved Disciple reached a fever pitch, the speculation remained confined within familiar boundaries: Magdalene as wife, lover, or mother of Jesus' children. Rarely did the theory advance toward the far more radical implication of what it would actually mean if Magdalene were the Beloved Disciple. This Disciple was not merely one among the twelve, or even simply the most important follower within the scriptural narrative. The text of John contains a remarkable claim: the Beloved Disciple is presented as the eyewitness whose testimony grounds the authority of the Gospel.

If Mary Magdalene was the Beloved Disciple, then she belonged to the inner circle of its formation—not as the Gospel's author in the sense of its final composition, but as the visionary witness whose memory and testimony the Gospel preserves, however much that testimony was shaped, edited, and reframed across generations of transmission.

This possibility does not require Leonardo to have hidden secret confessions within his paintings. Leonardo neither depicted Magdalene in any formally attributed survivng work, nor do his preserved notebooks contain overt theological revelations. Instead, his writing reflects an ardent fascination with nature: movement, water, anatomy, proportion, light, and the underlying order of the cosmos. "Nature," he mused, "never breaks her own laws."[4] That sensibility permeates his repeated images of the Virgin, contemplative and serene within natural landscapes, absorbed in moments of maternal tenderness toward her son.

The association between the feminine principle, nature, and divine wisdom would not have been foreign to Leonardo, particularly within the atmosphere of Renaissance Neoplatonism. Whatever Leonardo intended historically, the Beloved Disciple he painted evokes a feminine quality in spirit, a figure shaped less through masculine authority than through harmony, beauty, softness, and inward poise. It cannot be proven that Leonardo intended the Beloved Disciple in *The Last Supper* to be Mary Magdalene. Although its placement within a Dominican monastery, the same order of monks who preside over Sainte Baume may be more than coincidence. Yet the fresco nevertheless carries something of the feminine forward into one of Christianity's most iconic sacred images.

The fascination and controversy the fresco continues to inspire also point to an unresolved question surrounding the identity of the Beloved Disciple and the enduring mystery at the heart of John. Of all the canonical scripture, John has long occupied a distinctive place within Christian devotion because readers have sensed in it a more symbolic, philosophical, even mystical register. The *Book of Hours of Anne of Brittany*, for example, reserves one of its most lavish full-page miniatures for Mary Magdalene weeping outside the tomb, an image that has been lauded as the most poetic in the entire book.[5]

The question that follows, then, is not one of conspiracy but of perception. Leonardo communicated through symbolism, gesture, and layered meaning. The Gospel of John unfolds through a similarly indirect mode of realization, one that repeatedly asks its audience to see beyond the surface of things. Both invite the viewer and reader alike to attend more closely to what's been present all along, waiting to be recognized. Within its symbolic world, the possibility stirs. The anonymous Beloved Disciple may not be the figure tradition later claimed, but someone else unexpected, as of yet, unnamed.

For all the ways Mary Magdalene has been discussed, reimagined, defended, diminished, romanticized, and revealed, the least examined potential is the most controversial. Not that she was wife, lover, or even apostle, but that she was the Beloved Disciple.

Such a proposition may shake the foundations of apostolic authority more deeply than any sacred-marriage theory ever could. If Magdalene were the Beloved Disciple, then one of the four canonical Gospels may originally have stood not under the authority of a man named John, but of a woman named Mary. Christian tradition has rejected or ignored this possibility. Yet modern scholarship has increasingly destabilized the assumption that the Gospel straightforwardly belongs to "John" at all.

To perceive this possibility requires the patience to allow for revelation that rarely arrives directly. It emerges through signs, repetition, and even concealment. It requires a willingness to attend carefully to what the text reveals and what it withholds.

THE MAVERICK GOSPEL

The Gospel of John has always occupied a world of its own. Known as the "Fourth," it moves with a distinctly different cadence and character than the other canonical accounts of Jesus. Nothing else in the New Testament quite resembles it. Its origins, theological sophistication, and authorship have been subjects of fascination, controversy, and debate. Robert Kysar famously described it as a "maverick" gospel, a fitting term for one of the most inventive and controversial texts in Christianity.[6]

In the Fourth Gospel, symbol and story move together continuously. History is not abandoned but transformed into sacred meaning. Many have regarded this Gospel as less historically grounded than the Synoptics, while others have argued that this opposition misunderstands this text's methods. As Sandra M. Schneiders argues in *Written That You May Believe*, "because history itself is John's symbolic material, the more historical something is, the more symbolic potential it possesses."[7] This Gospel moves fluidly, resisting rigid literalism and flowing with the layered depth of ancient myth.

Repeated images and dialogues arrive in sequences that create deliberate returns, pulling the reader into an ongoing process of deepening recognition. Some scholars have even attempted to map the Gospel's structure to better understand these underlying patterns. In *The Genius of John*, Peter F. Ellis argued that the Gospel is constructed through intricate parallelisms and chiastic patterns, with sentences, scenes, and themes deliberately mirroring one another across the text. Ellis described how these techniques were common in ancient literature—found in Hebrew scripture, Homeric poetry, and other Mediterranean narrative traditions shaped by symmetry and symbolic architecture. In *The Good Wine*, Bruno Barnhart developed this concept further, mapping the entire narrative of the Gospel into a circular structure he called a "chiastic mandala." Barnhart discovered that the text moves through concentric circles of mirrored scenes, symbols, and revelations. Schneiders describes this movement as such: "The cyclical repetition in the Fourth Gospel is like a spiral staircase that takes the reader up higher, down deeper, passing again and again the same familiar points, giving an ever clearer and richer view of the One who stands in the center."[8]

The Fourth Gospel leads the reader toward meanings revealed gradually over time, a cadence initiated in the opening lines. Where the Gospel of Luke begins by invoking sources, the Gospel of Matthew by tracing a genealogy, and the Gospel of Mark by citing prophecy, the Fourth Gospel opens instead with poetry: "In the beginning was the Word, and the Word was with God . . . In him was life, and that life was the light of all mankind. The light shines in the darkness, and the darkness has not overcome it."[9]

The beauty of the Prologue can obscure the theological genius it introduces. Here, the Logos, translated as "the Word," presents Jesus not simply as a teacher or messiah, but as a divine presence existing before creation itself. As James D. G. Dunn argues in *Christology in the Making*, the Prologue marks a decisive development in the formation of Christian theology. Dunn demonstrates how the Logos theology of the Prologue builds upon the philosophical frameworks crafted by Philo of Alexandria, which blended Greek thought with the Wisdom traditions of the Hebrew scriptures. Dunn is emphatic: "There is no evidence in the earliest traditions of Jesus's ministry that he understood himself as Wisdom, or as the incarnation of (pre-existent) wisdom."[10]

This matters because divine Wisdom in Jewish tradition was personified in feminine form: she called, created, taught, and dwelled near God. In the Prologue, those older resonances are gathered into the Logos and identified with Christ. The result is brilliant and transformative, but also consequential. A feminine current of Wisdom within Jewish sacred imagination became absorbed into the masculine language through which Christianity would come to define the divinity of Christ.

Even as the Prologue transposes Wisdom into Logos, the narrative repeatedly places women at the center of revelation. While female figures appear across all the Gospels, the Fourth presents them with unusual depth and gravity. Women are depicted as those who perceive, remain, and understand. Some of the Gospel's most profound theological recognitions emerge through their voices. As Schneiders observes, the women of this Gospel appear as fully individuated characters who exist in intimate relationship to Jesus and his mission. No woman in the Gospel of John betrays Jesus, abandons him, or turns against his revelation. Instead, women consistently appear at moments of recognition, testimony, anointing, fidelity, and resurrection.

For these reasons and many more, this Gospel has fascinated Christians, theologians, mystics, and scholars alike. Its extraordinary theology, symbolic architecture, and distinctive portrayal of Jesus naturally provoke a deeper question that has persisted for centuries: Who could have stood behind such a text? Who created the Fourth Gospel?

MEMORY, AUTHOR, EVANGELIST

No other canonical Gospel binds its narrative so directly to the testimony of an eyewitness. At the height of the crucifixion scene, amid blood, grief, and death, the narrative suddenly pauses almost mid-breath to insist upon the truth of what is being witnessed: "The man who saw it has given testimony, and his testimony is true. He knows that he tells the truth, and he testifies so that you also may believe." By the Gospel's final chapter, the assertion resolves with even greater force: "This is the disciple who testifies to these things and who wrote them down."[11]

The Gospel grounds its authority directly in the testimony of the Beloved Disciple. Yet the figure of the Beloved Disciple is strangely elusive. The Gospel never names them directly. No hint of identity is provided, no genealogy, no hometown, no title beyond the mysterious designation "the disciple whom Jesus loved." The text insists upon the authority of this witness while simultaneously withholding the ordinary markers that would make any classification certain.

For centuries, Christian tradition understood these passages in largely straightforwardly, as evidence that a single man, identified as "John," had written the Fourth Gospel in one inspired act of composition. Modern critical scholarship has gradually dismantled that assumption.

Beginning in the nineteenth century and accelerating through the twentieth, historians increasingly dated the Gospel to the end of the first century or beginning of the second, making it the latest of the canonical four. Its sophisticated structure, polished Greek, highly developed theology, and the tensions it reflects between Jesus-followers and Jewish authorities all point to a long process of literary and intellectual development. The conceptual leap of Logos in the Prologue only intensifies that conclusion.

In the 1970s, Raymond E. Brown proposed one of the most influential models for understanding the composition of the Fourth Gospel. Brown identified three stages: an originating witness remembered as the Beloved Disciple, an evangelist who shaped those traditions into narrative form, and a later redactor who refined the text as the community evolved and the Gospel moved toward broader circulation. Brown's reconstruction became the foundation of the broader scholarly consensus that the Gospel developed over time and that the "Johannine" community preserving the text played an active role in its formation.[12]

As a result, the "disciple whom Jesus loved" came to be understood less as the direct author of the Gospel in its final form than as the originating eyewitness memory behind the tradition the text preserved. In many ways, this reflects the nature of all ancient sacred literature. The Gospels emerged first through oral tradition long before they existed as fixed written texts. Stories were remembered, repeated, performed, shaped, and transmitted communally across decades. It is widely believed that the canonical Gospels all circulated anonymously in their earliest forms.

Like all ancient works copied by hand across generations, the Gospels changed over time. Scribes clarified passages, editors rearranged material, communities harmonized disputes, and interpretation continued to evolve. A redactor could combine traditions, insert explanatory comments, shift emphasis, or restructure scenes so a text spoke coherently to a later audience and historical moment. Such changes were not necessarily evidence of corruption, but part of transmitting a living tradition across generations. What survives is therefore not a fixed artifact, unchanged from a single moment in history, but a layered text carrying the marks of centuries.

The story of the woman accused of adultery, among the most beloved in Christian memory, is absent from the earliest surviving manuscripts of John—it does not appear in Greek copies until around the fifth century. Elizabeth Schrader Polczer's work on Mary and Martha likewise demonstrates how even a name can shift during transmission, with consequences significant enough to alter a character's identity within the narrative. Beyond these specific edits, scholars like Rudolph Bultmann and J. Louis Martyn read the Gospel as preserving two distinct layers of historical memory, arguing that the entire text bears the marks of substantial editorial shaping across decades.

Despite the evidence of development and redaction, many continue to argue that the Fourth Gospel nevertheless bears the coherence of a single originating intelligence. The architecture of the text seems profoundly intentional: the patterning of the seven "I am" sayings, the sequence of seven signs or miracles, the careful symbolic structures, even forms such as the chiastic mandala identified by Bruno Barnhart. Debate continues over whether the Prologue was added later, or whether the final chapter represents a secondary conclusion appended to an earlier ending. Even among those who recognize multiple stages of composition, many still perceive a remarkable unity running through the Gospel from beginning to end.

It is possible that an original testimony connected to the Beloved Disciple once existed, whether passed down orally or written in an earlier form now lost. But the Gospel as it appears in modern Bibles stands at the end of a long process of composition, copying, editing, and transmission. The text readers possess today differs from earliest eyewitness memory behind the tradition as well as from the first version likely shaped by the Gospel's primary writer, or evangelist.

The questions that follow are unavoidable. What belongs to the memory of the eyewitness, and what belongs to later interpretation? What emerged from the life of the Johannine community as it reflected upon the meaning of Jesus across generations? What was shaped through redaction, harmonization, and theological development? And what arose from the singular literary vision that transformed these traditions into one of the most intricate and symbolically layered texts of the ancient world?

Through all these layers, where does the voice of the Beloved Disciple still shine through?

And if the relationship between eyewitness memory, authorship, editing, and tradition is far more complex than later Christianity assumed, then who exactly was "John"?

IN THE NAME OF "JOHN"

"John" has come to signify far more than a single Gospel. It now names an entire world of literature and interpretation: Johannine texts, Johannine theology, Johannine community, Johannine scholarship. The association between the Hebrew name Yohanan, meaning "God is gracious," and the Fourth Gospel runs deep. Yet the historical evidence linking that name securely to the text remains elusive.

The earliest clear attribution of the Fourth Gospel appears with Irenaeus of Lyon around 180, more than a century after the lifetime of Jesus. Writing in *Against Heresies* Irenaeus identified "John, the disciple of the Lord, who leaned upon His breast" as the author of the Gospel. In the same sweeping argument, he attached names to the canonical Gospels, all the while insisting the Church recognize exactly four Gospels. The reasoning, according to Irenaeus, was based on cosmic numerology: four corners of the earth, four winds, and so, four Gospels. Though the process of canonization would continue for centuries, this moment proved decisive for the future shape of Christianity and the consolidation of scripture into what would become the Holy Bible. In a single influential move, Irenaeus transformed four originally anonymous texts into the authoritative voices of "Matthew," "Mark," "Luke," and "John."[13]

From that point forward, the matter was increasingly treated as settled fact: a disciple named John was understood to be both the Beloved Disciple and the author of the Fourth Gospel. Eusebius of Caesarea reinforced this identification in his *Ecclesiastical History* in the early fourth century, helping cement it within the developing narrative of the Church.[14] Tradition maintained that Irenaeus inherited this understanding from earlier leaders and communities connected to the city of Ephesus. Yet the historical trail remains fragmentary and uncertain before Irenaeus.

Papias of Hierapolis, writing in the early second century, complicates the tradition rather than securing it. In a fragment preserved by Eusebius of Caesarea, Papias appears to have distinguished between "John the Apostle" and another figure called "John the Elder," without clearly attributing the Fourth Gospel to either. Though often invoked as evidence for Johannine authorship, Papias's testimony is ambiguous. Polycarp of Smyrna presents a similar problem. Irenaeus claimed that Polycarp knew "John" personally, making Polycarp an important link in arguments for Johannine authorship. Yet Polycarp's surviving *Letter to the Philippians* never identified John as the author of the Fourth Gospel. The association therefore depends on Irenaeus's retrospective account of Polycarp's writings, not what has survived of them.[15]

Justin Martyr, writing in the mid-second century, may have known the Fourth Gospel, but he was silent on its authorship. His work contains echoes of Logos and rebirth language, which scholars have taken as possible evidence that he knew the text or the Johannine tradition. He named "John, one of the apostles of Christ," as the seer behind Revelation. He also repeatedly referred to "memoirs of the apostles," or "memoirs composed by the apostles and those who followed them," indicating that he knew Gospel-like written traditions and treated them as apostolic memory. But still, Justin did not attribute the Fourth Gospel to a "John."[16]

Other second-century witnesses to Johannine authorship are similarly inconclusive. When Theophilus of Antioch quoted the Johannine Prologue, he referred to its speaker as "John," without clarifying whether he meant the apostle, the Beloved Disciple, or another individual. Polycrates of Ephesus, writing to Victor I, bishop of Rome, around 190, invoked "John who reclined on the Lord's bosom" as one of the great lights of Asia, buried at Ephesus. By then, the Beloved Disciple had acquired a local resting place, or at least a local claim to one. Whether that claim preserves historical memory or the concretizing of emerging tradition is difficult to know. And for all the weight Polycrates placed on John's memory, he stopped short of expressly naming him as the author of the Gospel.[17]

There is another source, one that may be roughly contemporaneous to Irenaeus, which names the connection directly—the Muratorian Fragment. It survives as a damaged seventh- or eighth-century Latin manuscript that was discovered in Milan's Ambrosian Library and published in 1740 by Father Ludovico Antonio Muratori. It clearly states: "The fourth of the Gospels, that of John, one of the disciples." However, the reference is grounded in a story, one that reads more like ecclesiastical legend than historical memory. According to the fragment, John wrote only after his fellow disciples and bishops urged him, fasted with him, and Andrew received a revelation that the Gospel should be written in John's name. The dating of the Muratorian Fragment's original composition remains disputed: some place it only a decade or so after Irenaeus; others locate it much later, closer to the era of Eusebius of Caesarea. Either way, it does not provide a secure attestation that clearly predates Irenaeus or stands fully independent of the tradition he helped consolidate.[18]

What earlier sources left suggestive but unresolved, Irenaeus fixed. He never explicitly called the author "John son of Zebedee," but his identification effectively fused the anonymous Beloved Disciple with the apostolic John known from the Synoptic tradition. This is especially striking because John son of Zebedee is never named directly in the Fourth Gospel, though "the sons of Zebedee" appear briefly near the end. In the Synoptics, John of Zebedee occupies a curious position. He is structurally present at the most significant moments of Jesus's ministry, and yet he rarely speaks, seldom acts, and his character is barely developed at all. When he does step forward, the portrait is unflattering. Mark gives him and his brother the Aramaic nickname Boanerges which suggests forcefulness and intensity. In Luke, the sons of Zebedee ask whether Jesus wishes to call down heavenly fire upon a Samaritan village. In Mark, the Zebedee sons angle for seats at Jesus's right and left hand in glory. Nothing in this portrait resembles the contemplative and quietly insightful Beloved Disciple of the Fourth Gospel.[19]

How, then, did the identification take hold despite the mismatch? In *The First Edition of the New Testament*, David Trobisch proposes that the Fourth Gospel was originally the work of an author "very interested in remaining anonymous," and that it circulated that way before Irenaeus.

The men who first gathered the four Gospels into a single published collection—the editors of what would become the New Testament—designed their edition to nudge the reader toward John son of Zebedee. The clues lie scattered across the collection. Acts of the Apostles reports that James, John's brother and the other son of Zebedee, was killed under Herod. The Synoptic Gospels identify Peter, James, and John as Jesus's three innermost disciples. And the final chapter itself implies that the Beloved Disciple outlived the others. A reader moving across those three texts is left with only one candidate from that inner circle: John son of Zebedee. Trobisch reads the closing lines of the Gospel, sometimes called the Epilogue, as the strongest evidence of this editorial hand, a publisher's sign-off appended to the body of the text.[20]

This closing line affirms the Beloved Disciple's testimony, its wording curiously similar to the language in 19:35. Then, the final narrative voice breaks even further from the rest. For a Gospel that opens with poetry, the final words are strangely stilted and editorial, reading almost like a postscript apologizing for the book's incompleteness: "Jesus did many other things as well. If every one of them were written down, I suppose that even the whole world would not have room for the books that would be written."[21] One word stands out—the sudden appearance of "I." This is the only time in the entire Gospel that the narrator uses first-person singular.

The shift is abrupt enough to suggest the presence of another hand. Trobisch argues that this startling "I" is not the voice of the Fourth Gospel's narrator at all, but the voice of an editor signing off the assembled book. Bultmann, too, treats the Epilogue as secondary, while Brown's three-stage model allows for a more complicated relationship between redaction and authentic Johannine tradition. Bauckham argues in the other direction, reading the Epilogue as belonging to the original testimony of the Beloved Disciple, with the closing attestation functioning as communal verification rather than late editorial overlay. Yet even across these competing models, the ending remains the place where the seams are most visible. Layered, though, is not the same as late: scholars who see editorial shaping at the end of John still locate the underlying material in the earliest Johannine tradition. The Fourth Gospel has already reached a formal conclusion at 20:30–31; then the Epilogue begins again, and by its final verses the voice has moved from communal attestation, "we know that his testimony is true," into the singular self-consciousness of "I suppose." Even the manuscript tradition preserves traces of discomfort around the final verse: 21:25 is absent from Codex Sinaiticus, although the verse is otherwise strongly attested and retained by modern editors.[22]

In sum, the weight of modern scholarship leaves the identity of the Beloved Disciple, and the authorial history of the Fourth Gospel, unresolved. A man named John may still stand somewhere behind the text, whether as source, elder, witness, editor, or evangelist. Yet it is far less likely that this figure was one and the same as John of Zebedee, the disciple named among the Twelve. Evidence has shifted; tradition has not. Centuries of attribution have proven remarkably difficult to dislodge, especially around the male names attached to the canonical Gospels.

THE JOHANNINE CONSTRUCTION

One of the greatest obstacles to disentangling the Fourth Gospel from "John" lies in the wider body of texts later gathered under that name. Irenaeus connected "John" not only with the Fourth Gospel, but also with the book of Revelation and the three Johannine letters. Through Irenaeus' influential synthesis, texts that may once have circulated independently came to be regarded as the work of one apostolic authority. "John" became not just a disciple but a visionary, a theologian, a community leader, and a scribe.

The final and twenty-seventh book of the New Testament, Revelation stands apart. Volatile, symbolic, and deeply contested, it differs starkly from the reflective tone of the Fourth Gospel. And unlike the Gospel, Revelation explicitly names its author in the first lines: "I, John, your brother and companion in the suffering and kingdom and patient endurance that are ours in Jesus, was on the island of Patmos because of the word of God and the testimony of Jesus."[23]

Ancient Patmos was a small rocky island in the Aegean Sea that may have been a site of worship for the goddess Artemis. Later, the Romans used it as a place of banishment. Although Revelation states that John was on Patmos, the text does not record that he was *exiled* there. The implication was that, amid persecution and isolation, this John had experienced the extraordinary visions recorded in the text: an ecstatic *revelation* shaped through the imagery and symbolic language of the Hebrew prophets. Any apostolic authority attributed to Revelation rested, yet again, with Irenaeus' claims. Even the idea that the John of Patmos lived long enough to have also been a follower of Jesus during his ministry is difficult to substantiate. Beyond sharing the name Yohanan—one of the most common male names in first-century Jewish society—there is no firm evidence connecting the possible authors.

At face value, Revelation bears little resemblance to the Fourth Gospel. It does not narrate Jesus's ministry through remembered scenes, sayings, or encounters. Rather, it presents the interior sights captured in prose by John of Patmos: beasts, angels, cosmic warfare, judgment, catastrophe, heavenly liturgy, and apocalypse unfolding through dramatic imagery. The atmosphere is violent and grand, standing in stark contrast to the relational and meditative world of the Fourth Gospel. Even in antiquity, readers recognized that the two texts did not sound like the work of the same person.

In the third century, Dionysius of Alexandria openly rejected common authorship between Revelation and the Fourth Gospel, arguing that the texts differed too clearly in language, style, tone, and theology to come from the same hand. He acknowledged that the author of Revelation called himself John but denied that this meant John the disciple or evangelist. Even Eusebius of Caesarea admitted uncertainty, listing Revelation among the most disputed Christian writings. This hesitation was especially pronounced in parts of the Orthodox East. Some eastern churches resisted using Revelation liturgically, while others questioned whether it belonged in the canon at all. The Syriac tradition, for example, excluded it from the Peshitta for centuries.[24]

Modern scholarship has only widened the distinction between Revelation and the Fourth Gospel, with scholars such as Brown, Adela Yarbro Collins, David Aune, and Bart D. Ehrman emphasizing how radically the texts differ in language, style, and symbolic world. One of the clearest discrepancies shows itself through language: Revelation's Greek is abrupt, grammatically irregular, and Semitic in texture, while the Fourth Gospel's Greek is controlled, sophisticated, and shaped by philosophical intent. R. H. Charles contended that the author thought in Hebrew even as he wrote in Greek—Revelation's broken grammar the very trace of a Semitic mind—and that he drew on and reworked older Jewish apocalyptic sources. Charles went further still, postulating that this prophet, a Jewish follower of Jesus, not an apostle, died before revising his work, leaving its disordered final chapters to a disciple who knew Greek better than Hebrew and little of his master's mind.[25]

Theologically, the two works move in vastly divergent directions with Revelation toward judgment and violence, and the Fourth Gospel toward realization and love. While both texts may reflect the upheavals of the Roman–Jewish War and the destruction of Jerusalem in 70 CE, they seem to integrate that historical trauma in radically different ways. The texts do share a focus on symbolism, including stars, light, heavenly imagery, and even the use of seven. However, this commonality points less to a single author than to the broader mythic environment in the ancient Mediterranean.

And if Revelation already strains the unity of "John," what happens when the Johannine letters begin to destabilize it further still?

Yet again, the authorship of the three epistles called "John" goes back to Irenaeus. In his writing, Irenaeus quoted from two letters and attributed them to "John, the disciple of the Lord." These became known as the First and Second Epistles of John. The Third Epistle of John was slower to gain recognition, but eventually it was absorbed into the same collection.[26]

The texts, however, do not naturally present the work of a unified author. First John reads less like a conventional letter than a theological sermon addressed to a community fractured from within. Second and Third John are brief personal pieces authored by someone identifying himself only as "the Elder." The name John never appears in any of the three texts. Why later tradition connected them to the Beloved Disciple remains uncertain.

Ultimately, the cumulative linguistic, literary, historical, and theological evidence has led the overwhelming majority of modern scholars to conclude that this collection of texts was not written by the same individual.[27] Still, this consensus rarely reaches ordinary Christians, where the idea of a single authorial "John" remains largely intact.

The broader implication is difficult to avoid. The more closely the Johannine writings are examined, the less stable the figure of "John" becomes, and the more consequential Irenaeus' synthesis appears. It is possible that Irenaeus was preserving earlier traditions now largely lost to time. It is equally plausible that gathering the Gospel, the epistles, and Revelation beneath a "John" and claiming him as the Beloved Disciple served an intentional ecclesiastical function.

Each of these texts contributed something highly valuable to the emerging Church. The Fourth Gospel supplied profound theology and intimate access to Jesus. The Johannine epistles reinforced communal boundaries and correct belief. Revelation extended the tradition into prophetic authority, cosmic judgment, and apocalyptic power. Bound together beneath the name "John," texts emerging from different authors, communities, theological concerns, and historical settings were unified beneath one authoritative identity, transforming what may once have been a diverse archive into a continuous line of apostolic legitimacy within a fragmented Christian world.

As the historical foundation of that construction fractures, the question of the Beloved Disciple opens again. If "John" was not a stable historical certainty but a later consolidation, then the anonymous figure at the center of the Fourth Gospel is no longer securely contained within the identity tradition imposed upon them.

The questions continue, and gain force: Why did Irenaeus boldly claim that this Gospel belonged to "John"? What possibilities became obscured once the text was fixed beneath a single apostolic male identity? And in all the claims surrounding "John," what does it really mean that this was the disciple that *Jesus loved*?

TO BE LOVED

The phrase is so familiar that its strangeness can easily disappear through repetition: *ho mathētēs hon ēgapā ho Iēsous*, "the disciple whom Jesus loved." These words appear five times in the Gospel, each at a decisive moment in the narrative: at the supper table, beneath the cross, at the empty tomb, and beside the Sea of Tiberias.

Of all the ways the Fourth Gospel might have defined this figure, it chooses the language of love. In a Gospel where Jesus places the new commandment to love one another at the center, the designation "beloved" carries heightened theological weight. The identity of the disciple is framed less through external authority than through intimacy, recognition, and relationship. Where others withdraw, the Beloved Disciple remains. In a story shaped by confusion, betrayal, fear, and revelation, this disciple consistently appears near the center of the Gospel's deepest moments of recognition and witness.

Even before the Beloved Disciple is explicitly introduced, many scholars identify an earlier unnamed disciple in the Gospel as the individual's first appearance. The scene is especially significant because it marks the initiation of Jesus's ministry. While all four Gospels connect Jesus to John the Baptist, the Fourth Gospel uniquely emphasizes that relationship.

In the first chapter, the Baptist is described standing with two disciples when he sees Jesus passing and declares, "Look, the Lamb of God!" At once, the two followers leave the Baptist and begin following Jesus. One is quickly identified as Andrew, who brings his brother Simon (soon to be Peter) along. The other disciple, though, remains unnamed—a conspicuous omission that has led many scholars to wonder if this is the Beloved Disciple.[28]

If this earlier figure is indeed the same Beloved Disciple who appears in the later chapters, the Gospel's narrative portrait of the Disciple comes into focus as a thread woven from multiple beginnings, traces of recognition, presence, and intimacy gathered under a single anonymous title. The deeper question is whose memory the figure most closely preserves, whose role in the movement the figure most clearly carries forward. The first place to look is the Last Supper, where the Disciple first receives the title "the disciple whom Jesus loved," the very scene Leonardo da Vinci would later immortalize.

In the Fourth Gospel, the Last Supper happens differently than in the Synoptic accounts. There is no clear Eucharistic sharing of bread and wine, but an extended meditation on love, fidelity, and relationship. Spanning several chapters, the discourse forms the theological center of the Gospel, much as the Sermon on the Mount does in Matthew. As it begins with the foot washing, devotion is defined through humility and care for others.

The emphasis on the feet also recalls the previous chapter, when Mary of Bethany anoints Jesus's feet, a connection often noted by scholars but rarely explored to its full interpretive potential.[29]

This first passage includes the intimate posture of the Beloved Disciple, with the Greek text literally reading: "there was reclining one out of the disciples of him in the bosom of Jesus whom loved Jesus." The verb *anakeimenos* refers to reclining at table, while *kolpos* means "bosom," "chest," or "lap." Though unusual to modern ears, the image carries theological weight beyond the physical scene. The language closely echoes the Prologue, where Jesus is described in older translations as dwelling "in the bosom of the Father," a phrase signifying profound intimacy and nearness. The point, therefore, is not necessarily romantic, but relational, intended to establish the particular closeness between Jesus and the Beloved Disciple.[30]

At this meal, Jesus shares his central commandment and continually returns to its theme: "Love one another. As I have loved you, so you must love one another." Greek contains several words for love, and the one used here is the same used for the Beloved Disciple. Not *eros*, associated more with desire, nor *philia*, the love of friendship or kinship, but *agapē*. In earlier Greek usage, *agapē* could simply mean affection or esteem. Within Christianity, however, it came to signify divine love: the love between Jesus and the Father as the model for faith, placed at the center of the Fourth Gospel and exemplified by the Beloved Disciple.[31]

The next time the Disciple enters the narrative is at the foot of the cross. In the other three Gospels, only women are listed by name as having been present for the tragic last moments of Jesus' life—Mary Magdalene usually listed first. The Fourth Gospel's witness list uniquely includes Mother Mary and the Beloved Disciple. From the cross, Jesus speaks. Addressing Mother Mary, he says, "Woman, here is your son." Then, to the Beloved Disciple, he continues: "Here is your mother." In this heartbreaking moment, Mother Mary and the Disciple are united, reinforcing the extraordinary connection between Jesus and the Beloved Disciple.[32]

The next scene involving the Beloved Disciple is at the tomb. After Mary Magdalene discovers that the stone has been moved, she runs to tell Peter and the Beloved Disciple that the body of Jesus is gone. The two race there together. The Beloved Disciple arrives first, pausing at the entrance while Peter walks in.[33]

Lastly, the Beloved Disciple appears in the Gospel's final chapter on the Sea of Tiberias. As the disciples struggle with an empty net, the Beloved Disciple recognizes the stranger standing on the shore, telling Peter, "It is the Lord." Otherwise, the Disciple stays quietly among the others in the boat.[34]

"If you love me, keep my commands." This line stands near the heart of the Johannine vision. In a Gospel where "believe" appears only as a verb and never as a noun in "faith," the Beloved Disciple becomes, as many scholars have observed, not simply a historical character but a model of discipleship. As in many ancient philosophical traditions, wisdom here is not only taught or admired, but lived.[35]

THE CARE OF THE FLOCK

Just as the Gospel's technical mastery appears in its rhythm and theology, its storytelling develops characters through deliberate contrast, using differences to define and teach. Repeatedly, the Beloved Disciple is set alongside Peter in a comparison that is unambiguous. Through scenes where their actions and responses diverge, the Gospel subtly advances a particular vision of leadership and authority.

Even before the Beloved Disciple is introduced by their designation, the contrast with Peter begins to take shape in the foot washing scene. When Jesus moves to wash the disciples' feet, Peter resists: "You shall never wash my feet." Peter's protest sounds reverent, but he seems to misunderstand the significance of Jesus's actions. "Unless I wash you," Jesus replies, "you have no part with me." Jesus insists that Peter, and all disciples, partake in his gesture of care and love.[36]

As the scene continues and Jesus foretells his betrayal, Peter turns to the Beloved Disciple and asks them to question Jesus directly. Peter himself does not ask, implying a degree of intimacy and access between Jesus and the Beloved Disciple that exceeds his own.

After Jesus delivers his central commandment of love, Peter interrupts: "Lord, where are you going?" Again, Peter seems to miss the moment, as his question breaks through the intimacy of Jesus's love to press at unanswered questions. When Jesus responds, "Where I am going, you cannot follow now, but you will follow later," Peter continues, insistent: "Lord, why can't I follow you now? I will lay down my life for you." Jesus immediately overturns Peter's claim: "Will you really lay down your life for me? Very truly I tell you, before the rooster crows, you will disown me three times."[37]

Infamously, the prophecy is fulfilled—Peter repeatedly denies Jesus during the arrest narrative. In the Synoptic Gospels, he fails to remain awake in Gethsemane, unable to stay present even for a single hour beside Jesus in the final moments before the arrest. There is also the fact that Peter is never named at the cross in any Gospel. (Besides, this list of Peter's shortcomings is not exhaustive.)

At the tomb, the contrast between Peter and the Beloved Disciple becomes obvious. The narrative places the two disciples in clear parallel: both run to the tomb, the Beloved Disciple arrives first and waits at the threshold. Peter enters immediately, examining the burial cloths with his own eyes, but seemingly unable to grasp their meaning. Once entering, the Beloved Disciple is described as having *seen* and *believed*—charged terms reserved for spiritual sight and knowledge in this Gospel.

By the final chapter, the comparison reaches its height. Among seven disciples gathered in a boat, Peter included, the Beloved Disciple is the one to recognize the risen Christ standing on the shore. When Peter hears this, he throws himself into the water with urgency, swimming to reach Christ first, just like he raced ahead to the tomb. Meanwhile, the Beloved Disciple remains with the group, the community, in the boat, a distinction that continues onshore.

As the twenty-first chapter goes on, Jesus turns to Peter. In a threefold rhythm recalling the earlier denial, he asks: "Do you love me?" Peter answers repeatedly, "Yes, Lord, you know that I love you." Each time, Jesus redirects him away from declaration and toward care and nurturance, varying his words: "feed my lambs," then "take care of my sheep," and lastly, "feed my sheep." Leadership, here, is clearly described through the pastoral language of tending. Love enacted through care is the basis of authority in this Gospel.[38]

Jesus continues on with one of the Gospel's more layered statements: "Very truly I tell you, when you were younger you dressed yourself and went where you wanted; but when you are old you will stretch out your hands, and someone else will dress you and lead you where you do not want to go."[39]

When held alongside his portrayal across the Fourth Gospel, these words evoke Peter's persistent sense of agency, even impulsiveness, shown in the way he speaks first, runs first, draws his sword first, jumps into the sea first. Jesus's words here describe a reversal. His reference to being dressed and led by another is suggestive not of self-direction but surrender. One way of reading this message is that Jesus is both calling Peter to leadership through loving care and asking him to relinquish the independence that defined him.

However, Church tradition has understood these passages in a very specific way since at least the second century. The verses were read as a prophecy of Peter's martyrdom, crucified upside down in imitation of Christ, while the earlier exchange about tending the sheep came to be interpreted as Jesus reinstating Peter as leader of the institutional church. There is a line in the text that clarifies plainly, "Jesus said this to indicate the kind of death by which Peter would glorify God."[40]

Perhaps it was a prophecy. Or perhaps that sentence was added later.

A difficulty in interpreting these final passages of the Gospel is that they are absent from some of the earliest surviving manuscript evidence. In Papyrus 66, the sheets of papyrus containing those final verses are missing due to damage, leaving it unknown whether or not the original scribe recorded those lines. The earliest surviving manuscripts preserving the full chapter are the mid-fourth-century Codex Vaticanus and Codex Sinaiticus. These copies emerged after the Council of Nicaea, after Eusebius of Caesarea wrote *Ecclesiastical History*, and after traditions of Peter's martyrdom and apostolic authority had become established in the Roman Church.[41]

There is one final comparison between Peter and the Beloved Disciple. Immediately after this exchange, Peter asks Jesus an almost petulant question, one in reference to the Beloved Disciple: "Lord, what about him?" Once again, the Beloved Disciple is set apart in an elevated position that Peter still seems unable to comprehend. Like a parent mediating between siblings, Jesus refuses the comparison entirely. Like with the sheep and lambs, Jesus draws Peter back to his model of leadership through humble care.[42]

The text again interrupts the dialogue with an explanatory clarification, this time insisting that Jesus did not mean the Beloved Disciple was immortal, but only that the figure's fate was irrelevant to Peter's own. What follows are the final words Jesus speaks in the entire Gospel. They are among his most cryptic and arguably the sharpest in tone toward Peter: "If I want him to remain alive until I return, what is that to you? You must follow me." Again, "him" seems to refer to the Disciple, and a special connection between them, though the intention remains indistinguishable.[43]

Because there are no complete pre-Nicene copies of these final passages, it cannot be known with certainty what may have been added, clarified, or smoothed over time. What the text preserves is a comparison of authority that would likely have troubled later Church leaders consolidating power through institutional hierarchy. The Fourth Gospel never, in all its pages, even uses the word "church." Instead, its vision of authority emerges through something far less imperial: not rank, rivalry, or comparison, but tender care for others—love expressed through the humblest acts of nurturance. Perhaps this is why the Beloved Disciple was *beloved*, what distinguished the figure above all others, even Peter.

And while Peter became the leader, the hero, and ultimately the foundation of institutional authority, the Beloved Disciple receded into the background as a secondary figure, memorialized more often in fine art than from the pulpit. Even still, no tradition could erase the force of the Fourth Gospel's claim of eyewitness memory, nor the influence of its poetic vision shaped through signs, encounters, and the commandment to love one another.

If anything, the question returns with renewed intensity. Who *was* the disciple whom Jesus loved, the figure placed closest to the living memory at the heart of the movement?

THE CASE FOR MARY MAGDALENE

For centuries, scholars and readers alike have searched the pages of this Gospel, tracing the Beloved Disciple through the text for clues. Though interpretations vary, certain features recur consistently across scholarly examination, like signals that seem to reveal something about the Disciple's identity. Several characteristics stand out, including that the Beloved Disciple appears to stand somewhat outside the formal circle of the Twelve while remaining closely connected to Jerusalem and, in particular, to the household at Bethany.[44]

Scholars such as Floyd Filson and James H. Charlesworth have suggested that Lazarus of Bethany may have been the Beloved Disciple. The textual case is substantial because Lazarus is the only person in the Gospel Jesus is explicitly named as loving, and the Beloved Disciple does not appear under that title until after Lazarus has been raised.[45] Yet the proposal stumbles on how little Lazarus offers as a figure in the narrative. He is not portrayed with receptivity or perception, has no ongoing theological engagement with Jesus, and once raised, scarcely reappears. His sisters feature far more prominently in the Gospel.

Other details suggest a person of rare social standing. During the arrest of Jesus, for example, an unnamed disciple gains access to the courtyard of the high priest, a level of familiarity difficult to explain if the figure were a Galilean fisherman. While the text never clearly identifies this anonymous person as the Beloved Disciple, some scholars have wondered whether they were one and the same. If so, the Disciple may have come from a priestly or aristocratic family.[46]

At first glance, observations like these seem to rule out the possibility that the Beloved Disciple could be a woman. Yet such assumptions move too swiftly past the complexity of the figure itself. The Beloved Disciple is characterized by intimacy, receptivity, and relationship. Much like Leonardo da Vinci's rendering in *The Last Supper*, this individual carries a sensibility, or a spirit, that can be interpreted as recognizably feminine.

So prominent is the feminine thread running through the Fourth Gospel that Schneiders has argued "whoever the author of the Fourth Gospel was, it was someone who had a remarkably rich and nuanced understanding of feminine religious experience." While such insight could be attributed to imagination alone, Schneiders believes the text reflects direct familiarity with the lives of women within the Johannine community: "It seems more than likely that real women . . . stand behind these Johannine characters." Schneiders even proposes that the Samaritan woman may function as a kind of "textual alter ego" for the author.[47]

Gathering the overt clues as well as the subtle ones, what the Gospel says along what it withholds, the portrait of the Beloved Disciple begins to resemble one follower of Jesus more closely than any other. The Beloved Disciple may, indeed, be Mary Magdalene. And once the evidence is surveyed, both within the canon and beyond it, the possibility begins to feel less outlandish.

Mary Magdalene's portrayal in the Fourth Gospel aligns closely in theme and function with that of the Beloved Disciple. Both figures are centered as witnesses present in moments of suffering, death, and grief. Each is portrayed with a unique closeness to Jesus. Their recognition of the risen Jesus arrives before the others, marking each with a faculty of perception and insight—of having eyes to see.

And if Mary Magdalene is also Mary of Bethany, the parallels draw the figures closer still. Both the Beloved Disciple and the siblings from Bethany are described as being loved by Jesus, not with a familial love but *agapē*. While the narrative emphasizes Jesus' love for Lazarus, it also states that "Jesus loved Martha and her sister and Lazarus." Many scholars have noted the echo between this phrasing and "the disciple whom Jesus loved," as being possibly more than coincidence.[48] Then, Elizabeth Schrader Polczer's work on Papyrus 66 makes this passage even more potent. If her research is correct, and there may be an earlier tradition where Martha was not present, then the "love" falls even more narrowly on Mary of Bethany. And the edits become all the more curious.

The emotional nature of the Bethany narrative deepens the connection further. When Mary weeps, Jesus weeps—the only moment in any Gospel where Jesus is described as weeping over a person.[49] The tears even anticipate later traditions surrounding Magdalene herself—the English word maudlin, meaning tearfully sentimental, derives from *Magdalene*. When Mary of Bethany anoints Jesus's feet, tears are absent. The unnamed sinful woman who anoints in Luke does cry at Jesus's feet, a detail utilized by Gregory the Great to shape Magdalene as sorrowfully penitent. In his conflations, the love and grief of the tears shared by Jesus and Mary of Bethany over Lazarus were forgotten.

When the evidence beyond the canon is considered, the case for Mary Magdalene as the Beloved Disciple gains momentum. Across texts such as Dialogue of the Savior, the Gospel of Mary, Gospel of Thomas, Gospel of Peter, Wisdom of Jesus Christ, and Pistis Sophia, Mary is repeatedly portrayed through the same qualities that define the Beloved Disciple in the Fourth Gospel: spiritual perception, privileged understanding, and remarkable closeness to Jesus.

The Gospel of Philip describes Magdalene as one of three women who traveled in surprising intimacy with Jesus: "There were three who always walked with the Lord: Mary his mother, and her sister, and Magdalene, the one who was called his companion." The text then adds: "His sister and his mother and his companion were each a Mary." Companion appears again in the famous passage describing Jesus "kissing" her, alongside the striking line that "Christ loved her more than all the disciples." Philip notes the resentment this provokes among the others: "Why do you love her more than all of us?" *Koinōnos* as companion could be shared participation, spiritual intimacy, and privileged understanding. The kiss, if spiritual not romantic, resonates with the Gospel's theme of recognition through spirit and inward perception.[50]

The Gospel of Mary mirrors the language surrounding the Beloved Disciple with striking similarity. Peter says to Mary: "Sister, we know that the Savior loved you more than all other women." He then asks her to share teachings hidden from the others. Later in the text, both Peter and Andrew challenge Mary, questioning her authority, insight, and connection to Jesus in a way that resembles the comparison between the Beloved Disciple and Peter. The same pattern of contrast between Magdalene and Peter is featured in the Pistis Sophia. Some scholars have suggested that the authors of the Gospel of Mary and Pistis Sophia may have drawn on this dynamic from the Fourth Gospel.[51]

Or, it is possible that the texts preserve an older memory, where Magdalene and Peter were in contrast. And where Magdalene was the Beloved Disciple.

Most scholars stop short of directly suggesting that Magdalene was the Beloved Disciple. For the most part, the possibility has remained a floating conjecture, touched on only indirectly in discussions, essays, chapters, and conferences. Scholars of the Gospel of Mary—Karen King, Sarah Parkhouse, and Esther de Boer—have noted that Mary is described in its pages as beloved. In 1998, Ramon K. Jusino published online what remains, to this point, the only dedicated, full-length essay arguing that Mary Magdalene may have been the Beloved Disciple and originating voice behind the Fourth Gospel. But tucked within her major Johannine study, *Written That You May Believe*, Schneiders suggests the possibility warrants serious consideration. In the chapter "Because of the Woman's Testimony . . . ," one of the most respected scholarly voices on the Fourth Gospel approaches the question with care and precision.[52]

A major objection is that in both the crucifixion and resurrection narratives, the text appears to present Magdalene and the Disciple as separate characters. The difficulty is obvious. How could they be one person if both are named within the same scenes?

In his analysis, Jusino argues that the crucifixion and resurrection narratives preserve signs of later editorial development. He points to what he sees as structural inconsistencies surrounding the Beloved Disciple's appearance in these scenes, proposing that the passages may have been reshaped during a later stage of the Gospel's composition, possibly amid the internal conflicts associated with the Johannine community. His argument draws on the work of Claudia Setzer, who described the Beloved Disciple's appearance in the tomb narrative as a possible "contrivance" reflecting editorial reshaping.[53]

The argument can sound speculative, until one notices that editorial reshaping of a woman's role inside the Fourth Gospel isn't hypothetical, as Elizabeth Schrader Polczer's work on Papyrus 66 has demonstrated. Her work revealed that the textual tradition replaced "Mary" with "Martha" at the scene where the Gospel's most decisive confession of faith is uttered. The kind of editorial reshaping Jusino proposes for the cross and empty-tomb scenes is therefore not an abstract speculation. It is the very kind of move the manuscript record has already shown happening to a woman, in this very Gospel, at one specific and decisive moment.

Masculine pronouns applied to the Beloved Disciple present an obvious challenge. Schneiders argues that this does not necessarily exclude a female figure. In Koine Greek, grammatical gender does not always track biological sex; masculine forms could function generically, and a singular masculine figure could stand for a wider community. At the foot of the cross, many commentators assume Jesus's words, "Woman, here is your son," establish the Beloved Disciple as male. Schneiders counters that "son" marks a representative role rather than a literal gender because the dying Jesus gives his mother a new son to stand in his place, so the masculine carries his role forward rather than fixing the sex of the disciple who embodies it—much as the risen Jesus's charge to my brothers is a generic masculine that plainly includes women. In fact, she proposes that the most natural reading is that the Beloved Disciple is already present among the women gathered at the cross, one of whom is Magdalene.[54]

Schneiders arrives at a stunning synthesis: "[Mary Magdalene] is the only figure in the Gospel who, by name, is presented as a witness of the death of Jesus, the discoverer of the empty tomb, and the recipient of the Easter protophany and of the only individual apostolic commission of the risen Jesus. If there is an eyewitness behind the Fourth Gospel, the most clearly designated embodiment of that role in the text itself is Mary Magdalene."[55]

In her conclusion, Schneiders proposes that the Beloved Disciple is not a single individual but a "textual paradigm," one who "concretely embodies in the text the corporate authority of the Johannine school" and is refracted across several figures. Even within that careful frame, she names "the most significant of these figures" as "certainly Mary Magdalene, who is the witness to and proclaimer of the paschal mystery."[56]

Schneiders herself never makes the identification outright, but it is telling that a scholar of her stature, following the evidence on her own terms, returns to the same figure: Mary Magdalene. Where Schneiders treats Mary Magdalene as the most significant refraction of a textual paradigm, the trajectory of her own analysis suggests something more: that Mary Magdalene may be not only the paradigm's most significant figure, but the figure the paradigm itself was constructed to honor and to conceal.

It is not that Mary Magdalene sat down and wrote the Fourth Gospel as it appears in modern Bibles. The Gospel stands at the end of a long process of community shaping, redaction, and transmission. The potential is more specific: that the originating eyewitness whose memory and testimony the Gospel preserves—the figure later remembered through the literary lens of the Beloved Disciple—may have been Mary Magdalene.

ON THE MARGINS

It is well established that the Fourth Gospel retains the imprint of the community that preserved and influenced it. So, if Mary Magdalene was its original witness, then traces of that community may also reflect something of her character. At least, understanding the shape and nature of that community could serve to strengthen, or to complicate, the possibility that she was the Beloved Disciple.

Modern scholarship widely agrees that ancient scripture preserves traces of the people who transmitted, edited, and interpreted them over time. The theology within bears the imprint of communal experience, preserving tensions, conflicts, aspirations, and evolving elements within the text. In the case of the Fourth Gospel, Brown famously argued in the 1970s that the Gospel developed through successive stages shaped by a Johannine community.[57]

The first chapter of the Fourth Gospel makes clear that the ministry of Jesus—and later the community that carried forward the movement after his death—emerged from the earlier circle surrounding John the Baptist. Brown extended this into his theory: the earliest stratum of the Johannine community originated among the Baptist's followers. As Schneiders describes, these "eager" followers were "highly religiously motivated Jews."[58] Those who were drawn to the Baptist had common traits they brought with them that can be sensed within the tone and theology of the Fourth Gospel, including a distance from established religious authority, an emphasis on inner transformation, and the symbolism of water as renewal.

The next layer of the Johannine community, in Brown's analysis, was Samaritan. In the first century, Samaritans were viewed by many Judeans as religiously suspect, ethnically mixed, and outside the bounds of proper worship. Yet the Fourth Gospel places a Samaritan woman at the center of one of its most profound revelatory scenes early in Jesus's ministry.

At Jacob's well, beneath the shadow of a sacred mountain, Jesus enters into the Gospel's longest recorded private conversation with an anonymous woman identified only as Samaritan. Through their dialogue, she moves from misunderstanding to recognition, seeing him first as a stranger, then a prophet, and finally as something far greater. It is to her that Jesus openly declares, "I am he"—one of the clearest revelations of his identity in the Gospel—and to her that he speaks of "living water." Wells and springs had long carried sacred associations throughout the Levant and wider Mediterranean world, often tied to the feminine as spaces of fertility, domestic life, encounter, and covenant. When the woman departs, she leaves behind her water jar, exchanging the vessel once used to draw water for the "living water" Jesus offers.[59]

In place of the water, she returns to her community with this message, and her testimony leads many Samaritans to join his movement. If the Samaritan woman and her community illuminate anything about the character of the Johannine tradition, it is that outsiders remain central to its vision. Repeatedly, the Fourth Gospel places revelation not in the hands of established religious authority, but among those standing beyond its boundaries: foreigners, women, the socially marginal, and those capable of recognition. Women, in particular, are repeatedly portrayed as bearers of spiritual insight and transformation.

The final widening of the community happened, according to Brown, with the inclusion of the Gentiles. One of the most distinctive elements of Christianity—rare in antiquity where religion came from place, from land, from tribe—was the idea that Jesus' message was for anyone, for everyone. This universal vision appears in the letters of Paul, but also in the Fourth Gospel, which includes Greeks and Gentiles more explicitly than the Synoptics. Even Luke, often considered Gentile-oriented, remains deeply rooted in Jewish scripture and tradition, while Matthew was almost certainly written within a Jewish Christian milieu, and Mark likewise reflects a community still shaped by Jewish concerns and traditions.

The Fourth Gospel does not reject Jewish tradition so much as radically reinterpret belonging within it. The tensions within its pages reflect a process of separation and differentiation occurring within first-century Judaism, not a rejection of Judaism as a whole. In its original context, the

Gospel reflects a struggle over authority, identity, and access to the divine, especially if its composition and editing took place in the wake of the Temple's destruction. What the Gospel seems intent on distancing itself from are structures that seek to interpret and mediate a faith the text locates elsewhere—within a process of inward orientation, recognition, and belief.

The pattern is evident: the Gospel consistently gravitates toward figures on the margins of established society—Samaritans, outsiders, women—and toward those willing to cross inherited boundaries in pursuit of truth. All of this complements the possibility that the central figure behind the text could have been a woman, even Mary Magdalene. This evidence, however, does not end within the Gospel's narrative—further clues can be found in what the historical record reflects about the Gospel's earliest interpreters and custodians.

A HERETICAL GOSPEL

In the very same text where he named John as the author of the Fourth Gospel and insisted upon a fourfold canon, published around 180 CE, Irenaeus criticized one group who had long been using and interpreting the Gospel in its own way. The connection was established enough that Tertullian voiced similar concerns. By that point, these communities had not only adopted the text, but developed interpretations centered on its mystical and symbolic dimensions, possibly even composing other writings shaped by Johannine themes. That group was the Valentinians—a Christian movement later denounced as heretical and gnostic.[60]

The Valentinians were a second-century Christian movement associated with the teacher Valentinus of Alexandria, and their embrace of the Fourth Gospel deeply alarmed the Church Fathers. Clement of Alexandria observed that Valentinian readers approached the Gospel symbolically, while Origen of Alexandria devoted extended analysis to the interpretations of Heracleon, a Valentinian teacher. Heracleon's commentary on the Fourth Gospel, surviving only in fragments preserved by Origen's own commentary, is the earliest known commentary on any Gospel. Previously lost or destroyed Valentinian writings rediscovered at the Nag Hammadi library further reinforce the relationship, repeatedly echoing themes familiar from the Fourth Gospel: spiritual awakening, symbolic language, and knowledge attained through recognition.[61]

The Valentinians were believed to use rituals meant to cultivate a direct relationship with the divine. Since they eschewed mediation, it is no surprise that their communities also appear to have resisted the emerging ecclesiastical hierarchies. Irenaeus connected these tendencies in his critiques, drawing on First Timothy's warning against "what is falsely called knowledge" to turn *gnōsis*—the Greek word for knowledge—into a term of derision. He even folded the charge into the title of his great refutation: the work now known as *Against Heresies* was formally "the Refutation and Overthrow of Knowledge Falsely So-Called."[62] He and other early Church leaders made plain their distaste for what they perceived as the Valentinians' emphasis on personal spirituality over institutional authority.

The chasm between orthodox and Valentinian Christianity raises logical questions about the Fourth Gospel. Were these early Christians simply drawing radically different meanings from the same text, or were they reading different versions of the same Gospel? Has the Fourth Gospel always possessed the capacity to sustain interpretations far removed from the way orthodoxy ultimately chose to define it, or were there earlier forms and readings later lost to suppression, editing, and time?

There is another conspicuous element to the connection between the Valentinians and the Fourth Gospel—Alexandria. The most significant second- and third-century commentaries on the Gospel emerged from this city: Heracleon, Clement, Origen, and the Valentinian texts all belong to the intellectual world of Alexandria. Moreover, the Gospel fits naturally within that philosophical environment. The Logos of the Prologue is clearly inspired by the work of Philo of Alexandria. The narrative's symbolic oppositions of light and darkness, above and below, flesh and spirit, blindness and sight reflect the symbolic and philosophical language of Hellenistic Judaism associated with Alexandria.

Alexandria could well have been the hometown of Mary Magdalene, a woman of independence, wisdom, financial means, and spiritual insight. Alexandria, of course, granted women extraordinary civic and religious freedoms for the era. Again, this converges with the Valentinians, whom

Irenaeus and Tertullian critiqued for allowing women to participate in prophecy, teaching, and rituals. More than that even, Valentinian literature portrayed female figures as bearers of revelation and wisdom—Sophia, the Holy Spirit, and Magdalene among them. The Gospel of Philip, which scholars link to the Valentinians, emphatically states that Mary Magdalene was the one Jesus "loved more than all the disciples."[63]

If an early Johannine community emerged within Alexandria, many features of the Gospel fall into a more coherent cultural setting. Its prominence of Samaritans, Gentiles, women, and figures like Mary of Bethany or Mary Magdalene aligns with the cosmopolitan world of Alexandria, where ethnic, religious, and philosophical boundaries overlapped more fluidly. So too does the Gospel's emphasis on personal revelation alongside its recurring suspicion toward institutional religious authority.

Based on these convergences the possibility no longer feels arbitrary. Valentinian communities were already reading the Gospel symbolically and venerating Mary Magdalene as a privileged spiritual figure, and so the identification of Magdalene with the Beloved Disciple is consistent with the trajectory of their interpretive practice.

The Alexandrian-provenance thesis is not new. It was argued explicitly nearly a century ago by the Yale scholar B. W. Bacon in *The Gospel of the Hellenists*, and developed further by J. N. Sanders and the English biblical scholar Edwyn Hoskyns in the 1940s. More recently, Charles E. Hill's *The Johannine Corpus in the Early Church* has documented the extensive Alexandrian reception of the Gospel, while April D. DeConick has placed the Fourth Gospel within an Alexandrian mystical-philosophical matrix. So while the strict Alexandrian-provenance thesis remains a minority position, it has not gone unnoticed or undefended.[64]

These connections make the traditional association between the Fourth Gospel and the city of Ephesus appear all the more tenuous. Yet again, Irenaeus is the earliest surviving source to make the connection. It is possible that an early community using the Fourth Gospel did exist in Ephesus. Critical scholars have also argued against the Ephesus theory, pointing instead to Syria as a possible provenance based on parallels with Ignatius of Antioch and the Odes of Solomon. But there are reasons, both textual and historical, to look farther south: to Alexandria.

Another explanation is that Irenaeus intentionally placed the Gospel in Ephesus in order to distance it from the heretical associations surrounding Alexandria. By contrast, Eusebius of Caesarea would later preserve the tradition that Mark founded the Alexandrian church.[65] Called an assistant to Peter, the Gospel attributed to him bears little obvious connection to Alexandria. Rather, the Gospel of Mark is rooted in Jewish communal life, apocalyptic expectation, and the world surrounding Jerusalem.

By the late second century, orthodox Christianity faced a serious problem with the Fourth Gospel. The text possessed immense theological authority, yet it was deeply entangled with communities increasingly defined as heretical: Valentinian Christians, mystical interpreters, movements emphasizing inward revelation, spiritual knowledge, and unusually prominent roles for women. Alexandria was a hotbed of diversity or dissension, depending on perspective. And the Johannine epistles may preserve traces of these very fractures, as Brown and Elaine Pagels have each argued.[66]

It is therefore worth asking whether these relocations of memory were entirely organic. Were names and places simply preserved, or were traditions strategically redirected and stabilized over time? Was the Fourth Gospel gradually drawn into a narrative designed to strengthen male apostolic succession and institutional authority? Ephesus and John may have offered a lineage far safer, more controllable, and less vulnerable to charges of heresy than Alexandria and Mary Magdalene.

The case for Mary Magdalene as the Beloved Disciple, then, rests on a convergence of textual clues, historical conditions, scholarly observations, and the silences a careful reader begins to hear within the text. Each link carries some weight, and none carries all of it. What makes the proposal worth taking seriously is the way the evidence accumulates precisely from the places where proto-orthodoxy pressed hardes—against women, and against the communities, like those at Alexandria, that read this Gospel symbolically. What the possibility reveals, more than anything, is how often tradition has been mistaken for history—and how little the historical possibilities around Mary Magdalene, and around Alexandria itself, have ever been examined on their own terms.

ANONYMITY

The unnamed status of the Beloved Disciple leaves the figure suspended between history and symbol, at once intimate and elusive. If Mary Magdalene was the Beloved Disciple, the Gospel's refusal to name her becomes easier to understand. The communities that preserved and transmitted the Gospel may have possessed many reasons not to foreground her identity openly—some protective, others critical. The precise mechanisms remain impossible to reconstruct, but the historical conditions for concealment were clearly present.

Schneiders articulates this possibility to its furthest implication: "If we are looking for a motive for the evangelist's deliberate obscuring of the identity of the Beloved Disciple in the Fourth Gospel, what better reason could there be than that the authoritative source of the Gospel was, or was connected in some way with, Mary Magdalene, the problematic woman protagonist in literature regarded as heretical at precisely the time that this Gospel was beginning to circulate at the beginning of the second century?"[67]

Schneiders further emphasizes the "high strategic importance" of ensuring that the Fourth Gospel did not become too closely identified with communities later labeled "Gnostic," particularly at the very moment emerging ecclesiastical structures were beginning to narrow female leadership. Within such a landscape, preserving the Gospel's authority while simultaneously obscuring a female eyewitness no longer reads as contradiction, but strategy.[68]

Even so, the anonymity of the Beloved Disciple need not be explained solely through disguise or later suppression. Scholars interpret it in different ways. Richard Bauckham argues that the disciple's identity may have been left unstated because the original community already knew who the witness was, making any further identification unnecessary. Bauckham himself identifies that witness as John the Elder, a figure he distinguishes from John son of Zebedee. Others, including Schneiders and Barnhart, interpret the anonymity as a literary and theological strategy. By withholding the name, the Gospel allows the Disciple to recede slightly from view, becoming a figure into whose place the reader may imaginatively step. Even among scholars who emphasize this symbolic dimension, however, most still conclude that a historical person stands behind that model.[69]

The literary reading and the historical reading need not stand in opposition. By the time the Gospel reaches its final form, the Beloved Disciple is a literary figure composed from many moments gathered under that single anonymous title. Inherently, the figure functions as a literary device because this is a Gospel designed for engagement. Every element is intended for the reader to become a *believer*. Anonymity allows the reader to imaginatively step into the Disciple's place and learn how to become the ideal follower of Jesus through *love*. Whether the anonymity was the evangelist's intention or a later redaction, and even if it obscures the identity of Mary Magdalene, the result is elegant and, in a way, miraculous. What might be concealment may serve to inspire the reader to greater faith—the highest concern for any sacred scripture.

Anonymity may therefore express something essential to the Gospel's character. In the Johannine world, authority shifts away from status, titles, and public power, and toward inward recognition and abiding love. Maybe the Beloved Disciple remained unnamed not only because later generations struggled over the memory of the witness, but because the community understood leadership differently from the beginning. The faithful one was not the one who claimed power most visibly, but the one who remained closest to the source—in divine love.

It is not impossible to consider that Mary Magdalene helped shape the figure of the Beloved Disciple. Could she have fashioned the character as a template for belief rooted within the self through love, recognition, and the heart? Could she have deliberately veiled herself, transposing personal memory into symbolic narrative, much as Jesus taught through parable? If the Beloved Disciple belonged, in some form, to her original vision, perhaps the anonymity was Mary Magdalene's own intention. Perhaps her own name receded so the message could remain central. Perhaps the Gospel was designed so that love would hold authority within its pages.

THE POWER OF LOVE

Exhilaration, skepticism, confusion, outrage. These are just some of the reactions provoked by the suggestion that the eyewitness memory behind one of Christianity's four Gospels may belong not to a man named John, but to a woman named Mary. The idea is unfamiliar enough to feel impossible at first, and threatening enough that, for centuries, it would have been treated as heresy. Yet just as often, the response arrives quietly, as curiosity, uncertainty, or the persistent tug of a possibility that refuses to disappear. Private realization may move in currents, rising and receding before it finds words. Publicly, however, the question is more complicated.

Among scholars sympathetic to her, the possibility that she was the Beloved Disciple of the Fourth Gospel is scarcely discussed. In Christian communities, even those open to feminist recovery, it may still be a bridge too far. Mary can be freed from the label of prostitute and restored as apostle to the apostles. She can be beloved as saint, witness, and woman of faith. She can even be imagined as Jesus's wife, a role the tradition can recognize and contain, one still a safe category for a woman. But to name Magdalene as the Beloved Disciple unsettles the status quo more than many are prepared to accept. For some, the claim is not simply unlikely, it is impossible. Heretical. Unthinkable.

The very nature of the Fourth Gospel presses against those restrictions of thought, defining belief not as passive acceptance, but as the responsibility to listen more deeply, to look again. Schneiders describes this beautifully when she writes that the Fourth Gospel invites a "fundamental openness of heart, the basic readiness to see and hear what is really there, the fidelity to one's experience no matter how frightening or costly it appears to be, the devotion to being that refuses to tamper with reality in order to preserve the situation with which one is familiar."[70]

Schneiders's words illuminate not only Mary Magdalene, but the long line of women who trusted what they had seen and heard beyond the limits their world imposed. Joan of Arc offers one of Christianity's most famous examples, but also one of its most revealing contradictions. Her boundary-crossing was spectacular, embodied in a peasant girl in armor, speaking with divine authority, entering war, advising men, and altering the fate of a kingdom. Yet the world that feared her could also understand her, because her visions served categories it already knew, including crown, country, Church, sacrifice, and holy war.

Born around 1412 in Domrémy, a village in Lorraine, she was the daughter of Jacques d'Arc, a farmer, and Isabelle Romée, whose name remembered a pilgrimage to Rome. Joan was raised amid the violence of the Hundred Years' War, in a fractured France, much of the north under English and Burgundian control. Villages like Joan's existed under constant threat, their farms stripped of resources, their women vulnerable to soldiers moving through the countryside. At least once, her family was forced to flee to safer refuge.

In Joan's world, violence was constant, and war was routinely justified in God's name. Revelation and the prophetic Old Testament texts it drew from had steeped Christian culture in apocalyptic expectation, giving sacred force to images of bloodshed, judgment, and divine victory. And beneath a single male name, tradition had long allowed a vision of judgment, conquest, and violent triumph to be joined with a Gospel rooted in recognition, intimacy, and abiding love. In a world where scripture was encountered less as a text to be read than as a tradition handed down through clergy, liturgy, image, and story, those differences were barely known by common people. "John" became a vessel large enough to hold both love and war.

And then there was *Jeanne*, her own name the French feminine of John. As a girl, she too began to receive visions, though hers didn't arrive as an apocalypse on an island, but as voices in a garden, saints and angels insisting she fight for France. She was thirteen when she first heard them, voices arriving in a great light with Archangel Michael, Catherine of Alexandria, and Margaret of Antioch. Centuries later, Jules Bastien-Lepage would paint it vividly: Joan in her garden, pink-cheeked and blue-eyed, leaning against a tree as the angel and saints hover behind her. For three years, Joan carried the voices in silence, still living the ordinary life of a peasant girl. When they persisted, she forced her way past mockery and dismissal until she reached Charles VII, where king and clergy tested her and failed to discredit her.

For a girl without education or rank, claiming such a vision was extraordinary. To speak it aloud was dangerous. To act on it would require her to cross nearly every line her world had drawn around her. And yet Joan was also a paradox. Her revelations were overtly political, aimed at raising the siege of Orléans, lead the dauphin to Reims, and see him crowned as king of France. Men who might otherwise have dismissed a girl's voices as delusion could hear them differently when the message answered the urgent needs of national survival. She moved into spaces forbidden to her, but the meaning of her mission remained legible and useful. She entered a system that might have crushed her and, for a moment, became one of its most effective instruments.

Joan's own heart ran truer than the uses to which it was put. Her desire was not violence for its own sake, but protection—of her village, her family, her people, and the world she believed sacred enough to defend. But this is what the language of holy war creates. It takes fear, desperation, and the hunger for security, then clothes them in images that feel ancient, powerful, and true. It makes violence feel ordained. It strengthens kings and generals, fills coffers, summons bodies, and comforts those left at home by telling them bloodshed has meaning. And within Christianity, no text gave that more sacred force than Revelation.

In Joan, faith and fight were bound together—the tenderness of devotion carried into the violence of command. What began as voices and light became cloth, armor, movement, and flesh. Riding into battle, Joan carried a banner with a white field scattered with fleur-de-lis, Christ in glory holding the world, two flanking angels, and the words "Jhesus Maria" written across the top in gold. By placing Maria beside Jhesus, Joan named the mother as well as the son, making the sacred feminine visible on the field of war. During one assault, a crossbow bolt struck her shoulder; she pulled it out herself and returned to the fight. Her relentlessness produced the line later attached to her memory: "I was born for this."

The transcripts from her trial at Rouen do not record Joan speaking those words. What they do preserve, even through the hostile machinery of interrogation, is something just as powerful: a young woman refusing to betray what she believed. Her trial was political murder dressed in the language of heresy, the destruction of a girl whose visions had made her invaluable to one kingdom and intolerable to another. Questioned, threatened, and cornered by men determined to break her, Joan remained steadfast. This is the courage that followed her into memory: a purity of purpose, a persistence so complete it became almost impossible to explain. Convicted of heresy, she was burned alive on May 30, 1431. She was already so beloved that English authorities ordered her ashes scattered in the Seine to prevent them from becoming relics.[71]

Joan was a fearless girl moving through a world organized by fear—fear of invasion, fear of dishonor, fear of divine punishment, fear of national ruin, fear of what would happen if the wrong king held the crown. Holy war takes those fears and gives them shape, turning dread into command, vulnerability into sacrifice, and violence into destiny. This is the power Revelation offered to Christian authority, and once that justification was placed beneath the name "John," it borrowed the authority of the Beloved Disciple, tethering it to apostolic legitimacy.

Joan, though a woman, was more legible than Mary Magdalene. She stepped beyond what was permitted but the meaning of her crossing could still be gathered back into a story Christianity already knew how to tell: the holy warrior, the obedient virgin, the sacrificed body, the victory of God in battle. Her courage was astonishing, but it moved inside a world where sacred authority could still be imagined through war.

Mary Magdalene offered no such benefit to the powers shaping institutional Christianity. She did not lead armies, crown kings, or sanctify conquest. In the traditions that surround her, she teaches, contemplates, and comforts. If she was the Beloved Disciple, she was not merely a witness but a leader of another kind, the one who knew him, the one entrusted with his mother, the one whose authority was rooted not in command but in intimacy, recognition, and care.

To disentangle fear from love, Revelation from the Gospel, the visionary man on Patmos from the Beloved Disciple, is about much more than Mary Magdalene alone. It is about returning to the heart of the Fourth Gospel. It is about returning to love.

Love is far more difficult to weaponize than fear. A Christianity whose most intimate witness may have been a woman is a challenge to the masculine line of apostolic authority. A Gospel whose authority arises through lived perception rather than domination offers little justification for empire.

Fire cannot destroy what is passed voice to voice, or carried within. Perhaps that is why the Beloved Disciple remained unnamed. Not because she lacked authority, but because the Gospel understood something far more dangerous to the powers that seek to contain us: fear is an illusion; there is only love.

Chapter 9

BASILICA DI SAN CLEMENTE

The Colosseum does not rise so much as remain, steadier than the centuries around it, recalling Lord Byron's famous lines, "While stands the Coliseum, Rome shall stand; When falls the Coliseum, Rome shall fall; And when Rome falls—the World."[1] Awed despite yourself, you walk amid a sea of tourists, speech jumbling across many languages as people lift their phones for selfies and modernity resounds against the travertine.

Eroded arches lift toward the Roman sky like the ribs of something that once breathed. Summer light pours through the broken arcades, bright and unrelenting. The arena floor lies open below, dust-fine and sun-bleached, the color of bone and ash. Grit clings to your soles, no different from how it would have when these walls first rose under the Flavian emperors, begun by Vespasian and completed under his son Titus. This was architecture designed to protect imperial authority and instill fear through death staged as entertainment.

You squint against the Roman sun, standing where gladiators once faced the roar of the arena, then slip out of the glare into a pocket of shade. Heat shimmers above the stone, trapped inside the amphitheater's enclosed spaces, and the relief of shadow is immediate. Each year brings stories of collapse, of visitors overcome and even seasoned guides suffering in the punishing temperatures. It is hard to escape the feeling that something of this brutality still clings to the place.

This was a space governed by ritual thresholds. There was a gate through which the dead were carried out, and another through which the victorious departed. The story did not belong only to gladiators; it gathered executions, animal hunts, condemned prisoners, and later, the tradition of Christian martyrdom into the same ring of stone. Violence was built into the movement, sightline, procession, and fear.

Once the gladiatorial games were restricted and then banned, this amphitheater was repurposed, neglected, and damaged by earthquakes. It became shelter, fortress, quarry, and, as ivy crept across its walls, romantic ruin. By the nineteenth century, that ruin had begun to exert another kind of power, drawing novelists and poets who wandered its perilous passages and found in its brokenness a strange enchantment. Nathaniel Hawthorne captured it in *The Marble Faun*:

> Within, the moonlight filled and flooded the great empty space; it glowed upon tier above tier of ruined, grass-grown arches, and made them even too distinctly visible. The splendor of the revelation took away that inestimable effect of dimness and mystery by which the imagination might be assisted to build a grander structure than the Coliseum, and to shatter it with a more picturesque decay.[2]

The beauty is difficult to hold against what occurred here. The ruins invite reverence, but they belong to a city shaped by structures of dominance that still command the landscape through triumphal roads, monumental arches, and muscular architecture proclaiming conquest and order. Even the fountains and piazzas carry this imprint, where river gods strain beneath obelisks while generals, saints, and emperors stand fixed in marble, authority given form and made to outlast everything it conquered.

Time has layered the Colosseum, turning the arena into ruin, ruin into shrine, and shrine into monument. That layering reaches beyond this place. It belongs to Rome.

*

When you depart the Colosseum, the present rushes back at once with traffic, voices, vendors, and the restless movement of the street. The stone that held you moments ago recedes behind iron railings and souvenir stalls.

Wanting a moment to settle, you duck into the refuge of a coffee bar across the street and stand at the counter like a Roman for *un caffè*.

Espresso cups clink against marble counters while, outside, fruit vendors arrange peaches, figs, and cherries in wooden crates. For a few minutes, you let the café hold you, the glass case bright with *cornetti*, while Vespas weave through traffic, and tourists pause over maps under umbrellas. Rome's sacred and imperial past sits everywhere beneath this tourist gloss of routes, tickets, photographs, and shade. Finishing your coffee, you step back into the warmth of the afternoon and continue on. Ahead, the Arch of Constantine rises over the road, another monument to victory, another claim of power waiting along the path.

Continuing east along Via San Giovanni Laterano, you feel the crowds begin to thin and the city ease its grip. The air remains warm, but the brightness softens as the street narrows and shade gathers along the walls. As the street quiets, the performance of Rome gives way to ordinary life with scarred facades, half-revealed courtyards, and laundry strung above streets layered with buried histories.

After only a few hundred feet, you reach Basilica di San Clemente, which is unassuming at first glance. One of Rome's earliest church sites, the upper basilica was built in the early twelfth century under Pope Paschal II. The official story holds that the lower church was damaged and abandoned after the Norman sack of Rome, yet the archaeology conflicts with this reading. There is no evidence of fire, no soot in the lower walls, no real indication of a sack.[3] From the street, it appears to be only one more church in a city dense with them, asking for covered shoulders and lowered voices. But even before you enter, the ground begins to drop.

You descend below street level, pass through a sheltered courtyard and portico, moving past yet another murmuring Roman fountain before entering the twelfth-century basilica. Unlike many churches in Rome, it makes little demand for grandeur. There are no Caravaggios tucked into side chapels, no iconic image waiting for a tourist's selfie, no grand papal tombs commanding the nave.

What lies here is cumulative rather than spectacular, historical rather than theatrical, and after the Colosseum, that absence of display feels almost startling. The space is sacred but restrained, its Romanesque order inviting attention instead of awe. No obvious image marks what you have come seeking. No, there is no plaque that directs you toward Mary Magdalene. But you have come because something happened here, in the basilica sealed beneath the present one, that would alter the story later told about her.

Walking in, your body is immediately oriented toward the far end of the church. Rows of columns line the nave, drawing your eye toward the mosaic glowing in the apse, while underfoot the Cosmatesque floor unfolds in ribbons of geometry. Circles of deep red porphyry and green stone are set within pale marble, linked by interlocking bands of squares and triangles that seem to move with each step. The design carries you forward, at once mathematical and strangely fluid. This language of stone would travel across Rome and far beyond, eventually reaching Westminster Abbey's Coronation Pavement. But here it feels especially alive, pulling your gaze between earth and heaven, floor and apse, movement and stillness.

You follow those patterned bands down the central aisle. As you draw closer, the stone canopy above the altar comes into view. The ciborium does not block the mosaic, exactly, but it interrupts your line of sight. You cannot receive the image head-on. Instead, you must look past its columns, beside them, through them. The frustration is immediate. You want to come close, to stand still and lose yourself in the gold-ground mosaic, to take in all the tiny details catching and scattering light. You consider shifting to the right for a cleaner angle, but the altar area is framed by marble screens and raised platforms that make the space around you more formal and bounded than it first appeared. As your eyes search for a way around, your attention snags on something unexpected: a small anchor fixed to the ciborium.

An anchor. At San Clemente, the symbol belongs to Clement of Rome, the early Roman Christian leader traditionally associated with First Clement, a late first-century letter from the church in Rome to the church at Corinth. Later church tradition folded him into Peter's lineage, naming him among Peter's successors as bishop of Rome, though this belongs more to the construction of apostolic authority than to secure history. The martyrdom came later. Clement was remembered as having been cast into the sea with an anchor tied to him, a legend that helped secure his place in Rome's papal memory centuries after his lifetime.

That distance between record and legend matters, because you realize that symbols rarely derive from the official record alone. The anchor may have been created for the ordinary needs of fishermen and sailors to hold a vessel steady against wind, tide, and drift. But beyond its functional purpose, it belongs to a larger language of water: danger and refuge, exile and arrival, depth and return. It calls up fishing villages and storm-tossed crossings, along with old feminine guardians—from Kwan Yin presiding over coastal villages in Asia to the Marys carried by legend across the Mediterranean.

Even the contested geography around Magdalene's name brushes against this watery world. No longer is "Magdalene" bound to "Magdala," a simple name for a town on the Sea of Galilee sometimes associated with fish and the idea of a tower. Recent scholarship has unsettled that connection, allowing other meanings of her epithet to come forward. Whatever the historical origin of the name, her later legends return to shorelines, boats, nets, and water, especially in southern France. There, in the same region said to have received her rudderless boat, the connection becomes explicit. The Camargue cross gathers anchor, heart, and cross into a single emblem: hope, love, and faith held together by the sea. From here, the marshlands of Camargue stretch along the Provençal coast, as Magdalene's story winds inland toward Sainte-Baume and its cave. Farther west lies Cathar country, whose ruined castles and memories of persecution preserve the sense that other versions of Christianity once endured under the official one, giving rise to a mythic landscape.

The anchor and the tower are different signs, but they belong to the same imaginative family, both forms of steadiness against uncertainty. One holds fast below; the other rises above. One grips the hidden depth; the other keeps watch from shore. Both offer a kind of maternal shelter and the promise of something that will hold when the waters move. Here in Rome, the anchor remains Clement's sign. You know that. And still, you cannot quite leave it there.

It is strange to focus on such a tiny detail, but the anchor does exactly what anchors do. It holds you in place.

You could remain above, mesmerized by the mosaic, its gold flashing differently in the changing light. But the anchor has already shifted your attention downward. You will return, but for now you want to descend, to move through the excavations that make San Clemente unlike anywhere else in Rome. So, you step to the counter, ask for admission, and tap your card on the reader. A small paper ticket is handed back to you, along with a map explaining the deeper layers you are about to navigate. From there, you follow the signs to the stairway, where the brightness of the basilica begins to fall away.

*

In the dim light below, you can make out frescoes from the ninth to eleventh centuries, their surfaces worn and faded. The outline of the original nave remains faintly legible, with aisles discernible underneath remnants of collapse. Above you, the living church carries on, all light, gold, and ritual, while you stand within the earlier church, one of Rome's earliest Christian spaces. But San Clemente was never only an architectural survival. Its gravity was liturgical, devotional, historical, and laced with power.

Old St. Peter's Basilica had already risen across the city in the early fourth century, but San Clemente retained its claim, rooted in Clement's nearness to Rome's apostolic beginnings and in the basilica's role within the city's station liturgy. Even after Rome's ceremonial attention shifted elsewhere, bishops and church leaders continued to return here on select feast days, preserving a memory that outlasted convenience and geography. This is why you came. Buried in the manuscripts of Gregory's Homily 33 is a small notation, *In basilica sancti Clementis*, "in the Basilica of Saint Clement."

The detail is easy to miss. But it places Gregory here, in 591, speaking the sermon that would fuse Mary Magdalene with Luke's unnamed sinful woman and make her a prostitute. From this very church, Gregory spouted the words that would become one of the most successful misidentifications in Christian history. After reading the anointing passage from the Gospel of Luke, Gregory opened his sermon: "When I consider Mary's penitence, I would rather weep than speak. For who, dearest brothers, considering the tears of that sinful woman, would not be softened to the example of penitence, even if he had a heart of stone?"[4]

The absurdity is immediate. Mary has entered the sermon already guilty. Before Gregory explains her, he has reduced her; before he names her, he has made her useful. Why did this woman, honored by some as witness and apostle, have to be remade as a lesson in sin, flesh, and sexual shame?

The answer requires looking beyond theology and into the politics of memory.

Gregory the Great presided over a hollowed-out Rome. The city had been a shell of itself since the fall of the Western Empire; his actual power was constrained, the seat of imperial rule now in Constantinople. Even so, he was constantly negotiating with Lombard invaders, navigating plague, and pushing back against Constantinople's claims to universal Christian jurisdiction. His strategy was humility—he took on the title "servant of the servants of God," doubled down on penitence as the path of salvation, and staked his claim to primacy on the oldest lineage available to him: Peter.

Mary Magdalene, meanwhile, had been narrowed in the West, while being exalted in the East, where women held property and inheritance rights Western women lacked, where empresses wielded real power. There, Mary was apostle to the apostles, a Myrrhbearer, a foundational witness honored in liturgy. When Gregory spoke in 591, it was not just a theological statement; it was a political one, lowering the status of a woman with an apostolic stake in a church whose foundations reached back to the first century. To reduce Magdalene was to subordinate the East—and to confirm that the path to apostolic legitimacy in Rome ran through Peter alone.

Her presence at the empty tomb was not erased but overlaid, rhetorically buried by a tall tale of sin, tears, and a sexual shadow that Western Christianity would carry for centuries. Apostolic witness became penitence. Recognition was redirected toward repentance. Testimony was reread as shame. This is what you have come to stand inside: not simply a ruined basilica, but the place where a memory was altered. And once you understand that the fragments around you begin to speak differently.

Turning through the lower basilica, you notice the images that line the walls before you. One of the most significant frescoes returns to Clement, depicting scenes from the legend surrounding the church's namesake and the saint believed to be buried here. But by now Clement feels less like a person than a structure built around a name, an office, a lineage, a martyrdom, and a symbol. Still, yet the place remains ancient and strangely alive, crowded with beginnings that do not need legend to make them matter. One wall even preserves traces of one of the earliest known examples of written Italian, vernacular speech embedded in paint as formal Latin gave way to something more local, spoken, and embodied. Nearby, another fresco depicts Christ seated among saints, both judge and teacher, part of an apse motif repeated across early Christian basilicas with only minor variation.

If walls could talk, you think, then here they truly are. And then one of them seems to answer, beckoning you toward a Madonna and Child in a rounded niche on the right, along the north aisle. She belongs to a larger decoration uncovered in 1857 through accident and loss. First, another Madonna fresco came to light, fragile and deteriorating, unable to survive exposure. Within days, it collapsed, and behind it this earlier Madonna emerged, as though the wall had finally spoken what it had been keeping.[5]

This Madonna, once concealed, sits enthroned. She wears strings of pearls, and you count five jewels set into her necklace. She is beautiful, almost modern in her immediacy, alive in a way that resists distance. Her eyes stare outward, alert and incisive. Her halo is edged in a dark red, nearly copper. A regal French blue surrounds her, the color so often associated with Mother Mary, though you wonder how much of these hues belong to the original surface. Beyond her beauty, the more pressing question is why was she covered at all.

The ornate headdress she wears is clearly Byzantine, though it remains uncertain when within that era she came to grace these walls. That uncertainty should have made her more arresting to historians and churchmen alike. An enthroned Madonna, possibly among the earliest of her kind in Rome, emerging from behind another image in this charged and layered space, should have demanded attention. But she is barely studied, rarely known and overshadowed by grander discoveries. And so she remains where you find her, potent in her dim light and buried space, commanding enough that even the ban on photography feels less like a rule than a warning.

Perhaps that is why she holds you. Not because she explains herself, but because she refuses to be made small. What this Madonna insists upon is authority: the frontal gaze, the crown, the stillness of command. This is not the softened, domesticated Mary that slowly emerged in later doctrinal imagination, even after she was exalted as Theotokos. This Madonna feels royal, and in this church, where Clement is traced back through a line of "holy" men to Peter and forward to a "great" man like Gregory, whose lies so successfully diminished a woman of apostolic standing in this very space, that royalty is no small thing.

Her lips curve in a restrained, ambiguous smile, with an expression difficult to discern, her interior life withheld. She recalls Theodora, the sixth-century empress and wife of Justinian I, in the unblinking eyes, the strong nose, the jeweled headdress, the bearing of a woman accustomed to command. The resemblance catches at you more than you expect, though at first you can only register it as similarity.

The official account locates her in the mid-eighth century as a Madonna in the style of a queen, called "Maria Regina." The *look* of this iconographic type of Madonna may be imperial, but she is, technically speaking, an image of Mother Mary. Still, there is another theory about the Madonna of San Clemente, even though it is one often discounted as conjecture. Leonard Boyle, a Dominican prior and later Prefect of the Vatican Library, identified this Madonna as Theodora herself and dated her composition much earlier, to the sixth century. What Boyle proposed was remarkable not only because it pushed the image centuries deeper into the past, but because it came from within the ecclesiastical scholarship itself. If he was right, the throne and the infant Christ may have been added later, additions that converted a regent into a religious image.[6]

Once you see the possibility of Theodora, the child becomes difficult to ignore. He does not quite sit in her lap so much as hover there, child-sized but in adult bearing, his presence more imposed than integrated. The image begins to feel less like a mother holding a son than a sovereign figure adapted into a Madonna. Then you begin to wonder whether she is even, technically speaking, a Madonna at all.

And once that question enters your mind, other details begin to slip loose from the official reading. Her right hand is raised, though the damage inflicted by the painting made over her obscures whatever object she may have once held. In the famous mosaic at San Vitale in Ravenna, Theodora holds a jewel-encrusted chalice, the wine of liturgy and a sign of her sacred role in imperial rule. There, the chalice functions as the key attribute of offering, while her headdress, jeweled collar, and hanging strands of pearls secure connection to Byzantine power.

Ravenna. This city had once been the western seat of the Byzantine Empire and long served as an ecclesiastical counterweight to Rome, the very eastern pressure Gregory had spent his life resisting. Decades before the lower basilica was filled in, the archbishop of Ravenna, backed by the emperor against the reigning pope, took the name Clement III and became a rival claimant to the papacy, a name tying him to Clement of Rome, and therefore complicating the meaning of San Clemente itself. Not long after Clement III's death, the lower basilica was deliberately filled in, with no evidence of fire. Whether or not the act was aimed directly at his memory, it sealed away an older, eastern-influenced layer of Rome, one bound to a venerable name and a rival lineage. Perhaps this is the power the Madonna, or Empress, of San Clemente represents: not a quiet devotional image, but a rival vision of sovereignty staring back from the wall.

And another question presses forward. If Boyle is right about the earlier dating, if this fresco was already here in 591, did her eyes look out from these walls as Gregory spoke? Did this Empress witness what was happening to the Mary Magdalene? Was the Roman sun still hot inside these walls, settling into the church as heat once settled into the arena of the Coliseum, while his words found their target? The thought pulls you because the parallels are difficult to ignore. Magdalene's witness would be overlaid, buried beneath repentance and sexual shame just as this Empress had been covered over, altered, hidden behind another before emerging again centuries later.

Held against the memory of Gregory's homily on Magdalene, the image seems to carry its own quiet argument. She stages a tension between two models of womanhood: one enthroned and glorified, the other recast through shame and repentance. The contrast makes you want to look deeper for Magdalene in Rome, because in this city the earlier layer is never fully lost, only covered, waiting to be found again.

So you move along another passageway, toward the first-century staircase marked on the map. Before you reach it, the sign returns: another anchor, this time worked into the iron gate. Technically speaking yet again, this is Clement's mark. But after the Empress, Clement no longer feels fixed either. Around him, as around Magdalene and perhaps even Theodora, memory seems to harden around what power needed most. A church leader becomes a pope. An Empress becomes a Madonna. An apostle becomes a prostitute. The anchor remains, but you cannot see any symbol of steadiness here without thinking of the woman Gregory's words tried to unmoor, or of the stories that fasten one version of a person in place and let the others drift.

Magdalene does not move through official channels because the church has not made room for her. She has arrived by another route, through symbols that catch and follow you, through what returns, through what is felt but not named. Her absence is not neutral. It is the aftermath of a story imposed on her, one that obscured witness with shame and then gave that distortion the name of tradition.

*

Deeper still, the air dampens as you descend steps from the world Mary herself would have known, the dimness closing around you. Your fingers trace soft Roman brickwork and dark mortar as water murmurs below, the subterranean stream still visible beneath the layers of the city. Here the ground shifts again as sparse light falls across thick masonry, weathered walls, and truncated rooms, remnants of a Roman building complex the official site of Basilica di San Clemente describes as a *domus* later adapted over time.

As you continue, a five-petaled flower appears faintly in the stonework. Around it, the ceiling drops and the chamber tightens into something almost cave-like. Beyond a gate lies a small enclosed room where benches still line the walls around a stone altar carved with the image of a man astride a bull. That figure is Mithras and this is a private, ancient temple called a Mithraeum.

Mithraism was a male-only mystery cult associated with the god Mithras, a figure likely connected in some way to the older Persian Mithra. Secretive and initiatory, the Roman cult spread widely in the first centuries, especially among soldiers. It emerged alongside early Christianity rather than before it, and some of their symbols and rituals feel strikingly familiar now: sacred meals shared among initiates, sacramental imagery of blood and wine, ritual hierarchies, and symbolic passage through death toward rebirth.

Perhaps these overlaps simply reflect the wider mythic landscape both traditions emerged from, or perhaps there is more to their convergence. In this moment, you resist collapsing one tradition into the other. The deeper you move into Rome, the less history behaves in clean lines, and San Clemente makes this tangibly apparent. As with Mary, as with the Empress above, the movement of history doesn't simply erase. It covers and revises, until a wall crumbles and the older face looks out again.

Standing in the dimness, with water moving somewhere through the stone, you feel the distance of that buried world almost physically: close below the surface, alive in shadow and mortar.

At the far end of the chamber, the floor slopes toward a metal grate set into the stone. A green light rises from below, dim and steady. There, the water gathers into sound and movement, rushing through a well-like opening hidden beneath city, church, basilica, and temple; persistent and unseen. This is the lowest point you can reach. Stone above. Water below. Everything else—centuries of worship and empire—pressed between.

Archaeologists believe this lower level may have been part of the imperial mint—the Moneta—an identification drawn in part from a fragment of the Severan marble plan. The water you hear offers an important clue. Metalworking required water at nearly every stage: to cool heated tools, quench metal, wash surfaces, carry away debris, and sustain the labor of workshops where fire met stone and metal rang against metal. The surrounding street patterns and industrial infrastructure support this interpretation as well. Even though no mint stamp has been found within the chambers themselves, the spatial logic remains persuasive.

If metal was worked here, authority may have passed through this place in its most portable form: coin. Struck, counted, and circulated, power was pressed into small, durable objects and sent out into the world. Before the faces of living rulers appeared on Roman coinage, divine figures dominated its imagery. From the beginning, coins bore goddesses and female personifications of prosperity, safety, victory, peace, freedom, and health, including Roma, Victoria, Fortuna, Pax, Venus, Libertas, and Salus among many others. Through their faces, coins carried the promises Rome made about itself, stamped into matter and passed from hand to hand.

At the grate, the thought becomes physical. You stand longer than you expect. Raw metal could become currency, and matter could become meaning, whether struck into coin or brushed into paint. A level above, the chipped, still half-hidden visage of the Madonna and Child bears the marks of revision and return.

What began as presence was gradually fixed, framed, and redistributed. Feminine power was not erased. It was recast in image, becoming beautiful, sexual, sorrowful, obedient, and containable; remembered less as leadership or sovereignty than as symbol. Yet she remains the source, like the water moving in the well you now stand before.

Your hand goes to your pocket almost without thought. A coin rests there, suddenly heavier than it should be. This is not a place where visitors throw coins into water, offering something small to the unseen below, yet you begin to understand the ancient impulse to surrender something of value in exchange for protection, blessing, or return. The coin stays in your pocket. But the intention does not.

If there is a prayer here, it is not for exchange. It is quieter and more difficult: that what was edited, corrected, and controlled might be remembered again.

You stay a moment longer, feeling the damp air, the sound at your feet, the weight of what remains overhead. Then you turn back.

*

The ascent is slower. Your body adjusts as the air warms, light returns in stages, and the sound of water recedes into memory. You pass back through stone and brick, through one threshold after another, until you emerge once more into the eleventh-century basilica. The space opens suddenly, almost too bright for your eyes now, its order briefly disorienting after the dark below. Only now do you realize that you have been carrying something unfinished. When you first entered, the mosaic had registered only in pieces: a blaze above the altar, curving high above the ciborium, too vast to take in before the anchor drew your attention elsewhere and descent pulled you below. You had promised yourself you would return.

This time, you take the side path toward it. The approach is indirect, almost awkward, as though the church still refuses to give the image all at once. But slowly the angle clears, and the mosaic comes into view, vast and gold-lit, almost impossibly alive. Christ hangs upon the cross, appearing strangely untouched by suffering, the crucifix transformed into the Tree of Life. Golden vines unfurl outward in spirals and tendrils carrying birds, animals, and human figures into branching abundance. White doves rest along the arms of the dark blue cross. Peacocks stand at the edges. The whole scene seems less made of stone and glass than of light briefly held in place.

The imagery belongs to a far older symbolic language where sacred trees stood as signs of fertility, wisdom, divine presence, and the axis between worlds. Echoes remain even within the Hebrew Bible, from Eden's Tree of Life to the condemned sacred poles of Asherah. Created in the twelfth century, as Kabbalistic symbolism was beginning to crystallize in southern Europe, the mosaic evokes a cosmic order later mapped through the ten Sephirot and the twenty-two paths of the Hebrew alphabet. Placed meticulously beside one another, thousands of tiny *tesserae* suggest a universe woven together through language, number, spirit, and creation, a living pattern branching endlessly between earth and heaven.

Your eye drops to the pastoral band of sheep below. One stands centered with a halo, twelve flanking him, six on either side. Your gaze descends again, past marble moldings and the ciborium, to a vast fresco stretching across the lower portion of the wall. You cannot see it all at once. Between the scale of the painting and the rope barriers controlling movement through the nave, the image can only be taken in fragments, forcing you to shift your body to follow the scene across the stone until the fresco slowly comes into view.

Below, mirroring the band of sheep above, a fresco repeats the same cadence: Christ standing at the center with the disciples on either side. They are not sheep now, but human figures, set against a dark indigo background above green grass dotted with white flowers. Each figure is robed in the restrained Byzantine style. These lower frescoes date from the ninth to eleventh centuries, meaning they had already been here for generations before the great mosaic above them was brought to life.

You observe the details surrounding the figure of Jesus. His hands are open: one raised in blessing, the other holding an open book. You strain to read the words across its pages until a phrase comes into focus: PACE MEA DO VOBIS. A quick search gives you the translation: "My peace I give you." Then recognition arrives. This line is from the Fourth Gospel's Last Supper, where Jesus tells his disciples, "Peace I leave with you; my peace I give you."[7]

The tenderness of these lines brings your eye back up to the mosaic crucifix, where a clearly male Beloved Disciple, stands just to the right of Jesus, with Mother Mary on his left. Then your gaze drops back down to the disciples in this fresco. The male figure on the right holds a scroll, so you scan his body for other icons to identify him. Perhaps it's the simplicity of the design that draws your attention downward. His feet are marked only by thin brown straps, almost like modern flip-flops. You look to Christ to see if the same detail appears there, but his feet are bare. Then your eye moves to the figure on his left. Shoes. Red ones. A quick look confirms it: among all the figures in the band, this is the only one whose feet are shod.

She is a woman. The rose-colored *maphorion* frames her face and falls close around her shoulders, making the identification certain. A halo graces her head. Her elongated eyes turn to Christ while still reaching outward to the viewer. Robed in red over blue, her entire body leans in his direction, arms lifted, hands rising in formal intercession. She does not lower her gaze in submission. She participates.

While the sandaled man on the other side of Christ folds his arms inward, hers extend remarkably close to Christ, nearly touching his arm. The space, or lack thereof, between the figures feels deliberate. Christ and the woman appear caught in exchange rather than hierarchy, joined within the visual logic of the scene. And still your eye returns to the shoes. Their redness feels too deliberate to ignore.

You know that red is associated with Mary Magdalene, the woman whose name was bound to sexual sin on this very ground fourteen centuries ago, the woman who anointed the feet of Jesus, in two Gospels. Feet, not the head. Love, not rulership. But you are in Rome, of course, where there is an established relationship between red shoes and the pope.

Since late antiquity, red footwear signaled imperial authority; emperors wore red or purple shoes. Popes later adopted the color to claim continuity with Roman sovereignty, martyrdom, jurisdiction, and the line of Peter. Immediately after his election in 2013, Pope Francis departed from the modern tradition of red papal shoes, choosing simple black shoes instead, a gesture that revealed how much symbolic weight the tradition still carried. But in the era that this fresco may have been painted, red shoes were not decorative. They belonged to the visual language through which Rome dressed power as succession. Which makes their placement here difficult to dismiss. Why would a woman be given the shoes of authority?

But succession can mean more than office. In Christian imagination, shoes also mark calling and proclamation. In the Letter to the Ephesians, the writer speaks of being "fitted with the readiness that comes from the gospel of peace."[8] You wonder: what if the shoes on this woman point to precisely that? Readiness. She is prepared to proclaim what she has heard and seen, the peace she has received, the love she has witnessed, the presence she believed before anyone else.

Red shoes. You know them from somewhere else, too. In *Women Who Run with the Wolves*, Clarissa Pinkola Estés calls up an old tale about a girl consumed by her desire for beautiful red shoes. They speak to vitality, desire, danger, *eros*, freedom, and the risk of losing oneself within systems that distort feminine power into spectacle or submission. Ultimately, in Estés' reading, the red shoes are what directs and animates the soul.[9]

As distant as all these stories might seem from one another, their connections no longer feel abstract as you stand and gaze at this unmarked, unnamed woman. She is among disciples. Only she wears red shoes. None of the male disciples do. The shoes begin to feel declarative. You know by now that in Christian iconography a woman like this would be interpreted as Mother Mary, or even a symbol of the "Church," but you cannot shake the red shoes.

The associations begin to lock into place: Roman authority, Christian proclamation, feminine life-force, Magdalene at the feet of Jesus, Magdalene sent from the tomb. The pattern feels almost too perfect. If shoes imply a readiness to carry a message, if red is the signature of feminine life force, if red shoes speak to the reorientation of the self into alignment with the soul . . . then, at least for you, this woman resonates with Magdalene.

Perhaps you simply have begun to see her everywhere. Or maybe your eyes have been trained by this place to notice female authority where it is not, technically speaking, supposed to appear. The walls here no longer seem content to whisper. They keep returning to the same truth in different guises: female authority has not vanished simply because official memory learned how to rename it. After all, this is a church tied to one of Rome's first supposed "popes," built above a lower basilica that may have remembered the image of a Byzantine empress, and marked by medieval arguments over apostolic authority in the long aftermath of the Great Schism.

Now you move back toward the entrance and pause at the shelves near the ticket desk. Because photographs are not permitted throughout the excavations, you look for something you can carry with you. You choose a postcard reproduction of the crowned Madonna—or Empress—who held you below. Then you begin flipping through guides to San Clemente. There are books on the excavations, the apse mosaic, Clement, and the buried layers beneath the church. One slim volume devoted to the Chapel of Saint Catherine of Alexandria catches your eye. On its cover, a woman in red clings to the foot of the cross. You recognize her immediately: Mary Magdalene, shown in the scene where three of the four Gospels place her by name as a witness to Jesus' death.

But the image you most want is not there. You want to find an account of the procession of apostles beneath the apse, to see what has been written about the woman in red shoes, the interruption in the pattern. You flip through pages, looking for some trace of her: a labeled detail, a reproduced image, some explanation of the figure that pulled your attention away from everything else. Nothing. In fact, in every reproduced view of the apse, the ciborium obscures the detail itself. The woman remains visible, but the red shoes disappear.

You buy the postcard, the Saint Catherine book, and a general guide, still hoping some detail might be hidden inside. But the image that seized you is not documented. You return for proof, or at least some way to keep what your eyes have discovered. Past the columns and the ciborium, you lift your phone, searching for the red shoes through the awkward side view. The picture is imperfect, but enough.

*

Photograph taken, you lower your phone. The red shoes are there now, held inside the frame at last. You have what you have come back for, or so it seems. With the books still in your hand, you turn toward the entrance and begin crossing the nave. But the cover of the Saint Catherine volume rises again in your mind: the woman in red at the foot of the cross, the only Magdalene named anywhere in the material you have just been flipping through. Just to the right, across from the center of the church, the chapel waits. It becomes your last stop before leaving. You already know whom you are going to see. What you do not expect is how much more powerful she will be beyond the cover, waiting in paint and plaster.

Mary Magdalene is at the foot of the cross, gripping it with both hands. Frescoed by Masolino da Panicale, she is vivid, clinging, robed in flowing crimson, her hair alive with movement. Nothing in her is still. Fabric pulls forward. Her whole body reaches for Christ. Even sorrow appears unable to remain contained. She gathers fervor, devotion, grief, courage, and love into one urgent form. She answers the red-shoed figure beneath the apse: red at the feet, red at the cross, nearness to Christ, witness made flesh. Movement is not power or status. It is love refusing to step away. Power, passion, action, and love converge in a single color: red.

Around Masolino's Magdalene, Saint Catherine's story unfolds in brilliant jewel tones—purple, pink, yellow, teal. Scene by scene, the virgin martyr is brought vividly to life. But who was Saint Catherine? You glance down at the book in your hands, curious whether she was a historical woman or more of a legendary figure, like Saint Barbara.

Catherine is said to have lived in fourth-century Alexandria, an aristocratic Christian convert who bested pagan philosophers in debate before being condemned to the spiked wheel. Flipping through the pages while continuing to glance at the frescoes of her life, you discover that Catherine belongs to that realm in between.

In the frescoes, Catherine appears through a Renaissance lens. Blonde-haired, delicate-fingered, golden-haloed, she teaches men dressed in black. Across the way, in another scene painted in periwinkle, burgundy, and gold, she gestures upward toward a statue, instructing those gathered before her. Above, the ceiling echoes the coffering of another nearby Roman monument: the Pantheon.

As you try to make sense of the layering of history and legend, your eyes are drawn again to this painted architecture, so evocative of the dome of the Pantheon. Built by Marcus Agrippa and later rebuilt by Emperor Hadrian, the Pantheon was not dedicated to one god alone, but to the divine cosmos. Tradition places Catherine of Alexandria in the late third and early fourth centuries, at least according to the book in your hands, during the volatile period before Constantine the Great transformed Christianity's status within the Roman Empire.

A widely held theory is that Catherine's life, her high education, her illustrious teaching position, and her tragic end were all modeled, at least in part, upon another woman of late antiquity: Hypatia. She was an Alexandrian noblewoman, mathematician, and philosopher. Renowned in her own time for her wisdom, Hypatia's qualities of intelligence, eloquence, and spiritual authority appear to have been transposed onto Catherine. The story of a "pagan" woman killed by Christians was inverted into the story of a Christian woman murdered by pagans.

And while Renaissance artists often chose architectural settings simply for their elegance, geometry, and grandeur, the environment becomes more charged now. In Catherine's lifetime, the Pantheon was still a "pagan" sanctuary and would not be consecrated as a church for roughly another three hundred years. To see a Christian virgin martyr painted inside that space creates a strange dissonance when her story was borrowed from a pagan woman killed by Christians. The inversion is almost too neat: one woman absorbed into a narrative of piety, the other discarded.

You're standing in the same church where Magdalene's story was changed. Her narrative was inverted: from a woman bearing the good news, commissioned by Jesus, possibly even the Beloved Disciple, into a penitent prostitute. And suddenly Magdalene does not seem alone. She stands in the company of other women whose stories have been rewritten, absorbed, corrected, or made useful to the traditions that inherited them. Catherine. Hypatia. The Empress. Women remembered, but not always as they were.

You could collapse into fatigue, into disillusionment—and you do feel the strain of it. You are moved, but not in the way you expected. You thought you might feel anger in a place where she had been defamed. Instead, your shoulders drop. You stand taller. With them. With *all* of them.

Remembrance is present in San Clemente, but so is reclamation. The red shoes have led you to this revelation: from the hidden woman beside Christ to the named Magdalene at the cross. *It is love refusing to step away.*

Chapter 10

OF PINECONES AND PEACOCKS

With ears pricked forward, her gaze reaches beyond the frame, alert to something unseen. Her arched brows and unblinking eyes hold an expression that resists naming. She is watchful, tender, almost incredulous. Her mouth parts slightly, as if you might hear her panting breath. Cast in bronze, her body stretches into a wide, grounded stance, faint ribs visible as her flanks pull taut around teats heavy with milk. This is the mother of Rome, the *Lupa Capitolina*, her weathered golden form poised above two infants who kneel beneath her, reaching upward to nurse.

For centuries, the wolf was thought to be Etruscan, cast in the fifth century BCE. But tests done in the early 2000s suggest the bronze may instead belong to the eleventh or twelfth century. The twins were later additions, widely attributed to Antonio del Pollaiuolo around 1471.[1] However, their story reaches back toward Rome's beginnings.

Romulus and Remus, the sons of Mars and the Vestal priestess Rhea Silvia, were abandoned in a wooden basket and set afloat on the Tiber River, in the city's legendary founding age of 753 BCE. A she-wolf became their first adoptive mother, nursing and guarding them in the wild near a cave, until they were taken in by a shepherd and his wife. As the first guardian of Rome's founders, the wolf still keeps watch on Capitoline Hill, one of the seven hills on which the Eternal City was built.

The Eternal City rose upon seven hills, little more than ridges above the marshy bends of the Tiber. Over generations, its slopes and valleys were shaped by human hands, stone by stone, as moved through the low ground, homes clustered around busy marketplaces and public squares. The heights of the hilltops, closest to the heavens and the gods, remained reserved for what was sacred. One offering became many. Shrines formed and eventually gave way to the more formal designs of temples. Jupiter and Mars were honored, but so were presences even older than them—the perpetual fire of Vesta, the watch of Juno, the groves of Diana.

Each of the seven held its own story. Palatine Hill, where the mythic twins were said to have been born, was once home to a temple of the goddess Cybele, known as Magna Mater. On the Aventine stood the temple of Diana, the Roman Artemis, she of the moon, the forest, the hunt, and childbirth. Capitoline Hill, where the she-wolf still stands, hosted the great Temple of Jupiter Optimus Maximus, the supreme male deity of the Roman state. Yet it also honored Juno Moneta, guardian of the city and patron of women. Moneta became the origin of the word "money," for the first Roman mint was attached to her sanctuary. Another shrine to Juno, associated with the protection of childbirth, stood on Viminal Hill.

Almost nothing remains of these feminine sanctuaries today, but their memory serves as a reminder that the protective mother wolf was not an isolated image. She belongs to an ancient world where the goddess functioned as source and safeguard, as she was birth, vitality, and continuation. One particularly beloved Roman goddess was Salus, whose Latin name shares its root with the English "salvation." To the Romans, *salus* meant wholeness—protection, health, safety, and collective flourishing.

The Temple of Salus was dedicated in 302 BCE on Quirinal Hill. For centuries, Romans approached her sanctuary through prayer and ritual practice. A devotee might first wash to purify before ascending the slope carrying a small offering of incense, wine, grain, honey cakes, or flowers. At the altar, prayers were spoken simply, ones for relief from illness, protection from plague, or the safe delivery of a child. Offerings would be burned or left behind, often alongside a vow to return in gratitude if the request were answered. Over time, these promises accumulated: inscriptions and small votive gifts, tokens of hope reflecting the sacrality of survival.

In moments of uncertainty, Salus's presence extended beyond her hilltop sanctuary. As protectress of the state's fragile well-being, she was the figure citizens, senators, and emperors all reached for. Her image appeared on Roman coinage from the Republic through the late Empire, circulating as continuity stamped into form, reassurance carried and exchanged. Delicate silver or heavier copper alloy, the coins remembered her with a curved nose and composed profile. Sometimes she held a scepter. Other times a snake emerged beside her, often rising toward a bowl, or *patera*, in her hand. The icon of snake and bowl blended Salus with Greek Hygeia, daughter of Asclepius, each a figure where female and serpent meet in the alchemy of healing.

The sanctuary of Salus on the Quirinal Hill was the site of the annual Augurium Salutis, a public festival of prayers and offerings made for the safety of the city and its people. The surviving *fasti*, Rome's ancient religious calendars, preserve its date as the same one associated with the founding of Salus's temple: August 5. This date is still remembered in Rome, but as a miraculous day for another woman and another sanctuary. Tradition holds that on the eve of August 5, a wealthy childless couple prayed to the Virgin, asking how they should use their fortune in her honor, and they were answered by her in a dream. She told each of them to build a church wherever snow fell that night—snow in an Italian summer was, of course, preposterous. Astoundingly, Liberius, then bishop of Rome, received the very same message the very same night. Impossible snow, the legend says, fell on Esquiline Hill, a hill that had been home since 375 BCE to a Temple of Juno Lucina, a goddess of light and protector of women in childbirth. Exact footprints are disputed, and this sanctuary to the feminine had likely fallen into disrepair after the temples had been legally closed, the old rites made illegal. Within that altered sacred landscape a monumental basilica began to take form: Santa Maria Maggiore, which has stood now for almost 1,600 years.

Construction began less than a year after Mary was proclaimed Theotokos at the Council of Ephesus. The next bishop of Rome, Sixtus III, raised the basilica and completed it by 440. As the first great Marian church in the West, Santa Maria Maggiore was a monumental answer in stone and mosaic to the doctrine the Council had just settled. A gilded coffered ceiling shimmers overhead, said to contain some of the first gold brought from the Americas. Fifth-century mosaics line the nave and triumphal arch, glinting in filtered light, their surfaces alive with gold and glass. Beneath them stretches a Cosmatesque floor of inlaid marble, porphyry, serpentine, and colored stone.

In one of the city's grandest and most enduring sacred spaces, devotion converges not around a male apostle, martyr, or bishop, but around a woman.

Within its walls rests one of the most revered Marian icons in Christian Rome: Salus Populi Romani, "Protectress of the Roman People." Traditionally dated between the fifth and eighth centuries, though more recent technical analysis has suggested later elements within the panel, the image presents Mary in a deep midnight-blue mantle, her gaze steady and forward, watchful in its stillness.[2] Her posture is upright and formal but embodies an easy grounded grace that extends a maternal sense of shelter. She holds the Christ child, rendered in warm copper ochre, securely within her arms. The gilt backdrop and subtle halo catch the light behind her; she appears luminous, ancient.

Like the coins bearing Salus's image, this Marian icon functioned not only as a symbol, but as a living presence invoked for protection. In 590, as plague swept through Rome, Gregory the Great ordered a Marian icon—later associated with Salus Populi Romani—to be carried through the streets in solemn procession. Amid clouds of frankincense and myrrh, and the low rhythm of chanted hymns, the Madonna passed through the plague-stricken, an image of maternal resilience moving amongst the suffering. More than a millennium later, Pope Francis repeatedly came to pray before Salus Populi Romani, making a small pilgrimage across the city before journeys abroad, and upon return. His papal tomb lies not in St. Peter's Basilica, but, as requested, close to her.

No explanation is necessary for continuity so plainly visible. Her name had changed, her theology had shifted, but her role was the same. What once belonged to Salus now rests with Mary. But from Mary to Salus to the goddesses before, what can be glimpsed is the broader truth—not only was the feminine a central presence in the spiritual imagination, but her heritage is still present in Christianity even if unacknowledged. What the lasting power of Salus, Mary, and Magdalene insists is that the official story of early Christianity is far more complicated than how it has been told. Its progression resembles less a single straight line running cleanly from Peter through structures of male authority, than a feminine curve—one that loops and spirals, disappearing beneath the surface and returning again.

Defying gravity, what is ancient becomes future when the memory of a woman who lived two thousand years ago arrives bearing answers to questions long surrendered to the unknowable. Defying gravity, what is ancient becomes future when the memory of a woman who lived two thousand years ago arrives bearing answers to questions long surrendered to the unknowable. History itself records that Mary Magdalene has been inextricable from the sacred feminine as far back as the second century, and very likely extending into her own lifetime, through her own words, what she taught, felt, and believed. For all that has been lost, what remains is the truth that Christianity did not rise in isolation, nor did it develop solely through a Jewish world. In the earliest centuries of the first millennium, life in the Mediterranean was rich with goddesses, priestesses, gods, priests, pantheons, incense, offerings, prayers, incantations, and amulets—sacred ways of believing, seeing, and knowing that had existed for centuries, each unique to its land and culture. The feminine was present and alive in this world from which Christianity emerged, and Mary Magdalene would have been legible as a leader, a teacher, and an embodiment of the feminine principle in ways little imagined or understood in a modern culture shaped by a predominantly masculine monotheistic paradigm for at least seventeen hundred years.

Mary Magdalene was not simply a flashpoint in Christianity arising from the prominence of Christian women leading, teaching, and baptizing—she was a fault line because of the prominence of women in sacred life and the feminine in the divine as a whole. In the very same period that Christianity was developing, the worship of Isis was expanding across the empire, her image and stories a source of maternal strength and comfort to sailors, women, slaves, and nobles too. What Isis and Magdalene hold in common is not some esoteric conflation, but a real historical parallel of feminine sovereignty rising in the first and second centuries, ones so powerful and prominent in daily life their authority was a clear and obvious threat to a new religion seeking to gather new believers, and the economy of that belief. It was not as simple as Gnostics, who followed an inner path, against the proto-orthodox leaders who desired mediation through hierarchy—though that dynamic was significant. What led to the diminishment of Mary Magdalene, and the feminine, was wider, greater, and even more profound than that—and it was carried out through not just laws, decrees and creeds but through the power of storytelling, the twisting of words, the omissions of excluding texts, and the control of a narrative that still grips Christianity and Western culture to this day.

A NASCENT RELIGION

The rise of the movement around Jesus in the first century has long been presented by the Church as a unified story, coherent from the beginning. The surviving historical record points instead to an organic development across communities, shaped by competing memories, interpretations, beliefs, and leadership. Even the earliest sources offer little agreement about what occurred in the decades following Jesus's death and how a grassroots movement became organized.

Within the New Testament, Acts of the Apostles offers the clearest vision. Tradition attributes the text to the author of the Gospel of Luke, a connection first recorded by Irenaeus of Lyon.[3] Acts was not unique in its time but belonged to a wider literary tradition of apostolic "Acts." These were stories in which figures like Peter, Paul, and Thomas preached, performed miracles, confronted rivals, gathered followers, and met dramatic deaths. Scholars now date Acts later than tradition had claimed, placing its composition at the end of the first century or into the second. Rather than a factual chronicle of apostolic history, Acts appears to be a theological narrative shaped to form doctrine and unify early Christian communities. Mary Magdalene is not mentioned in Acts at all. By contrast, Acts privileges the male apostolic leaders, Peter and Paul.

A very different picture is given by the letters of Paul the Apostle, generally dated to the 50s CE. Earlier, less polished, and far less resolved than Acts, the Pauline letters reflect communities struggling to define themselves in real time. What feels most authentic about Paul's letters is the conflict they preserve: disputes with Peter, arguments over Jewish law, tensions surrounding Gentiles, rivalries over leadership, divisions within communities, and ongoing negotiations over theology. Curiously, Paul's letters quote none of Jesus's parables, recount almost none of his miracles, and give no indication that he knew the Gospel traditions in written form. Outside of Paul's letters and the later Acts of the Apostles, there are no clear first-century references to Paul.

Only seven Pauline letters are now widely regarded as first-century, while several others are believed to have been composed, or finalized, in the second century. But by that era, Paul's writings appear to have become central to Christian debate. This was largely due to Marcion of Sinope, a wealthy shipowner from Asia Minor who came to Rome in the 140s and became one of the most influential and most controversial Christian thinkers of the second century. Marcion taught that the God revealed by Jesus was distinct from the God of the Hebrew scriptures, and on that basis, he excluded them altogether. What he assembled in its place may have been the first Christian canon: ten Pauline letters and a Gospel resembling Luke. But Marcion was condemned as a heretic. Nearly everything known about him survives through hostile Church Fathers, since all of his own writings disappeared.[4]

Though still outside the mainstream, some scholars, including David Trobisch and Markus Vinzent, argue that Marcion's canon may have preceded the canonical Gospels, at least in their later forms. Others pushed further still. The nineteenth-century Dutch Radical School denied the authenticity of the canonical Pauline letters altogether. More recently, Nina Livesey has argued that the Pauline letters were not authentic first-century correspondence, but pseudonymous literary compositions that likely emerged in the mid-second century, in or near the Roman school of Marcion.[5]

Outside the New Testament, the record for early Christianity is remarkably sparse. One of the few major witnesses is Flavius Josephus. In one brief passage, Josephus mentions "James, the brother of Jesus who was called Christ," placing Jesus's followers within the volatile world of first-century Jerusalem. Another passage, known as the *Testimonium Flavianum*, describes Jesus more directly, though most scholars believe the text was at least partially reworked in Christian transmission. Even so, Josephus offers a compelling glimpse into the diversity of first-century Judaism, a picture later deepened by the Dead Sea Scrolls, whose texts preserve evidence of multiple Jewish sects, interpretive traditions, and scriptural debates.[6]

That same diversity would characterize early Christianity, described as a "riot of pluralism" by Cynthia Bourgeault in *The Meaning of Mary*

Magdalene.[7] Deserts, ruins, jars, monasteries, marketplaces, and forgotten collections all reveal buried voices. In earlier centuries, these writings might never have reached the public at all, disappearing instead into locked archives or lists of forbidden books. But they resurfaced in a modern world able to circulate them rapidly through universities, publishers, translations, bookstores, and eventually the internet, revealing a far stranger and more contested landscape than many had imagined.

Reading the archaeological traces, scattered manuscripts, and fragments that survive, nascent Christianity appears to have spread first through people rather than institutions, moving through conversation, memory, oral tradition, shared meals, and teachings carried from household to household and city to city. Missionaries and evangelists proclaimed the message, but so too did merchants, sailors, artisans, migrants, and families moving along the trade routes of the Mediterranean world. What made Christianity distinctive was its increasingly universal vision of salvation, one that crossed ethnicity, geography, and rank in ways that were revolutionary for the ancient world.

Its earliest form, however, was intimate and domestic. Early Christian assemblies, *ekklēsiai kat' oikon*, met in adapted houses where meals, prayer, ritual, teaching, and debate unfolded. Stories were repeated, letters copied and read aloud, teachings revised and passed onward. In this environment, influence flowed not only to those claiming spiritual authority, but to those with charisma, persuasion, education, social standing, and the power to shape how the story was told. And because Christianity first moved through the intimate spaces of ordinary life, women naturally became central to the formation and transmission of the growing religion.

THE FIRST WOMEN

Beyond Mother Mary and Mary Magdalene, the Gospels are crowded with women: Mary and Martha, Joanna, Susanna, Salome, Elizabeth, Anna the prophet, the Samaritan woman, the woman with the issue of blood, the Syrophoenician woman, the widow of Nain, the women at the cross, the women at the tomb, and the unnamed woman who anoints Jesus, of course. From its earliest moments, the Jesus movement was populated by women, but their names and identities would be pushed aside by a tradition interpreted and codified almost entirely by men.

For centuries the silence held, with women absent until they gained the intellectual freedom to reopen the record themselves. Elizabeth Cady Stanton's *The Woman's Bible*, published between 1895 and 1898, was one of the first major attempts to reread scripture through a female lens. In the generations that followed, female scholars brought renewed attention to women's prominence, focusing on the textual and historical processes through which women had been diminished, obscured, or edited out altogether.

The undisputed letters of Paul preserve vivid glimpses of women as leaders, patrons, and teachers in first-century Christian assemblies. Paul names Phoebe as a *diakonos*, greets Prisca as a teacher alongside Aquila, and identifies Junia among the apostles. He praises the labor of Mary, Tryphaena, Tryphosa, Euodia, Syntyche, and others who worked beside him in the movement. Brief as these references are, they demonstrate that women were integral in leadership and expansion.[8]

Even second-century critics of Christianity remember women moving through positions of authority. Writing to Emperor Trajan, Pliny the Younger described Christian gatherings that included women serving as *ministrae*. Celsus referred to female-led Christian movements naming Helen, Marcellina, Salome, Martha, and Mariamne. This is the same Celsus who mocked Mary Magdalene's resurrection encounter.[9]

As Christianity spread, women continued to appear in positions of spiritual authority across its literature. In the Acts of Paul and Thecla, considered a legendary text, Paul is accompanied by a young and courageous teaching companion, Thecla. As they travel, she baptizes followers, preaches publicly, and ultimately survives repeated attempts on her life. She even miraculously escapes the lions of the arena. In the Acts of Philip, Mariamne—identified by François Bovon as a literary heir of Mary Magdalene—travels alongside Philip performing healings and acting openly as an apostolic figure. Later accounts such as the Life of Saint Nino credit a woman with converting an entire region. Meanwhile, Marian traditions increasingly elevated Mother Mary into a teacher, visionary, intercessor, protector, and queenly presence among the apostles.[10]

Bishop Epiphanius of Salamis complained that certain groups ordained women as bishops, while funerary inscriptions near Rome refer to women as *episcopa*. Research by Ally Kateusz traces that female leadership through literature and art, revealing women depicted holding censers, standing at altars, processing publicly, and occupying central devotional space. The exact meaning of these titles and images remains debated, but together the evidence shows that women held visible leadership roles even as institutional pressures against them intensified.[11]

Among the "heretical" Christians, the pattern of female authority was even clearer, more pronounced, and irritating to Church leadership. Even through an incomplete record, women's names persist: Marcellina led a Christian school in Rome; Prisca and Maximilla prophesied publicly alongside Montanus; and Quintilla gave her name to an entire prophetic movement. The communities of Valentinus and Marcion of Sinope were said to have granted women unusually visible roles.[12]

The Gospel of Mary is widely acknowledged by scholars to epitomize this struggle over female power. Composed during the second century, just when these gendered conflicts intensified, the text vanished for centuries. Strangely, it was never directly addressed in the writings of the Church Fathers—maybe its vision was too dangerous to confront. The surviving text features Mary Magdalene rising among the gathered disciples, her voice carrying hope through their uncertainty and despair. Of all those present, Peter is the one to ask Mary to share previously unknown teachings. His words reflect that he recognizes her wisdom and that Jesus *loved* her. What follows is a radically interior spirituality rooted in revelation, vision, and transformation.[13]

In texts like Dialogue of the Savior, Pistis Sophia, and the Gospel of Philip, Mary Magdalene, Mother Mary, and other women speak, interpret, question, and teach. Persistently, women appear not at the edges of spiritual life, but near its center, receiving and transmitting sacred knowledge. More extraordinary still, within these traditions the feminine was expressed through the language of divinity itself: the Holy Spirit appears in maternal form, divine Wisdom descends as the revealer Sophia, heavenly pairings and feminine emanations are woven into the structure of creation.

Once the frame widens to include the plurality of the Christian world in the first and second centuries, the identification of Mary Magdalene with the Beloved Disciple no longer appears far-fetched, but deeply coherent. Her prominence, and the later effort to diminish and contain it, suddenly make historical sense. Reducing Mary Magdalene served the effort to narrow the memory of women within the early Jesus movement. Yet the anxiety behind her diminishment likely extended beyond women's presence in Christian circles. During this formative period, across the empire, female sacred authority still commanded devotion, influence, and wealth.

A FEMININE INHERITANCE

Christian history is often filtered first through Jewish history, and for good reason, but Judea was not sealed off from the world around it. By the first century, the Diaspora stretched into Alexandria and across the Mediterranean. Through empire, Judea, Galilee, Samaria, Syria, Egypt, Ephesus, Greece, and Rome were bound together. Roads, ports, trade routes, the movement of armies and pilgrims, and the exchange of goods carried ideas, stories, rituals, and even deities.

Female divinity remained visible everywhere in the first and second centuries. Isis was growing in popularity, beloved as mother, mourner, magician, and protectress. At Dendera, Hathor's great temple had risen again under the last Ptolemies, in spectacular cosmic fashion. Cybele, the Magna Mater, had already been brought into Rome as a state goddess. Artemis presided over Ephesus. Demeter and her daughter Persephone, also called Kore, remained bound to mysteries of death, fertility, and return. Aphrodite, Venus, Fortuna, Pax, Victoria, Salus, and countless local goddesses permeated temples, coins, festivals, household shrines, and civic life. And women were much more than just worshippers—they were priestesses, initiates, patrons, chantresses, and more. Beyond the temple, women presided over the sacred thresholds of daily life, tending of household shrines, keeping the rites of childbirth, preparing bodies for burial, and singing, and praying over babies, blood, illness, marriage, and death.[14]

Female deities did not stand outside the great male gods of the ancient world. They moved beside them, as consorts, mothers, sisters, rivals, and sovereign powers in their own right, within pantheons that shaped the civic and spiritual life of the Mediterranean for centuries. Even in this established cultural landscape, newer spiritual currents were gaining force parallel to Christianity. One was Mithraism, a male-only cult that was not secret, but private, practiced in underground sanctuaries where initiates passed through seven graded ranks and shared meals bound to death, rebirth, and salvation. Popular in Rome from the late first century onward, especially among soldiers and merchants, Mithraism traveled as far as Britain and North Africa. The syncretic Greco-Egyptian cults of Serapis and Isis spread far out of Egypt, as Isis became celebrated as a universal Mediterranean goddess from the banks of the Nile to the shores of Provence.

Wherever the empire reached, her temples followed. The heartbroken and downtrodden, those suffering under poverty or enslavement, sailors and laborers who lived daily beside danger, and women, so many women, were drawn to her as a figure who promised divine protection and personal salvation. Mistress of Magic, Lady of the Sea, Mother of the Gods, Isis was beloved because she promised continuity beyond death with a presence both maternal and cosmic. In the first and second centuries, Isis worship became one of the most powerful religious practices in the empire. Authorities tried to restrain her, emperors paid her honor, and her devotion remained ascendant.

Across the Campus Martius in Rome, her sanctuary, the Iseum Campense, was a vast sacred complex of courtyards, colonnades, water basins, and shrines. Obelisks, sphinxes, river gods, fountains, and Egyptian figures in bronze and granite filled the precinct, marking it as hers through visual language. Priests and priestesses walked through its courts in linen garments. Sistrums sounded, incense drifted, water moved through basins of purification, reflecting the columns and sky. On the same expanse, the Pantheon was built, the great domed temple that still defies easy comprehension: the cosmos made manifest in air, circle, and light.

Christianity did not emerge apart from this environment, but from within it. The study of this evolution has become a major center of scholarship, notably in Paula Fredriksen's *Ancient Christianities*. One of Fredriksen's pivotal observations is that religious identity in this era was remarkably porous—Jews, Christians, and pagans did not always inhabit sealed worlds. Josephus, Epictetus, Juvenal, and Tacitus all attest, in different registers, to Gentile interest in Jewish practices. Fredriksen describes how women appear as patrons and participants, communities not isolated but overlapping in shared resources, rituals, and scriptures. Julia Severa, a first-century aristocrat and priestess of the imperial cult, built a Jewish assembly place, and Capitolina, a third-century wife of a senator and priest, furnished synagogue mosaics.[15]

Just as polemics against Asherah suggest that Jewish women were venerating her, Christian polemics against the feminine may reveal an anxiety, not only about Christian women, but about the wider cultural landscape. This is how Mary Magdalene and Isis are interconnected. Beneath esoteric conflations, there was a real resonance between their symbolism as female figures within resurrection narratives. But even more than their mythic connections, Magdalene and Isis are inextricable because each female figure was, seemingly, alive and thriving in religious memory in the same time period. The diminishment of Magdalene in orthodox Christianity is interwoven with that of the goddess, just as the persecution of heretical Christians and non-Christians would move hand in hand.

Isis was simply too powerful to vanish. Some of her visual elements passed into Marian iconography, especially in the image of the divine mother and child. The Madonna motif remains deeply evocative of statues and reliefs of Isis nursing Horus, a resonance scholars have long noted and debated. Many early images of Mary and Jesus show her nursing him, before the Christ child came to be depicted as more frontal, formal, clutching a scroll or book. Even the prevalence of Madonnas with dark countenances, the Black Madonnas, seems to carry a trace of this older sacred world. Some were darkened by time, by smoke, some by intention. Given the charged, miraculous, magical, and communal folktales that surround so many of these images and sculptures, it is hard not to see remnants of Isis in their forms.

It was never only art, or only belief. Behind vehement polemics like those of the Church Fathers against the feminine, there was always something tangible: power, resources, money. Money was, and remains, a central element of organized religion and a driving force behind the need to engage believers. For Christianity to grow required entering a world already saturated with the feminine divinity, woven through civic and communal life for generations, sometimes millennia. A world where wealth flowed through women into temples, mysteries, festivals, priesthoods, and cults.

A world where feminine deities absorbed attention, devotion, influence, and resources. To gather enough faithful followers to sustain an expanding institutional religion within such an environment was a staggering feat. A feat that cannot be separated from the intentional suppression against "heretics" and pagans that followed.

Within this world, the prominence of Mother Mary becomes more legible. The virgin mother of God was not a new narrative or unique story, but an ancient mythic pattern revised for a religion centered on a man both human and divine. Her titles, her imagery, her role as mother and protectress were continuations of the ancient goddess—only now left unacknowledged. They were a way to draw in people who had long worshipped the mother, though her image and function would change dramatically over the centuries of doctrinal development.

While the image of Mother Mary could be reworked in ways that preserved much of older feminine divinity beneath a Christian surface, even if never openly acknowledged, Mary Magdalene's story posed a different challenge. Whether or not she was the Beloved Disciple, the rediscovered texts reveal that she was being elevated as a teacher, visionary, and companion of Jesus. Magdalene's story, symbols, and legends lingered dangerously close to the powerful female figures of the ancient world to be absorbed. She and Isis held too much in common. She had to be rewritten.

THE POWER OF STORY

The earliest Christian scriptures demonstrate just how soon the anxieties around female power emerged. Statements such as "women should keep silent in the churches" became foundational prooftexts, cited for centuries to restrict women's speech, teaching, and participation in sacred life, regardless of whether the letters themselves were authentically Pauline.[16] The book of Revelation casts female figures through imagery of corruption, danger, and threat. By the time the Church Fathers began defining orthodoxy more systematically, female authority was not just questioned, but increasingly constrained, recast, and treated as suspect.

Tertullian was among the harshest voices of all. In *On the Veiling of Virgins*, he wrote: "It is not permitted to a woman to speak in the church;

but neither is it permitted her to teach, nor to baptize, nor to offer." In *On the Apparel of Women*, he went further, addressing women as daughters of Eve: "You are the devil's gateway," the ones through whom death entered the world.[17]

Irenaeus repeatedly linked women with deception, disorder, false prophecy, and heresy in his critiques of rival Christian groups. Women, in his telling, were especially vulnerable to manipulation by "heretical" teachers, easily drawn into ecstatic practices and spiritual error. His episcopal seat was Lyon, inland but connected by the Rhône corridor to the wider religious world of southern Gaul and the Mediterranean coast. Historians and archeologists have clearly traced goddess worship to ancient Gaul. Centuries later, this same region would be central to the legends of Mary Magdalene in Provence. At the very least, Irenaeus read about Magdalene in the Gospels and chose to ignore her, and was well aware of the popularity of goddesses like Isis, Venus, and Diana.

Tertullian and Irenaeus wrote during the second century, arguably the most charged period in the struggle over female authority within Christianity. It was the same cultural moment in which someone composed the Gospel of Mary.

In its closing scene, Mary's authority is challenged by Peter and Andrew not on doctrinal grounds, but because she is a woman. Levi intervenes: "If the Savior made her worthy, who are you then to reject her?"[18] The conflict centers not on theology, but on a woman's right to speak and teach. If Mary Magdalene was the Beloved Disciple, perhaps the text preserves something older still: memory. Perhaps the women remembered in Paul's Romans did not lead without apostolic authority of their own. Perhaps Mary Magdalene was their model and claim to legitimacy.

Regarding models, it is curious that second-century leaders like Irenaeus did not use "John" as their model for apostolic succession. Given they believed he was a male disciple, one of the Twelve, and the only eyewitness to have penned a Gospel, "John" appears to be the ideal not only as a model of Christian devotion, but as a figure through whom authority itself could be traced back to Jesus. Who could be more perfect than the disciple Jesus loved? But "John" was not chosen. Nor was James, the brother of Jesus, who was remembered by Josephus as a major authority in Jerusalem. Perhaps James was too deeply tied to Jewish communities to be useful to an increasingly Roman Church. Instead, these leaders used another as their model, their claim to proximity with Jesus: Peter. Simon. "The Rock."

Like Magdalene, Simon Peter survives almost entirely through Christian tradition. "Peter" was not even his birth name, but rather a nickname or title given by Jesus: Cephas, "rock," later rendered in Greek as Petros. Across the Gospels, Peter is prominent but unstable. He speaks often, but repeatedly misunderstands. He falters at critical moments. After Peter resists Jesus's prediction of suffering and death, Jesus publicly rebukes him, calling him "Satan." Peter appears less as an unshakable foundation stone than as a man heavy like *rock*: stubborn and resistant.

Only the Gospel of Matthew transposes his nickname into leadership: "You are Peter, and on this rock I will build my church." Notably, the earliest surviving substantial copies of Matthew date to the third and fourth centuries, precisely as claims of apostolic succession intensified. Over time, this single line became the central scriptural justification for Peter's elevation. To this day, the glittering mosaic interior band under the Dome of St. Peter's Basilica proclaims these words in indigo and gold.[19]

However, the earliest extra-canonical sources do not present Peter as the singular leader later tradition would make him. First Clement names Peter alongside Paul as a martyr, not a bishop. Ignatius of Antioch refers to him respectfully, but without assigning unique authority. Papias connects Peter to traditions behind the Gospel of Mark but says nothing about institutional governance or succession. By the second century, the Apocalypse of Peter, Gospel of Peter, and Acts of Peter attest to his growing prominence without clearly establishing him as the basis of Christian authority. Even the New Testament letters attributed to Peter strain historical credibility.[20]

Early traces linking Peter to Rome do exist, most notably in a fragment attributed to Dionysius of Corinth, though the passage survives only through Eusebius's *Ecclesiastical History*. Clear first-century evidence for Petrine supremacy, however, remains absent. What tradition demonstrates instead is a gradual development that deliberately centered Peter, transforming him from disciple into foundation.[21]

Yet again, Irenaeus appears early in the construction of Peter's leadership narrative, explicitly advocating for a line of apostolic succession running from Peter and Paul through the bishops of Rome. Even more revealing is that Luke and Acts do not simply elevate Peter—they diminish Mary Magdalene and female authority alongside him. As Ann Graham Brock argues in *Mary Magdalene, The First Apostle*, the author of Luke consistently reshapes earlier traditions to privilege Peter while reducing the apostolic significance of women, recasting them into acceptable roles. Of all four Gospels, Luke alone diminishes Mary Magdalene's role as witness to the resurrection. It appears the most pro-Petrine of the canonical Gospels is also the one in which Magdalene's authority is most abridged.[22]

In *The First Edition of the New Testament* and *On the Origin of Christian Scripture*, Trobisch proposes that figures such as Irenaeus were not merely preserving tradition, but actively organizing, editing, naming, and reframing earlier materials into a coherent narrative of Christian origins. That is, the books of the Christian New Testament were consciously gathered, shaped, and even produced by a collection of second-century proto-orthodox leaders. Trobisch even suggests that the mysterious "Theophilus" addressed in Luke–Acts may have been Irenaeus.[23]

In sum, Irenaeus was at once the principal source of the names of the Gospels, the insistence there should be exactly four, and their attachment to certain figures and places. He argued all of this in *Against Heresies*, alongside his case for Petrine apostolic authority, and the awkward admission that the Fourth Gospel was already in the hands of the Valentinians. Irenaeus is the first clear and explicit figure in the historical record to even cite the Acts of the Apostles; there is no clear trace of the text before 150. He is the source of the strange tradition that the author of Luke and Acts was a physician—a detail Irenaeus draws from a single line in the Letter to the Colossians, which many modern scholars regard as pseudonymous.[24]

Irenaeus, the same one to never name Magdalene at all. The same one to advocate for a solely male apostolic lineage from Peter to Paul to bishops like himself. Like many of history's most effective architects of power, Irenaeus appears to have understood that stories shape belief, and belief in turn shapes populations, economies, institutions, and history.

But Irenaeus was not alone in this work. Many others were laboring on parallel projects of similar force and scope. Eusebius of Caesarea's *Ecclesiastical History* reflects the same impulse, arranging legends, fragmentary documents, martyr stories, and emerging traditions into a clear arc of apostolic succession, episcopal authority, persecution, and eventual triumph. Within that narrative, authority flowed through male lineage and institutional continuity. Magdalene is not named, though "Marys" are mentioned. Augustine of Hippo, renowned for his prolific writing, used the power of words to shape a powerful theological vision, including the doctrine of original sin. Augustine addressed Magdalene only briefly, in his commentary on the resurrection, with little recognition of her significance.

If there had been any doubt that Mary Magdalene specifically was perceived as a problem, a figure whose memory might let women claim formal spiritual authority, the Didascalia Apostolorum removed it. A Syrian church order composed around 230, the text states the matter directly:

> For He the Lord God, Jesus Christ our Teacher, sent us the Twelve to instruct the People and the Gentiles; and there were with us women disciples, Mary Magdalene and Mary the daughter of James and the other Mary; but He did not send them to instruct the people with us. For if it were required that women should teach, our Master himself would have commanded these to give instruction with us.[25]

Her name is present, but her authority is carefully contained. This restriction stands in direct contradiction to the words attributed to Jesus, where he explicitly commissions Magdalene: "Go instead to my brothers and tell them, 'I am ascending to my Father and your Father, to my God and your God.'" The Didascalia attempts to resolve that discrepancy by redefining the scope of her role, arguing that women were never sent to teach, only to bear witness, and then keep quiet.

While the Church made this effort to demote women, it made a parallel effort to retrospectively build back papal authority. It is little recognized that the titles of the early popes are all tradition, not history. Peter was never called pope during his lifetime, nor was Gregory the Great called Pope Gregory I. The term derived from papa, "father," a broad honorific once used for many bishops across the Christian world. In the early seventh century, the Byzantine emperor Phocas recognized the see of Rome under Boniface III as "head of all the churches." But the idea of "the Pope" as a singular supreme ruler over all Christianity emerged gradually, reaching a new level of authority only under Gregory VII in 1073.[26]

What is in a name? What is in a title? What is in a story? In the history of Christianity, it turns out: everything.

STICKS AND STONES

Constantine the Great was not baptized until the end of his life. His relationship to the rapidly expanding faith was shaped as much by statecraft as by claims of divine visions and favor. Famously, he attributed his victory before battle to a vision of the cross, while the influence of his mother, Helena, also drew him toward Christianity. The Edict of Milan in 313 marked the first major step toward a Christian empire, though it granted toleration to both Christians and non-Christians. Roman emperors had presided over sacred order as *pontifex maximus*, and Constantine applied that same imperial logic to Christianity, positioning himself as a guiding force within the faith.

From the beginning, he favored Christian groups whose hierarchy and structure mirrored the administrative order of the empire. Constantine established a massive transfer of imperial wealth and patronage toward the Church. He oversaw the confiscation of certain temple properties, the removal or melting down of cult statues, and the redirection of resources, even grain distributions, toward favored clergy and communities. By the end of Constantine's reign, bishops could adjudicate civil disputes, receive state privileges and financial exemptions, and travel under imperial support. This transformation of power manifested in monumental architecture as Constantine erected the Old Saint Peter's Basilica.

Constantine's most consequential intervention was his sponsorship of ecumenical councils, empire-wide assemblies of leaders, all of whom were male. Bishops gathered together, traveling from Asia Minor, Syria, Egypt, and North Africa, to formally debate theology and organizational matters. From their inception, these councils were a primary mechanism for defining right belief and condemning heresy. The First Council of Nicaea is often misunderstood in the popular imagination, due in part to the Dan Brown era. It was not the moment the biblical canon was created. It was, however, a pivotal turning point in the formation of the Creed—not what was written, but words spoken in unison.

In all religions, speech carried sacred force, even reflected in the Logos: "In the beginning was the *Word*." Words were used to invoke, bind, protect, and transform: Egyptian hymns, temple liturgies, Greek and Roman oaths, invocations, and ritual formulas articulated in precise sequence and communal rhythm. Sanctified words were *magical*, by function. The Creed functioned similarly, since to speak it was to belong, and to refuse it was to stand outside. By the Council of Constantinople several decades later, one defining phrase had been fixed: "one holy, catholic, and apostolic Church."

Among the immediate consequences of Nicaea was an imperial command that Arius's writings be destroyed. Arius had argued that the Son was distinct from, and subordinate to, the full divinity of the Father. After the council, Constantine ordered his books burned and threatened punishment for anyone who hid them. From Nicaea onwards, Christian theology was no longer only belief, but doctrine: one interpretation of Jesus and the scriptures surrounding him increasingly bound to imperial power, enforced through law.

The Council of Laodicea in 363–364 marked a crucial turn for women. Canon 11 prohibited the appointment of *presbytides*, a term interpreted to mean elder women, widows, or female presbyters. The very existence of the prohibition suggests that women held forms of religious authority significant enough to require suppression. It was not the final word on formal roles for women. Layers of regulations were progressively instituted, while some women continued to defy them. For example, as late as 829, bishops in Gaul (later France) were still complaining that women were performing functions associated with the Eucharist.[27]

In the years following Laodicea, the powerful episcopal seat of Alexandria was held by one of orthodoxy's fiercest defenders, a bishop named

Athanasius. Locked in conflict with Arian Christianity and competing visions of the faith, before Easter of 367 Athanasius issued his Festal Letter 39. Scholars now widely regard it as the earliest surviving list of the twenty-seven books of the New Testament. But his letter did more than define an emerging canon. Athanasius condemned noncanonical writings, describing them as dangerous inventions capable of leading believers astray. Festal Letter 39 evinced a growing effort not just to define orthodoxy, but to control the voices, texts, and memories that could continue. It is possible, scholars like Elaine Pagels believe, that the Nag Hammadi codices were concealed during this threshold moment.[28]

The most powerful development in this consolidation of authority came through the Theodosian Code, enacted across the late fourth and early fifth centuries. Initiated under Theodosius I and expanded by his grandson Theodosius II, the Code imposed escalating restrictions on heretical Christians and non-Christian traditions alike through fines, legal penalties, confiscations, and limitations on ritual practice. Across Rome, Greece, Egypt, Asia Minor, and the Levant, these laws accelerated the collapse of religious pluralism. Increasingly, imperial subjects were expected to conform or risk exclusion, punishment, or loss of civic standing.

Ancient accounts describe the great temple complex, the Serapeum, dedicated to Serapis and Isis in Alexandria as one of the largest sacred complexes of the Mediterranean world. Monumental stairways rising above the city, colonnades, libraries, ritual chambers, and vast courtyards where priests and priestesses moved among worshippers. In 391, the temple complex was destroyed amid escalating anti-pagan legislation. Christian sources record violent clashes surrounding the destruction, culminating in accounts of the colossal statue of Serapis being hacked apart and paraded through the streets before being burned.

In the decades that followed, Manichaeans, Donatists, Eunomians, Montanists, Arians, and other groups faced increasing restriction through fines, exile, confiscation of property, loss of inheritance rights, and bans on assembly. In 435 Theodosius II mandated that the writings of Nestorius, the Patriarch of Constantinople who opposed the Theotokos doctrine, must be burned. By 438, the Theodosian Code gathered generations of legislation into a single legal framework.

These laws reached into private homes. What had once been intimate acts of protection, mourning, healing, gratitude, and devotion, enacted in kitchens, courtyards, thresholds, and at the beds of the sick, became crimes punishable under imperial law. Household altars and shrines were stripped of their ordinary offerings: no incense, no garlands of flowers or herbs, no candles or ritual lamps, no wine poured before sacred images. Penalties ranged from fines and confiscation of property to loss of legal and social standing. In some cases, particularly sacrifice and divination, the punishment could be death.

Still, belief persisted. The Berlin Codex copy of the Gospel of Mary, written in Coptic and dated to the late fourth or early fifth century, belongs to the Christian manuscript culture of Egypt, where texts continued to be copied, hidden, preserved, and transmitted. Manuscripts like it may have moved through the monastic networks of Upper Egypt, near the world of the White and Red Monasteries, where literate communities of monks and women alike copied and circulated texts. Far from Rome, the shadow of orthodoxy eventually reached these monasteries through figures of authority like Shenoute of Atripe, a powerful abbot who led campaigns against rival religious traditions.

Shenoute's most active decades, from the 380s into the 440s, overlap directly with the period in which the Berlin Codex was likely copied. In those same years he was raiding pagan shrines, suppressing rival Christian communities, and ruling his federation with notorious severity. Even in theory, Shenoute would not have allowed the Gospel of Mary to be copied. An unorthodox text in the name of a woman was already dangerous to preserve by this era; his rule made it more dangerous still.

Did a female scribe bend over the manuscript by lamplight, line by line, moving Mary's voice forward into a world narrowing around her? Was her writing an act of courage not fully recognized as such, a task that could have resulted in penalty, exile, or worse? Did she seal away the codex in the dry Egyptian earth, intent to preserve its sacred words? Could she ever have imagined that centuries later those pages would rise again and travel across the world?

Even into the sixth century, the Temple of Isis at Philae remained active, among the last living expressions of ancient Egypt. Its closure in

535–537 under Justinian I marked more than the end of a sanctuary. Priestesses, chantresses, female scribes, musicians, and statues of the goddesses all vanished. What had once lived openly in temples, festivals, and homes receded into fragments, whispers, and silence. An entire world, one in which feminine divinity had been visible, embodied, and woven into daily life for millennia, was gone. Not simply through the evolving currents of faith or a gradual tide of conversion, but because older ways of worship were made illegal. A landscape once dense with gods and goddesses narrowed into a single sanctioned tradition, one that severed itself from the layered truths of its own beginnings.

VEILS, VISIONS & FLAMES

The influence of Gregory the Great's homily in 591 on Mary Magdalene and the Christian feminine cannot be overstated. Whatever suspicions had circulated around Mary before him, Gregory crystallized them into one of the most enduring narratives in Western history. The tale he crafted around Magdalene became accepted Church tradition not because it was factual, but because it was useful. Like Irenaeus, Eusebius of Caesarea, and even Augustine of Hippo, Gregory understood the power of story.

With Mary Magdalene fixed as a penitent prostitute, the model of sacred womanhood increasingly narrowed. Through Marian doctrine, Mother Mary's image became centered on perpetual virginity, purity, obedience, and submission. Female saints were burdened with legends of sacrifice. The story for Christian women became centered on denial and abandonment: of the self, the body, and even one's own children. As Kathleen Gallagher Elkins shows in *Mary, Mother of Martyrs*, this image of the self-sacrificing mother was not inherited but constructed, emerging in precisely this first-to-third-century window.[29] The older Egyptian and Greco-Roman mother had been imagined as formidable and influential in her adult children's lives while the new Christian mother was being remade as a vessel of suffering and surrender.

Nowhere is this transformation more visible than in the *Passion of Perpetua and Felicity*, a martyrdom account composed in Carthage around 203. At its center are first-person prison writings widely believed to come from Perpetua herself, though the surrounding narrative may have been shaped by Tertullian or someone within his circle. A young mother who left behind her nursing infant to face death in the arena, Perpetua entered was killed while her postpartum body was still flowing with milk in a story that sanctified the severing of mother from child.[30] A century later, in Iberia, Eulalia of Barcelona would carry the logic of this violence to its extreme. A thirteen-year-old girl was glorified as being martyred by through thirteen tortures—hooks, fire, a barrel lined with knives and broken glass—and through the miracles said to attend her death: a dove flying from her mouth, snow falling to cover her naked body. Augustine of Hippo himself praised Eulalia as a model of Christ-like endurance.

This is the feminine in Christian history: the tortured bodies of women and girls remembered as triumph, suffering made sacred, destruction turned into devotion. Across centuries, male theologians and churchmen refined the pattern, praising feminine sanctity when it appeared as sexual renunciation, obedience, anguish, or martyrdom. Clement, Tertullian, Origen, Cyprian, Athanasius, Gregory of Nyssa, Jerome, Ambrose, Chrysostom, Augustine, Gregory the Great, Bernard, Aquinas, Peter Damian, Bonaventure, Jacobus de Voragine, and Thomas à Kempis. The names change, but the demand remains. Women were valuable when chaste, submissive, anguished, or dead.

Outside martyrdom, virginity was elevated while motherhood became spiritually suspect. The domestic and maternal lives of women, once central to family, ritual, and community, were treated as spiritually compromised rather than sacred vocations. Cyprian, bishop of Carthage, declared that virgins alone escaped the curse of Eve. Ambrose was known to compare children to "troubles" and focused on the "dangers" of childbirth and motherhood: "Why speak of the troubles of nursing, training, and marrying? These are the miseries of those who are fortunate. A mother has heirs, but it increases her sorrows." Jerome was sharper still: "I praise marriage," he wrote in his *Letter 22 to Eustochium*, "because it produces virgins for me." Motherhood, in their logic, was valuable only insofar as it produced future women who would refuse it.[31]

This emphasis on chastity was not unique to early Christianity. Greek philosophical schools, including Stoics, Pythagoreans, and Platonists, had long prized continence as a spiritual virtue, and Christian asceticism extended that tradition into a more absolute form. Historians generally agree that the movement of consecrated virgins, or "Brides of Christ," emerged from a confluence: devotion, escape from arranged marriage, fear of childbirth, and the intellectual and spiritual liberties the life could afford. The legendary heroine Thecla embodied this defiance by breaking her engagement, following Paul, and rejecting the life her family had arranged. Her story circulated so widely because so many women recognized something of themselves in her. And it was precisely that sovereignty, that authority over their own bodies and faith, that prompted male leaders to contain it.

"Unruly" was the word Tertullian used to describe the consecrated women in his city of Carthage, a clue to the independence these virgins may have held when he set out to discipline them. In his 207 treatise *On the Veiling of Virgins*, Tertullian quite literally veiled these women, using a garment as a means of suppression. An unveiled virgin, he wrote, was indistinguishable from a prostitute, her body inviting the gaze of men and angels alike. "Every public exposure of an honorable virgin," he insisted, "is a suffering of rape." A generation later, Cyprian expanded the program in his treatise *On the Dress of Virgins*, warning consecrated virgins against makeup, jewelry, and ornament. Any beautification of the body was, in Cyprian's eyes, a betrayal of the virgin's vows to her husband, Christ.[32]

As Christianity was legalized, virginity became the new martyrdom, at least for women. In the fourth century, Ambrose introduced the *consecratio virginum* ceremony, a literal wedding rite, replete with a white dress, vows of chastity, a bishop placing a veil on the bride, and a public procession before a gathered congregation. Naturally, there were economic aims behind the theology. In Roman society, a daughter's marriage required her family to pay a substantial dowry, and Ambrose pitched consecration partly as the cheaper alternative. Athanasius gave these vows the force of canon law, binding a woman to Christ as wife to husband and therefore to the institutional Church itself. Wealth flowed into Church coffers through dowries paid at consecration, family donations, and inheritances willed by consecrated women, as the estates of women rich and poor alike passed into monastic hands. If a woman tried to leave the bond, the Church enforced its canonical authority through excommunication, public discipline, and the loss of her status as a Christian.[33]

For a period, in the Christian East, women retained authority that was already eroding in the West. Theodora, the Byzantine empress and wife of Justinian I, intervened directly in law and church politics as she advocated for women, supported female religious communities, and expanded protections for vulnerable women across the empire. Pulcheria, a vowed virgin who ruled as regent and then empress in the fifth century, used her authority to advance Marian devotion across the empire and co-convened the Council of Chalcedon, one of the most consequential gatherings in Christian history. Macrina the Younger founded a major monastic community in Asia Minor and was remembered by her younger brothers Basil of Caesarea and Gregory of Nyssa as "the Teacher." Olympias served as deaconess of Hagia Sophia in Constantinople and founded one of the city's largest monasteries. The office of deaconess, vanishing in the West, persisted in the East for centuries, where women were honored more visibly as ascetics, mystics, patrons, and saints. Mary Magdalene, too, has always been less diminished there.[34]

As Christianity moved westward across Europe, spreading slowly, unevenly, and by force, it entered landscapes already alive with local cosmologies, seasonal rites, sacred wells, rivers, and land-based traditions. Women played an unacknowledged but essential role as mothers and wives influencing conversions through households and kinship networks. For example, Bertha of Kent helped prepare the way for Augustine of Canterbury's mission to England, while Clotilde is traditionally credited with helping pave the way for the conversion of the Frankish kingdom through her marriage to Clovis.[35] Through syncretism, older sacred worlds were absorbed and reinterpreted: goddesses became saints, sacred sites were rededicated, older symbols survived beneath new names.

Beginning in the late eleventh century, the Crusades were launched under papal authority, framed as sacred duty and rewarded with promises of salvation. In reality, these were wars for land, resources, and control: Jerusalem was captured in 1099 in a massacre remembered for blood filling the streets. Even in this environment, examples of powerful Christian women persisted. Melisende, the twelfth-century queen of Jerusalem, ruled in her own right, challenged her husband's authority, expanded the Church of the Holy Sepulchre, and established a convent at Bethany under the leadership of her sister. In doing so, she preserved a female religious presence within the sacred geography of Bethany, the village associated with Mary and Martha, and therefore linked with Mary Magdalene.[36]

One woman, Hildegard of Bingen, defied these narrowing norms to an extraordinary degree. A medieval Benedictine abbess, composer, theologian, artist, and natural philosopher, Hildegard wielded influence at the highest levels of the Church. She corresponded with popes, preached publicly, and was celebrated in her own lifetime as a visionary whose intellect approached that of the great philosophers. At the heart of her theology was *viriditas*, "greenness," a living creative force she described as flowing through plants, stones, bodies, music, light. In her natural works *Physica* and *Causae et Curae*, she catalogued the spiritual and therapeutic properties of more than five hundred plants, herbs, gems, animals, and minerals; sapphire, jasper, and emerald, in her writing, were not decorative but charged with divine force. Hers was a Christianity in which the natural world was densely meaningful, alive with the same power that moved through prayer and song.[37]

The brilliance of Hildegard did not go without scrutiny. She was discussed at the Synod of Trier in 1147, where the Cistercian abbot Bernard of Clairvaux advocated on her behalf and Pope Eugene III formally endorsed her visions. Bernard himself would become one of the great architects of medieval bridal mysticism, reading Song of Songs as an erotic and universal drama between the soul and Christ. That language did not remain confined to monks or virgins; it swept up wives and mothers as well—a transformation Dyan Elliott brings sharply into focus in *The Bride of Christ Goes to Hell*. Stepping into the role of the Bride, Elliott argues, "offered select women an unprecedented degree of freedom and privilege in the church." Their visions moved along the line between literal and symbolic, recording epiphanic and even erotic experiences in their "marriages" to Jesus.[38]

Margery Kempe, born around 1373, married for decades and mother of fourteen children, dictated a book in which Christ appears not only as savior but as intimate beloved. In one vision Christ ravished her spirit and commanded her to call him Jesus, her love, for he was her love and would be her love without end. In later visions, she described herself as Christ's Bride and spouse, the union between them passing beyond worldly bonds. Margery was rare but not an anomaly. Self-sacrifice was often woven into the way these women pursued and validated their spiritual lives. Dorothea of Montau, a fourteenth-century Prussian Bride of Christ, claimed divinely sent wounds and exacerbated them through extreme self-mortification—burning her own breasts, fasting to the edge of death, exposing herself to winter cold. Eight of her nine children died in infancy. After her husband's death, Dorothea had herself sealed alive inside a cell at Marienwerder Cathedral. This was a recognized form of extreme medieval female spirituality called being an "anchoress" where a woman was sealed in a tight enclosure attached to a church and fed through a slit in the wall, until death.[39]

Not every bridal mystic swung to the extremes of Dorothea's tragic life. Some channeled the same visionary intensity outward, into political power. Birgitta of Sweden—wife, mother of eight, and widow from a noble family—reported mystical pregnancies, including a famous vision of Mary giving birth on her knees, the Christ child on the ground emanating radiant light that reshaped Nativity iconography for centuries. She founded the Bridgettine Order of nuns, moved to Rome, and pressed for the papacy to return from Avignon, where seven successive popes had been seated since 1309 under French influence. Catherine of Siena, working in parallel a generation later, claimed her own mystical marriage to Christ, inclusive of an invisible wedding ring, and used her visionary authority to push the same papal return in 1377. Catherine and Hildegard were both later named "Doctors of the Church," a title the Church reserves for saints whose writings shape doctrine.[40]

For women to claim access to the divine outside of male mediation was a hazardous line to walk; to have experienced the influence, authority, and respect that Birgitta, Catherine, and Hildegard did was exceedingly rare. The same gifts that elevated some toward sanctity could just as quickly expose others to accusations of deception, or demonic influence, and heresy. Marguerite Porete, the Beguine mystic, was burned at the stake for refusing to renounce her work, *The Mirror of Simple Souls*. The book reads almost like a Platonic dialogue—an allegorical conversation between figures named Love, Reason, and the Soul, it contrasts institutional religion with personal spiritual responsibility in it. Porete imagined the highest spiritual state as complete surrender in divine love, the soul emptied of will, ego, and possession.[41]

Seven governs the soul's ascent in *Mirror*, the number so closely bound to Magdalene. Within that structure, Porete presents Mary Magdalene as a soul remade by love beyond measure, beyond calculation, beyond Reason itself. Magdalene was, of course, beloved in the medieval imagination, but the resonance between Porete's vision and the Gospel of Mary is startling, especially given that Porete almost certainly could not have encountered that long-lost text in the early fourteenth century.

At the end of the Gospel of Mary, the soul rests in silence. Porete, too, became known for silence during a trial that stretched over more than a year, while she was imprisoned and examined under the Dominican inquisitor William of Paris. She refused the required oath and would not answer theological questions. Her book was condemned as heresy, and on June 1, 1310, she was publicly burned in the Place de Grève as onlookers wept. More than two hundred years later, another mystic, Teresa of Ávila, would publish a similarly sevenfold framework of spiritual ascent in *The Interior Castle* from 1577. Teresa would not be executed, but elevated and canonized.

Decades before Teresa wrote, another woman approached the same dangerous interiority from within the French court. In 1531, Marguerite de Navarre—not a nun, but a royal—published *The Mirror of the Sinful Soul*, a devotional poem steeped in bridal mysticism and inward spirituality. The work was criticized, even called heretical, by contemporary theologians. Yet for all that "dangerous" interiority, and even with the echo of Porete in its title, Marguerite's poem remained doctrinally contained. It did not carry the soul beyond sin, as Porete had dared to do. It returned the soul to Augustine's old wound—humanity as fallen, helpless, and dependent on grace.[42]

Sister of Francis I of France and sister-in-law to Claude of France, she almost certainly shared the milieu Anne Boleyn occupied during her years at the French court—and that same reformist circle had been entwined with the humanist scholar Jacques Lefèvre d'Étaples. Years earlier, in 1517,

Lefèvre had approached the central tangle around Mary that remains today, and not only in conversation within royal residences, but in print. In his treatise, he argued that Mary Magdalene, Mary of Bethany, and the sinful anointing woman of Luke were three separate women—a position that freed her from tradition's image as a penitent prostitute. The response was swift. A flurry of books rose against him, and in 1521 the theology faculty of the Sorbonne formally condemned his claim as heresy. He was protected by Francis I and by Marguerite herself.[43] Anne's daughter, the future Elizabeth I, would make the earliest known English translation of Marguerite's poem at only eleven years of age.

Taken together, these threads—the chain of royal women, the scholarly attempt to divide Magdalene and the heresy it drew, the penitential theology of Marguerite's poem, and the 1516 pilgrimage to Sainte-Baume by Claude, Marguerite, and possibly Anne—reveal the devotional gravity Mary Magdalene held for them.

A common belief, one that underwrites the bloodline-bride thesis as well, is that royal families, and especially royal women, have always known more about Mary than meets the eye, carrying secrets hidden from public view. This is possible, of course. But the theology of *The Mirror of the Sinful Soul* suggests something slightly different. The text does not dispel the framework of sin and obedience for women; it works within it, building upon Magdalene's inherited image as the penitent sinful woman. What seems more likely than mysterious royal secrets is that women like Marguerite sensed a truth around Mary Magdalene, a force that exceeded the categories they had been given. They followed the symbols, images, and fragments available to them as far as their world allowed.

Royal status did not necessarily give them special knowledge. It may have given them something else: the education, protection, and proximity to preserve what other women could only feel. But this devotion to Mary Magdalene, and to another way of being Christian, was not confined to nobles. It moved among ordinary people too, taking shape outside the sanctioned walls of the Church. In the medieval south of France, a community of Christians lived outside the authority of Rome. They elevated women, rejected the hierarchy of the Church, followed an interior path, and were later said to have revered Magdalene. They held the Fourth

Gospel in special regard. They called themselves *bons hommes* and *bonnes femmes*, "good men" and "good women," or simply Good Christians. History calls them the Cathars.

THE CATHARS

Something resembling an older current surfaced again in early medieval southern France. Not a relic bone or fragment of a saint, but a living Christian movement that seemed to preserve echoes of an older spiritual world. Almost none of the Cathars' own writings survive. What remains instead are inquisitorial records, theological attacks, and accounts written by the very institutions seeking their destruction, leaving the movement filtered through accusation, fear, projection, and the voices of its enemies. Stephen O'Shea's *The Perfect Heresy* remains one of the most careful and illuminating modern histories of the Cathars and of the persecution that followed, the Church's war against them remembered as the Albigensian Crusade.[44]

The Cathars appear to have understood their Christianity as ancient, perhaps even tracing it back to traditions Mary Magdalene was believed to have brought to southern France. Scholars cautiously connect them to the Bogomils, a dualist movement that spread westward from the Balkans and merged with older traditions in the Languedoc. Stretching from Provence to the Pyrenees, the region that Catharism inhabited was prosperous, decentralized, and comparatively resistant to both northern French and Roman authority. Its language was Occitan, not northern French, and its culture had its own legal, literary, and political traditions. Women could inherit land in their own names, rule fiefs, exercise political authority, and even participate in the literary culture of the troubadours, the poet-musicians of courtly love.

From what can be reconstructed of their beliefs and way of life, the Cathars sought to embody the goodness their name claimed—visible in the body and enacted in the world. They practiced voluntary poverty, dressed plainly, abstained from meat, and refused to bear arms or swear oaths. Of the scriptures, they especially revered the Fourth Gospel, whose central call to love and care for one another echoed their communal way of life. Their spiritual leaders did not bear titles; they were simply *bons hommes* and *bonnes femmes* though the later records would render them "Perfect." The highest sacrament was the *Consolamentum*, a ritual where the laying on of hands bound them to a lifetime of poverty, chastity, and nonviolence.

Critics accused the Cathars of dualism, a term that meant privileging the spiritual over the material; some sources suggest they may also have believed in the soul's return through multiple lives. But the deeper threat lay in their refusal to recognize the Church's claim over the soul. They would not sanctify Rome's wealth, violence, hierarchy, or systems of power as divinely ordained. They rejected Roman authority in belief, ritual, and structure alike. They did not recite the Nicene Creed, center worship on the cross, or participate in the Eucharistic system of the institutional Church. They refused spiritual taxation and denied that priests alone mediated access to God.

Women occupied unusually visible roles in Cathar life as wives, mothers, teachers, patrons, and Perfects. This culture was rooted in their interpretation of Christian theology, since the soul was beyond gender, the body merely material and temporary, and women and men were imagined as spiritual equals. Even their communal lifestyle supported it, as gatherings met in households rather than churches, naturally placing women at the center of religious life. Women Perfects preached, ministered, and performed the sacred rite of the *Consolamentum*. As Stephen O'Shea observed, "not since the time of the Gnostics had women had such a say in the affairs of the hereafter."[45]

As the authority of Rome intensified and the French crown expanded, the Languedoc became both a theological threat and a territorial prize. The land was rich, autonomous, and home to a Christianity that could not easily be governed. At its height, Cathar belief may have reached a third of the population in parts of the region. It was, in effect, a parallel religious system, with its own bishops and sacraments, drawing loyalty, influence, and wealth away from the institutional Church. For a papacy increasingly insisting on a unified Christendom under Roman authority, this was no longer regional dissent.

Envoys and reformers were sent south to debate Cathar Perfects in public squares and noble courts, among them Bernard of Clairvaux, whose earlier campaigns against heresy helped shape the Church's response. But persuasion failed. Noble families refused to turn against their neighbors. Pope Innocent III escalated pressure through threats of excommunication and confiscation of lands. When this too proved unsuccessful, he turned to the northern French crown for military support. In 1209, a Crusade was called—not against distant lands or foreign armies, but against a peaceful community of fellow Christians.

What followed was not a correction of heresy, but the massacre of innocent women and children. Its opening act came at Béziers. On July 22, 1209—the feast day of Mary Magdalene—a papally sanctioned crusading force descended upon the city. Béziers was home to some Cathars, but mostly to Catholics—to faithful people who refused to give their neighbors up for slaughter, a distinction that ultimately did not matter. Men, women, and children were murdered indiscriminately; the dead numbered at least 20,000. The papal legate Arnaud Amalric gave the order that would become infamous: "Kill them all; the Lord knows those who are his." Whoever escaped the sword died in the fire when the papally sanctioned army burned the city.[46]

One year later, on the feast day of Mary Magdalene, more than 140 Cathar Perfects were burned alive at Minerve. These acts, genocidal in their scale and intent, were only the beginning.

Over two decades, the Languedoc was dismantled: autonomy broken, culture fractured, communities subjected to siege, starvation, and terror. Amid immense suffering, resistance continued, led in part by women. Noblewomen such as Geralda of Lavaur and Esclarmonde of Foix sheltered Cathar leaders within their walls, fully aware of the consequences. Many were imprisoned, tortured, or killed for their actions, yet the networks these women cultivated proved more resilient than the structures aligned against them. Women were, in many ways, inherently protective of the movement itself: as O'Shea observed, "it was asking too much of anyone to hunt down his mother."[47]

The campaign intensified under the regency of Blanche of Castile and Pope Gregory IX. When force alone failed, new methods followed. Lands were seized, orchards cut down, vineyards uprooted, settlements burned, and wells fouled. Communities were stripped not only of belief, but of the means to survive. Then came a deeper rupture: once bounties were offered for heretics, neighbors were compelled to testify against one another. In an atmosphere where accusations could remain anonymous and testimony was extracted under threat, confession became survival. Families that had held through decades of war were torn apart. In time, a permanent court system was created, one that would become the basis for the Inquisition.

People found guilty of being heretics were stripped of any wealth, imprisoned, and executed. Many were forced to sew yellow crosses onto their garments, their bodies transformed into visible markers of shame, surveillance, and submission. What the persecution of the Cathars reveals is that wherever spiritual authority moved inward, it became intolerable to a Church increasingly built upon controlling the connection between people and God. And where women moved openly within that authority, they became inseparable from the threat.

It did not matter how closely their lives aligned with the teachings attributed to Jesus, nor that they called themselves Good Christians. What mattered was that they could not be governed. And so, they were erased.

MAGIC MADE EVIL

For centuries, anyone who veered too close to what was pagan—too close to the earth, to herbs, to healing, to old and ancient ways—was seen through a lens of superstition, but not heresy. Around 900, a document called the *Canon Episcopi* argued that women claiming to fly through the night with pagan goddesses or spirits were deluded by the Devil.[48] In this paradigm, a woman accused of such practices might be made to do penance or face her community's distrust, but she was not, as a rule, put to death. Magic was wrong, but not heretical—it was a different kind of error from false belief. Until the paradigm shifted.

After the Cathars, everything changed. The Church now had an apparatus of systems of surveillance, interrogation, forced confession, and theological policing. In 1184, Pope Lucius III issued a warning against heresy and in 1231 Pope Gregory IX formalized the papal inquisitorial structures. Thomas Aquinas argued in the thirteenth century that demons could interact, and humans could consciously collaborate with them. By

1450 the witch trials had begun, though in Europe they would continue across nearly three centuries. In 1484 Pope Innocent VIII formally authorized inquisitors to prosecute witchcraft as a real and dangerous form of heresy and an existential danger to Christian society.

Two years later, Heinrich Kramer, a Dominican friar, published the *Malleus Maleficarum*, which theologized and systematized the condemnation of "witches." Kramer built upon many centuries of thought: Tertullian's description of woman as the "devil's gateway," to Augustine of Hippo's association of sin with Eve, to the more dramatic examples of bridal mysticism. He argued that women were especially vulnerable to demonic influence because they were morally weaker, carnal, emotionally unstable, and spiritually impressionable. But the *Malleus* offered more than theory: it provided courts and clergy a blueprint, fusing theology, fear, and legal procedure into a machinery of accusation.

In *Witches, Midwives, and Nurses*, Barbara Ehrenreich and Deirdre English argue that the witch trials coincided with a major transfer of authority away from local female networks of communal knowledge and toward male institutions. Not only to the Church, but to universities, emerging state bureaucracies, and especially the professionalization of medicine. For centuries, ordinary people had encountered healing primarily through the wisdom of women, with midwives, herbalists, caretakers serving as the authorities in traditions surrounding birth, illness, and the body. As Ehrenreich and English write:

> The witch-healer's methods were as great a threat (to the Catholic Church, if not the Protestant) as her results, for the witch was an empiricist: She relied on her senses rather than on faith or doctrine, she believed in trial and error, cause and effect. Her attitude was not religiously passive, but actively inquiring. She trusted her ability to find ways to deal with disease, pregnancy and childbirth—whether through medications or charms. In short, her magic was the science of her time.[49]

With no mediator and no external authorization, this was exactly the kind of knowledge that threatened institutional control. Ehrenreich and

English described the witch hunts as "a calculated ruling class campaign of terrorization directed against the female peasant population," carried out through "well-organized campaigns, initiated, financed and executed by Church and State." Thousands upon thousands were executed, many burned alive. Modern historians debate the highest estimates, but women made up roughly 75–85 percent of the accused across Europe.[50]

Old women, young women, widows, healers, mothers, daughters. Generations of female knowledge were shattered, with practices outlawed, authority stripped away, and expertise reassigned to emerging male institutions. Age and class offered only partial protection. Women in power continued to be perceived as spiritually dangerous, especially when they moved beyond sanctioned female roles and into theology, reform, or influence over the Church.

Anne Boleyn was never formally accused of witchcraft, yet the language used against her carried many of the same anxieties visible in the European witch trials. Anne was portrayed as dangerously seductive and capable of bewitching Henry VIII, her sexuality as threatening, her fertility as insufficient. Anne had helped open the breach with Rome, but she may not have agreed with what followed. Some historians argue that her growing conflict with Thomas Cromwell reflected two diverging visions of reform. Anne had a more humanist and devotional vision, shaped by charity, education, and religious renewal, while Cromwell desired and implemented a ruthless consolidation of royal power, wealth, and control through the machinery of the English Reformation. Cromwell was instrumental in her execution, which was carried out on May 19, 1536.

Anne died when Elizabeth was not even three years old, yet devotional books associated with Anne may later have found their way into Elizabeth's hands through women who had served her mother. Perhaps something of her mother's inner world reached her. In her own book of hours, Anne had hand-written three words in French in the margin of the page—*le temps viendra*, "the time will come." Beside her words, she drew a small drawing of an armillary sphere, an emblem of cosmic order her daughter would one day take up as her own. What Anne intended by those words cannot be known, but read across the long chain of these women, the phrase reads like a quiet signal of a truth rising through generations. The path cannot be proven, but the story remains—a daughter inheriting, however faintly, the currents of faith her mother had known. By the time Elizabeth became queen, fears surrounding witchcraft and magic were intensifying across Europe. Her reign witnessed growing anxiety around astrology, prophecy, and demonic influence. Elizabeth was known to rely upon the mathematician, astrologer, and occult philosopher John Dee. For centuries astrology had existed comfortably within educated life, practiced by physicians, scholars, rulers, and clergy alike. But by the sixteenth century, practices once associated with natural sciences were being increasingly recast as forms of divination linked to the demonic.

Elizabeth I navigated these tensions with extraordinary precision. She consciously shaped herself through sacred feminine symbolism: the Virgin Queen, Astraea, Gloriana. Her image drew upon classical goddesses, Marian imagery, and cosmic order. Admirers elevated her almost to divinity, while enemies attacked her through familiar polemics of female power, painting her as manipulative, seductive, unnatural, dangerous. Elizabeth's mastery of symbol, performance, and myth became its own form of protection: she controlled the story and knew just what of the feminine could be made visible.

Meanwhile, Mary, Queen of Scots became surrounded by rhetoric of dangerous femininity amid religious conflict and political chaos. Protestant opponents deliberately portrayed her as morally corrupt and fatally alluring, in part because she was a Catholic queen whose claim to the English throne threatened Protestant England. Mary was a woman born into power, forced to defend her body, crown, faith, and name in a world determined to make all four suspect. Her sovereignty, lineage, and refusal to fully submit to English control ultimately led to her execution. Historians remain divided over how directly Elizabeth I desired her cousin's death. In one of history's ironies, it was Mary's son, James VI and I, who ultimately inherited Elizabeth's throne, carrying forward many of the Renaissance currents and relative political stability associated with Elizabeth's reign.

James, however, became darkly fascinated with witchcraft. After storms disrupted the voyage bringing his bride, Anne of Denmark, across the North Sea, he grew convinced that demonic conspiracies threatened the crown. He presided over the North Berwick trials, among Britain's most infamous witch hunts, and in 1597 James wrote *Daemonologie*, defending belief in witches and their prosecution. In another strange twist, he also patronized the earliest survey of Stonehenge, bringing the ancient pagan sun-marking circle back into the cultural imagination. James oversaw the English Bible that bears his name, completed in 1611. The same king who hunted witches authorized a translation whose rendering of Exodus 22:18 would echo through later trials. "Sorceress" became "witch," giving persecution a darker, more specific scriptural charge.

Even as the age called the Enlightenment dawned, Christian Europe began to tell a new story about itself: that reason, science, and progress would free humanity from superstition. Yet this new world did not restore what had been lost. Older forms of feminine authority remained marginalized, recast now as irrational, emotional, primitive, or unscientific. The witch became the hysterical woman. The prophetess became mad. The healer became unqualified. The mother, continually, became useless. Accusation shifted from soul to mind. Female authority was no longer based on demonic influence, but women were still too emotional, too extreme, too bodily, too much, and never quite enough. Saint and sinner, the old polarities remained, still exalting female perfection, purity, and compliance.

By the twentieth century, Church and state had largely separated in function. The Holy Roman Empire had fallen in 1806, ending nearly a thousand years of political-religious union. In most of the Western world, the institutional Church no longer ran courts, levied taxes, controlled marriage law, or commanded armies. Christian institutions had splintered into countless denominations, diffusing the concentration of power once held by Rome alone. Old doctrines softened in some places and held firm in others. Women gradually entered ordained ministry across many Protestant traditions, the Lutherans first, in 1948, while the Catholic and Orthodox churches still do not ordain women. The deeper assumption has been harder to dislodge, rooted in the belief that women's spiritual authority must be constrained in a religion that gave women Eve as blame, Mary as impossibility, and God as Father, Son, and Spirit without a mother.

And Magdalene's story has undergone a gradual rehabilitation, at least in scholarship, liturgy, and popular devotion. Yet for the most part, those who know her name still think of her as a prostitute, a sinful woman, or a footnote in the biblical story. The post–Vatican II reforms began to loosen that inherited image, with the Catholic Church elevating her July 22 memorial to the rank of feast day and honoring her again as apostolorum apostola. Still, these gestures amounted to little more than belated acknowledgement, whispered into a crowded atmosphere of assumption. In Sunday worship, and in Christian culture more broadly, Magdalene remained caught in the same old narrative of projection—wounded woman, dangerous woman, sexual woman. Even now, television retellings turn trauma into her defining feature, while popular fiction continues to eroticize her beyond recognition. et fiction, when crafted with care, can reach into the silences of a record where women's voices were erased. In her Magdalene and Anne Boleyn novels, Kathleen McGowan opened narrative space for readers drawn to the intuition that the feminine spirit in pursuit of the sacred had never fully disappeared. The recovery of Mary Magdalene has come this way, whether through scholarship, mystical writing, or fiction—each carrying forward what the others could not.

The work of recovery has been led instead by female theologians, priests, leaders, scholars, and the countless women drawn to Mary Magdalene who are speaking and writing her back into view. Mary did not need Rome to elevate her again. Nor did the women who have carried her memory need institutional permission to begin. Stories carried across centuries are not undone by a single decree, a single generation, a single voice, or a single book. And because Magdalene's memory has never belonged only to her, its restoration is collective too: women remembering her, claiming her, and singing her back to life with their breath.

FROM THE ASHES

A giant bronze pinecone towers at the center of the Vatican's Cortile della Pigna. On either side stand two much smaller bronze peacocks, delicate beside its mass, while below, a pair of dark stone lions anchor the composition. This is a threshold space, where visitors pause in Roman sunlight before entering the vast vault of the Sistine Chapel. Set into the Renaissance architecture of the Belvedere Court, these objects seem to belong here, but they don't. Their presence reaches back to Old St. Peter's, but they are not originally Christian.

The pinecone and peacocks share a green-blue patina that hints at a shared outdoor life, though they did not come from the same place. Small perforations at the base of the pinecone reveal that it once functioned as a fountain, likely within the sacred landscape of the Campus Martius, perhaps even belonging to the Iseum Campense. The peacocks, meanwhile, are believed to have come from Hadrian's tomb, an imperial monument across the river. Remarkably, they were not melted down for their valuable metal, as the bronze of the Pantheon's portico later would be, stripped and recast for Christian use. Pinecone and peacocks were kept whole, moved, and absorbed.

Pinecones were everywhere in antiquity, appearing in Roman frescoes and household shrines, in ritual, fountains, finials, and processional staffs. The *thyrsus*, the pinecone-topped staff carried by Dionysus and his maenads, was a widespread fertility emblem that crossed languages and empires. Pine was sacred to the goddess Cybele, whose consort Attis was said to have died beneath one; her priests carried pinecone-topped staffs in procession. The cones appear far earlier still, in Sumerian palace reliefs, held by the winged wise men, the *apkallu*. Pinecones never became a central Christian symbol, yet they did not disappear. The Vatican's bronze giant is one survivor. Another rests in the small fist of the infant Jesus at Montserrat, where he sits in the lap of his dark, gentle mother, La Moreneta, the Black Madonna and patroness of Catalonia. Two more flank her throne. There, the pinecone is more than ornament. It is a seed-bearing vessel held by the child of a mother long approached for protection, blessing, and new life.

Peacocks, by contrast, appeared everywhere in early Christian art: in the mosaics of Santa Costanza, within the great Tree of Life at San Clemente, and throughout Ravenna, where Empress Theodora still gazes outward in gold and purple from the walls of San Vitale. Over time, the peacock yielded to more dominant Christian signs, among them the cross, the lamb, the dove, and the fish. But its jeweled body never vanished entirely. It resurfaces unexpectedly in Provence, where two blue-and-white peacocks appear in the central floor roundel of the French Orthodox church at San Michel du Var, the same church that holds an image of Mary teaching in a coral-pink cloak of compassion.

Originally, the peacock belonged to Hera-Juno, queen of the gods, whose chariot was drawn by peacocks marked with the eyes of Argus. In Rome, the bird, even in its full masculine plumage, continued to carry a feminine charge. At an empress's funeral, peacocks were released to bear her soul heavenward; an emperor's ascent was signaled by eagles instead. So although the Vatican's peacocks can be traced to Hadrian's Mausoleum, they may have belonged symbolically to his wife, Vibia Sabina, revered as a goddess after her death in 136.

Early Christians absorbed the peacock by tying it to resurrection. Augustine of Hippo, once again making the figurative literal, claimed in *The City of God* that peacock flesh did not decay, turning an odd fiction into proof of Christ's bodily resurrection. In the medieval era, bestiary texts described peacocks as killers of poisonous snakes. Yet beneath the Christian overlay, peacock and serpent were less rivals than equals. The peacock sheds its spectacular plumage each year, mirroring the snake's release of skin and placing both creatures within the same ancient grammar of life, death, and return.

But the peacock was never only Christian. It became one of the great images of transformation in the philosophy of alchemy: blue into red, green into gold, dissolution into radiance. Medieval and early modern alchemy sought to turn the lower into the higher, the base into the precious, pursuing the literal transmutation of metals into gold as an outer mirror of the soul's refinement. One stage of the work was called the *cauda pavonis*, the peacock's tail, named for the sudden iridescence that appeared between dissolution and purification. Beyond it lay "the reddening," the final intensification where the phoenix was burned and reborn from its own ashes.

Fire is where peacock and pinecone meet. The pinecone is female, a seed-bearing vessel sealed until heat opens it, with the ash left behind to nourish what takes root. Evergreen trees have long carried the promise of eternal life, their green, Hildegard's *viriditas*, holding through winter when everything else falls dormant or appears to die. For all that fire could maim, burn, and kill, its flames were also a source of life, cooking food, giving light, warming bodies into morning. Consuming and creating in the same motion, fire became a language of transformation, answered by its opposite in water, inside Christianity's canon and beyond it.

At the desert's edge in Middle Egypt, in a garbage dump among the ruins of ancient Oxyrhynchus, a small piece of papyrus was found. Scholars now call it P.Oxy. 5577. Between 1896 and 1907, British papyrologists excavated Oxyrhynchus and brought roughly half a million papyrus fragments back to Oxford, overlapping with the year Carl Reinhardt claimed to have purchased the Gospel of Mary from an antiquities dealer. For well over a century, P.Oxy. 5577 sat in archival storage before anyone identified what it contained. Juan Chapa, the Spanish papyrologist who first translated and published the fragment, unveiled it at a Vienna conference in 2023. At that same event, scholar Silke Petersen suggested that the scrap might preserve a missing section of the Gospel of Mary. Sarah Parkhouse made the formal case in print in 2024; Elizabeth Schrader Polczer followed in 2025. Neither of their explorations claims certainty—the fragment is too small for that—but their cases are persuasive.[51]

The broken lines of P.Oxy. 5577 begin with the words "good Father," a turn of language that distantly echoes the Cathars' own vocabulary, their *bons hommes* and *bonnes femmes*. The lines continue on. "Simple and incorruptible," the same words Augustine of Hippo would later use to defend the flesh of peacocks as proof of bodily resurrection. "Therefore I say, Mary." *Mary*. The speaker is unidentified but understood to be a Jesus-figure, who says: "I showed myself as the artificer mind in the *logos* made flesh." The "artificer mind" is the *nous*, the same term the Savior uses in the Gospel of Mary: "Where the *nous* is, there is the treasure." The Logos is pre-existent divine Wisdom transposed into masculine Greek, Jewish thought meeting Platonic.

"Awakening through my kindness," the speaker continues, words that seem simple and universal. Then John the Baptist enters the narrative, quoted: "I bathe you with water, but a man will come and will bathe you with fire and spirit." The phrase is resonant with similar words found in Luke and Matthew, but in P.Oxy. 5577, the elements surrender their sequence and hierarchy—water and fire meet. The speaker continues: "Therefore I say to you, Mary: seek to mix water and fire and you will no longer appear as an image of the flesh, but an image of the eternal incorruptible light, bringing together for you, Mary, the intellectual spirits from two intertwined and dissolved elements." Mary, named three times in one small torn piece, entrusted with a transformation she is intended to perform.

"Duality" was the charge leveled at the Gnostics, the Cathars, and the heretics across the ages, accused of treating flesh as bad, the body as lesser than the soul, matter as inferior to spirit. Such ideas could not be sustained, the Church insisted, if Jesus was fully human and fully divine in equal measure. Even the fragmentary passage in P.Oxy. 5577 could be read along these lines: spirit and flesh, water and fire. Yet what this scripture, and many like it, including logion 114 of the Gospel of Thomas taught was not separation. It was a theology of discernment, of distinction without division and ultimately of integration.

Underlying this theology of integration was a notion older than Christianity itself, that spirit and matter were never truly separate. Plato gave words to it, but this is a story far older than philosophy, far wider than any single tradition. The Egyptians called it Ma'at, the cosmic order woven through truth, balance, and justice. The Lakota, Navajo, and Hopi held the spirit world and the material world as one inseparable weave. The Chinese named it the Dao, the eternal way that runs through all things. The Japanese saw the *kami* in every grove, every stone, every river. The Australian Aboriginal traditions called it the Dreamtime, the eternal creative present in which ancestors still live. Every people, in every age, has sensed the same thing: that there is another realm beyond this one, that the body is temporary, that life itself is eternal. Divine and human, heaven and earth, are one. Separation is an illusion.

In a religion that staked itself on Jesus as the first to bring eternal life, this older intuition had to be rewritten. The communities that held the old wisdom alongside the new—that blended water and fire, body and soul—could not remain. Power, when it insists on ruling alone, cannot tolerate partnership. The fragment of P.Oxy. 5577 was thrown away and buried in an Egyptian garbage dump not for wrong belief, but for the reality it contained. Water and fire generate together: fire releases the seed, water swells it, roots descend into the soil, and the incorruptible light of the sun calls the hidden life upward. Together, the elements will new life into being: an olive sprout that may transform into a great tree, a pinecone that may, in time, release a forest of its own.

What was condemned as evil by some was, for others, the language of change and renewal. To expand beyond old ways of being and seeing is a release that can feel like burning. In the way a peacock releases its feathers and a snake sheds its skin, what seems to break down becomes the ground of regeneration. To rise is to embrace a winged immortality—the courage to resurrect the feminine divine through the memory of Mary Magdalene. As new life springs green from the dark, nothing is ever lost.

Chapter 11

SANTA MARIA MADDALENA

You begin in Pigna, the old Roman neighborhood named for the bronze pinecone whose story has begun to trouble you. Maybe it is the shape, its resemblance to the pineal gland, to hidden sight and inner knowing. Maybe it is the way Rome preserved the object while severing it from the world that gave it meaning. Because the pinecone is gone, carried long ago to the Vatican, where it now stands within the walls of an enclosed courtyard called the Cortile della Pigna.

Here, only the name remains, which leaves almost nothing to see and everything to imagine. Around Piazza della Pigna once moved the world of Isis as mother and mourner, healer, and restorer, goddess of loss and return. Water was drawn and poured over waiting hands. Bodies were washed, lamps were lit against the heat and shadow, and prayers rose softly for fertility, protection, and renewal. In the dry summer heat, you can still picture the bronze pinecone, thirteen feet high, water spilling from its scales into this sacred precinct below.

Thirteen. Unlucky or holy, depending on who is counting, a number that has always belonged to thresholds, to what falls outside the neat order of twelve.

*

As you begin walking westward, you round a corner past an "I ♥ Roma" sign and a shop overflowing with souvenirs, trinkets of memory for sale above ground where the Iseum Campense once stood. Not far on, the street opens into the piazza before Santa Maria Sopra Minerva, where the absent pinecone finds its counterpart in another displaced object. This one is visible: a small Egyptian obelisk, its hieroglyphic shaft crowned by a cross and carried, almost absurdly, on Bernini's elephant. Solar, royal, unmistakably masculine, it rises from the earth like a stone ray, Ra made manifest. Yet these vertical forms also became processionary markers, lining the goddess's path. Taken from Egypt in the first century, though likely erected centuries earlier, it was unearthed from the garden beside the church in 1665, lifted from the buried world of Isis and set once more in the Roman sun. The Latin inscription at its base offers instructions for its interpretation, presenting the monument as a lesson in the wisdom of Egypt and the strength required to sustain it, while placing that wisdom under papal authority.

You pause at the edge of the piazza where the elephant, obelisk, and cross rise before the church's twelve-point rose window, one symbol stacked above another. Its stone and glass geometry already hints at the celestial order within, though you remain outside, before a restrained façade that conceals one of Rome's only surviving Gothic interiors, vaulted in deep blue and scattered with golden stars. There rests Saint Catherine of Siena, the woman who dared advise popes and speak with startling authority to the heart of the Church. She died in Rome at the age of 33 after spending her final years urging the papacy out of Avignon, away from the Provençal landscape already thick with Magdalene memory, and back toward the old seat of power.

It's hard not to hear in Catherine of Siena an echo of Catherine of Alexandria, the philosopher-saint whose wisdom likewise challenged empire. With these women of counsel and philosophy moving through your mind, you remember another image across the city, where Catherine is teaching in the frescoes of San Clemente with the Pantheon rising behind her in the background. And now, as if summoned, that same ancient building has begun to surface down the street to your left. Once the Pantheon, the temple of all gods, it is now Santa Maria ad Martyres, Saint Mary and All Martyrs. You realize the names begin to align: Mary over the martyrs. Mary over the pagan temple. Mary, the name that could sanctify what Rome could not destroy.

Standing here before another Santa Maria, the reading becomes hard to avoid. The cross crowns the obelisk just as the church rises over the memory of Minerva. Santa Maria sopra Minerva. Mary over Minerva. Mary over the goddess of wisdom. The phrase carries too much history to feel accidental. In Rome, after all, names are never neutral, and this layering points you toward the Dominicans. They settled here in 1256 and received the church in 1275, within a generation of the Albigensian Crusade's formal end, after their order had helped hunt, condemn, and crush the Cathar world of southern France. These were the same Dominicans who, by 1295, had been entrusted with Mary Magdalene's Provençal shrine and the shaping of her legend. In Rome, they made this place their *insula sapientiae*, their "island of wisdom," as if wisdom had to be claimed, housed, corrected, and watched.

Island. The word strikes you with unexpected pressure, and from the space between France and Rome, Glastonbury Tor rises again through the mist of memory, the old hill long braided with Avalon, the "Island of Apples." Another sacred place poised at the edge of disappearance and survival, where older feminine power was not so much erased as renamed into forms Christianity could keep. So this is how it endured. Minerva could stay, so long as Mary stood over her. Magdalene could be venerated, so long as her cave remained under guard.

Truth, too, could be policed. This Dominican convent became one of the chambers of Christian certainty, tied to the Roman Inquisition, where the old crusading impulse found a new form in tribunals. Here, in 1633, Galileo was forced to recant the motion of the earth around the sun. He was not killed but silenced and sentenced to live under watch for saying what was true. In the so-called island of wisdom, even the heavens had to be corrected. Yes, the church could render celestial order overhead, but when Galileo named the living order of the sky, it put him on trial

Leaving the claimed wisdom of Piazza della Minerva behind, you approach the Pantheon from the rear. As you make your way toward its crowded square, history and architecture begin to stack. First comes the great curve of the rotunda, where the ancient circular heart of the temple is still open through its oculus. Its dome was a feat even the dome of Saint Peter's could not surpass, the kind of mastery Raphael honored when he asked to be buried there. Then comes the rectilinear mass of the portico, once a threshold of gods, empire, judgment, and old philosophy. And finally, the gigantic columns, stone moorings between earth and empire, carrying the weight of nearly two thousand years. You pass it all in one sweep, through tourists gathered around the haunting melody of a violinist playing with his case open at his feet. For a moment, the music feels older than Rome, older even than the empire that claimed so much wisdom as its own, the kind of song the ancients might have traced back through Orpheus and Greece to Egypt.

Alexandria. Catherine's legendary city, and Hypatia's real one. Two women whose names became inseparable from wisdom and authority, and perhaps from one another. One imagined speaking in the city's churches, the other known to have taught in its halls of philosophy. The Pantheon behind Catherine in San Clemente returns to mind again, but differently now. It seems less like an architectural detail than a quiet clue. Seen beside Alexandria and the centuries of devotion that followed, the name Catherine became a vessel for woman's wisdom, allowing philosophy to survive under the protection of sanctity.

By the time you reach the Pantheon's façade, its pull is nearly impossible to resist. A line stretches from the portico toward the fountain at the center of Piazza della Rotonda, but you do not turn left to join it today. Instead, you cross the open space, noticing an immense Marian image gracing the wall on your left, spanning two stories. She leaves you with a flicker of intrigue, just enough to make you promise yourself you will return to her. But for now, another destination is pulling harder and you are already bearing right into Via della Maddalena.

The walk is brief. Almost at once, the street gives way to Piazza della Maddalena, where Chiesa di Santa Maria Maddalena rises to your right.

Yes, there is a street, a square, and a church all bearing her name in the old heart of Isis's Rome. Maddalena. Magdalene. *That* Mary. On this same ground, where sacred women once thrived before their rites were forbidden, their temples buried, and their names rewritten, Mary Magdalene remains too. Not free of the pattern, but caught within it, tangled in the very net that allowed her name to survive.

*

At the foot of the church, you pause and let the shock of it settle. How had this place never appeared before? Not in the books. Not in the conversations. Not in all your searching for Magdalene. You had found it almost by accident, on a whim, certain that nothing bearing her name would appear so plainly here. Then three simple words brought it forward: "Magdalene in Rome."

Maybe because it's small, you think. Maybe because there is nothing here. Or maybe because her name has been folded so completely into the familiar story that few stop to look again, or even try to find her. As you begin to climb the steps, the eighteenth-century Rococo façade rises above you, theatrical and restless. Magdalene and Martha are carved into its restless surface together, sisters in stone. Magdalene with loose hair, cross, and a jar. Martha with the conquered monster at her feet and the holy-water sprinkler in her hand. After tracing the places where Mary seems to slip behind Martha, here they are again, cleaved together under ecclesiastical authority, side by side on the outside of Mary's church. You pass through the doors, and the movement in the stone follows you inside.[1]

Within Santa Maria Maddalena, that restlessness becomes one of Rome's rare Rococo flourishes, its curves refusing to settle, its stucco seeming to ripple across the surface. What begins on the façade carries inward, where flowing forms shape everything from architectural details to painted frescoes above. Rococo takes its name from the French *rocaille*, meaning shell-like ornament, and that is certainly what you see here, in such abundance that you begin to wonder if Botticelli's Venus, painted nearly 250 years earlier, might rise again from her half shell. But this space belongs to a later Rome, closer to where you stand in time than much else you've encountered in the city, and all the more unexpected for being dedicated to Magdalene.

As the shells settle and your gaze adjusts to the overwhelmingly feminine imagery, color arrives first, abundant in colored marbles, gilded wood, stucco ornament, frescoed vaults, and veined illusions of stone. Rococo excess was long dismissed as *zuccheroso*, the Italian word for "sugary" or overtly sweet, a judgment perhaps aimed less at style than at essence, at what was felt to be feminine and therefore suspect. Whether that reaction names something real or diverts attention from what is actually happening here is harder to say. At least, surrounded by all this color and curve, you begin to wonder whether what was dismissed as sweetness is also the surface through which the room begins to speak. Only after a moment do you realize that all this ornament is directing your attention toward a single figure.

Everywhere else, you have had to search for Magdalene where she is unnamed, half-hidden, secondary, and present only when you knew how to look. Here, the reversal is immediate. Scanning the walls, you realize the name outside was only the beginning. She is not a detail to notice and leave behind. She is the path the church asks you to follow.

An elaborate "Magdalenian" cycle opens across the nave vault, then moves deliberately along the arches toward the altar. In churches, sustained painted narratives usually belong to Christ, the Virgin, or saints whose lives have been stabilized by devotion and doctrine. In this case, the very idea is startling, because Magdalene's scriptural presence is scattered—her legends dispersed, her identities debated. Yet here, for better or worse, they cohere. Rather than resolving the tensions surrounding her, the church binds them into a single narrative, giving them sequence, continuity, and form.[2]

The central panel pulls your attention first. It is the Raising of Lazarus. Near the miracle, a woman kneels at Jesus's feet in awed gratitude, her bright golden-yellow mantle one of the first colors to leap from the scene, catching again in the robe of the angel above. Yes, scripturally, this radiant woman is Mary of Bethany, not Mary Magdalene. But inside Magdalene's church, the distinctions seem to soften.

To the right, there is no ambiguity. *Noli me tangere*: Magdalene in the garden, Magdalene at the empty tomb, Magdalene hearing her name and turning toward the risen Christ. She is wrapped in that same golden-yellow mantle over a pale dress.

Then the left panel changes everything. Jesus has been taken down from the cross, and Magdalene, with her hair loose and her mantle falling in folds of amber and yellow gold across her lap, cradles his body in grief. Head-to-head. Not only present, which would already be rare enough, but holding him in the place Christian art usually reserves for Mother Mary. In this panel, though, just behind Mary, the one called Magdalene, stands Mary the mother of Jesus, wearing the traditional powder-blue mantle, her head covered and her hands folded in prayer. Yes, Mother Mary is there, but she is not the center. At Sainte-Baume, you had seen Magdalene in a Pietà, but lower, at his feet. Here, the image turns itself around.

And once it does, a question slips loose. How fixed was that role ever meant to be? How many Pietàs have we been taught to see through the certainty of Mother Mary, when the image may be more intimate, less determined? It is a possibility Michelangelo seemed unable to leave alone, damaging one late Pietà and leaving his final one unfinished, as if even he could not carve the answer safely into stone. Who, then, was cradling Jesus in that unscripted moment Christian art made unforgettable?

Too overwhelmed by Magdalene in that charged position, you can barely take in the smaller scenes around her. But there she is again draped in that honeyed-yellow fabric, with the jar and an angel: myrrhbearer, witness, the woman who came to tend the body. Nearby, another yellow-robed Magdalene peers into the tomb with a man behind her. You pause. This should be Peter behind the Beloved Disciple.

Between this tomb scene, the Pietà, and the central panel that first drew you in, the church has given you more than you can absorb. Magdalene as Mary of Bethany. Magdalene holding the body like the Mother. Magdalene where the Beloved Disciple should be. The sequence reveals her everywhere tradition has taught you not to look for her. In Rome, of all places. You cannot follow that thought far enough to understand what it means. Not yet. You follow the yellow instead.

That thread draws you toward one of the largest scenes near the altar. A table. Feet. Water. Hair. Oil. You try to discern the gospel source of this anointing scene, but it refuses to stay still. Mary of Bethany is there at Jesus's feet, with Martha serving in the background. Luke's unnamed woman shadows the scene through the Pharisee-like figure nearby, and you can almost hear Jesus speaking of the greatness of her love. Yet what you see is not penance. It is love, made visible and lifted into light. Her garment spills across the floor at the feet of Jesus in vibrant golden-yellow, falling toward the edge of the painting in the brightest hue of the scene, turning the old conflation into something resplendent. Only then do you realize what has been moving fluidly through the cycle: not the story, but the color.

You are so accustomed to Magdalene in red that even after you begin following the yellow, it takes time to understand what the color is telling you. Red usually speaks along a range from passion to penitence, from blood to devotion. Here, though, she appears repeatedly in a yellow robe that drapes over white garments. Butter-yellow. Honey. Amber. Ochre. Gilded sunlight. The color travels with her until it becomes impossible to ignore, lifting even the most damaging distortions out of shame and into illumination.

Had she been painted in red, the old story might have tightened around her again. But yellow changes the atmosphere. It does not deny the confusion. It transfigures the way you see her within it.

Is she Mary, the one from whom seven *daimonia* had gone out? Or is she Mary of Bethany, whose role seems to expand each time you look more closely? Or is she Magdalene as witness, standing at the cross and called by name in the garden? Or, more radically still, is she the Beloved Disciple, the eyewitness memory behind the Gospel as we have received it?

Across this painted cycle, somehow, she is all of them. Not reduced to a woman defined by demons but rendered in the color of revelation made visible. Tones of a color as bright as the sun, the source, the same warm hue that shines on the petal of a buttercup or suffuses a woman in aged glass on the forty-fourth step in a Gothic cathedral. And when a Gospel shaped around seven great declarations of identity, seven unveilings of "I am," meets Magdalene in this golden splendor, the seven *daimonia* no longer read as a stain against her but as a sign of spiritual mastery: seven forces known, faced, and overcome.

What gives this golden thread its weight is that across Rome, you have learned to read this palette as more than decoration. Gold belongs to Rome's language of authority. It recalls Peter clothed in yellow-gold tones in Santa Maria Maggiore, his keys and staff in hand, marking apostolic office. White and gold grace the flag of the Holy See and Vatican City, and appear again in papal heraldry and vestments, where gold carries the prestige of the keys and the office they represent.

Against that backdrop, yellow becomes startling here. Within the very system that so often diminished Magdalene, the color does not accuse her. It crowns her. And through that same color language, you think of

Joan too, her white banner strewn with golden fleurs-de-lis and marked with Mary's name, carrying the colors of divine authority into history. The effect is immediate and disarming. Magdalene appears in the color you have learned to read as power.

Here, she is, in every sense of the phrase, the apostle *to* the apostles.

*

After yellow makes its case, you find yourself scanning the cycle again, testing the recurrence. Was it really her each time? Had you made too much of it? No. The yellow is there. Only at the high altar does the palette shift, the familiar bright yellow softening into a butter-cream dress while a deep blue mantle lends her new gravity. Luxurious folds of rich fabric spill toward the skull near her feet, but her gaze rises toward a cross borne by angels and putti. The scene has moved beyond the body, beyond suffering. This is Magdalene in contemplation, fully clothed in majesty, composed, almost regal. It feels less like an ending than a preparation, as if the church's whole painted program is lifting her upward and your eyes follow the elevation.

Above, in the dome, the colors shift again. Magdalene is clothed in Marian red and blue, the palette of heavenly ascent. The yellow has not vanished so much as completed its work, carrying her from witness into glory.[3]

From that height, your eyes begin to descend through the church's color and motion. Rococo splendor presses from every side, vivid, crowded, almost too much to take in. Then something restrained interrupts it. A muted panel within her life cycle, painted in monochromatic antique yellow, nearly disappears into the ceiling, as though it expects you to miss it—or notice that it's different from the rest.

But inside that subdued panel, you count five figures crowding a narrow vessel on open water. The sea is rough, there is no sail and no oars, and the figures huddle together in uncertainty, except for one. A woman stands upright and calm, her raised hand steadying the fear of the others. Your breath catches at the sight of Magdalene's "rudderless boat" painted overhead, almost hidden in plain sight.

As with most of the scenes drawn from Magdalene's life that unfold across the church, this image belongs to her legend, not scripture, specifically to the Provençal tradition that brought her by boat to the shores of southern France.

Staring at this unexpected scene, your mind wanders to other boats of biblical telling. On stormy seas, Jesus rises and orders the wind and waves into stillness. Now, you cannot unsee the parallel. Here, Mary calms the fear. Yes, she is the one who steadies the vessel. She may be shadowy and indistinct in the sepia tones of the painting, but she is nevertheless commanding in posture.

Her arm rests across the shoulders of another figure. Her other hand lifts toward the sky. The gesture is clear. She is the one orienting the boat, holding its center, imparting its direction, and drawing meaning from what surrounds them, almost as though she has become its anchor. Upright, she carries faith while the waves break around her, borne adrift but not undone.

You know her "golden" legend. You've chased it across France. But now it rises in you with a different kind of force. The Dominican-shaped medieval story tells of escape, of persecution, of a boat set out with no sail or oars. But what if that is only how the narrative was later shaped, a way to account for her survival, for the absence of martyrdom? For all her proximity to Jesus, for all her witness at the cross and in the garden, Magdalene was not remembered as one who died for the faith. Instead, the traditions keep sending her onward. To cities. To the wilderness. To a cave. To old age.

And if her story did not need martyrdom to make it holy, another possibility opens. Mary Magdalene was among the women who provided for Jesus and the disciples out of their own means. She was no passive witness. She had resources. She had agency. A woman capable of sustaining a traveling ministry may also have been capable of securing passage across the sea.

What if Mary did not flee at all? What if she sailed deliberately, even peacefully? The seas may still have turned. She may still have needed to steady those around her, to guide the vessel forward. But the journey itself may not have been an act of desperation, but of choice, of setting out toward a place where they could rest and flourish together.

And then, just as you begin to imagine her arriving on the shores of Provence with the wisdom, wealth, and regal force of the queen of Sheba, the realization is almost disorienting: you are not in France. This image waits in the Italian city at the center of the very authority that tried to manage her story.

As your mind returns from memory and dream, you begin to account for what you have seen. The legend carries Magdalene across the sea, but this image—Mary in the boat—is rarely given visible form. You did not find it at her grotto, or either of the basilicas that claim her relics. Aside from Giotto's more penitent cycle in Assisi and a magnificent modern fresco in Saint Michel du Var, iconography is sparse.[4] A fragment in stained glass. A triptych. The occasional object, detached from place and history, circulating quietly through private hands. That is all.

Which makes this boat feel impossibly rare. Not evidence of a legend preserved intact, but a remnant of something tradition never quite knew what to do with. It has not disappeared exactly. It has receded into the category of things easy to miss, easy to soften, easy to explain away—like an ankh woven into a tapestry, a boat-shaped cookie, red shoes on a female apostle, a lost feminine gospel structured around seven, or an anchor whose meaning refuses the official story.

Yes, it is as commonplace as a fleur-de-lis, or as regal as the gaze of a lion, watching the rising of Sirius on the twenty-second day of July—but once you see the sphinx weathered in Egyptian sands waiting for the name of the star to be restored, you cannot unsee it. Sopdet is no more a dog than Magdalene was a prostitute, and the distance between an Egyptian goddess and a Christian woman only appears to be vast at first. With practiced perception, time and space collapse, like stars traced into an abstract figure.

Still, you are standing in Rome, inside a sanctioned church. And there she is, Magdalene, holding the center of it all like the golden sun that descends through the body of Nut only to rise again, reborn.

*

This is not the story you set out to find. But it is the one you recognize. Not a single path, but a way of seeing, emerging through signs too potent to hide and too familiar to question. Subtle, if one can call it that, as a thirteen-foot pinecone severed from its sacred precinct. Inconspicuous, as thirteen Egyptian obelisks planted across the Eternal City.

By now the signs have begun to spin. You are inside the tornado, caught in a whirlwind of stories, symbols, and history. Blue and white, as Dorothy, rather than the Virgin, slipping into glittering red shoes and setting out along a yellow brick road, following color as if it had become instruction. Ahead: a field of poppies, and a city rising green and glimmering at the center.

Or was that the path through La Forêt Domaniale, just beyond the wash of red, green and gold, where a buttercup first asked you to look down before the cave asked you to look within?

It begins to blur—the cave and the heart, the road and the return—not as a journey marked out ahead of you, but as a practice of sacred attention, found in small things. A five-petaled yellow buttercup underfoot at the beginning of your ascent. A five-petaled pink flower growing from stone near the summit, at Magdalene's grotto. Five petals, like the five senses, or five fingers on your hand, even the five wounds of Christ. Five figures in the "rudderless boat" on the ceiling above you in this Roman Catholic church. Five times the beloved disciple is named by love. Five claims that, once restored, lift Mary beyond the place tradition assigned her: beloved, anointer, confessor, witness, source. Yes, truth persists, even when it must rise through a crack in the rock. A small earthly pink star, Venusian in its geometry, lifting your gaze from ground to heaven, revealing the feminine as inextricable from the whole, the pentagram restored to its innocence.

And somehow that celestial rosette, hidden in the sky, feels inseparable from the Empress at San Clemente, buried beneath all those layers, with a pearl-strung crown above her regal eyes, bearing witness to the ecclesiastical diminishment of Magdalene's name. At her throat, five gems gleam like gifts carried in from a sea of tears cried over all that was slandered and silenced. Tears are water too. Not weakness, but movement: lunar, tidal, womb-deep, the element that receives without surrendering, carries without breaking, and remembers what was never theirs to wash away.

Perhaps this is what Glinda meant when she told Dorothy she had always possessed the power but had to learn it for herself. And to learn, we must be willing to be changed. We must trust ourselves enough to feel our way through what we cannot yet understand, moving through grief, wonder, fear, and joy without demanding that each emotion justify its presence. Water does not apologize for flowing. Neither does the womb for its tides, nor the snake for the skin it must shed. The path of becoming asks no less of us.

Maybe that is why every vessel needs enough water beneath it to move. Feeling becomes not something to shut down or hold back, but a current to follow, a force that carries truth through obscurity. A knowing that moves almost like a sixth sense, noticing what reason might never explain—how seven goddess-haunted hills rise within Rome's twenty-two rioni, echoing Magdalene's feast day on the twenty-second day of the seventh month, and carrying Sopdet's Egyptian lesson that time reveals itself through return.

For now, you make your way into the eye of the storm. Once feeling is allowed to flow beyond the dismissive meaning of maudlin, intuition opens through what mystics have called the eye of the heart.

Which means the great reveal is not only where Mary Magdalene is within the churning sea of obscurity, but how authority has taught you to look. How it tells you what you are meant to see, as with the elephant made to carry an obelisk, even as Isis and her solar barques drift through your mind beside Magdalene steering a boat of her own.

You do not need to climb a mountain to find her, not physically. It is a matter of seeing anew, though at times that seeing requires a kind of ascent, a rising of perception. And seeing means recognizing the role of the wizard, peering out from behind his velvet curtain in the Emerald City, his authority sustained by the illusion of distance. In Santa Maria Maddalena, it takes another form as a priest in white vestments steps out from the sacristy as the midday Mass begins.

Suspended between pattern and presence, between the strange convergences that have been gathering around you and Magdalene bathed in butter-yellow light, you find yourself far from the familiar fields of Kansas, drawn instead into an adventure of your own choosing. And though you have not arrived on foreign shores, like Mary, you have traveled far and wide all the same, along a yellow brick road that has wound its way through mind, heart, body, memory, and spirit, until the five begin to feel less like separate faculties than elements awaiting transformation.

And yet before you click your ruby heels and return to the ordinary, the church is not finished with its sermon. It continues at the altar where matter is asked to become mystery. You watch from where you are standing near the back of the pews, beneath the painted boat, as the linen is unfolded, the paten set, the chalice left covered: the vessel that will hold the blood, they say.

Soon, he will lift the consecrated bread, and you cannot help but think of the woman with the tower in the glass at Wells, circumpuncts scattered across her cloak, her left hand raised around a golden disc. Sun sign, host, golden center—the symbols seem to rhyme across centuries and across your own seeking, each speaking in its own language of presence and transformation, as small and insistent as the buttercup that followed you from Sainte-Baume to Glastonbury Tor, shining among women searching not for a chalice to guard, but for a sacred presence they could approach without permission. Here, that gesture belongs only to male hands.

But you remember the women who once held hosts, who carried cups, even as priests and bishops from neighboring churches condemned them. And then there were the women who led without altars. Without Eucharist. Who taught, guided, and sustained communities beyond the reach of sanctioned structures.

Women like Geralda of Lavaur, a noblewoman who established a community of female Perfects within her home in Languedoc, the heart of Magdalene country. She fed and sheltered them, tended to their bodies as well as their devotion, sustaining them through the quiet, unceasing work of care, even as the world tightened around them. When the crusading forces arrived at her doorstep, she did not relinquish her women. She remained where she had always been, calm at the center, holding.

After the city fell and hundreds of Cathars were burned, Geralda was singled out, not for what she believed, but for what she had sheltered. She was tossed alive into a well, and stones were thrown down until her body disappeared beneath them.[5]

It is not only Geralda that you feel with you now, but the long procession of women you have encountered by following Magdalene. Their voices, their memories, their courage, and their suffering, wash over your body with both heaviness and electricity. And threaded through it all is yellow again, no longer only Magdalene's golden robe above you, the buttercup underfoot, a woman in glass, or the keys to what should be a metaphorical kingdom. Now it is also the yellow crosses sewn onto the condemned as marks of heresy, and the flames rising from pyres on the twenty-second day of July, in a century when orthodoxy was enforced with fire.

How can the same color lead you through wonder and then return like this, stitched to suffering? How can a journey feel so enchanted and still break your heart?

At the very moment your eyes could lower, close, or turn away, they do not. The tears rise and fall. Salty, the water moves in rivulets down your face, salt long understood in scripture as covenant, preservation, and offering, something that binds rather than dissolves. Maudlin, they would say. Magdalene, you think. Tears not as weakness, but as witness. The courage of the heart is to see it all and still choose love. It is love that remains. Love that refuses to step away. So you do not drop your gaze. Through tears, you follow what rises.

Your eyes lift from the golden cup at the altar, the cup the Cathars refused, following the thin trail of candle smoke upward from the six candles beyond the contemplative Magdalene in her blue robe. There, you realize, the most commanding image in the entire space has been held in reserve all along, spread across the great vault above the altar, governing the church from its architectural center.

At first, the scene seems to echo Christ among the Doctors, the familiar image of the young Jesus in the Temple among learned men. There is the spirited exchange, the circle of listeners, and Jesus at the center with his arm lifted in the classical gesture of philosophical discourse. But unlike the traditional scene, he is no child here. He is a man in ministry—preaching, teaching, and answering. And beside him, at his right hand, stands Magdalene, her butter-yellow robe unfurling around her with a kind of abundance, securing her undeniable place of honor.[6]

You stop and remind yourself to take a breath, realizing only then that you have been holding it again. In so many images, Magdalene kneels, bends, weeps, repents, or receives. But here she rises, even towers, alongside Jesus. The composition revolves around their shared verticality, held in place above you. At first, it is her authoritative presence that startles you. And then, her hands.

Her left hand lowers toward Jesus, close, receptive, as though receiving something not spoken aloud. Her right hand lifts outward, palm open, offering it into the space around her. Her gaze does not waver. Where the others look on, chatter, gesture, or drift into distraction, she remains utterly focused. And suddenly, you hear it, rising from the still, small voice within: "I will teach you about what is hidden from you." After the words from the gospel written in her name move through you, a phrase that survived among writings condemned as heretical, another line follows from within the selected canon: "Blessed are the pure in heart, for they will see God." As the teachings meet, the scene feels less like an illustration than a correction. The Sermon on the Mount and the Gospel of Mary suddenly occupy the same imaginative space. One preserved. One suppressed. One amplified. One diminished. And standing between them is Magdalene herself.[7]

Looking up into the vault, you realize how much work it took to contain a Magdalene this potent within the preferred tradition: silent, penitential, kneeling in shame, defined by exorcism rather than wisdom. But here, containment fails. Now you see her as you believe she was, elevated above the altar in a form you have never encountered anywhere else, most especially not in a sanctioned religious space, and perhaps only in your own mind, where the surviving fragments of "Mary" have already taught you to imagine her this way.

Here, in Santa Maria Maddalena, Mary Magdalene appears composed as a philosopher, sage, and mystic at once, upright and attentive, mediating between what is received and what is revealed. More words return: "You are blessed, for you did not waver at the sight of me."[8] Was she sinner, saint, bride, mother, muse? Each name made use of her, turning her into a vessel for someone else's meaning. But beyond these familiar projections rises something newly visible and far more dangerous to the powers that be: a woman connected directly to the source of wisdom.

Wisdom. Witness. Beloved. The words build differently now. If Mary is the Beloved Disciple, then she is not only the one who saw and testified, but the one who reveals where true authority begins: not in title, rank, or sanctioned permission, but in intimacy with the source. In love. In recognition. In the courage to trust what the heart has seen.

That is the revelation hidden in belovedness. No, the power was never somewhere else. It was never locked behind the curtain or held only in consecrated hands. And Mary does not keep that power for herself. She teaches you how to see from within it.

*

You stand there for a long minute taking it in and realize that from the shadowed boat above you, through ascent into glory, the gold-washed anointing, to Magdalene beside Jesus in the posture of teaching, then down through the royal contemplative in blue to the six candles, the chalice, the robed priest, and the ritual at the altar, the church has drawn one continuous line of sight.

You do not yet know the artist of the yellow threaded Magdalenian splendor, who commissioned it, or what conversations surrounded its creation. What you do know is that once it is seen, the line becomes difficult to unsee. For the moment, her story moves in a single arc, like the sweep of a compass drawing hidden correspondences into form.

Standing beneath it all, you cannot help but wonder whether the deepest truths survive not because they are proclaimed, but because they are held with such love and faith that they can wait until someone is ready to see them. Perhaps that is what this church has somehow, miraculously, preserved. Not the memory of Mary as history has written her, but the invitation to see from the place of the beloved, where nearness becomes knowledge, love becomes authority, and the unseen waits to be recognized.

Il Signore sia con voi.

A voice drifts through the stillness, and only then do you realize the ritual has begun. Around you, the small congregation rises into the familiar rhythm of call and response, locals and scattered visitors alike settling into words known by heart.

E con il tuo spirito.

The spell does not so much break as settle. The paintings remain overhead. The incense still hangs in the air. The beauty of the devotion is real too, held in the voices, the gestures, the faith that has carried people through centuries of longing. The place is not perfect. It bears the markings of the institution that preserved and limited Mary in equal measure.

But because of it, we still have her: not whole, not untouched, but present in fragments, in contradictions, in wounds that became clues, in images that ask to be looked at again.

You take a step back, careful not to disturb the Mass, and turn around intending to leave. Only then does the organ catch your attention across the way, exuberant with carved figures, gilded scrollwork, and upward thrust. Drawn toward it, you cross beneath the painted ceiling to the opposite end of the church and find yourself standing beneath its gilded vertigo. Your eyes tumble from figure to flourish with no obvious place to land, so visually consuming that it threatens to be the last thing you remember.

Almost. Because by now you have learned that looking beyond is how one begins to see beyond. Above the organ, another fresco emerges from the shadows, antiqued in the same muted palette as the boat scene. It rests between two more familiar images, one recalling Mary's choice of the better part, the other her vigil beneath the cross.

Before you study the details, craning past the organ as you once craned past the ciborium to see the red shoes in San Clemente, you turn back across the church and notice how deliberately the two scenes seem to answer one another. There, Mary in her boat. Here, another muted panel. Both are tucked into the folds of Rococo grandeur, easy to overlook because they are quiet, and impossible to miss because they are different.

Your gaze returns to the fresco above the organ and begins to take in the details. A long table stretches through the scene, disciples gathered around it. Bodies cluster and lean, forming a low horizon of motion and exchange. The space feels dense with voices, reaction, response. At the center, Jesus and a feminine figure are joined in a way that creates a V-shaped axis you almost refuse to see. Because for one dizzying moment, it looks as though Leonardo da Vinci's Last Supper has found its way into Magdalene's cycle.

You sigh. Surely not. How much more could there possibly be? There comes a point when even wonder turns into fatigue. And still, the scene pulls you back to the scriptural place where love is embodied as a title, to "the disciple whom Jesus loved." There, nearness is no longer only position at the table. It becomes an invitation to the reader, the receiver of the Logos, to step into the place of belovedness.

"In the beginning was the word . . . " The line moves through you as you turn toward the exit. Near an offering box, a small stack of leaflets catches your attention, almost the only information the church seems to offer. You take one, hoping to carry away some trace of the space you have just encountered, some record of the Magdalene portrayed here. Then you step outside and back into the August glare, noticing that the Roman heat is waiting exactly where you left it.

Before you have even descended the church steps, you glance down. Across the stapled three-page "pamphlet," fluorescent yellow highlights a question shouted in red, all-capital Italian letters: "MA CHI FU VERAMENTE MARIA MADDALENA?" Who really was Mary Magdalene?[9]

The irony is almost too much. Red letters under fluorescent yellow, on something that looks like a school handout, as though the question has been caught between two Magdalenes: the one labeled by tradition and the one you have just seen illuminated above it.

You don't need to translate the words to understand how they have colored the "real Magdalene." The cover image has already supplied the answer beneath the scarlet letters through a somber, marbled woman kneeling against a black background. She is nude but for the thin drapery barely clinging to her body. Her long hair is loose and she gazes down at a cross in her hands. Beside her, a skull completes the lesson.

Still, after everything you have just seen inside the sanctuary dedicated to its namesake "saint," some part of you wants to believe the pages might begin there only because that is where most people begin: with the reputation, the assumptions, and the old slander cast across her name. But as you move through the images, that hope thins quickly.

The scenes are as eerily familiar as the golden thread you had traced inside, only here it has been dragged through mud. Magdalene at the foot of the cross, thrown forward in sorrow. Magdalene in the garden, called by name, yet still kneeling, reaching, restrained. Magdalene as myrrhbearer, rendered in gray, her face drawn with sorrow, holding the jar that should have marked devotion, but is so easily turned back into a marker of her supposed sin. And then a lamentation, overwrought in its violence. Magdalene arrives like a storm, mouth open, garments flying, her grief turned into a grotesque tableau.

It is all here, folded into a flimsy little guide to the old charge of female excess: the weeping woman, the fallen woman, the irrational woman, the woman overcome by her body, the woman whose love must be translated into frenzy before it can be understood. Different artists, different centuries, yet somehow the same Magdalene emerges each time, branded again in scarlet, as if the mark could still keep her contained. Gregory the Great himself might as well have stood behind every brush, gathering centuries of suspicion about women, desire, and the body into a single figure and fastening it to her name. And this, after the church had offered something so much more radiant, so much more spacious, so much less afraid of her. Instead of reproducing the Magdalene its own sanctuary has dared to imagine, or even identifying the artists who gave her such elevated form, the pamphlet circles back to the old wound. It culminates in the most devastating image of all: Donatello's *Maddalena penitente.*

Here, Augustine of Hippo's celebrated theology of restraint takes form in a woman made almost unrecognizable. Hair is all she has left, falling in tangled strands around an emaciated frame, covering her where clothing does not. Her cheeks are hollow. Her eyes sink deep into their sockets, almost skull-like. Skin clings to bone. Ribs press through thinning flesh. Even her posture collapses inward, as though the self has been worn away through years of deprivation. She appears less like a living woman than a body slowly disappearing from the world.

The sculpture asks you to see holiness in the wasting. Virtue in the hunger. Sanctity in the erasure of the flesh. Her body is made to testify not to wisdom, witness, authority, or love, but to deprivation. A woman made small enough to be called redeemed.

You are not unfamiliar with the swing from sinner to saint, from ruined woman to redeemed woman, from desire to deprivation. But to see it in images tied to the same place is something else entirely. Inside the sanctuary, Mary had stood beside Jesus, hands lifted, present and radiant, allowed the fullness of witness and authority. In the pamphlet, she cowers in a wasting body, stripped down until holiness looks almost indistinguishable from punishment. The contradiction is not subtle. It is visual, immediate, almost unbearable. Why preserve one Magdalene in gold and circulate another in ruin? What, exactly, is the church so afraid of?

You stare at it for a moment, fighting the immediate impulse to rip the pamphlet into pieces. But you don't. The little brochure could not repair centuries of suppression and violence, even if it had told the truth. But neither can it erase the truth Santa Maria Maddalena has already shown you. The recognition remains because it is no longer only an idea. It is something felt, something sensed, something known. And this, too, is part of following Magdalene: learning to live with the dissonance around her. The image and the interpretation will not always agree. The symbol and story will continue to pull against one another. Your task is not to reconcile them, but to hold fast to what you know to be true. That lesson could hardly be clearer than it is here. The very church that preserves such rare, glorifying art of her still curates a misogynistic caricature with no scriptural foundation instead of the woman bathed in golden light. And still, she rises, even from a text intent on diminishing her. Can you feel her? Can you see her? You do not have to make peace with the wound to know what survived it, or to outgrow what it made of her.

Perhaps this is where refusal begins, not in argument, but in the body. Not as theory, but as sensation. Your feet ache. Your eyes feel oversaturated with color and image. Only now do you realize how hungry you are, and there is nothing symbolic about it. After the flood of images asking women's bodies to explain, confess, suffer, or disappear, your own hunger feels almost like a return. Your desire for nourishment does not need to be purified, punished, explained, or made holy. It only needs to be answered. You decide to trust it.

*

Almost without thinking, you drift down the steps and toward a line spilling down the block outside a small corner shop, the kind Romans and travelers alike seem to know instinctively. The smell of toasted bread and olive oil lingers in the air. People cluster beneath a chalkboard scrawled with combinations of cured meats and cheeses, each sandwich wrapped in paper and eaten standing in the street.

After Santa Maria Maddalena, even the menu feels abundant in its own way, its names stacked with meats, cheeses, herbs, and oils until choosing becomes part of the feast. In the end, you order the simplest thing. "La Summer": *prosciutto toscano, fiordilatte* mozzarella, tomato, and basil.

While you wait, something catches your eye beyond the line of people. Just over their heads, a painted woman gazes down from an oval frame fixed to the corner of the building.

Of course.

By now you are half convinced Rome is doing this on purpose, but there she is. Painted in a side profile, long bright red hair spills over bare shoulders. Her head tilts upward against a dark background. No veil. No crown. Mother Mary would never be shown with bare shoulders. It's Magdalene, held in a perfect oval, watching over the Piazza della Maddalena, just across from the church dedicated to her, on the very street that bears her name.

You cannot help but laugh. And after so much revelation, the laughter feels almost human. So does the hunger. So does the simple, stubborn fact of being alive.

By the time the sandwich reaches your hands, the bread is still warm. The paper crackles as you unwrap it and standing under Magdalene's gaze, you take a bite. Tomato juice and olive oil run down your fingers. The mozzarella is soft and milky, softening the salt of the prosciutto. Then the basil comes through, sweet and peppery. It is almost embarrassingly good. For a moment, there is nothing to solve, nothing to defend, nothing to interpret. Only hunger answered, pleasure allowed, and your body welcomed back into joy.

You look up again, taking in a woman with red hair and bare shoulders watching over the piazza as if she has been there all along. Then you notice the red in your hands too, the tomato slipping from the bread, ripe and bright in the sunlight. After all the yellow inside the church, red has found you again, no longer as the scarlet lettering of accusation, but as tomato and sunlight, as juice on your fingers, as appetite, as life.

Though the golden thread in her church was uplifting, the red so typical of Magdalene need not be abandoned. After all, it belongs to power alongside that white and gold of the Vatican flag, to cardinals, martyrdom, passion, papal shoes crossing marble floors. Or carried by a woman standing as close to Christ in her red robe and shoes in San Clemente as the woman in gold and white in Maddalena. Seen this way, you think, perhaps red was never the problem.

The problem is how the thread is followed. From Magdalene's hair, it is easy to trace red back into accusation, but red is one of the oldest threads there is. Long before it entered scripture, human hands were grinding red ochre into pigment and carrying it into caves, onto bodies, into burials. Red already belonged to blood and earth, to life, death, return. When scripture takes up the color, it does not invent that charge so much as carry it forward. In Genesis, a scarlet thread marks the child emerging from Tamar's womb; in Joshua, a scarlet cord hangs from Rahab's window as a sign of protection and survival. Red is birth, bloodline, boundary, rescue. It marks the body at the place where life comes through. Like the serpent, it has always carried the double charge of danger and protection, wound and remedy, venom and antidote. So why, when it gathers around Magdalene, does one side of that power so often swallow the other? Why does vitality become accusation?

It is not only Magdalene. You can trace the red thread through fairy tales, women's stories, and old myths, where the color keeps appearing at the threshold between girlhood and danger, desire and punishment, body and awakening. It appears as an fruit, cloak, shoes, lips, and blood. Snow White's poisoned fruit. Little Red Riding Hood's cloak. The girl in Andersen's *The Red Shoes.* The pricked finger of Sleeping Beauty. Persephone's pomegranate seeds. The color is present in stories that teach the same lesson in different forms: a woman's appetite must be watched, her beauty must be moralized, her longing must be punished, her crossing must be feared.

But here, on Magdalene's own street, the red feels less like warning than enchantment, less like a mark against her than a thread you want to tie around your wrist, something worn in remembrance of what was distorted, buried, and nearly taken. It does not deny the danger. It carries it differently, with pride, with power, with the pulse of blood that sheds and returns, sea foam, and women rising from more than one world. It remembers what survived.

And because red has already begun to move like water, another red-haired woman rises almost inevitably into memory. Ariel, Disney's little mermaid, with her impossible red mane, carries the old signal in a modern song.

She sings from the depths, among broken things, wanting to be part of a world from which she is excluded. She lifts a fork as if it were a treasure, draws it through her hair, and calls it a dinglehopper, misnaming it but sensing that it matters. She does not know what the object is for, only that it belongs to a world she longs to enter. Moments later, she turns toward another mystery entirely. "What's a fire and why does it, what's the word, burn?"

And there, in the middle of "Part of Your World," a bright Disney song from 1989, Magdalene appears beside the flame Ariel reaches toward. Framed among the treasures in Ariel's grotto is Georges de La Tour's *Magdalene with the Smoking Flame*, a woman in contemplation before fire, skull, mirror, light, and pearls. The image is so obvious it almost escapes notice. Suddenly, her cave in the depths is not only a chamber of collected things, but another grotto of longing, where objects of a forbidden world gather around a woman before a fire she cannot fully possess and cannot stop seeking. The scene is not a throwaway—not a childish accident, but a woman's longing written into a song everyone thinks they already know.

Disney softens the ending, but the cost is still there. A woman must give up her voice to be transformed, to cross into the world she longs for. Even Andersen's tale turns on the same wound. To cross over, the little mermaid must surrender her voice. Her body is altered, pain is made beautiful, her longing is punished and spiritualized. The old bargain returns: transformation at the cost of speech.

You continue south along Via della Maddalena, back toward the Pantheon, thinking of the cost, and of how often women are asked to pay for passage with some part of themselves. Magdalene is not voiceless exactly. Scripture lets her speak. She tells the disciples, "I have seen the Lord." But the witness who speaks is not the same as the authority later allowed to interpret. Her testimony survives, yet the tradition around her keeps lowering it, translating witness into penitence, intimacy into scandal, presence into grief. A voice can be recorded and still be contained. A woman can speak and still be made smaller than what she saw.

Maybe that is why the mermaid's bargain cuts so deeply here. What happens to a woman's voice after she speaks? Who carries it forward? Who is allowed to hear it, and who is told to mistrust the sound? Magdalene did not disappear into silence. Her voice moved differently. Follow that song far enough, and it leads beyond the mermaid, beyond even Magdalene's wounded transmission, toward an older figure whose power was voice from the beginning: the Siren.

Before the fish-tail fixed them to water, the earliest Greek sirens belonged to the air. They were part woman, part bird, appearing in archaic art with wings, claws, and human heads. Sometimes beautiful, sometimes uncanny, and almost frightening. In the ancient Mediterranean, birds belonged easily to the soul, to prophecy, to divine messages, to the dead, to crossings between worlds. The dove, before it became Christian shorthand for the Holy Spirit, moved through Inanna, Tanit, Aphrodite, Venus, and Asherah.

In Homer, the Siren's danger was knowledge: she knew too much, she promised to tell what happened at Troy. She tempted men away from ordinary life not through the body, but through fascination, memory, wisdom, and transcendence. Sirens were dangerous because they possessed what ordinary limits cannot contain.

Perhaps this is why the golden Magdalene could be preserved in the church but not trusted on the pamphlet. She calls too clearly. She stands too near the truth the story tried to bury. A Magdalene bathed in light, beside Christ, radiant with witness and authority, does not ask to be pitied. She does not kneel low enough to be managed. She summons. She remembers. She knows. And somehow, because she knows, something in you knows too.

And there it is again, the siren's call you first heard reverberating against Provençal limestone, now echoing through Roman streets, church ceilings, painted bodies, red hair, hunger, and song. Truth finds its pitch inside you. For a moment, the scattered notes seem to answer as a secret chord you have been learning, all along, to hear. And once heard, it becomes difficult not to understand what followed.

In the medieval imagination, the Siren becomes something else, no longer the woman of dangerous knowledge, but the woman of dangerous flesh. The mirror appears. The comb appears. Wings give way to the fishtail. Beauty becomes vanity. Voice becomes seduction. Female power becomes temptation. In bestiaries and church art, the warning hardens: a woman who draws the eye becomes the distraction that pulls man from God. A Jezebel, they would say. But who, exactly, were the victors who made her death by dogs into a triumph?

By the time the fork appears in Ariel's grotto, the distortion has become ironically exact. Made for hunger, it is lifted to the hair. Made to feed the body, it becomes a tool of beauty. The mistake is funny, but it is also perfect. Even appetite has been trained to pass through vanity before it can be seen. The charge keeps changing its costume, but never its aim. If a woman hungers, she is suspect. If she adorns herself, she is suspect. If she sings, shines, knows, or longs beyond the place assigned to her, she becomes the danger. Make her dangerous, then call the cage protection. Make her song threatening, then wonder why the caged bird sings.[10]

*

Via della Maddalena spills you back into Piazza della Rotonda, where the crowds gather around the Pantheon and the city widens around its ancient center. Across the square, beyond the fountain, you see the image you came back to find and begin moving toward the woman watching over this storied place.

But a few steps in, you stop. From somewhere along the edge of the square, another red-haired woman's voice catches your ear through a restaurant patio speaker.

"Run fast for your mother. Run fast for your father. Run for your children, for your sisters and your brothers."

You recognize her immediately. Florence Welch is singing "Dog Days Are Over." You smile before the thought finishes forming. Maybe this is how the call works. Not one voice, not one place, but a current that keeps finding you.

Dog Days. The old name returns once more.

Magdalene, Isis, and Sopdet have more in common than boats, barques, and vessels—and dawn, return, and renewal. Each has been renamed into something smaller than she was. Magdalene into prostitute. Isis into idol and superstition. Sopdet into a dog. But *the star is not a dog*, you think. Yes, this is what you now *know*.

The cobblestone streets you trod down were once walked by priestesses, by priests, by women and men, making offerings, lighting candles, amidst the shrines, obelisks, fountains, lamps, to the goddess. And you feel it with the same certainty that has been gathering since the beginning. Through ordinary days and English fields. Through Provençal limestone and Roman streets. Through paintings, stories, churches, songs, and symbols. Not because every question has been answered, but because something in you has learned to recognize the difference between what is true and what was laid over it.

"Can you hear the horses? 'Cause here they come."

The lyric rushes past like hooves on stone, carrying with it the peculiar exhilaration that arrives when something long obscured begins to emerge back into view. Not a discovery, but a remembering. Something older than the names that covered it. Older than the stories that claimed it. As ancient as flood and star, as mysterious as the pyramids in Egyptian sands.

The song follows you across the square as you continue toward the image waiting beyond the fountain, your thoughts already returning to her hands and the question of what they might be holding, when a woman passes carrying one of those oversized lemons hollowed out and filled with ice. After the salt of the prosciutto and the sun-warmed tomato, it looks impossibly good, and for a second your gaze follows the pleasure of it through the crowd.

Bright yellow, cupped between her hands, it moves like a small vessel of sunlight as she drifts away toward the Pantheon, disappearing into the movement of the square. By now, you know better than to dismiss the ordinary thing that appears at exactly the right moment, not as proof, but as an invitation.

So you keep the promise you made when you first crossed the piazza, walking from the neighborhood named for a missing pinecone toward the church dedicated to Magdalene. With the yellow light still in your eyes, you turn back toward the woman watching over the square, toward the hands you now *know* you need to see. Surely there is something there . . .

Chapter 12

THE MIRACULOUS CATCH

Her chariot wheels struck stone, iron ringing sharply against the pavement as the sound carried ahead of her through the worn streets of Alexandria. Matched mares moved together with contained precision, their black flanks dark with sweat and harnesses flashing as they pulled forward through the cacophony of noise. Hooves, wheels, shouting vendors, and bodies parting in the street sounded chaos around her, but her voice still carried—low, measured, and confident, guiding the horses with ease and grace. At the center of it all, she stood upright and balanced inside the chariot box, one hand steady on the reins as the axle turned beneath.

She wore a philosopher's mantle; its gray wool plain enough to refuse display and distinct enough to mark her authority. Yet it was not the dress of a philosopher, nor the singularity of her position as a woman driving her own chariot, that distinguished her against the gleaming brightness of the broad white streets. It was the manner of her demeanor, the fluidity of her passage, the way she could move among the people with the unguarded confidence of someone accustomed to leadership in public life. Her femininity did not keep her from following her duty to wisdom, choosing to teach among the people, even if that visibility made her vulnerable as a woman.

She was Hypatia of Alexandria, daughter of Theon, a scholar formed in the last echoes of the Mouseion's world. But she was far more than the daughter of a learned man. Hypatia became a mathematician, philosopher, and teacher in her own right, one of the final great minds shaped by Alexandria's ancient tradition of inquiry before that world began to disappear.

What Hypatia achieved did not make her anomalous, but exemplary, a culmination of what her city's intellectual culture could still contain in the late fourth into the fifth century. She embodied an older possibility of what a woman could hold and carry, first in the temple, later in the library, across ritual, philosophy, mathematics, and sacred order. Even as Christian Rome tightened its hold on Alexandria, Hypatia exemplified that a woman could still learn, guide, and gather community as a recognized authority.[1]

Hypatia may have been among the most accomplished female philosophers in antiquity, but almost nothing securely attributable to her survives. The tenth-century Byzantine encyclopedia known as the Suda credits her with three commentaries: on Diophantus's *Arithmetica*, on the *Astronomical Canon* of Ptolemy, and on the *Conics* of Apollonius. Book III of her father Theon's commentary on Ptolemy's *Almagest* contains the heading: "Commentary by Theon of Alexandria on Book III of Ptolemy's *Almagest*, the edition revised by my daughter the philosopher Hypatia." The classicist Alan Cameron has argued that this attribution is genuine and it is in fact Hypatia's edition.[2]

Several ancient and medieval sources preserve Hypatia's legacy. Her student Synesius of Cyrene, later a Christian bishop, left seven surviving letters asking her about mathematics, astronomy, and the design of scientific instruments, including the astrolabe. Socrates Scholasticus praised her as a woman of surpassing learning and philosophy. Damascius, the last head of the Athenian Neoplatonic school, wrote of her beauty, her purity, and her public visibility in Alexandria. Three further notices complete the record from Philostorgius, Hesychius of Miletus, and John of Nikiû, the seventh-century Coptic chronicler whose hostile account recast her as a pagan witch and magician.

Hypatia was not a Christian, though many of her students were, several of them future bishops. By her lifetime, Alexandria's old religious plurality had been narrowed by Christian public power as Theodosius I's edicts had outlawed pagan sacrifice and authorized the closure of pagan temples. Hypatia was alive to witness the devastation of the Serapeum in 391, to see centuries of sacred ground taken down in swift procession. Yet the destruction of temples did not erase the philosophical world that had formed her.

What Hypatia believed, and how she gave form to that belief, likely moved through the language of her life's work, which was Neoplatonism. For Hypatia, philosophy was a way of living, a discipline of the soul meant to bring a person into harmony with the truth of existence. In Neoplatonic thought, all life flowed from a single source called the One, or the Good, and the philosopher's task was to turn back toward that source through contemplation, study, moral discipline, and purification. Hypatia embodied this discipline as devotion through balance, harmony, restraint, and peace.

By Hypatia's time, the great libraries had faded and civic balance was strained, yet philosophical life persisted. As leader of the Neoplatonic school, Hypatia moved where Alexandria's intellectual and political worlds overlapped, commanding what Socrates Scholasticus called "extraordinary dignity and virtue." Her reputation for wisdom, moral clarity, and rare trust across divisions made her advisor to Orestes, the Roman prefect whose office carried imperial authority in Egypt and unusual independence from Rome. Socrates Scholasticus records that Orestes visited her often and consulted her on the city's affairs, making Hypatia visible within the highest reaches of civic authority just as Alexandria's order began to fray. Orestes was Christian, but his faith did not spare him a protracted conflict with the city's new bishop, Cyril.

Cyril of Alexandria was the same man who would defend Theotokos at the Council of Ephesus in 431, where he manipulated the proceedings to destroy his rival Nestorius. Four years later, Theodosius II ordered Nestorius's writings burned. But that was his future. When Cyril succeeded his uncle Theophilus as bishop in 412, he plotted to expand episcopal authority from church to state. He was scheming to make the bishop, not the prefect, the true ruler of Alexandria. Cyril laid the groundwork for this crisis by assembling the *parabalani*, lay-monks who served as an ecclesiastical militia. Loyal to Cyril alone, and known for their violence, the *parabalani* would spiral out of his control; perhaps chaos itself was part of what he was engineering. When Cyril expelled the Jewish community from Alexandria in 414 and seized their property, he tore out one of the city's oldest and most integral populations. Orestes appealed to the emperor, insisting that Christian authority could not excuse public violence or the seizure of private property. From this moment, the conflict between the two men sharpened.

One morning, as Orestes was passing through the city in his chariot, he was attacked by a group of Nitrian monks who were supporters of Cyril. Calling the prefect a sacrificer and heathen, they pelted Orestes with stones, and one, hurled by a monk named Ammonius, struck him on the head and drew blood. Orestes had Ammonius arrested, publicly tortured, and put to death, actions that fell within the brutal logic of Roman authority but infuriated Cyril. Rather than condemning the act of violence against Orestes, Cyril briefly elevated the assailant as a martyr, a move that upset many Alexandrian Christians. Orestes, shaken, grew more cautious in his public appearances. But Cyril, having failed to bring the prefect to heel directly, turned his attention to the woman Orestes kept consulting.

To Cyril, Hypatia appeared not as a woman of wisdom, but as a threat to his power that could not easily be overcome. Cyril could hardly attack Hypatia for not being a Christian while men loyal to him were attacking a Christian Roman prefect. What scandalized him was not her beliefs, but the visible fact of a powerful man listening to a woman who answered to no one but herself. The only weapons remaining at Cyril's disposal were words. He began spreading a rumor, or even more cunningly, had members of his circle begin it for him. The slander claimed that Hypatia had bewitched Orestes, that her influence over the prefect came from magic and illicit knowledge, that she alone stood between him and reconciliation with the bishop. These lies carried through the city until accusation became permission. What followed was sudden, horrific, and irreversible: an eruption that caught Hypatia, and the city itself, unprepared.

It was Lent, March 415. Hypatia was moving through the streets in her chariot, as was her custom; unguarded, accessible, the way she had always been. She did not know that the rumors had hardened into intent, that Cyril's *parabalani* and the crowd his lies had incited were lying in wait for her. Socrates Scholasticus recorded that the men had "waylaid" her as she returned home, a word that preserves the ambush without softening it. The ringleader was Peter the Lector, a reader in Cyril's church. The mob pulled Hypatia from her chariot and dragged her to the Caesareum, a former temple of the deified Caesar converted into a church. There they stripped and killed her, tearing flesh from bone with *ostraka*, the broken potsherds used for everyday writing and counting, before dismembering and burning her remains outside the city.

The shock was immediate. News of Hypatia's brutal murder spread to Constantinople and to Rome. Even Emperor Theodosius II, hardly sympathetic to non-Christians, responded with decrees placing the *parabalani* under closer scrutiny. Socrates Scholasticus, a Christian writing for Christian readers, still declared that the murder brought "no small opprobrium upon Cyril and upon the Alexandrian Church."[3] Cyril would not be remembered for his hand in the death of a peace-seeking woman, but for his triumph at Ephesus, where he defended Mary as Theotokos. Yet secular historians would return to Hypatia's murder as a fault line: a change in eras, a divide in time.

Her death marked a turning point in the history of the West, and in the history of Christianity. What disappeared with Hypatia was not only a woman, nor even only a philosopher, but a way of approaching truth.

The Gospels describe Jesus moving through crowds, speaking in parables and engaging in exchange, drawing listeners into self-examination. He invited his people to perceive differently, to recognize what had been hidden, to encounter the Father as present and active, and to awaken to that reality within themselves. Even the language with which Jesus spoke, in phrases that may seem confusing, demanded the hearer's own work. The Church Fathers would gradually reverse this way of teaching. A religion that began on the dusty roads of Judea and Galilee, among working people, women, and the marginalized, became increasingly led by highly educated men from comfortable, often elite backgrounds. Many, Augustine of Hippo included, had been trained in philosophy and rhetoric as well as Christian scripture.

Augustine was nearly Hypatia's exact contemporary, having been born within a few years of her, he was almost certainly aware of her death in 415, the year he was at work on *The City of God*. His own theology drew deeply on the Greek tradition, the same Neoplatonism that Hypatia was an expert in. But his doctrine of original sin took classical assumptions about the female body and transposed them into something Greek philosophers would not have recognized. Beyond the harm Augustine's theology would inflict upon women existed an irony: Western Christianity would be built from a philosophical inheritance it refused to recognize, then turned against.

After Hypatia died, to be educated in the ancient knowledge of philosophy, and even the natural sciences came to be suspected as being pagan. The reasoning was simple. The great philosophers were not Christian, their cosmos was not created by Jesus, and so the entire tradition was not to be trusted. Under Justinian I, the same imperial campaign that brought the last temple of Isis at Philae to an end also closed the Athenian Academy, the last home of Greek philosophy. School and temple, philosophy and goddess, fell simultaneously. The bridge between critical inquiry and Christianity would not be rebuilt for nearly a thousand years.

Before that severing, Alexandria had been a rare place where philosophy continued to flourish into late antiquity, an environment that had long made room for women. Even after Egypt became the personal possession of the Roman emperor, Alexandria remained a world apart, a gleaming crossroads where languages, gods, and ways of knowing met without losing their shape. But Alexandria was still Egypt, and Egypt's ancient traditions had granted women legal, religious, and symbolic authority in ways few Greek or Roman cities allowed. That inheritance helped make the city a world where brilliant women could flourish.

For all the names that have been lost, enough examples of Alexandrian female minds survive intact to offer a portrait of what might have been possible. Cleopatra VII, of course, remains one such reminder—remembered not only as a queen, but as a scholar-philosopher. Too beloved to be erased, her story was secured on Rome's terms, with her power preserved and her sovereignty contained. Yet the throne was not the only route to an education for a woman in this era and city. Some Alexandrian women entered history through stranger remnants, leaving behind an apparatus, a recipe, a title, or a fragment of mastery preserved by those who came after.

Mary the Jewess, also remembered as Mary the Prophetess or Mary the Copt, may have lived between the first and third century. Zosimos of Panopolis credited her as the founder of alchemy itself, the inventor of the *kerotakis*, the *tribikos*, and the *bain-marie*. Her name preserved the Axiom of Maria: "One becomes two, two becomes three, and out of the third comes the one as the fourth." Cleopatra the Alchemist left the *Chrysopoeia*, preserving diagrams of furnaces and the ouroboros. Pandrosion, an Alexandrian mathematician, received Book III of Pappus's Collection, where he addressed her as "most learned." Aedesia, a Neoplatonist in the century after Hypatia, carried the tradition forward. Even the *Therapeutrides* on Lake Mareotis, the Jewish female contemplatives Philo described, reflected this lineage.

Beyond those who entered history through formal roles, many women of Alexandria's wealthy and educated households were schooled alongside their brothers. More than anything, an educated Alexandrian was taught not what to think, but how to think. In *Cleopatra: A Life*, Stacy Schiff vividly reconstructs Cleopatra's training, not only the tutors who formed her or the subjects she mastered, but the habits of mind her education was meant to cultivate. Her royal example opens a window onto a wider Alexandrian reality: women, too, could be formed in that disciplined art of reading, reasoning, and discernment.[4]

Girls of educated households would have begun with Aesop's fables, learning to find the moral hidden in the story. Older students moved to Plato's allegories and Homer's Odyssey, reading narrative for philosophical and spiritual meaning. Truth, students male and female learned, arrived veiled, waiting to be drawn out. They would have been raised on Homer and Euclid, Sappho and Archimedes, and on Egypt's history, Alexander's triumphs. Like their brothers, girls could write with stylus on wax and reed pen on papyrus, hold compass and straightedge over trays of fine sand, and trace circles and intersecting lines while learning Euclid's first proof.

Mary Magdalene may have been a Jewish woman born and raised in Alexandria, arriving in Jerusalem at precisely the right moment to find her way to the Jordan River and cross paths with a teacher from Galilee. Or she may have been a woman from a small fishing town on the Sea of Galilee, a place known for its salted fish. Somewhere within that spectrum of possibility, a real woman lived and breathed. The intricacies of her path escape the record of history, yet the force of her memory remains remembered within one of the greatest stories ever told.

There is nothing implausible about imagining the author of the Fourth Gospel, and perhaps the eyewitness behind it, as a highly educated Alexandrian. The Gospel invites that world, with Logos, Wisdom, Jewish scripture, Greek thought, and traces of Egyptian sacred imagination all moving together. Scholars have no trouble placing the text in that kind of intellectual atmosphere. The difficulty only begins when the mind imagined behind it belongs to Mary.

Because if Mary Magdalene had been a man, she would already be treated as one of the most serious candidates for the Beloved Disciple. If Magdalene were a man, she would easily have been the most prominent disciple, the figure from whom apostolic authority was built, on the eminence of her resurrection witness alone. But because she is a woman, the possibilities around her have been dismissed as implausible before they even enter argument.

The excuse of ancient gendered norms dies the moment Alexandria enters the story. Women in Mary's lifetime could be educated, mobile, wealthy, philosophically formed, and religiously consequential. If Mary needed wealth to enter those worlds, the Gospel of Luke records that she had it. All the same evidence that led to the possibilities of wife, priestess, and even leader, can be reinterpreted with even greater gravity, as noblewoman, patron, philosopher, theologian. As a woman like Hypatia, but four hundred years prior: educated, intellectually serious, spiritually disciplined, and dangerous to the structures that could not contain her.

Between witness and author, legend and theology, history and symbol, Mary begins to come into view. Perhaps Mary Magdalene never held the pen that composed the Fourth Gospel. Or perhaps the text retains traces of her own story, her memory, her theology: not only in the events it records or the phrases it preserves, but in the language of faith woven throughout. If history left only fragments of Mary's life, the Gospel may have kept another kind of record—not a name written plainly at the surface, but a presence carried through the story like thread through cloth.

A BOAT AT DAWN

The Fourth Gospel's Prologue opens onto the cosmic vision that would shape Christian theology; the Epilogue turns to something intimate and mythic. Light and darkness define the opening, while water, boats, nets, and fish organize the close. The Prologue is saturated with philosophy and symbolism traceable to the Alexandrian imagination, and the Epilogue may be read through that same world. In a Gospel built on signs, recognition, double meaning, and hidden identity, every word matters: the hour, the water, the side of the boat, the number of disciples, the weight of the net, the fire on shore, the meal already waiting. Each becomes a clue to follow. Its provenance remains contested: some scholars see it as a later addition, some as the work of a redactor, others as the hand of the Beloved Disciple. More than one may be true.[5]

The Epilogue opens at dawn, the hour of Venus as morning star, the threshold between night and day, dark and light, when the veil between worlds was imagined to grow thin. It is also the hour for fishermen—when cooler water and lower light draw fish toward the surface, less wary, more likely to feed. Peter initiates the scene: "I'm going out to fish." Six more disciples join him, counted as Thomas, Nathanael, the sons of Zebedee and two unnamed disciples. "We'll go with you," they reply as the fishing begins with seven total in the boat.[6]

The Sea of Galilee opens the passage into water, the oldest source of origin. Across the ancient world, water carried the same meanings: life begins there, danger waits there, and hidden things rise from its depths. To cross it by boat was never only travel, transport, or labor; it was passage, preservation, the fragile vessel by which life crosses what it cannot control. And to fish was to go farther still: to cast below the visible surface and draw up what had been hidden in the deep.

By dawn, the seven disciples have been fishing all night, their nets coming up empty. This chapter follows the resurrection, but no other detail is given to explain how the risen Christ appears or speaks. "Early in the morning, Jesus stood on the shore, but the disciples did not realize that it was Jesus. He called out to them, "Friends, haven't you any fish?" "No," they answered. He said, "Throw your net on the right side of the boat and you will find some."

To an ancient ear, especially one trained in philosophy or theology, the phrase would have resonated with more than the movement of a net in one direction. Throughout the Mediterranean world, the "right" carried favor, recognition, and right relation, making it less a physical position than a sign of alignment with truth and order. In Hebrew scripture, the "right" hand was the hand of power and blessing: the hand God stretched out to deliver, the hand Jacob laid upon the son he blessed, the place of highest honor where the king was told to sit. Pythagorean thought, preserved in Aristotle's catalogue of opposites, paired the right with limit, light, and virtue, the left with the unbounded and material disorder. Greek omen-reading, too, often made the right the side of coherence and good fortune.[7]

For the Egyptians, the words for west and right were one and the same, *imnt*. The Beautiful West was the mythic direction of the afterlife, and at its threshold stood Imentet, a goddess and a facet of Hathor, a sacred place personified as a woman. In the *Book of Coming Forth by Day*—the corpus modern scholars later named the Book of the Dead—she appeared crowned with a falcon, sometimes winged, sometimes as a kite linking her to Isis and her sister Nephthys. Imentet's image appeared on tomb walls and coffin lids, her arms opened wide, a maternal presence gathering the dead into shelter. At the desert's edge, the goddess waited in the sycamore's shade, offering the parched soul a meal of bread and water.[8]

At Jesus's instruction, the disciples cast again, moving not the boat but the net. With that shift, the miracle comes: "they were unable to haul the net in because of the large number of fish." Three more times the narrative will return to the catch: the fish too plentiful to haul in, the heavy drag toward shore, and the net that, despite the weight, is not torn. The miracle is not abundance alone, but containment. The net bears what should have broken it.

Nets were richly symbolic in antiquity because they gained strength through relation: slight strands knotted into a structure able to receive weight, pressure, and movement. Fluid and pliable, they adapt to what they carry. They catch, separate, sort, and release what they gather now transformed. To make a net, or any woven structure of similar force, was women's work, mundane and sacred at once. In Greek imagination, thread and weaving were inseparable from feminine power: Ariadne's thread opened the labyrinth, Athena presided over the loom, and the Moirai spun, measured, and cut the thread of human fate. In Egypt, the goddess Neith was said to have woven the world upon her loom. Isis and Nephthys wrapped Osiris in fine linen and worked their magic with knotted cords; the *tyet*, or Knot of Isis, became one of the most powerful protective amulets in funerary practice.

What was gathered in this net, of course, was fish. Throughout the Mediterranean world, fish were first and foremost sustenance: the objects of hunger, labor, food, and survival. In the unpredictable environment of their watery home, fish moved in patterns that could be traced; sometimes fish were abundant, other times painfully elusive, their source and cycles all the more mysterious in antiquity. To catch fish was to be able to read these rhythms—a good fishermen still is the one who possesses the perception required to "see" below the surface, to somehow know what is present in its depths. In Mesopotamian myth, Oannes, half fish and half man, emerged from the sea to teach humanity writing, mathematics, agriculture, and the foundations of civilization, one of the seven *apkallu* sages. Nanshe, too, governed fish, fishermen, water, marshland, birds, and dreams. In Syrian and Levantine cults, Atargatis, or Derceto, was associated with fish and doves, transformation, rescue, and fertility, her worship spreading across the region.

In Egypt, fish belonged to the register of creation and rebirth. Fish were essential to Egyptian life, and their slender forms appear across temple walls, amulets, tomb imagery, and river scenes. The tilapia, which carries its young in its mouth before releasing them alive into the water, became a sign of regeneration. The fish-goddess Hatmehit, of Mendes, embodied the Nile's abundance. There were even cults to specific species of fish: the *lates* fish at Latopolis, and the *oxyrhynchus*, or *medjed* fish, at Oxyrhynchus. The funerary texts, too, including the *Book of the Coming Forth by Day*, are filled with boats, nets, fishermen, and the perilous work of passing through what lies beneath the visible world.

So when *ichthys*, the Greek word for "fish," became the acronym ΙΧΘΥΣ, "Jesus Christ, Son of God, Savior," it entered a world already crowded with hunger, mystery, wisdom, rescue, fertility, and hidden life. And when Mary became "Undoer of Knots," Christian devotion inherently drew on a Mediterranean language of binding, loosening, fate, protection, and release, even if Irenaeus inverted the older benevolence of the knot when he recast it as Eve's sin untied by Mary's obedience.

These symbols found their way into other Christian stories, including the feeding of the five thousand men in chapter 6 of the Fourth Gospel. It was a miracle of hidden sufficiency: what appears too little becomes more than enough when taken, blessed, and distributed. The twelve baskets of leftover barley loaves become theology in the Bread of Life discourse that follows: "I am the bread of life," and "whoever eats this bread will live forever."[9]

The Gospel of Luke recorded its own catch of miraculous fish. On the Sea of Galilee, the fishermen, including Peter and the sons of Zebedee, have worked all night and caught nothing—the story is strikingly similar to the Epilogue. Yet in Luke, Jesus's instructions are much simpler: go out into deep water and let down the nets. Peter is central, portrayed as willing and listening, bringing in a catch so plentiful that the net does begin to break while the boat even starts to sink. Peter chastises himself as a sinful man, but Jesus replies telling him not to be afraid. Moments later, Jesus seems to choose Peter as a leader: you will be *fishers of men*.[10]

Perhaps this is just another memory, another event, a story transposed for a different audience. But if David Trobisch is correct, and the Gospels were smoothed to cultivate apostolic authority by ecclesiastical leaders in the late second century, and if Ann Graham Brock is right that Luke works to privilege Peter, then the Lukan catch may represent more than a parallel. It may be a literary counterclaim—a story shaped to elevate Peter, diminish the Epilogue's force, and withdraw authority from the Beloved Disciple.[11]

If Luke's catch redirects authority toward Peter, then the Fourth Gospel's Epilogue asks to be read with even greater care. What was this story meant to teach, preserve, or encode, and why would a rival version need to shift the weight back toward Peter? What do the Gospel's symbols, signs, and silences reveal? Here, every word turns and every image opens a landscape of meaning. Just after the miraculous catch is secured in the net, one disciple recognizes Jesus: the Beloved Disciple. "Then the disciple whom Jesus loved said to Peter, 'It is the Lord!'"

In Greek, *kyrios* could mean sir, master, or lord. But in Jewish and Christian scripture, "Lord" bore a weight beyond everyday meaning. For observant Jews, the divine name—the four Hebrew letters YHWH revealed to Moses at the burning bush, the tetragrammaton—was too sacred to pronounce. When reading scripture aloud, the reader would substitute Adonai, Hebrew for "my Lord." When the Hebrew Bible was translated into Greek in the third century BCE, YHWH became Kyrios. This is why every English Old Testament, even today, still renders the divine name as LORD in small capitals, a typographic signal that "Lord" is standing in for the unspeakable name beneath it. So when the Fourth Gospel's characters call Jesus Kyrios, they are using that same divine-name substitute.

"Lord" is bound to recognition throughout the Fourth Gospel; to call Jesus by that title is to show that one can see his divine identity. In chapter 9, the theme becomes literal: the man born blind moves from darkness into sight and finally says, "Lord, I believe." Continually, the Gospel entrusts this deepest recognition to women: the Samaritan at the well, the Bethany sister, and Magdalene in the garden. This bond between Magdalene, sight, and recognition follows her into legend. In *The Golden Legend*, the man born blind in chapter 9 becomes St. Cedony, sailing in the rudderless boat with Mary Magdalene, Martha, Lazarus, and the others to France. Later, another blind man is led toward the church where Magdalene's body was venerated; he begs to see it, and his eyes are opened.[12]

The name rings out over the water: Kyrios. When Mary Magdalene first sees the risen Christ in the garden, she calls him Rabboni—the familiar teacher—but before and after that personal recognition, she also speaks of him as Lord: "They have taken the Lord out of the tomb," and then after the garden, "I have seen the Lord!" If the Beloved Disciple is Mary Magdalene, then the Kyrios she speaks across the water in the Epilogue is the third time she has named him by that sacred title since his resurrection.

Across the ancient world, names carried sacred power, part of a broader conviction that words could reveal, summon, bless, bind, or transform. In Egypt, the *rn*, the name, was one of the essential parts of a person's being, often counted among five. To preserve a name was to preserve a life; to erase a name was to threaten a soul. Beneath the public name lay the hidden one, the *rn imen*, the secret name that held the deepest force of a person or god.

That power of divine naming took a specific literary form in the centuries leading up to the Fourth Gospel: the aretalogy, a hymn in which a deity declares her own attributes and acts in the first person. *I am this. I am that. I am the one who has done this.* The most famous aretalogies belonged to Isis. The *Kyme* aretalogy, inscribed in stone on the coast of Asia Minor in the first century BCE or first century CE, opens, "I am Isis, ruler of every land," and continues for nearly fifty lines of self-declaration. Others survive from Maroneia in Thrace, Andros in the Aegean, and Oxyrhynchus in Egypt, each preserving the same first-person form: the goddess names herself over and over again. Though many surviving inscriptions are Greco-Egyptian, scholars believe they preserve older Egyptian formulas of divine self-declaration, spoken in Isis's voice long before they were carved in stone.[13]

The same tradition of divine self-naming echoes in Thunder, Perfect Mind, where a feminine voice declares herself through paradox, gathering opposites into a single sacred identity: first and last, honored and scorned, knowledge and ignorance. Yet this was a text not included in the canon, one that would only resurface in the Nag Hammadi discovery.

The Fourth Gospel draws on sacred-name logic not only through titles like "Lord" and "Messiah" spoken at pivotal moments of recognition, but through Jesus's seven "I am" statements. *Egō eimi*, Jesus declares throughout the narrative, each name joined to a teaching metaphor: the bread of life; the light of the world; the door; the good shepherd; the resurrection and the life; the way, the truth, and the life; the true vine. The standard Christian interpretation traces these declarations to the burning bush in Exodus, where God reveals his name to Moses—I am who I am, the phrase from which the tetragrammaton, YHWH, was formed. But the force of divine self-naming did not belong to Exodus alone. It moved through that older and wider sacred grammar, one the Fourth Gospel may have gathered from.[14]

As soon as the words leave the Beloved Disciple's mouth, Peter is in action, in dramatic fashion. "he wrapped his outer garment around him (for he had taken it off) and jumped into the water." Another small detail might easily slip by unnoticed: Peter clothes himself before entering the water. In the world of Judean and Galilean fishing, laborers commonly set aside their outer garments in order to work freely. So, Peter was not naked in the modern sense; clothing himself before entering the water had its own purpose. Garments belonged to both social order and symbolic transformation: in antiquity, dress marked status, while in myth, the putting on or removal of clothing could alter identity or fate. To be clothed was to be placed within an order; to be stripped was to be exposed, humbled, or remade.

Taking off garments is central in the ancient poem The Descent of Inanna from Sumeria. As the goddess Inanna descends through the seven gates of the underworld, she is made to surrender, piece by piece, the emblems of her power: her crown, jewels, breastplate, ring, measuring rod, and royal garment, until she arrives stripped of status, authority, and protection.[15] In Egyptian funerary practice, the dead were wrapped in linen as Isis had once wrapped Osiris. Across the ancient Mediterranean, priests, initiates, mourners, brides, kings, and the dead were clothed for passage from one state into another. Jewish priestly vestments belong to this same ritual grammar: the high priest entered the Holy of Holies clothed for the crossing, wearing the linen garments prescribed for that sacred threshold.

To get dressed, as Peter did, was to prepare oneself for an encounter. Or, at the very least, it marked the sense of something changing. But Peter's specific gesture may also signal something more particular to his characterization across the Gospel: a concern with appearances and actions, with what is shown rather than what is recognized. Garment aside, the jump and swim physically separates Peter from the six disciples still in the boat. Peter moves ahead of them, seemingly intent on reaching Jesus first, just like he raced to the empty tomb. But Jesus does not greet him as special in any way, rather Jesus waits with a meal ready for all.

After the long night on the water, the scene turns toward morning, warmth, and food: "When they landed, they saw a fire of burning coals there with fish on it, and some bread." The breakfast is already waiting before the disciples come ashore with the full net. It is humble, but not ordinary: a meal set at the threshold between night and day, hunger and provision, labor and recognition. What follows is a form of communion, different from a formal Eucharist, but deeply aligned with the Gospel's theology.

The language of body and blood, bread and wine, which became central to Christian sacramental doctrine, is primarily derived from the Synoptic accounts of the Last Supper. The Fourth Gospel's Last Supper contains no institution of the Eucharist. During the gathering, Jesus washes the disciples' feet and offers an extended teaching on love, service, and self-giving: "Greater love has no one than this: to lay down one's life for one's friends." Many interpreters have read the beach meal in the Epilogue as a communion scene, a eucharistic moment of recognition and provision. The only comparable passage comes in chapter 6, where the feeding of the five thousand turns into the Bread of Life discourse.[16]

The narrative moves by interruption and return: the feeding of the five thousand ends with Jesus withdrawing alone to the mountain. But then he is described walking on the sea to rescue the disciples in a storm and the last sections circle back to the bread from the start. These final passages begin in the Gospel's familiar symbolic mode of bread becoming a sign. Jesus declares, "I am the bread of life," linking the miracle back to Israel's scripture, the manna from heaven. But then the discourse sharpens into vocabulary unusually close to Eucharistic doctrine: "unless you eat the flesh of the Son of Man and drink his blood, you have no life in you." It is this turn that has attracted scholars attention.

In *Das Evangelium des Johannes*, when Rudolf Bultmann famously argued that the Fourth Gospel had been shaped by later ecclesiastical redaction, chapter 6 was one of his clearest examples. It is not only the bread, flesh, and blood that stand out, but the sudden attention to "the Twelve," atypical in the Fourth Gospel, and Peter's perfectly placed confession: "You have the words of eternal life." For Bultmann, these details reflected the marks of a later hand that intentionally aligned the Gospel with Church's emerging Eucharistic doctrine and gave Peter retrospective authority.[17]

If communion was always meant to be about joining with the divine and carrying that life within oneself, then the Epilogue meal exemplifies it. Throughout the Gospel, what is needed has already been given—the fish were always in the water, the meal already waits on shore, and abundance arrives with recognition. In morning light, bread and fish are broken and shared equally. There is no priest, no altar, no ritual gate. Only the risen Christ at the fire, calling everyone to breakfast, even Peter, who had denied him three times before his death. This is the communion the Fourth Gospel weaves: love, repair, and fellowship.[18]

And in a story where every word matters, even the fire is named with precision, like another clue to follow. Charcoal. The Greek noun *anthrakia* appears only twice in the entire New Testament: both in this Gospel, both in scenes with Peter. It was over a charcoal fire in the high priest's courtyard that Peter denied Jesus three times. Charcoal is wood altered by slow, oxygen-starved burning into something denser, darker, and longer-lasting. It is matter that has passed through fire and been remade. In

Isaiah's vision, a burning coal touches the prophet's lips to purify unclean speech. And it is by a charcoal fire that Peter's threefold denial will meet its answer, when Jesus asks him three times, "Do you love me?"

Before that moment, Jesus asks the disciples to bring some of the fish they have just caught. Peter is the one who goes and hauls the net ashore. It is a small action, but it continues the pattern already established throughout the Gospel: Peter moves first, visibly and alone, while the Beloved Disciple recognizes first and remains in relation. The group that began as seven fishermen is now divided, with one swimming ahead, six rowing behind; one moving to the boat for the net, six remaining beside the fire together.

Six was the perfect number, the Greeks believed, because its divisors add up to itself: one, two, and three. To the Pythagoreans, six was an integer of proportion, harmony, balance, and union. In geometry, six was the foundation of hexagonal symmetry: the honeycomb, the snowflake, the crystal lattice, the most efficient packing form in nature. In Jewish tradition, six was the stage that preceded completion: human beings were created on the sixth day in Genesis, and the six days of labor preceded the Sabbath. And in the Fourth Gospel, the most significant six before the Epilogue was the six stone water jars at the wedding at Cana that Jesus transformed into wine—the Gospel's first sign, the first miracle, initiated by his mother.

So when Peter went to retrieve the net from the boat at Jesus's request, the gesture was double: he acted on command, yet once more singled himself out from the community, the bonded, balanced group of six that includes the Beloved Disciple. As the focus moves from meal, to boat, to catch, the narrative repeats the unbroken net and abundant catch for a third time, now described in quantity: "It was full of large fish, 153 of them, but even with so many the net was not torn."

The earliest surviving witness to this passage appears in Papyrus 75, dated to the late second or early third century. The Epilogue is heavily damaged in Papyrus 66 and does not preserve the line. In Papyrus 75, the number appears in Greek numerals: PNΓ': 100, 50, 3. No clear symbolic tradition connected to the number 153 survives before its appearance in the Epilogue. Even so, generations of readers became convinced the number could not be accidental. Theologians, philosophers, mystics, and mathematicians repeatedly returned to it, searching for the logic concealed beneath its precision.[19]

DECIPHERING THE 153

By the first century, numerical harmony, geometry, and proportion were deeply woven into philosophy, theology, and cosmology alike. Pythagorean traditions treated number as the hidden structure beneath reality itself; Platonic thought understood mathematics as a pathway toward eternal order. The Alexandrian intellectual world integrated these traditions more thoroughly than any other in the Mediterranean. Jewish theology, Greek mathematics, and Egyptian cosmology weaving together in what would later flow into the Hermetic tradition. Within such a world, a number like 153 would not have been dismissed as meaningless or accidental; it would have appeared as a sign waiting to be read.

Mathematically, 153 possesses a number of unusual properties. It is the seventeenth triangular number, formed by adding every number from one to seventeen into a single geometric whole: a perfect triangle of 153 points. For ancient mathematicians, triangular numbers revealed arithmetic as geometry, number becoming visible as form. 153 emerges through repeated tripling: $17 \times 3 = 51$, and $51 \times 3 = 153$. Then, it equals the sum of the cubes of its own digits: $1^3 + 5^3 + 3^3 = 153$. Both those properties relate to tripling, three, the number of harmony. 153 is also the sum of the first five factorials: $1! + 2! + 3! + 4! + 5! = 1 + 2 + 6 + 24 + 120 = 153$, meaning it bears the weight of the cumulative multiplicative weight of the first five integers. And 153 is the ninth hexagonal number; hexagonal numbers are the figures built by nesting hexagons inside each other, the same six-sided shape that builds the world.

These properties belong to the number itself; they are mathematical facts before they are symbolic claims. Some would have been familiar within ancient mathematics, others are modern observations. In antiquity, numbers moved naturally between arithmetic, geometry, and meaning. One signified unity and wholeness; three, harmony and balance; five, the marriage number, joining the first feminine integer, two, to the first masculine, three. The digits of 153 also add to nine: three squared, a figure of completion. Considered together, these qualities make 153 especially available to interpretation: shaped by triangle and hexagon, by three and five, by accumulation, harmony, and visible form.

But if the reading stays in numbers alone, it drifts too far from its origin: the Epilogue, and the specific function of 153 within the story. The earliest Christian commentators who took up the number understood this. They worked from the inherited Greek tradition of reading numbers for meaning, but held it to the narrative discipline of the Gospel itself. Chief among them was Origen of Alexandria, writing in the early third century. Origen treated 153 as deliberate and symbolically charged, reading it through the layered allegorical method his Alexandrian school had perfected. His interpretation became the foundation on which later Christian readings of the number were built, carried forward from North Africa to Rome to medieval Britain.[20]

At roughly the same time Origen was reading 153 inside the Gospel, pagan philosophical writers were preserving a similar story around Pythagoras. Neopythagorean writers Porphyry and Iamblichus recounted a tradition in which Pythagoras foretold the number of fish caught in a net, had them counted, and then ordered them released alive. Fishermen, nets, counting, a wise man, philosophical insight, all the elements appear together. By this point the Fourth Gospel had been circulating for more than a century. The Pythagoras story may reflect borrowing from the Epilogue, or both stories may draw from an older shared symbolic vocabulary. Crucially, however, no number is given to the fish, 153 was absent.[21]

Writing in the late fourth century, Jerome connected the 153 fish to the prophetic river vision of Ezekiel, where abundant fish gathered in the life-giving waters flowing from the Temple. Drawing on Oppian's *Halieutica*, Jerome claimed that the sea contained 153 kinds of fish, interpreting the miraculous catch as a symbol of all nations gathered together. Modern classicists have noted that Oppian himself never lists 153 species, so either Jerome misunderstood, conflated, or retrofitted the number to the Gospel. His argument ultimately rested less on zoological precision than on symbolic totality, a synthesis that was characteristic of his era.[22]

In the fifth century, Augustine of Hippo developed the most influential early mathematical interpretation of 153. In his *Tractates on the Gospel of John*, Augustine observed that 153 is the seventeenth triangular number. The *tetractys*, the triangular number ten, had long been revered in Pythagorean tradition as a figure of cosmic harmony, and Augustine was right to see that the Epilogue's number belonged to a world in which geometry could carry meaning. Augustine then divided seventeen into ten and seven, associating ten with the Ten Commandments and seven with the Spirit's sevenfold work, connected to Isaiah. The catch became, for him, a symbol of grace, spiritual fullness, and the saints gathered into the end-time Church. That interpretation reflects a later Christian framework, or even Luke's separate miracle catch, rather than a reading tied to what the Fourth Gospel's writer would have intended.[23]

Two centuries later, Gregory the Great carried Augustine's reading forward in his *Homilies on the Gospels*. Gregory kept Augustine's ten-plus-seven reading of seventeen as Commandments plus the gifts of the Spirit but layered further meanings onto the count: the three of the Trinity, the fifty days between Easter and Pentecost, the gathering of the elect through grace. After Gregory, Christian interprative frame grew more elaborate still. Medieval commentators such as Honorius of Autun and Hugh of Saint-Cher would divide 153 into 144 + 9, joining the 144,000 elect of Revelation to the nine orders of angels, or into 100 + 50 + 3, read as Gentiles, Jews, and the Trinity. What began as a narrative detail became an inexhaustible mystery—a number precise enough to demand explanation, and elusive enough to keep generating speculation.[24]

Across time, the number kept finding new Christian forms. The Dominican rosary eventually expanded to 153 Ave Marias, corresponding to the 150 Psalms framed by three additional prayers. In modern Marian devotion, observers have also noted that the six apparitions of Our Lady of Fátima in 1917 unfolded across 153 days, from May 13 to October 13. Each of the integers, one, five, and three seemed to carry special attention: three for the Trinity and the days in the tomb; five for the wounds of Christ and the Joyful Mysteries of the rosary; one for divine unity, the one body of Christ, the one shepherd and flock. These numbers, patterns, and shapes found expression not only in ideas and prayers, but in stone, carried by geometers and master masons into Gothic cathedrals. Their work was framed through the architectural imagination of scripture, especially the

Temple of Solomon, though the sacred geometry encoded stretched back far before Christianity itself.

In the modern era, 153 inspired renewed fascination in nineteenth- and twentieth-century mysticism and esotericism where increasingly elaborate systems tried to account for the figure. Yet these readings tended to drift from the Gospel's narrative, while projecting meaning and ideas backward, rather than considering the time period of composition. Today, biblical scholars tend to agree that the number must be intentional in some way, but most explanations remain within the Bible and none has fully accounted for the figure's precision.

It may be that the number has resisted interpretation because it has so often been approached from the wrong horizon. It has been read through Rome, later theology, and the Hebrew scriptures, but rarely through the Alexandrian imagination capable of transforming Philo's Logos into the Prologue's opening hymn. In late-first-century Alexandria, theology and philosophy, mathematics and cosmology, allegory and sacred symbolism still moved within a single imaginative field. Whether the Epilogue came from the Beloved Disciple's own memory, a later writer, or the Johannine community, the mind that held the pen that first wrote in "153 fish" was formed through an Alexandrian lens.

So the question becomes: how would someone like Hypatia have read 153? She would have started where any Pythagorean reader started—with the number's triangular root, the integer from which the larger number unfolds. The triangular root of 153 is seventeen.

SEVENTEEN

Numerically, seventeen sits at an edge. Not as ordered as the twelve of the zodiac, the tribes of Israel, and the apostles. Not as irregular as nineteen which resists almost every symbolic system. Seventeen is structured but not closed, prime but adjacent to perfection. In Pythagorean thought, sixteen and eighteen were considered uniquely perfect plane numbers because each is the only figure of its kind in which the perimeter equals the area. The Pythagoreans treated this rare coincidence as evidence of cosmic order, and seventeen as an integer that broke two patterns at once.[25]

Seventeen is the sum of the first four primes, 2 + 3 + 5 + 7, and the seventh prime number. It can be split into two squares, $1^2 + 4^2$, giving it a hidden geometric coherence prized in Pythagorean thought. Among odd primes built from two unequal squares, seventeen is the third: after 5 and 13. Multiplied by nine, it produces 153. And nine is three squared: the triad brought to completion. In Pythagorean and later Christian terms, three carried the weight of the sacred small integer while nine fulfilled it.

In the Hebrew scriptures, the most striking appearance of seventeen comes in the Genesis flood narrative. The flood begins on the seventeenth day of the second month, when "all the fountains of the great deep burst forth, and the windows of the heavens were opened"—the ark comes to rest on the seventeenth day of the seventh month, on the mountains of Ararat. The same number frames the beginning and the end of the waters of judgment. As in the Epilogue, water mediates the passage from one order to another. The world before the waters, and the world remade after them.[26]

At times, the peculiar nature of seventeen migrated into popular culture. In Italy, seventeen is considered so unlucky in folk tradition that some hotels skip the 17th room, airplanes omit the 17th row, and *venerdì* 17 functions as the Italian equivalent of Friday the 13th. The usual explanation is older than simple superstition. The Roman numeral for seventeen, XVII, can be rearranged to spell VIXI, Latin for "I have lived." That is, *my life is over, I am dead.* Stranger still, in French, *dix-sept* and *déception* ring against each other in the ear—a number that breaks and the experience of being caught between two truths. The resonance must be coincidence because their roots are not shared: dix-sept descends from the Latin *decem* (ten) plus *septem* (seven), while *déception* descends from *dē-capere*, or to take down, to capture, to ensnare.

Writing in the early second century in *De Iside et Osiride*, Plutarch provides two ancient explanations for the anxiety surrounding seventeen. First, he preserves the Pythagorean account of seventeen as a numerical obstacle, a cut placed between the harmonious figures of sixteen and eighteen. Then in his account of the Egyptian myth of Isis and Osiris, he notes that Osiris was killed on the seventeenth day of the month of Athyr, the period associated with Hathor. Recounting the myth for a Greek-speaking audience, Plutarch describes Osiris's death and Isis's searching, recovering all but the part consumed by fish, as she resurrects him and conceives new life through magic, grief, tears, breath, and embodied devotion.[27]

The boats, the fish, the nets, and the women at dawn. Women weeping for broken men, women whose faith took its place in the work of resurrection and communion. The Pythagorean obstacle, the death of Osiris, triangular numbers, these may seem disparate and obscure in modernity, but in antiquity they were well-known and integrated. Not for everyone, but for someone highly educated in philosophical schools, especially in Alexandria, they would have been present, palpable, readable. Plutarch happened to be remembering and repopularizing the myths of Isis and Osiris, and the number seventeen, in the early second century—the same era, the same intellectual atmosphere, within which the Fourth Gospel was circling through communities of readers.

THE SHAPE OF 153

If seventeen was legible from an ancient Alexandrian perspective, 153 was still too specific to dismiss and too strange to explain easily. Why not seventeen fish in the net, or 1,700, or some round number like the Gospel's other miracles? Since at least Origen, readers have searched backward through the ancient record for a source. But unlike nard in the anointing, whose sole precedent lies in the Song of Songs, 153 has no obvious home in Jewish scripture. The clearest pre-Gospel appearance of 153 comes in a third-century BCE treatise still foundational to mathematics more than two thousand years later: *Measurement of a Circle.*

Is there anything more primordial than a circle? A line returning in echo of moon and sun? The revolution of the wheel, the perfection of a berry, the pupil of the eye, the form of many seeds, the wandering visible bodies in the sky tracing their way in slow circles against the shimmering fixed dots of stars. Seasons returned in a circle; life death rebirth; planting, growth, decomposition. The circle was pressing, immediate, haunting. Enclosure, unity, totality, mystery, the cosmos itself—all read as one.

The circle can be seen in the markings at Newgrange in Ireland, in the great rings of Avebury and Stonehenge in England, on the ancient pottery of Old Europe. Not just circles, but spirals—like the snake goddesses illuminated by Marija Gimbutas, figurines painted with meanders tracing a path like a river, inverted triangles upon her body.[28] The circle holding sacred ground: the temenos, the mandala, the omphalos, the axis mundi enclosed by a ring, the ouroboros, the circumpunct, the sun disk, the clock, the halo, the Eucharistic host. Wedding rings, prayer wheels, the round dance, the circular fire pit. A circle makes a world. A circle is the place of birth. A circle holds what seems impossible.

It was the Greek philosophical tradition that turned the mystery of the circle into a problem of reason. In Plato's world, geometry disclosed the structure of reality itself, and the circle became its central figure. About a century later, Archimedes approached it not as symbol but as proof. A mathematician, physicist, engineer, astronomer, and inventor, Archimedes is still remembered as one of the most innovative thinkers of the ancient world. In *Measurement of a Circle*, he asked one of geometry's most difficult questions: how can the curved be measured by the straight?[29]

To measure a circle, Archimedes had to bring circumference into relation with line, curve into relation with polygon, wholeness into relation with number. He did this by placing many-sided figures inside and outside the circle, tightening the bounds until the circle could be approached through reason. The most important building block was the equilateral triangle—the figure from which the regular hexagon, his starting polygon, was built.

The equilateral triangle is governed by a single irrational ratio—the square root of three, $\sqrt{3}$—which defines the triangle's height and underlies 60-degree symmetry. $\sqrt{3}$ could not be expressed exactly, so Archimedes worked with it through two bounds, upper and lower, that allowed precise calculation. Together the two bounds contained $\sqrt{3}$ between them; close enough to the true value that a mathematician could work with it. The upper bound set the value's ceiling; the lower bound set its floor. For $\sqrt{3}$, Archimedes calculated the lower bound as 265/153. 153 did not appear in isolation, but as part of a pair. As the denominator, 153 held the value just below $\sqrt{3}$—close enough to be accurate, yet small enough to remain usable.

In Archimedes's text, 153 carries no special emphasis—the number was not intended to mean anything beyond the function it served in calculating $\sqrt{3}$. One of the greatest misunderstandings around Archimedes is the claim that he used circles to arrive at his proof of $\sqrt{3}$ and its lower-bound ratio involving 153—this is a modern conflation. The shape itself is simple, consisting of two circles intersecting to form a narrow, lens-shaped space between them. Later tradition would call that space the *vesica piscis*, Latin for "fish's bladder," and some websites and sacred geometry books even attribute the name to Archimedes. But the term is medieval. Archimedes wrote in Greek, and no equivalent expression appears in his surviving texts. And Archimedes's own work reflects only polygons like the hexagon, not the two overlapping circles.

That intersecting form belongs to the most basic language of geometry, an ancient figure that would carry symbolic meaning for centuries before the medieval name *vesica piscis* arrived. The name has stuck to the circle form, nonetheless, in part because the lens-shape does resemble a fish. Another misunderstanding lies between the *vesica piscis* and the ichthys, the early Christian acronym developed in the second or third century. There is no tangible, ancient connection between them, but because both involve fish, modern thought has long fused them. From there, the vesica was folded into the Magdalene tradition as well, however sideways. The most visible modern example is the cover of the Chalice Well in Glastonbury—the wrought-iron lid atop the red spring was designed in 1919 by Frederick Bligh Bond, an architect who had directed excavations at Glastonbury Abbey. The cover renders two interlocking circles in the classic vesica form, and the well sits at the heart of the Glastonbury legendary complex, where Magdalene meets Avalon meets the Holy Grail. Beneath these conflations there are intuitions, and beneath the intuitions connections, just ones not fully untangled.

While Archimedes did not use circles to derive the ratio 265/153, $\sqrt{3}$ is the ratio that governs the equilateral triangle and in antiquity the most common way to construct an equilateral triangle was through drawing two overlapping circles. To create the form, a geometer would begin with a single point, the circumpunct, placing the compass there and sweeping a circle around it. Then, placing the compass point on the circumference of that first circle, they would draw a second circle of the same radius. The two circles overlap, sharing a single radius between them. From there, the geometer would connect the two centers with a straight line, and then draw further lines from each center up to one of the points where the circles cross. The result is an equilateral triangle: three sides, each equal to the radius. Within the lens shape between the circles not just one triangle could form, but two—one with its apex pointing up, one pointing down.

Therefore, the ratio 265/153 *is* present in the geometry of the two overlapping circles. It just cannot be safely or accurately tied to Archimedes, specifically. But this exact two-circle construction of an equilateral triangle opens Euclid's Elements, Book I, the basic geometry text every educated student would have learned. And when Archimedes's ratio is applied to that construction, 153 becomes the width of the lens shape between the circles—the distance from one center to the other, along that shared radius—and 265 becomes the height, from the top intersection point to the bottom. The lower boundary of $\sqrt{3}$ sits, literally, inside the lens shape of the two circles joined.[30]

To an ancient eye, the resonance would have been immediate. Upright between the circles, the lens shape could register as an almond, hence the Italian *mandorla*, or as a seed, a doorway, even the female body—a vulva. Turned on its side, the pointed oval became a fish, an eye, a boat, a vessel. This flexibility helped the form endure, giving it an inherent sense of sacrality. In Christian devotional art, the *mandorla* often appears as the radiant enclosure around holy figures, including Christ, saints, and Mother Mary, most famously in the image of Our Lady of Guadalupe. Across traditions, the opening between the two circles has most often been read as a portal, a bridge, a meeting point between heaven and earth.

Within this mathematical and geometric context, 153 transforms from a blank unknown into a field of possibility so crowded with meaning. Yet when the numbers and shapes lead, rather than the story, interpretation goes astray. 153 does not float free. It is anchored to within a story, to fish it counts, held whole within the net. And there happens to be a confluence between the number 153 and the miraculous strength of the net.

The defining feature of 153 is its position within the mathematics of the equilateral triangle as the denominator of the lower boundary ratio. Its function is to hold the form: 153 is the smallest denominator that can be paired with 265 to keep the ratio just below $\sqrt{3}$; if it were any smaller, the ratio would slip above $\sqrt{3}$, and the proof would collapse. The equilateral triangle was considered by ancient geometers foundational, stable, and perfect in form: the simplest possible polygon, three sides bound into a single irreducible whole. It was the first form from which all others were built. Without 153, the triangle slips, the harmony fails, the foundation cannot hold.

Therefore, 153 speaks directly to the logic of the unbreakable net mentioned three times in the narrative. Just like the miracle of the net's strength, the number 153 does not break. That net gathered a specific object 153 counted: fish. If 153 is described as the maximum amount the net could hold without breaking, while 153 appears as the minimum denominator needed in Archimedes's proof, then the symbolism works by inversion: mathematical sufficiency becomes narrative fullness.

The shape of the count even mirrors the shape of the catch. A triangular number is built by stacking—one in the first row, two in the second, three in the third, and so on up to seventeen. Fish captured in a net pile in much the same way, layer upon layer settling into the form of the container.

Then the fish symbolically layer in more meaning. At their simplest, fish are food carrying life into the body, the basis on which any individual, family, or community thrives. But at this scale, fish become abundance drawn from the depths. So, fish represent the hidden made visible, they signal life-force pulled up from the realm beneath the seen.

Weaving each thread together, 153 becomes an elegant minimum that yields wholeness met, plenty contained. Further, the connection between the function of net and containment of the denominator makes it all the more likely that in some way 153 did, in fact, derive from Archimedes's text. And if the Gospel's author could be inspired by Philo's Logos, why couldn't that same mind, or minds, place 153 with equal precision?

THE SPACE BETWEEN

If the Prologue has long been read as a new creation story, the Epilogue becomes a poetic completion of the Gospel's arc. On the Sea of Galilee at dawn, words cross the water and the miracle of 153 fish followed. That words precede form and exceed Logos is an idea as old as scripture and story go, one manifest in the I am statements of Jesus, the I am aretalogies of Isis, the ancient concept of spells, and the Christian repetition of creeds. Words create and words arrive through communication: the divine speaks, the receiving listens, and what was hidden becomes seen.

Both Euclid's two circle geometry and Archimedes involve the meeting, and the spaces between them, as a means of measurement. Archimedes often used a regular hexagon, because a hexagon inscribed in a circle has a special property—its side length equals the radius. A regular hexagon is built out of six equilateral triangles radiating from the center; each triangle has all sides equal to the radius. So, the hexagon is the equilateral triangle, six times, creating $\sqrt{3}$ and 153 within it. Then the Euclidean construction every geometer learned of the two circles overlapping, with equilateral triangles between, was just the beginning of geometric construction. A third circle was drawn on the intersection of the first two, a fourth on the next, the pattern extending outward. Two becoming three, three becoming six circles arranged around a center, becoming a hexagonal arrangement of overlapping circles. So each design, polygon or circles, that create the equilateral triangle of $\sqrt{3}$ and 153, resonates with the hexagon, with six.

Modern writers in the esoteric tradition have called this hexagonal circle pattern the "Seed of Life," a name that is a twentieth century creation, not an ancient term, but shape itself has been drawn for thousands of years. At some point, geometry crossed into divine meaning, because that same hexagonal circle form, or flower, has been found across sacred architecture. It appears in Greco-Roman floor mosaics around the Mediterranean from the first century BCE onward as a standard geometric motif. It became foundational to Islamic geometric ornament from the eighth century forward, serving as the construction grid behind nearly every classical Islamic geometric tiling, from the Alhambra in Granada to the Dome of the Rock in Jerusalem. It has been found in the margins of medieval Christian manuscripts, in the architectural plans of monasteries and cathedrals across Europe, and in the notebooks of Leonardo da Vinci, who drew the shape multiple times in the *Codex Atlanticus*.

The hexagonal circle form has even been found in red ochre on a granite pillar in the Osireion at Abydos, in Egypt. While this particular inscription has been dated to the Roman or early Byzantine period, it was made in a temple already a millennium and a half old. The Osireion is a strange, sunken ritual structure behind the Temple of Seti I at Abydos, one of Egypt's holiest sites and the city most deeply tied to the worship of Osiris. The chamber lies below ground level, built of enormous stone blocks as a symbolic tomb to Osiris. Its central space holds an island surrounded by water, a layout that evokes the primeval mound rising from the waters of creation. It joins two ideas at once: creation from the deep, and resurrection from death, with the hope of afterlife.[31]

Symbols are never placed accidentally or unintentionally in holy places. That the hexagonal circle pattern was drawn here, in a chamber devoted to generation and resurrection, conveys that this form was understood, in some way, to align with the generative nature of the Osiris-Isis-Horus story. The pattern begins with the circumpunct, then opens into two, six, and beyond, multiplying outward like creation itself. The hexagon's six-fold symmetry appears in snowflakes, in honeycomb, in basalt columns left behind by cooling lava. Even in the hidden structures of life, six-membered rings recur in organic chemistry and in some of the molecular forms that carry genetic information. So if seven marks completion, perhaps six marks the fullest expansion of divine creativity just before it.

What the geometry of the overlapping circles makes visible is that creativity may culminate in six but it begins with just two. Only two overlapping circles are needed to create the lens shape in between, the *vesica piscis*, whose shared radius generates the equilateral triangle and measures as 153. That shape reads visually as creative—a portal, a fish, an eye, a seed, an opening.

Within the body of a woman, these forms become even more visibly and powerfully generative. The vulva resonates with that elongated lens shape. The uterus was rendered in symbolic art as an inverted triangle. The microscopic egg, the placenta, the amniotic sac, each a ring of creative potential. When the baby moves down the birth canal during labor, he or she spirals in descent. The child emerges through a portal created by the meeting of two—masculine and feminine. And in that sacred shape, the feminine half of the equation conceives, contains, labors, births, nurses, and tends that new life into being. Geometrically, while two circles of male and female create life, the feminine performs the creative labor through nature's design.

This is mirrored in creation stories, where male and female divine pairs generate gods, worlds, and humans, yet the feminine embodies a distinct creative force. She is not merely a consort or counterpart, but as the matrix from which life emerges—this was the origin of *parthenos*, a word that conveyed this sovereign creativity. In myths, creation begins in breath, water, darkness, depth, and wisdom, all images repeatedly marked as feminine. Primordial waters are imagined through goddesses and feminine powers: Naunet in Egypt, Tiamat in Mesopotamia, Nammu in Sumer, Thalassa in Greek imagination, and even Aphrodite-Venus. In Hebrew scriptures there is the feminine *ruach*, Spirit, hovering over the waters and Wisdom herself standing beside God at the beginning, rejoicing as the world comes into being. When this creative principle was later transposed into the masculine Logos and Jesus in the Fourth Gospel, the feminine language was lost, but the sacred power of breath, water, and speech remained.

In the Epilogue, the creative function that brings forth 153 fish begins as words exchanged between Jesus on the shore and the disciples in the boat. The speech is received, enacted upon, and that action becomes a miracle.

Another subtle element of the story is that the disciples did not know who Jesus was when they listened to his words. The reader did—the narrative made clear it was Jesus. But to the disciples, he was a just figure on shore speaking across the water. The disciples acted on the stranger's words before they knew who spoke them, trusting that a simple instruction might carry more than it first appeared to hold. Divine speech, human labor—and between them, trust, two parties, or circles, meeting.

After the catch, the Beloved Disciple speaks the decisive name: "It is the Kyrios." This sequence—hearing, abundance, recognition—reveals still more about the Disciple's identity, role, and singular capacity to listen.

HOW TO SEE AND HEAR

By the Epilogue, the Gospel has already trained its reader in recognition: the Samaritan woman, the Bethany sister, and Mary Magdalene in the garden each come to know Jesus through a movement of encounter, perception, and naming. The Beloved Disciple belongs to that same theology of recognition—it is no surprise that they, of all seven disciples in the boat, are the one to recognize Jesus.

In the boat, the Beloved Disciple has been hidden among the seven, one disciple within the group rather than a figure set apart. Even Jesus, standing on the shore, remains strangely indistinct. The narrative does not say how far the disciples are from land, what he looks like in the morning light, or how clearly his voice carries across the water. Jesus's words arrive, but the Disciple remains silent. Only after the net rises full of fish does the Disciple speak aloud, making *the catch, the 153 fish in the net*, the visible sign of Jesus's presence that the Beloved Disciple can perceive, read, and name aloud.

One chapter earlier, there is a similar moment at the empty tomb. Though Jesus's body is gone, the linens remain behind, and the way the narrative moves, the linens become a sign that the Disciple is able to read and understand. Upon seeing the linens, the Disciple "sees and believes," a recognition of Jesus's resurrection arrives silently and remains personal.

So one chapter later, this pattern is continues and expands. The Beloved Disciple does not respond to Jesus's voice, but to the sign of the net. As with the linen, the Disciple reads a symbol. And if at the tomb, they only saw, now in the boat they hear, see, and speak. And by verbalizing that realization, the Disciple's recognition becomes a shared group revelation.

At the tomb, the body has passed into the unseen, but the linen remains. On the water, the fish rise from the depths, held in a net that does not break. In both scenes, woven matter becomes a legible symbol. Across cultures and centuries, fabric and net have served as images for the way reality itself holds together. In Egyptian thought, Neith was said to have woven the cosmos on her loom; creation emerged as fabric, and the order that held it was Ma'at. The Greeks imagined the Moirai spinning, measuring, and cutting the threads of every life. In Hindu and Buddhist thought, the same vision took form in Indra's Net: a vast net strung with jewels, each one reflecting every other jewel without end. Even modern science reaches for similar language when it tries to describe invisible fields and relations beneath the material world.[32]

If linen and net disclose the invisible order beneath reality, then the Beloved Disciple's ability to read them makes them an even more profound figure of spiritual perception. Across philosophy, mathematics, geometry, and religion, human thought has long tried to read that order: to perceive it, name it, translate it, and make the hidden structure of things tangible. The 153 fish belong to that same impulse: to make the ineffable visible through a number whose mathematical and geometric coherence becomes symbolic. Placed within the sacred context of the Fourth Gospel, 153 becomes the moment when quantity turns into revelation: the hidden order of things rising visibly in the net.

The Gospel of Mary opens from within that ancient effort to perceive the unseen pattern beneath reality. Following the lost pages, the surviving dialogue begins: "All natures, all formed things, all creatures exist in and with one another, and will be resolved again into their own roots. For the nature of matter is dissolved into the roots of its nature alone. Whoever has ears to hear should listen." This is not simply a lesson about sin, but a teaching on the metaphysics of return. The Savior's teaching is simple: all things exist in relation, and all things move back toward their source.[33]

As the dialogue goes on, more of the Savior's vision is revealed. When Peter asks, "What is the sin of the world?" the Savior answers: "Sin as such does not exist; you are the ones who make sin when you do the things that are like the nature of adultery, which is called sin." He continues: "For this reason, the Good came among you, to the essence of every nature, to restore it to its root." The Savior is not describing sin in a Pauline or Augustinian framework. Sin in the Gospel of Mary is misalignment from source, and the Good is what restores nature to itself.

The Good is the Greek philosophical concept still visible beneath the Coptic text: not goodness as moral virtue, but the hidden source of order, the radiance by which reality becomes intelligible. In Plato, the Good is compared to the sun, the power that allows things to be seen and known. By the first century, that idea had entered the wider philosophical air of Middle Platonism—the same world in which Philo spoke of the Logos as the divine ordering principle, and the same world from which the Fourth Gospel's Prologue opens.[34]

But Greek philosophy centered around the Good did not arise in isolation. Egyptian theology had long articulated Ma'at as truth, balance, justice, and right relation woven into the cosmos. Ancient writers repeatedly described Greek wisdom as derived from or inspired by Egypt; Pythagoras,

Solon, Thales, Eudoxus, and Plato were all linked, historically or traditionally, to Egyptian learning. So, the Greek Good is at the least a striking parallel to Ma'at—and the ancient tradition itself insisted Greek wisdom drew on Egyptian learning—even if modern scholarship treats direct derivation with caution.

The Gospel of Mary's articulation of the Good aligns with Middle Platonism for the most part, but it varies in one crucial respect. The Savior says it "came among you, to the essence of every nature, to restore it to its root." Plato's Good does not come or descend; it is transcendent, the soul must rise to meet it. What the Savior describes—the Good entering every nature to restore it—resonates more closely with Egyptian and Hebrew traditions. Ma'at was not an abstract ideal, she was embodied through kingship, enacted in temple ritual, sustained by priests and priestesses, and made visible wherever order overcame chaos. Wisdom, personified as feminine in Hebrew scripture, came down from heaven to enter holy souls. "In every generation she passes into holy souls and makes them friends of God," the Wisdom of Solomon says. The Savior's teaching moves in this same current: divine order does not remain remote, but descends to act, to restore, to bring each nature home.

Only after this teaching does Mary step forward. The Savior has departed, and the gathered disciples have fallen into grief and despair. Mary rises with words of comfort: "Do not weep and be distressed nor let your hearts be irresolute. For his grace will be with you all and will shelter you. Rather we should praise his greatness, for he has prepared us and made us true Human beings." Peter then asks her, "Sister, we know that the Savior loved you more than all other women. Tell us the words of the Savior that you remember, the things which you know that we don't because we haven't heard them." It is hard to imagine the Peter of the canonical Gospels calling Magdalene "sister," let alone admitting Jesus's love for her and her knowledge of teachings he has not heard. Mary replies: "I will teach you about what is hidden from you." This is the premise of the scene: Mary is the disciple who knows what is hidden, who can hear what others have not heard, and teach what others have not understood.

When Mary begins to reveal the teachings Peter has asked for, the first thing she says is, "I saw the Lord in a vision." Her words make clear that what follows is derived from interior experience, not a bodily-resurrection encounter of the kind the canonical Gospels record. The Savior validates her perception: "Blessed are you that you did not waver at the sight of me. For where the *nous* is, there is the treasure." In Platonic philosophy, the *nous* was the faculty by which the soul perceived the underlying order of reality.[35]

Listening, watching, waiting: these are the faculties Mary and the Beloved Disciple each exemplify. Mary's not-wavering, her calm and undisturbed reception of the vision, is what makes her able to receive the teaching. When Mary says, "I saw the Lord in a vision," and the method of her recognition is named as the *nous*, the text evokes the Greek concept of the higher mind, an inward faculty of spiritual perception by which the soul apprehends what lies beneath appearance. The *nous* is distinct from the senses and from ordinary reasoning. It is closer to what modern vocabulary might call contemplative insight, or intuition in its older philosophical sense. It is what is awake in a person who recognizes something true the moment they encounter it—not by reasoning toward it, but by seeing it whole.

In the Hellenistic Jewish tradition, that same *nous* was the faculty through which Wisdom was received. Philo himself identified the *nous* as the divine image within the human being and as the very means by which Wisdom entered the soul. The Wisdom of Solomon and Proverbs 8 each describe Wisdom herself as a presence that moves and reaches toward the soul. Philo identifies the awake nous as Wisdom dwelling in the soul. The Gospel of Mary names Mary's faculty as the *nous*. The claim is specific: Mary's perception is Wisdom's perception. She is Wisdom, embodied.

Mary Magdalene's name marks a Gospel that gathers Jewish, Egyptian, and Middle Platonic threads into a single Alexandrian synthesis and within it, she is the figure who knows what is hidden and perceives the underlying order through the *nous*. These are the same faculties the Beloved Disciple embodies in the Epilogue: each is a master of spiritual perception, each remains steady at decisive moments, each waits until the sign has disclosed itself before speaking the sacred name. Each models the same kind of faith—not belief imposed from outside, but recognition arising from within. Mary and the Beloved Disciple share the same way of seeing, the same way of hearing, the same way of waiting.

No other figure in early Christian literature occupies the position

Mary Magdalene does. In the canon she is first witness; outside it she is recipient and revealer of hidden teaching, questioner and companion. Other disciples receive revelation in noncanonical texts, but none holds the dual position across traditions that Mary commands. If she was Mary of Bethany, her place in the early Christian imagination is singular. If she was the Beloved Disciple, it is without parallel. And no other disciple or figure in the Christian tradition matches the model of the Beloved Disciple more than Mary Magdalene.

In the Gospel of Mary, Magdalene moves to extend the methods behind her vision to the disciples and the reader: how to see, hear, and know from within. Mary asks the Savior: "Lord, does a person see a vision with the soul or the spirit?" He begins to answer, but the narrative stops. The pages are missing from an otherwise remarkably intact and well-preserved codex. The answer is gone. But the question itself reveals that Mary was not guarding her gift privately. She meant to model what she herself had done, to offer how any soul might receive the divine directly. As institutional Christianity narrowed the paths to divine knowledge, routing them through priest, bishop, doctrine, and Church no message could have been more threatening.

Even if the Savior's answer is lost in the missing pages of the Gospel of Mary, the Epilogue of the Fourth Gospel may preserve it in another form. When Jesus instructs the disciples, he does not simply tell them to cast again, nor does he tell them to "go out into deep water," as he does in Luke. He gives a precise command: "Throw your net on the right side of the boat." From that small reorientation, abundance appears, the net fills, the number arrives and the Beloved Disciple sees. This phrase, when read closely, is not simply a how-to for fishermen, it is an instruction in how to see, hear, and perceive, and to know what might seem hidden.

FISHING ON THE RIGHT SIDE OF THE BOAT

The Fourth Gospel's creator could have written the phrase as *eis ta dexia tou ploiou*, "to the right of the boat," and the phrase would have been clear—a simple direction, a place to cast a net, easy to express in everyday Greek. But the originator of this phrase chose to insert *merē*, making the phrase *ta dexia merē tou ploiou*. Adding *merē* converts the instruction from a direction into a destination, from a which way into a what place, from the right side to the right realms. Translated literally, the instruction reads: cast the net into the right regions, the right domains, the right realms of the boat.[36]

A realm or domain is a field of possibility, a bounded place where certain things can appear. The sea is one domain, the boat another, the shore another still. A domain is an area held together by a shared logic, a place where meaning coheres. These words are often used to express what lies beyond literal or even visible understanding. Realm especially is a word that is reached for when ordinary place-language fails: the unseen realm, the invisible realm, the divine realm. And just as side opens beyond location into realm, right moves beyond direction or correctness.

In Middle Platonism, *right* was an indicator of alignment, a meaning inherited from the Pythagoreans, who had organized the cosmos into pairs of opposites and placed right on the same side as good, light, and order. The right hand was the hand of blessing; the right side was the auspicious one in omen-reading; right reason was the soul's posture toward what was true. So when the Savior spoke of casting to the right, an educated listener heard not a direction but an instruction: turn the soul toward the Good. And when the soul turned rightly, what the source held flowed in to meet it. The net heavy with fish was that meeting made visible.

Yet there is another way to read the phrase, one that remains within Alexandrian symbolic grammar. In Egypt, the right was literally a realm. The word for "right" and the word for "west" were the same: *imnt*, the realm of the sunset, of the afterlife, of the hidden, ruled by Imentet, the goddess of the threshold. To go right was to go west; to go west was to go into the hidden. Read through this Egyptian lens, the Gospel's phrase becomes Egyptian thought in Greek words: *dexia merē*, the right that is a realm. And in Egyptian cosmology, the *imnt*, that realm of the right, was filled with boats, fishermen, and nets.[37]

The deceased soul had to pass through this realm to reach the Hall of Two Truths, where the heart would be weighed against the feather of Ma'at and the journey was perilous. The *Book of Coming Forth by Day* preserved the spells the soul needed to pass safely—sacred utterances inscribed on tombs, coffins, and papyri, formulas of right knowledge that guided the deceased through each gate and test. The path through the broader realm of *imnt* was called the Duat: the underworld route Ra also traveled each night in his solar barque. Along that path, the soul encountered divine nets cast by fishermen-spirits who would ensnare any who were unprepared. To pass through, the soul had to know names—the names of the threads and parts of the net, and even of the fishermen-spirits themselves. To know these names and speak them with clarity allowed the soul to continue to the right realm, because it demonstrated that the soul was in alignment with Ma'at and ready. One of these spells addresses the net-passage with particular clarity and when the nineteenth-century editors numbered the corpus, this spell was given the mark: Spell 153.[38]

In Egyptian thought, the right was the realm where Ma'at existed, not as a principle to reach toward, but as the fabric of being. Its opposite was the *iabt*, the left, the realm of the visible, the everyday world. To fish on the right side wasn't to perform an act that produced alignment; it was to enter the realm where alignment already existed. So, "cast the net into the right realms of the boat" could be understood through Egyptian theological language: enter the *imnt*, the hidden realm where Ma'at holds, and bring forth what you find there into the *iabt*, the visible—the catch made real, the abundance of Ma'at manifest.

To read a Christian text through Egyptian theology may seem like a stretch, yet the comparison between Christian ideas and Egyptian wisdom is neither new nor fringe. April DeConick, Birger Pearson, Esther de Boer, and Erik Hornung have each, from different angles, helped recover the Egyptian and Hellenistic-Egyptian inheritance running through early Christian, Gnostic, and esoteric traditions, including the texts most closely tied to Mary Magdalene. This does not prove direct dependence, but it makes the symbolic proximity harder to dismiss. What remains suggestive in the Fourth Gospel becomes explicit in the Gospel of Mary, particularly in the soul's mysterious sevenfold ascent.[39]

This is the passage that picks up after the missing pages preceded by the Savior answering Mary's question about interior vision. As the text resumes, it continues with a dialogue already in process, in language unfamiliar in any standard Christian context. Sarah Parkhouse has called it an eschatology, the ascent of the soul to heaven. The soul is speaking with a power named Desire, which challenges her: "I did not see you descending, but now I see you ascending. So why do you lie since you belong to me?" The soul answers: "I saw you. You did not see me nor recognize me. I served you as a garment, and you did not know me."[40]

As the dialogue continues, the soul rises through power after power—first Darkness, then Ignorance, and finally the most complex of them, Wrath, which itself appears in seven forms: Darkness, Desire, Ignorance, the Death-instinct, the Kingdom of the Flesh, the Foolish Wisdom of the Flesh, and the Wrathful Wisdom. Each power challenges her; each claims dominion, and each time the soul answers as she answered Desire. She names what the power has missed and refuses its claim—naming allows safe passage. By the time she has crossed all seven forms of Wrath, the soul has transcended. The structure unmistakably echoes the Egyptian theology and eschatological journey of the soul through the right realm and the Duat. In Spell 125—which records the heart-weighing in the Hall of Two Truths—the soul must move through stages, pass tests, and articulate the correct words, names, and answers. So while the boats, fishermen, and nets are not present in the Gospel of Mary, the theology beneath them is—Egyptian theology in a Coptic Christian gospel.

When Jesus commands the disciples to throw the net on the right side of the boat, he relays through the language of fishing what the Savior in the Gospel of Mary was beginning to teach when the pages broke off: how the soul sees, how the spirit perceives. If the Gospel of Mary records the question, then the Fourth Gospel's Epilogue may remember the answer, at least in part. And the figure who knew enough to ask the question in one Gospel may have been the same figure who, in the other, knew enough to see what the answer drew up in the net: Mary Magdalene, the Beloved Disciple.

When Mary finishes sharing the Ascent of the Soul in the Gospel of Mary, the text records that "she was silent, since it was up to this point that the Savior had spoken to her." She says no more and no less than what the Savior shared with her—though that doesn't keep Andrew and Peter from criticizing her for being a woman who was favored by the Savior, a woman who is teaching. While many scholars have understood this as the central drama of the Gospel of Mary—a gendered conflict that speaks to the broader environment of second-century Christianity—the theology the text contains appears to be much more significant than merely a female political polemic.

The *nous* and the right realm, the Gospel of Mary and the Fourth Gospel, each becomes the place through which the hidden is made manifest, be it wisdom or 153 fish in an unbroken net. Both gospels point to the same place. And across the ancient Mediterranean, that hidden was understood as feminine. In Egypt, it was governed by goddesses—Ma'at, cosmic order itself; Imentet, who welcomed the dead at the threshold of the West; Isis, who gathered Osiris from death and ruled with him over the hidden realm. In Greece, the Pythia spoke for the hidden—the priestess of Delphi through whom Apollo's truth descended to humans—while Athena and Minerva personified wisdom as a woman. In Hebrew scripture, Wisdom is radiant, easily seen by those who love her, found by those who seek her, greater than every constellation, more powerful than light, the breath of God moving through holy souls. And in Gnostic theology, Sophia both descends and makes return possible; she is salvation imagined as the recovery of relation, recognition, and alignment with the divine source.

It is a pattern as old as story, as old as faith: the hidden realm was feminine; the wisdom that emerged from it took the form of a goddess, or a woman speaking in her name.

MEASURE OF THE REALM

Once Jesus's command to draw up the catch is understood, the number becomes inseparable from the scene itself: word and symbol, figure and sign, the one who speaks, the seven in the boat, and the Beloved Disciple who reads what has risen from the depths. Then there is the mathematics: 153 as the seventeenth triangular number, an integer whose meaning this chapter has traced through Plutarch's Pythagorean obstacle, the Egyptian myth of Osiris, and the waters of renewal in Hebrew scripture. And the geometry: the harmony of the equilateral triangle, the unity of the two overlapping circles, and the portal shape created between them that holds the denominator 153 as width.

The ancient Mediterranean world had another way of reading this same order—not through the proportions of shapes, but through the sound and sum of letters. Greek letters, Hebrew letters, all could be counted. A phrase could become a number. A number could carry the trace of a name. In Greek, this practice was called isopsephy: a form of equal counting where words or names with the same numerical value could be placed in relation to one another. In Jewish interpretive tradition, the related practice came to be known as gematria: a way of allowing meaning to take shape as number, something that could be heard, seen, counted, and even concealed.

Modern scholarship has long treated isopsephy and gematria with skepticism. But the dismissal is beginning to give way. In *The Testimony of the Beloved Disciple*, Richard Bauckham argues that ancient texts, including the New Testament, were deliberately composed with numerical encoding, and that the 153 fish may belong to that pattern.

Bauckham follows the seventeen behind 153 to connect the figure to the same passage Jerome linked it to: Ezekiel 47, where life-giving water flows from the temple and fishermen stand between En-gedi and En-eglaim. Bauckham also notes that the Hebrew phrase *b'nei ha-Elohim*, "children of God," sums to 153 in gematria. The phrase appears in the Prologue of the Fourth Gospel—in Greek as *tekna theou*—the children of God promised to all who receive the Logos. Though the Gospel is written in Greek, the exchange between Greek and Hebrew was a common interpretive methodology in this period. An Alexandrian author would have known both and may have encoded the bridge that runs from the Prologue's children of God to the Epilogue's 153 fish. So while Bauckham does not engage Archimedean geometry, he arrives at a related vision: 153 as a figure of abundance, harmony, and gathered relation.[41]

Bauckham goes further, he proposes that the techniques of gematria and isopsephy may have encoded some hint towards the Beloved Disciple. His method involves counting words and even multiplying them by triangular numbers—though he does not arrive at a clear conclusion. And he does not consider the phrase Jesus speaks to pull up the catch: *ta dexia merē tou ploiou*, the right side of the boat.

Counted as a whole, the phrase sums to 1,964—a total without obvious meaning. But one word in the phrase adds up to 153: *merē*, realm. Its letters add as follows: m (40) + e (5) + r (100) + ē (8) = 153. The odds that any random Greek word equals 153 are roughly one in several hundred.

The odds that this specific word—the one that converts a direction into a realm, the one that is grammatically unnecessary to the sentence, the one that appears in the very phrase that brings up 153 fish—would happen to sum to 153 by chance are slim. What is far more likely is this word is the mark of deliberate composition.

For the word "realm" to sum to 153 is even more extraordinary when set beside the geometry. 153 is the measurement that creates the realm: the width of the lens between the two overlapping circles, the threshold shape that has long been read as a portal between worlds. The word names the realm; the number measures it, both marked as 153.

Perhaps the simplest way to understand how the symbols, story and geometry meet is through the metaphor of birth. Both right and left, feminine and masculine, are needed to bring a child into the world. The right circle is the womb—the hidden generative space, the perfect triangle, the dark waters where a soul takes form. The *imnt*, the hidden realm, the feminine. The left circle is the world the child enters—air, light, the visible. The *iabt*, the material world, the masculine. The lens between them is the birth canal: the portal the child passes through. Without the womb, there is nothing to bring forth. Without the world, there is nowhere for the child to arrive. The baby is made from both circles, drawn into being through their union, carried in the hidden mysterious realm and brought into the light through the threshold their union creates.

And if the two circles are read as parties in communication—Jesus and the disciples in the story, the divine and the individual more broadly—then 153 is what opens between them. It is the measurement of the realm—the *imnt* without, the *nous* within—where the treasure lies, where the 153 move from ocean to net.

In Egyptian theology, this right realm was feminine, ruled by a goddess who held creation in balance. But in Christianity, no such realm survived. The feminine—as communicating spirit, as creative source, as the principle that made the cosmos intelligible—was silenced or transposed. The Spirit, once feminine, was rendered masculine. Wisdom was overwritten by the Logos. Sophia was banned as heresy. Mother Mary was elevated not as the creative source of all life but for her obedience, her perfection, her sinlessness. Christianity preserved only the masculine: Father, Son, male

Holy Spirit; twelve male disciples; only male clergy. And Magdalene—made sinful and penitent, her role as witness diminished, her own gospel that taught how to perceive directly buried for centuries before rising again like a miracle.

Magdalene has a count too, one that was discovered by Margaret Starbird years ago, when gematria and isopsephy were still scoffed at within academic circles. In *The Woman with the Alabaster Jar*, Starbird established that the Greek isopsephy of Mary's title, the Magdalene, sums to exactly 153.[42]

In Greek letters, ἡ Μαγδαληνή, "the Magdalene" can be counted as: ἡ (8) + M (40) + α (1) + γ (3) + δ (4) + α (1) + λ (30) + η (8) + ν (50) + ή (8) = 153.

In full, Maria hē Magdalēnē yields a higher number. Maria alone measures 152—one short. But the distinctive title—the Magdalene—lands precisely on 153. Isopsephy is internally consistent; the math cannot be manipulated toward a desired result. The probability that a random Greek phrase would sum to a specific number like 153 is roughly one in several thousand—closer to one in ten thousand for a phrase the length of hē Magdalēnē. Combined with the geometric role of 153, the narrative precision of the unbroken net, and the isopsephy of *merē* as realm, the combined likelihood drops into one in many millions.

153 does not measure Mary, or even Mary Magdalene. It measures the Magdalene—the title, the place, the elevation, the key to Mary's identity hidden in plain sight. In Hebrew and Aramaic, the root m-g-d-l means tower: a structure that rises, that stands at a height, that magnifies. The Aramaic *gadal* means to be great. And just as "Mary" carries an Egyptian phonetic resonance with *mry*—beloved—so does "Magdalene" sound itself out in Egyptian. In antiquity, this kind of cross-cultural sound resonance was part of daily life, especially in the Roman Mediterranean where languages and cultures met constantly. The Semitic syllables of Magdalene, heard in Egyptian, resonate with *mḥ*—cubit, the act of measuring—and *ḏr*—boundary, limit, threshold. In Egyptian, "the Magdalene" would sound like: the one who stands at the edge, the one at the threshold, the one who measures the boundary.

The title encodes what 153 measures in geometry, the portal to the hidden place, and what Mary embodies—the one who listens through the *nous*, the one who sees and recognizes the risen Christ, the one who knows the truth. Mary is not the catch—she is where the catch arrives from, the hidden place where abundance is drawn forth to be made real. The Magdalene is not just the vessel, the container, the womb—she is the entire circle—from seed to sprout to flower, from life to death to rebirth, from thought to prayer to manifest reality.

A number, a word, a name—a pattern that repeats throughout divine stories across antiquity. The right name, the right word, the right phrase, the right number brings forth what is needed; the names change through time, their faces transforming, but the truth beneath them remaining. Rabboni becomes Kyrios; "I am" spoken by Jesus and by Isis; the names of goddesses moving: Aphrodite to Venus, Artemis to Artemis Ephesus, Isis to Isis Panthea, Hathor to all the goddesses at Dendera, "Lady of Heaven" moving from Sumerian goddess to a title of Virgin Mary. Mary Magdalene to Mary of Bethany to Martha of Bethany to the anonymous anointing woman to the anonymous Beloved Disciple. Magdalene is that sort of name—a name that could not be erased, a name no one would fully understand, a code, a truth, allowed to remain in plain sight, for those with eyes and ears, like the miracle of 153 fish.

THE MISSING CIRCLE

One of her earliest traces is her feast day: July 22. Christian figures began to be remembered as saints as early as the late second century, their death days—and sometimes birth days—becoming moments of celebration and feasting, much like the feast days that preceded them in the pre-Christian religions. These commemorations were preserved through local practice rather than centralized decree, so their origins are difficult to pinpoint. Though Mary was not martyred, her name and her feast of July 22 appear in Bede's early eighth-century martyrology. And in the South of France, from Provence to the Pyrenees, locals will tell you she truly lived there; that her story is as old as the soil, passed down through their own lineages. There, July 22 carried such force that Rome's crusaders chose her day for the massacre at Béziers.

In the first century, July 22 fell in the heat of high summer, when the Mediterranean sun stood at its fiercest, grain fields had yielded their harvest, figs and grapes were ripening, and the land was heavy with abundance. Even the sky carried the language of power and change, marked by constellations ordinary people would have watched and the educated would have known how to read.

In the early first century, July 22 would have fallen near the Sun's passage out of Cancer and toward Leo. Cancer is one of the faintest regions of the zodiac, yet it holds Praesepe, the Manger—a dim cluster imagined in Greek as a feeding trough where two celestial asses, the Aselli, came to be fed. Greek texts named Cancer the crab, but across older sky traditions this summer creature could appear as a crayfish, water beetle, scarab, or turtle: hard-shelled, water-bound, and associated with darkness, return, and rebirth. In astrological symbolism, Cancer became the watery, feminine threshold of the mother. This interpretation was already present in the first-century systems that linked Cancer to the Moon, which signified the mother, nurturance, the breasts, and receptivity.[43]

In Greek myth, the constellation Cancer commemorates the crab Hera sent against Heracles; she placed it in the stars in honor of its service when it snapped at the hero's heels. This detail is small but charged—a creature sent by a goddess strikes the hero's heel and is crushed beneath his foot. The image resonates with Genesis 3:15, Revelation's woman clothed with the sun, later Christian prophecy, and the Marian imagery that would place a serpent beneath the feet of Mary.

Cancer marked the summer solstice—the moment the Sun reaches its highest point and turns. The Greek *tropos*, the turning, creates "tropic" and the Tropic of Cancer is named for this celestial threshold, the gate where the Sun stops climbing and begins to return. By July 22, the Sun stood at the boundary between Cancer, ruled by the Moon, and Leo, ruled by the Sun—the meeting place between water and fire, mother and father, feminine and masculine.

In Egypt, the stars of Cancer were seen as a scarab beetle, rendered in turquoise on the famous zodiac wheel from the temple of Hathor at Dendera, carrying a solar disk. The scarab beetle belonged to the god Khepri, the morning form of the sun god Ra. But Egyptians did not track these ecliptic constellations; they tracked time by the fixed stars. And around July 22—closer to July 19 or 20—the brightest fixed star in the sky was reappearing at dawn after seventy days of invisibility: Sopdet. This was Wepet Renpet, the Opening of the Year, the sign that the Nile would rise and life would return to the land.

The twenty-second day of the seventh month—it is impossible to prove Mary Magdalene's feast traces to the first century, or to know how it might have been written, remembered, or shifted in the centuries between. But in an astonishing coincidence—or perhaps, for a reader who has followed Magdalene through 153, a sign—the number 22/7 is itself mathematical: the classical approximation of π, pi. And it comes from the same Archimedean text that yielded 265/153: *Measurement of a Circle.*

Pi is one of the most extraordinary numbers in mathematics. It governs the relation between any circle's circumference and its diameter—the universal constant every circle obeys regardless of size. It surfaces in places far beyond circles: in probability, in the geometry of waves, in the equations that describe the structure of physical reality. Ancient civilizations spent centuries approximating it. The Egyptians put it at roughly 3.16; the Babylonians at 3.125; the author of First Kings, describing Solomon's bronze sea, gave it as exactly 3. Archimedes did better, proving pi must lie between 22/7 and 223/71.

But none of these is pi exactly. Pi cannot be expressed exactly. Its decimal expansion never terminates and never repeats. It is irrational—incapable of being written as a ratio of integers—meaning every fraction we use for pi, including 22/7, is an approximation. In a way, pi makes the ancient mystery of the circle more manifest, not less: the circle is the form that resists final capture by number, the figure that always exceeds the straight line trying to contain it.

If pi reveals the uncontainable truth at the heart of the circle, then the circle becomes ever more clearly a figure for the divine—and especially for the feminine. The feminine has long been called irrational by polemic, and dismissed for it: too emotional, too uncontrollable, too uncontainable by reasonable systems. But what pi shows is that irrationality is not a flaw of measure. It is the property of certain fundamental realities—the circle, the depths, the source—that they cannot be captured by integer ratio. The feminine that accesses the depths, where Ma'at lies, where the Good resides, is irrational in this older and more accurate sense: it is the form of being from which all measure emerges, and which no measure can finally contain.

By some strange miracle, Mary Magdalene's feast day is a circle's ratio—22/7, the classical approximation of π—and her title the gematria of 153, the integer that holds the equilateral triangle in proportion. Two circles meeting to create a triangle. Two becoming three. The fishing on the right side of the boat that accesses the hidden feminine realm and draws abundance into the visible. Magdalene becomes circle and triangle at once—completion and harmony, the half of the whole that was left out, the feminine divine absent from Christianity.

She was a companion to Jesus—perhaps as a follower, perhaps as an apostle, perhaps as a wife, perhaps as an equal in teaching. She was a vessel—perhaps not a chalice or the mother of a bloodline, but the container of a teaching no doctrine could fully receive: how to see, how to hear, how to perceive the hidden, how to bring forth what was waiting there. Her gospel was buried for fifteen centuries. Her name was made a sinner's. But like the catch of 153 fish that came up from the depths into the light, Magdalene is rising. The missing half of the divine, returning. The goddess. The woman. The mother.

THE KINGDOM WITHIN

To follow Mary Magdalene, a sacred story, or a number like 153 is a process of revelation. It requires a search: gathering, learning, stretching toward possibilities that may feel unfamiliar, through symbols, methods, and languages one may not yet know. The work, not the solution, is what produces the realization—not through clean sums but through a messy process of discovery. The net may have been thrown to the right, but what mattered was the passage between. Not the finding, but the seeking. Not the kingdom without, but the kingdom within.

After the 153 fish are quantified, the Epilogue turns to the dialogue between Jesus and Peter, where Jesus asks Peter three times if he loves him, and in turn he replies "feed my lambs," "take care of my sheep," and "feed my sheep." Sheep and shepherds, this metaphor is perhaps the most familiar of all to Christians. In Luke, the lost sheep is the sinner, lost by failure and found in repentance. In Matthew, the lost sheep are the little ones, the vulnerable, and the Father steps in as their protector. But outside the canon, the sheep are remembered differently.

The Gospel of Thomas, Logion 107, contains a parable about one sheep going missing among one hundred and the sheep that strays is the largest. The shepherd leaves the ninety-nine to search for the one, and when he finds it, he says: "I love you more than the ninety-nine."[44]

The Gospel of Truth tells the same parable, but adds a methodology: "For ninety-nine is a number expressed on the left hand. But the moment one is found, the whole number passes to the right hand." The Gospel of Truth is a Valentinian text. In ancient Greek finger-counting, numbers 1 to 99 were counted on the left hand. Only at 100 did the count move to the right. So when the missing sheep is recovered, the entire flock shifts from left to right. From the hand that holds the lesser to the hand that holds the divine, from lack to completion.[45]

The shepherd leaves the ninety-nine to find the one not because he is searching for a sinful sheep, as in Luke, but because goodness seeks what is missing, because goodness desires the whole. And the sheep has not gone astray because it is weak or sinful. It departed the conventional flock in pursuit of something greater. That is why the shepherd in Thomas says "I love you more." The seeking is what makes the sheep beloved.

In Valentinian theology, there is no original sin in the garden at all. Eve does not bring the fall—she reaches for wisdom. Sophia does not bring catastrophe—she goes seeking beyond the boundary. The "fall" is the divine spark descending into matter, and the descent is itself the seeking. Their wandering, their going "astray," is what produces the world and the possibility of reunion with the divine. The fall is the initiation and the recovery is what completes the whole. That seeker is Mary Magdalene, she is Eve, she is Sophia. And she is anyone willing to leave behind old beliefs, inherited structures, and settled doctrine to follow the intuition that something essential has been missing—and can still be found.

In Logion 3 of Thomas, Jesus says: "If those who lead you say to you, 'Look, the kingdom is in the sky,' then the birds of the sky will go before you. If they say to you, 'It is in the sea,' then the fish will go before you. Rather, the kingdom is inside you and outside you."[46]

The seeker carries them all along, following wisdom that does not move in straight lines but in spirals, in circles meeting other circles, in the thresholds between. What is needed is not the answer alone—but the courage to leave the first known, to step into the place where the visible touches the hidden, where one circle joins another, where what has been waiting in the fertile darkness can finally be fully seen in the day's light.

Conclusion

A JAR OF HOPE

TOTA PULCHRA ES
AMICA MEA
ET MACULA NON EST
IN TE
CANT. IV

The Latin words are inscribed on an *edicola sacra*, a sacred architectural street shrine that frames the painted figure of a woman. Among the largest *madonnelle* in Rome, she stretches across a two-story building on the west side of the piazza outside the Pantheon. Unlike many *madonnelle*, which offer only a face or bust, this woman appears whole, her body visible between two faint angels within the weathered surface. A delicate halo still encircles her head, while a red gown and sweeping blue mantle envelop her figure. At her feet, a sinuous serpent winds through the fading lower edge of the fresco. The image seems suspended between presence and disappearance, its details slowly worn into one another by centuries spent in the elements.

The frame that surrounds her is elaborate. Above the niche, a dove radiates from the center of a crest, its rays spreading through curling scrollwork and floral ornament. Below, Latin words are carved into a decorative, cartouche. A *rocaille* flourish cradles the inscription, surrounded by more stylized flowers. The verse names itself as CANT. IV, Song of Songs 4:7: "You are altogether beautiful, my beloved, and there is no flaw in you."[1]

Tota pulchra, words lifted from this verse, became a visual tradition intended to portray Mother Mary in her ultimate perfection. Officially known as the Madonna Immacolata di Piazza della Rotonda, this fresco belongs to that lineage. Its painter is unidentified, and its composition is dated to the mid-eighteenth century, but its title anticipates the doctrine that formalized Mother Mary's Immaculate Conception in 1854. This is the belief, formally held by the Catholic Church, that Mother Mary alone was spared the inheritance Adam and Eve passed on to humanity—she is not divine, but the only human soul ever conceived without original sin.

This figure is exquisite, but something in her resists perfection. Serene in feature, gentle in posture, and ethereal in her simplicity, she breaks from many conventions of Marian imagery. There are no stars above her head, she gazes downward but does not seem submissive, her body appears in motion, almost as though she is carrying something forward with her, beyond the frame. Aside from the drapery of her garments and the *putti* around her, complete with bare bums, the only icon that reads clearly is the serpent—present in a still vivid green, her feet hovering above it. Undefeated and whole, its emerald body is a reminder that what was given to Mary did not originate with her.

Serpent, stars, and moon become primary Marian symbols. Potent and recurring, they shape the way the feminine appears throughout Christian iconography, their source recalling the symbolic language of Revelation 12, the Woman and the Dragon: "A great sign appeared in heaven: a woman clothed with the sun, with the moon under her feet and a crown of twelve stars on her head."[2]

The pregnant woman, the dragon, and the rescued child are not inventions of Revelation, but older mythic symbols seized and recast by its apocalyptic vision. Isis survives in the mother hidden in the marshes, protecting the child who will rise against his father's enemy. Tiamat reappears in the primordial sea-dragon slain by the storm-god Marduk, her divided body made into heaven and earth. Artemis of Ephesus is echoed in the tower-crowned figure marked by the zodiac. And the Queen of Heaven, once named through Inanna, Ishtar, Asherah, and Isis, returns under Mary's name as the woman crowned with twelve stars.

Radiant mother became the heroine set against another female, the

Whore of Babylon. The split is so clean it is impossible to miss. Mother Mary made a perfect, virgin, sinless mother. Mary Magdalene made a fallen, sexual, sinful prostitute. The feminine divided against itself.

By calling the dragon "that ancient serpent," Revelation reaches back across the canon to Eden. The garden snake becomes a red, seven-headed dragon.[3] The old enmity between woman and serpent widens into the opening movement of an apocalyptic war. The first book and the last are made to share a single arc: serpent, woman, child, curse, sin, and battle.

Yet for all that later Church Fathers would make of Eve, Genesis does not record a curse on her. What was spoken over Eve was *ʿitsabon*: sorrow, hardship, pain, the same word given to Adam in the next verse. Only with Eve did *ʿitsabon* become pain in childbirth, and from that narrowing came one of the most devastating inversions in the history of faith: the body that carries, nurtures, grows, screams, weeps, and loves new life into the world was inverted into evidence of divine punishment. The womb became a wound. Birth became blame. Creation was taken from the mother and reserved only for the father.

When God pronounced the curse on the *ʿarum* serpent, the crafty garden creature became *ʾarur*: cursed, made to crawl on its belly, divided from humanity by enmity. The serpent would strike the heel; the woman's seed would strike the serpent's head. But for all that Revelation and centuries of Marian imagery would place the serpent beneath the feet of the woman, that is not what the Hebrew records. The word for offspring is grammatically masculine. Somewhere in the Latin transmission, the gender turned. Not the woman's seed, but the woman herself, would crush the serpent's head. *Ipsa conteret caput tuum*: "she shall crush your head."[4]

This is how a creation story about separation from the divine, and the human longing for return became a story of cosmic rupture, where a wound between soul and God was caused by the act of a woman. Eve ceased to be a foremother of wisdom and became evidence against her daughters, her actions recast as proof of a weakness believed to belong to all women by nature. Her story was transposed onto every expression of the feminine until the body became temptation, the womb became a source of suffering, and blood became impure. Beauty was endangerment, knowledge disobedience, intuition deception, and the voice seduction.

Mother Mary alone was spared, but only by being lifted out of womanhood altogether—rendered unstained, untouched, and obedient. A mother of God divided from humanity. This is the doctrine the image is meant to proclaim, and the words beneath her body seem to seal it: *There is no flaw in you.*

"Flaw" is *mûm*: a blemish, defect, or mark, most often named in relation to the body, especially the bodies of priests and sacrificial animals. It is the language of a body in which nothing is missing, broken, or visibly marked. How did a word that named bodily wholeness become a doctrine of moral absence? What happens when a body without blemish becomes a soul without sin? These are the shifts, of a word, a story, a symbol, that change the entire narrative. The whole becomes broken. The woman becomes the sinner. The serpent becomes evil. The mother goddess becomes an abomination.

With *ruach*, the feminine breath of life recedes beneath a masculinized Spirit. With *ḥawwāh*, the mother of all living becomes the mother of sin and death. With *'ezer kenegdo*, a corresponding strength becomes a subordinate helper. With *ṣēlā'*, a chamber becomes a rib, and woman is severed from origin. With *'itsabon*, toil and sorrow become the burden of childbirth. With *ipsa*, a masculine "he" becomes a feminine "she," and Mary is made to crush the serpent once linked to the goddess. With *mûm*, a body without blemish becomes a soul without sin, set against the imagined flaw in all other humans. With Logos, Sophia becomes the Word, and Wisdom is written into a masculine form. With one iota, Mary becomes Martha, and the authority of sacred witness is displaced.

Magdalene: a title of exaltation, a tower of faith, collapsed into a seaside town known for fish salting. Seven: a number of divine completeness, inverted into a count of mortal sins. *Daimonia*: a passage of spiritual power, remembered as demonic possession. Vision: the direct reception of divine knowledge, treated as danger because it did not pass through the sanctioned mouths of men. *Nous*: the faculty of recognition and inner seeing, dismissed once it appeared in the body of a woman. Apostola apostolorum: the apostle to the apostles, first witness and first messenger, yet pushed to the edge of the Easter story, if she is named there at all. And the jar: a sign of devotion, recognition, and sacred anointing, turned into the mark of a prostitute through the sinister projections of one bishop's sermon.

But once a sermon changes the meaning of a symbol, images begin to obey. What had once marked witness could be repainted as shame, softened into ambiguity, or removed altogether. A word spoken from a pulpit can enter paint. It can teach the eye what to see, what to suspect, what to erase.

The woman hovering over the green serpent does not read as praying, contemplating, or submitting. Her eyes are lowered, not in penitence, but with quiet certainty. Her body moves forward slightly, her arms held as though guarding something no longer visible within the frame.

A jar.

Perhaps she is just touching her heart, but this is not quite the posture of devotional surrender. The gesture carries through her body, from the angle of her arms, to the distribution of her weight, and the quiet tension of a protected grip. It is not the stance of emptiness. Nor does it resolve into the familiar image of mother and child. No one holds an infant that way. Or a scroll. The arrangement is too rounded, too contained, shaped for something with weight and hollow.

The colors are worn down, the edges muted, the lines blurred until the form seems blended back into the wall itself. However cautiously one tries to reconstruct it, only the outline survives preserving a small vessel with a rounded body and narrowing neck, the kind one hand might support from below while the other steadies near the mouth. The erasure is clean enough to remove the object, but not thorough enough to undo the gesture. Her hands remember its gravity. They are shaped to cradle something sacred.

Only then does the absence become legible. The symbol can be removed, but the body remembers. The narrative can be twisted, a word can be changed, a doctrine can be laid over an older meaning, but the threads remain. Faith does not mean surrendering to every story told in its name. It can also mean looking again, refusing the distortion, and trusting that what survives beneath the official story may still be true. It can mean widening the gaze until the single sanctioned story gives way to the larger pattern: the whole tapestry, the weave that still holds what was altered, hidden, and nearly torn, but not destroyed.

A woman holding a jar. This is how Mary Magdalene was remembered, carrying a vessel scripture never placed in her hands. But the jar was never only a jar, just as following Mary Magdalene was never only about one woman. It became a sign of the feminine as vessel and threshold: what holds, what opens, what pours forth, what changes that brings new life forward.

The jar belonged to Pandora too, the woman who opened not a box, but a vessel, another small translation shift from *pithos* to *pyxis* that diminished the fullness of the symbol. Even in the sky, where Aquarius is named as masculine, the image betrays an older truth: water jars belong to women, to the ones who carried, filled, poured, and kept life moving. Pandora, Eve, Sophia—again and again, a woman stands at the threshold of a creation story, at the origin of a tale about how the world changed, how humanity awakened, how life passed from one state into another. Each time, the story was turned against her. Still, the symbols retain their form.

The jar holds. The serpent transforms. The water pours out. The fruit awakens. Memory belongs to shape, to what the eye recognizes and the ear hears before institution intervenes. It cannot be taken, revised, or renamed, because it speaks not to the surface but to the soul, not to what is taught but to what is known. Truth does not burn in fire. It is not swallowed by the waves. It rises with the tide, regenerates within its own ashes, and returns by its very nature, remaking itself from within like the generative goddesses from the earliest reaches of memory.

The feminine is life, creation, transformation, return. The Mother remains under every name placed over her, no matter how many times her story is rewritten. She abides at the center of the circle, where she has always been, and where she will always be.

When the symbols and stories are seen again, the myths return to their origin place: a woman, a vessel, an opening, a world altered by what crossed the threshold and could not be called back. Once the jar is opened, nothing returns to what it was before. What pours out may spiral beyond control, but it is not evil. It is not the ruin of the world any more than a scar is the ruin of the body. It is the force that proves life has not stopped moving. It persists, though unpredictable.

In Pandora's story, one thing remained inside the jar. *Elpis*. The word can be translated as hope, though it carries something older and less certain too: expectation, waiting, the unknown still held in reserve. Hope is not what escapes the jar. It is what survives inside it. And if hope remains within the jar, then the entire story turns again.

The jar becomes a sign of abundance, wisdom, and life kept in trust. The serpent beneath her becomes the living shape of regeneration. The words she rises above become a song that recognizes wholeness. Even the scar belongs to that truth, made beautiful because healing left its mark. And hope becomes the quiet knowledge that fear is not the deepest truth. Love is.

Love as the force that calls life back when the world breaks open. Love as the capacity to contain what exceeds control without surrendering to despair. A love wide enough to hold serpent and jar, wound and healing, darkness and light, without dividing one from the other.

It is love that sees her whole.

You are altogether beautiful, my beloved, and there is no flaw in you.

Epilogue

THE TWELFTH HOUR OF DAY

London, 2024

A woman's voice was already carrying beyond the fortress walls as we walked out beneath the thick stone arch and through the timbered gates. We moved side by side, her familiar song rising into our silence.

That wordlessness had settled earlier, on the raised platform beside the White Tower, when a passerby offered to take our photo. We stood just beyond the stone parapet, with the Tower Bridge rising behind our shoulders and the Thames moving steadily below—its surface pulling the last of the light westward. October dusk hovered over the water, and something in us moved with the river.

Change rarely arrives in a single moment. More often, it moves like a current you enter without noticing, until you look back and understand you have already been carried somewhere new.

And then there are moments when the ground gives way beneath you.

*

In our shared quiet at the Tower of London, we drifted toward a bench in the inner ward, settling along the open sweep of green where a queen once stood at the edge of her final moments.

It was not the first time we had noticed Anne Boleyn circling.

Like the fleur-de-lis that moves across European courts and gleams from the Crown Jewels, Anne seems to appear where religion, authority, and symbol converge, like an ermine painted into the folds of royal imagery or the maiden with the unicorn torn from the tapestry. Given her fate at this very place, it should not have surprised us to feel her here. And yet we were stilled by the sense of a woman not entirely gone, just as we had come to recognize with Mary Magdalene. More and more, we noticed that Anne traces a path beside Mary. She is a woman once central, then torn from the heart of a story, like a tattered tapestry whose remaining threads can be pieced into an outline of what is no longer there.

No Tudor gallery will name her, though she wore a king's crown and bore the white falcon. What marked her was ordered stripped away. Walls were repainted and insignia removed, not unlike the early Christian texts that were burned or left to vanish when no one remained to copy them. Memory does not always fade on its own; sometimes it is deliberately erased. The sky remains, and only fragments of a missing maiden linger amid a fence strewn with red and white roses, their petals now blending into an echo of the Tudor emblem.

As we settled into the unexpected ending of our Magdalenian journey at the Tower of London, we sat feet from where Anne was executed and Elizabeth imprisoned before rising, against all expectation, to rule as one of the most successful monarchs of her age. Mother and daughter seemed suspended there, held between them in prayer books, jewelry, memories, and the women who carried those fragments forward, refusing to let them be lost.

That's when a raven cut through our astonishment, heavy, glossy, and deliberate, her black feathers catching the last light with an oil-dark sheen. She moved with the authority of a creature that had outlived every story told about this place, crossing before our bench as though the Tower were her own. Not a wild bird free to depart, but one of the kept ones, the necessary ones, for if the ravens ever leave the Tower, the old legend says, the kingdom will fall.

A bird that remains, her wing clipped for the sake of legend, though nothing in her carriage admits the wound. She appears as she should be, but she is not. Her wings may open, but they cannot carry her beyond these walls, not as far as a raven was born to go.

The same might be said of the women whose stories were not left in their own hands, drawn from their centers and kept within bounds not of their own making.

*

Our park bench moment inside the Tower was not where we expected to arrive, let alone where we anticipated our pilgrimage would end, having begun just forty-eight hours earlier on a transcontinental overnight flight from New York to London.

Somewhere over the Atlantic, in the small, improbable miracle of having escaped the demands of two large, growing families, we paused at *Mary, Queen of Scots* while scrolling through the in-flight movies. We hadn't planned to watch it. It was simply there and fitting enough, given where we were headed to Glastonbury. We pressed play on our separate screens in tandem, expecting nothing beyond distraction.

The film opens with Mary's execution, ordered by her cousin Elizabeth I. Mary walks into the great hall at Fotheringhay Castle, where the scaffold has been raised, dressed in black velvet mourning, composed and deliberate. Her attendants remove the cloak, revealing a red petticoat, set against the white of her veil. As the outer layer falls away, the contrast sharpens into a language of color she chose, carried forward in symbol where words no longer suffice.

A crucifix in her hand and rosary beads at her wrist, she lifts the cross briefly to her lips, praying aloud in Latin: *In manus tuas, Domine, commendo spiritum meum.*

She declares her faith, forgives the executioner, and continues in prayer as the moment closes around her. She kneels at the block, placing herself into position. The veil is adjusted, her eyes covered, her lips still moving as she lowers her head, steady in the final seconds before the blade falls.

It is said the execution was not swift, unlike the clean stroke given to Anne by the French swordsman whom Henry VIII had brought in at great cost. And for Elizabeth, whose signature had set Mary's death in motion, shaped by the fall of one mother and the rise of another, by the father whose will had defined her life before she could define herself, and by a court where survival required distance, it becomes difficult to say where her will ends and the machinery around her begins. What unfolds between them is less a contest of queens than two women ruling within forms already set, shaped by men, by doctrine, by a faith that both anoints and contains.

After the film opens with her ending, it returns to Mary at the beginning of her rule. A ship approaches a cold Scottish coast, unfamiliar after the years she spent at the French court. The camera lingers on what is carried with her: woven tapestries, a small casket, and a devotional image of the Virgin, all lifted from the vessel and brought ashore with the rest of her household.

From our seats above the ocean, the moment startled us, not for what it showed, but for what it seemed to suggest. A tapestry, something like a maiden and her unicorn, the kind that would have filled the courts she had just left; a Marian image, darkened into something closer to a Black Madonna; and the boat, borne into land.

Not the rudderless vessel carried toward the shores of Marseille. Not that story directly. Yet the Magdalene echo was as insistent as the red dress Mary Stuart had chosen at her end.

We exchanged a glance. A pattern was already forming between us, though not yet named. It could have been dismissed as coincidence, or nothing at all. But in that moment, we knew. What we were seeing was the first points of a constellation, before any lines were drawn: stars not agreed upon, but already gathering into something that asks to be told.

To trace even the faintest line between the disparate stars we saw in our inky sky was to risk being called crazy. To see connection where none had been formally named, to speak it aloud, especially as women, was to step just beyond what is considered safe. Because there has always been a space reserved for what does not fit, and women have often been placed there: present, attentive, yet discredited the moment they begin to name what others refuse to see.

First it is called conflation. Then superstition. Then something closer to danger than wisdom.

The unease around a wise woman is not unlike what clings to the figure of the witch, those cast to the edges, imagined in circles of thirteen, in covens, their knowledge turned to threat. Thirteen takes shape there first, not simply a number, but a formation, suggesting a force just beyond what can be ordered or fixed in place, not fully seen or understood, and therefore feared.

Violence and secrecy converge around what does not fit, as with the blue moon, sometimes associated in folklore with the old word *belewe*, "to betray," an extra moon that falls outside the twelve-month calendar and exposes the limits of the system meant to contain it. Ophiuchus, the serpent bearer, follows the same logic. It is the thirteenth constellation crossed by the sun's path, present along the ecliptic yet excluded from the twelve-part zodiac. What is difficult to reconcile becomes easier to ignore. Still, the bearer and the serpent are there, just outside the sanctioned sky.

And how striking that image becomes beside the Marian imagery of the Miraculous Medal. "There was also a serpent, green in color with yellow spots," Catherine Labouré said of her vision. In the hands of those who received, edited, and authorized her story, the serpent was pressed beneath Mary's feet and bound to Genesis 3:15; on the reverse, twelve stars closed their circle around the great M. What Ophiuchus holds together, the medal divides: woman, serpent, and the missing thirteenth presence. The circle appears complete, yet something vital has been left outside the count.

Not imposed, but given—thirteen, whether we recognize it or not.

In the living world, the spiral held in the pinecone already carries this count. Thirteen emerges as structure, the seventh number in the Fibonacci sequence, appearing among the patterns held in the fern, the nautilus, the seed-head of the sunflower, and the ordering of blossoms such as the lily and the buttercup.

What, then, is it that Venus traces across the sky?

A fivefold path across eight years—five and eight returning into a rhythm that does not resolve into twelve, even as it inscribes a pentagram above, long demonized for what it suggests. But the sky does not hold the shape in a single pass. It returns. And returns again, until what first appeared as a star begins to open, its lines no longer fixed, but turning, layering, softening at the edges, no longer a pentagram at all, but something fuller, something living: a rose.

So too, wherever the count is set at twelve, thirteen marks what does not disappear, but is not fully admitted, as at the table in Leonardo's *Last Supper*.

And there she is, Mary Magdalene, if she is understood as the thirteenth disciple, not counted among the twelve, still present where it matters most, beside Jesus, the space between them forming the open V of a chalice. Not only a disciple, but something more. A teacher with him. A philosopher in her own right. A leader of one of the earliest Christian communities. Even, "impossibly," the author of the Fourth Gospel.

But what if thirteen has never marked what is dangerous, only what refuses to be contained?

We know this vision, too. It floats in our modern consciousness. Taylor Swift, who has long claimed thirteen as her personal talisman, ascends onto a stage of her own making, shattering records and expectations on the Eras Tour in a serpentine costume to ". . . Ready For It?"

Are we ever ready—for change, for revolution, for new ways of seeing, for the apocalyptic moment of revelation?

The lights rise anyway, and a stadium of screaming voices breaks open as the infamous serpentine costume she has worn all along transforms from black and red to black and gold—not as a change, but as a culmination, the turning of an era into something else entirely.

It can be overwhelming. In the frenzy of a sold-out arena, it is almost too much to fully take in, that a woman could stand at the center in such a role and imagery. And she does. Not hidden, not diminished, but revealed: woman and her serpent, a goddess no longer bound to shame, rising before a watching crowd, the old sign of threat transfigured into power. No white horse, no rider sent to conquer, only the world rearranging around her, and her voice.

It is a show, yes, but something else is breaking through, something long present and now impossible to ignore. The fans answer her as witnesses turned passionate participants, hands marked with her thirteen, singing every lyric of a career already written into them.

Reputation.

Not simply the name of the album from which the song arises, but the thing itself: what is made, imposed, sustained. The story told about a woman until it begins to take her place, until she is named a whore, as in Babylon, or a prostitute, as in the rumor that has haunted Magdalene since a "great" man gave it voice.

Yes, this recasting, this lie, is not unlike the diminishment of Mary Magdalene, whose name has been burdened with what was never hers to carry, obscured and made to hold a version that could be managed.

Something like that moved beneath what we were seeing, something just beyond reach, or just beyond permission, as difficult to fix as the mists of Avalon, or Mary herself.

It was not new to us. These moments, these flashes of alignment, had long threaded through our lives, appearing without warning, asking to be followed or dismissed.

"Why does she matter so much to you, anyway?"

We knew that question. We had lived inside it, feeling the resistance to Mary, the quiet pressure to look away, to leave certain connections unmade, so that everything might remain as it was.

And still, we kept following.

What we had been tracing had already begun to organize our days through our work on *The Magdalene Thread*, our growing publication, following the fragments, the images, and the stories that refuse to settle into a single telling about the most elusive and misunderstood woman in the Christian story. What appeared scattered to others had, over time, begun to assume its own coherence—not by forcing a pattern, but by returning again and again until the lines could no longer be ignored.

On pilgrimage, it intensified.

Twenty-two hours in the English countryside, and the scattered pieces seemed to clarify. The sense of wonder we felt standing before Stonehenge gave way to our walk through the Chalice Garden, the shock of cold in the white spring, and our climb up and down the Tor just before the rain swept in.

From there, a storybook bed and breakfast awaited us, a sanctuary among its watching lions. It just so happened to be only minutes from Wells, the cathedral we visited only on the insistence of a friend and because there was spare time—nothing more than that, or so we thought.

Yes, we were delighted by a buttercup in a Somerset pasture and its return to painted form in subtle places within this gothic cathedral. Maybe that's why the glimmer of yellow caught our eyes after walking up a sea of steps and through a forest of stone, to uncover our stained-glass Magdalene with a host in hues as golden as a five-petaled chalice-shaped flower in midday sun—waiting there, as if expecting us. How could we ever explain to anyone what we see, and how it forms, we wondered, how one thing answers another across distance, across time?

We arrived, almost reluctantly, at the realization that what we had begun to build with *The Magdalene Thread* would need to be set aside so a book could be written.

We returned to London knowing what that required, to bring her forth not as she had been given to us, but as she had been kept: passed hand to hand, preserved where she could not always be spoken, but never entirely lost. It was a task neither simple nor without risk. No longer hidden but seen as she is.

And yet she is everywhere, if one learns how to see. Or perhaps more precisely, we were beginning to understand that this way of seeing, this attunement to story, symbol, and what returns, was a form of faith.

That understanding followed us to the Victoria and Albert Museum, where we went to see Raphael's *The Miraculous Draught of Fishes,* drawn there by our growing questions around the miraculous catch and the mysterious 1-5-3. The cartoon is usually identified with Luke's version of the catch, not the one in the Fourth Gospel. But to us, that displacement only deepened the question. What if Luke's cleaner call story had been laid over the Fourth Gospel's more potent scene, where the clue is not only the catch, but the command to cast the net on the right side of the boat? What if the confusion was not ours alone, but part of the very history of covering, borrowing, and renaming that had helped move Magdalene out of view?

We did not expect to find Magdalene there, inside a museum named for a queen, at least not explicitly or in any obvious way. But there she was: unlabeled, recurring in triptychs and painted scenes, among altarpieces, devotional panels, and fragments of stained glass. She was recognizable through the symbols that persist, through red, through the jar, through her place among the Marys, and through her presence at the cross.

Why is she unnamed, even here, even by those entrusted with preserving and interpreting these works, when her presence is not in question, only unspoken?

Raphael's image had not remained confined to sketch. Woven into tapestry, it traveled, carried north and taken up again under another crown, another telling. The museum plaque made note of it. And there, then, was the Stuart line, from James, the son of Mary, Queen of Scots, to Charles, who carried Raphael's cartoons into England, rising where we had not expected it, as so many things had emerged on this journey: out of stone, out of story, out of what seemed at first like coincidence and then no longer did.

"In my end is my beginning."

Words long associated with the woman who had followed us from that overnight flight into this unfolding end, said to have been carried, perhaps even stitched, into the red dress she wore at her death. We would only later come upon them in the sea of our research, but by then we were already living inside the story as it was taking shape, following the smallest, most obscure details wherever they led, no stone unturned, no footnote unread, no book too strange, no fragment too tattered to matter.

And perhaps that was the question running through it all: whether Mary, and these women, and even we ourselves, were more than what had been told.

*

Amid the ramparts standing watch for centuries, we walked through those gates, tickets in hand for the sixteenth of October, with minutes to spare before the final entry. Our timing felt almost meant to be, especially given that we had missed the Magdalene chapel in Glastonbury by the same margin the day before.

Sixteen.

Not a number we had been looking for, nor one as immediately charged as thirteen, or even as 3.14, the ratio of the circle that returns on her feast day through its fractional equivalent of 22/7. It held its own quiet insistence: the number of the Tower in the Tarot deck, the card of a structure split open, a crown dislodged, lightning exposing what cannot remain as it was.

Tarot, of course, sits uneasily beside the Christianity of our upbringing, often dismissed as superstition or even sorcery. For others, however, it became one of the symbolic languages through which older stories survived when more direct ones could not.

In any language, and from whatever side of the pew or mat one comes, this is what it is to follow Magdalene: less a path toward comfort than a movement toward disruption, toward the sudden flash that splits the surface of things and reveals what has been there all along.

She is, in a way, a golden bolt of lightning, both illumination and consequence.

Because once something is seen in a new and moving way, it does not return easily to where it was. The structure has already been struck. What is opened does not close without a trace; the mark remains, like a scar, like a crack that alters the shape of what can be held.

And sometimes, from that fracture, something as small and persistent as a five-petaled pink wildflower blooms on a Provençal mountain, its delicate form turning again in Venus as she rises in the evening sky.

That recognition asks something of us now. It asks to be gathered. It asks for the patience of hands that will tend what remains. And then—for voice, for breath, for song. And in the singing, what's broken begins to mend. For as Clarissa Pinkola Estés writes, "Stories are medicine."

We moved with that knowing, not as singers or scholars, but as writers and mothers, shaped as much by what we had lived as by what we were beginning to see. We crossed the Tower grounds and came to rest on the open sweep of green where Anne and Elizabeth had each been kept, at different moments, under different hands. The space held both mother and daughter at once—not as separate histories, but as a single field of tension where power was revealed, contained, and rewritten.

In that quiet, everything we had passed through in those two whirlwind days returned, not in sequence, but all at once. The film. The fragments. The crossings. The images that had first felt incidental now striking back into view, colliding with the stories of our own lives and the recognition of what motherhood has carried, and what has been made to disappear with it.

As the raven picked its way across the grass, stopping, pecking, lifting again, scanning the ground, and us, it felt less like a passing presence than a witness. It was impossible not to imagine Anne glancing over her shoulder, a gesture some say was her last hope that Henry would pardon her—a looking back that did not end with her but became the work of those who kept looking for her, seen or not.

What was cut down in her did not disappear. It changed form, passed into the daughter who would follow, as in the ring Elizabeth kept close, long thought to hold her mother's image, hidden and revealed at will.

Elizabeth, in one of her carefully managed portraits, reigns with the serpent at her left sleeve. Elsewhere, the serpent was painted out, its body covered over by flowers. Her symbology carefully shaped, her authority projected through image as much as decree. The Virgin Queen is not simply a title, but a construction, a figure made to hold what could not be openly claimed.

Still, the serpent remains: held, subdued, never entirely gone, like the jar in the hands of a woman near the Pantheon, painted over but not erased. Its presence shifts between concealment and display, less an enemy than something absorbed, turned inward, made to serve the image that contains it. Something not unlike the ouroboros, an older form of the snake that turns back upon itself, not as ending but as return. A form older than court, older than crown, carrying within it the trace of something once held differently, before it was pressed into obedience—before Isis, before Egypt, were folded into forms that could be sanctioned.

The synchronicities were no longer subtle.

It felt as though the Tower card had been thrown down into this moment of our lives, for we knew the work could no longer remain where we had placed it. It would have to be carried now, as other women had carried what could not be lost, and something would have to be left behind. Time would have to be set apart, with a willingness to answer the calling fully, even without knowing what it would become, like following stars westward toward a boat not yet seen.

We sat with that for a while, the aftershock still moving through us, not yet resolved but already altering the shape of what would come next.

Then, almost at the same moment, we rose, the raven still moving at the edge of our awareness, her clipped wing no longer something we could look away from.

As we walked farther from the Tower and closer to the sound, the woman's voice came clear. Contemporary worship rose into a space that had once bristled with royal supremacy and papal defiance:

When You don't give the answers / As I cry out to You / I will trust, I will trust / I will trust in You

It was a Lauren Daigle song, carried here by a street singer—the kind of worship anthem as at home on the radio as in a sanctuary, devotion folded into the wider sweep of popular sound, now echoing through a medieval threshold. Ancient and modern, Christian and something older, sacred and pageantry braided together without asking permission, like the tapestry we felt ourselves beginning to weave.

She stood just beyond the gates as tourists drifted loosely around her, shopping bags swinging from their wrists—Union Jack flags, sweatshirts stamped with *LONDON*, velvet boxes cradling replicas of the Crown Jewels, toy swords and plastic shields marked with Tudor roses. Red and white flashed in the fading light as evening settled, conversation and footsteps weaving through her refrain.

And it was there, in that convergence, that we began to understand. What we had taken for an ending was, in fact, a beginning. Not a line closing, but something turning toward its source. Not forward, but back through what has been set aside, until what was excluded becomes the expression of the whole.

It is, of course, about Mary. But not only Mary, and not only the Tudor women whose stories rise so visibly around her. It is about something that moves through them all, through every woman misunderstood.

The question was never simply what to say, but how to follow what had already begun to stir, a question that had been there all along, until lightning struck at the Tower, and the raven seemed to ask whether we would have the courage to say what needed to be said.

The day was already leaning into its final hour, the light thinning as it drew us inward, the long passage approaching its close: the twelfth hour, as the Egyptians marked it, just before the sun's passage into darkness and its return to light again.

Leaving was no longer what it had been. By then, we understood that freedom was not in the flight, but in what might rise from the ashes of what we were willing to let burn.

As it is written in the Fourth Gospel: "Then you will know the truth, and the truth will set you free."

Alicia & Kelly at the Tower of London, October 2024.

NOTES

Unless otherwise noted, New Testament quotations follow the New International Version (NIV) and Old Testament quotations the New Revised Standard Version (NRSV); where a passage uses another translation, or the author's own rendering of the original, that is indicated in the note.

Introduction

1. C. Tuckett, *The Gospel of Mary* (Oxford, 2007). See also K. L. King, *The Gospel of Mary of Magdala* (Santa Rosa, CA, 2003), for an accessible scholarly translation and discussion.
2. J. P. Allen, *Coptic* (University Park, PA, 2020).
3. King, *Gospel of Mary of Magdala*, 6, citing C. Markschies, "Lehrer, Schüler, Schule" in *Religiöse Vereine in der römischen Antike* (Tübingen, 2002), 97–120 (here 98).
4. The Niceno-Constantinopolitan Creed (381 CE).
5. M. Meyer, *The Nag Hammadi Scriptures* (New York, 2007).
6. A. Kateusz, *Mary and Early Christian Women* (Cham, 2019).
7. *The Thunder, Perfect Mind*, in Meyer, *Nag Hammadi Scriptures*, 372.
8. C. P. Estés, *Women Who Run with the Wolves* (New York, 1992), 24.

Chapter 1: La Grotte de Marie-Madeleine

1. J. de Voragine, *The Golden Legend*, trans. W. G. Ryan (Princeton, 2012).
2. Voragine, *Golden Legend*, trans. Ryan, 380.
3. J. Guy and J. Fox, *Hunting the Falcon* (New York, 2023), 65–67.
4. K. L. Jansen, *The Making of the Magdalen* (Princeton, 2000).
5. Guy and Fox, *Hunting the Falcon*, 65.

Chapter 2: The Missing Mother

1. J. J. Rorimer, "The Unicorn Tapestries Were Made for Anne of Brittany," *Metropolitan Museum of Art Bulletin* n.s. 1 (1942): 7–20.
2. A. S. Cavallo, *The Unicorn Tapestries at The Metropolitan Museum of Art* (New York, 1998), 45–49; M. B. Freeman, *The Unicorn Tapestries* (New York, 1976).
3. J. Williamson, *The Oak King, the Holly King, and the Unicorn: The Myths and Symbolism of the Unicorn Tapestries* (New York, 1986).
4. Song of Songs 2:16.
5. Williamson, *Oak King*.

6. Gregory the Great, Homily 33 (on Luke 7:36–50).
7. J. Schaberg, *The Resurrection of Mary Magdalene: Legends, Apocrypha, and the Christian Testament* (New York, 2002); S. Haskins, *Mary Magdalen: Myth and Metaphor* (New York, 1993).
8. Luke 1:28.
9. Luke 1:34.
10. Luke 1:38.
11. B. E. Reid, *Choosing the Better Part? Women in the Gospel of Luke* (Collegeville, MN, 1996).
12. Suetonius, *Lives of the Caesars*, "The Deified Augustus," 94, trans. J. C. Rolfe, Loeb Classical Library 31 (Cambridge, MA, 1914).
13. Matthew 1:23.
14. Isaiah 7:14.
15. R. E. Brown, *The Birth of the Messiah: A Commentary on the Infancy Narratives in Matthew and Luke*, updated ed. (New York, 1993).
16. A. Kateusz, *Mary and Early Christian Women: Hidden Leadership* (Cham, 2019), 121 (Kindle).
17. Kateusz, *Mary and Early Christian Women*, 30 (Kindle).
18. Justin Martyr, *Dialogue with Trypho* 100, in *Ante-Nicene Fathers*, vol. 1, trans. A. Roberts and J. Donaldson (Buffalo, NY, 1885; repr. Peabody, MA, 1994).
19. Irenaeus of Lyons, *Against Heresies* 3.22.4, in *Ante-Nicene Fathers*, vol. 1, trans. Roberts and Donaldson.
20. S. Wessel, *Cyril of Alexandria and the Nestorian Controversy: The Making of a Saint and of a Heretic* (Oxford, 2004).
21. Galatians 1:19.
22. J. Campbell, *Goddesses: Mysteries of the Feminine Divine*, ed. S. Rossi (Novato, CA, 2013).
23. Genesis 2:7.
24. Genesis 2:18; see P. Trible, *God and the Rhetoric of Sexuality* (Philadelphia, 1978).
25. Genesis 2:22.
26. L. Berne DeGear, "(m)Adam: Adam's Rib Reframed," YouTube video, premiered April 5, 2020, https://www.youtube.com/watch?v=j147Kd_JDhw.
27. Sirach 25:24.
28. Galatians 3:28.
29. 1 Timothy 2:11–14.
30. B. D. Ehrman, *Forged: Writing in the Name of God—Why the Bible's Authors Are Not Who We Think They Are* (New York, 2011).
31. G. A. Anderson, *The Genesis of Perfection: Adam and Eve in Jewish and Christian Imagination* (Louisville, KY, 2001).
32. Tertullian, *On the Apparel of Women* 1.1, in *Ante-Nicene Fathers*, vol. 4, trans. S. Thelwall (Buffalo, NY, 1885; repr. Peabody, MA, 1994).
33. John Chrysostom, Homily 9 on 1 Timothy (on 1 Timothy 2:11–15), in *Nicene and Post-Nicene Fathers*, 1st series, vol. 13, trans. J. Tweed (Buffalo, NY, 1889; repr. Peabody, MA, 1994).
34. Jerome, *Against Jovinianus* 1.16, in *Nicene and Post-Nicene Fathers*, 2nd series, vol. 6, trans. W. H. Fremantle (New York, 1893; repr. Peabody, MA, 1994).
35. S. Greenblatt, "How St. Augustine Invented Sex," *The New Yorker*, June 19, 2017.
36. Greenblatt, "How St. Augustine Invented Sex."

37. Augustine, *Confessions* 6.15 and 8.11.
38. Greenblatt, "How St. Augustine Invented Sex."
39. Augustine, *The Literal Meaning of Genesis*, trans. J. H. Taylor, Ancient Christian Writers 42 (New York, 1982), 9.5.9.
40. Augustine, *City of God* 14.16–24; *On Marriage and Concupiscence.*
41. For the Kuntillet ʿAjrud inscriptions: W. G. Dever, "Asherah, Consort of Yahweh? New Evidence from Kuntillet ʿAjrud," *Bulletin of the American Schools of Oriental Research* 255 (1984): 21–37; and Z. Meshel et al., *Kuntillet ʿAjrud (Horvat Teman): An Iron Age II Religious Site on the Judah-Sinai Border* (Jerusalem, 2012). For the Khirbet el-Qom tomb inscription: J. M. Hadley, "The Khirbet el-Qôm Inscription," *Vetus Testamentum* 37, no. 1 (1987): 50–62.
42. T. Römer, *The Invention of God*, trans. R. Geuss (Cambridge, MA, 2015).
43. T. Frymer-Kensky, *Reading the Women of the Bible* (New York, 2002); see also Römer, *Invention of God.*
44. Proverbs 8:22–31; E. Pagels, *The Gnostic Gospels* (New York, 1979).
45. Irenaeus, *Against Heresies* 1.11, in *Ante-Nicene Fathers*, vol. 1, trans. Roberts and Donaldson.
46. Hippolytus of Rome, *Refutation of All Heresies* 9.13, in *Ante-Nicene Fathers*, vol. 5, trans. J. H. MacMahon (Buffalo, NY, 1886; repr. Peabody, MA, 1994).
47. Jerome, *Commentary on Isaiah* 11.2; for text and discussion, see *New Testament Apocrypha*, ed. W. Schneemelcher, rev. ed., trans. R. McL. Wilson, 2 vols. (Louisville, 1991–92), 1:177.
48. Apocryphon of John, in M. Meyer, ed. and trans., *The Nag Hammadi Scriptures: The Revised and Updated Translation of Sacred Gnostic Texts Complete in One Volume* (New York, 2007).
49. Gospel of Philip 55, in Meyer, *Nag Hammadi Scriptures.*
50. S. Brock, "The Holy Spirit as Feminine in Early Syriac Literature," in *After Eve*, ed. J. M. Soskice (London, 1990).
51. F. Bovon, "Mary Magdalene in the Acts of Philip," in *Which Mary? The Marys of Early Christian Tradition*, ed. F. S. Jones (Atlanta, 2002).
52. A. Kateusz, *Finding Holy Spirit Mother* (Kansas City, MO, 2013).

Chapter 3: Campagne Provençale

1. V. van Gogh to T. van Gogh, Letter 619, Les Saintes-Maries-de-la-Mer, on or about 3–4 June 1888, in *Vincent van Gogh: The Letters*, 6 vols. (Amsterdam and Brussels, 2009).
2. W. Shakespeare, *Romeo and Juliet*, act 2, scene 2.
3. S. Haskins, *Mary Magdalen* (New York, 1993).
4. Voragine, *Golden Legend*, trans. Ryan, 376–377.
5. V. Flayol, founder, Magdalene Sacred Journeys.
6. P. Verlaine, "Clair de lune," in *Fêtes galantes* (Paris, 1869).

Chapter 4: Tower of Faith

1. J. I. Dirvin, C.M., "The Miraculous Medal," in *A Woman Clothed with the Sun* (Garden City, NY, 1961).

2. Dirvin, "The Miraculous Medal," in J. J. Delaney, ed., *A Woman Clothed with the Sun*, 48–49.
3. Ibid., 49.
4. Ibid., 55.
5. Ibid., 60.
6. Ibid., 66.
7. Origen, *Contra Celsum* 2.55.
8. Jerome, *Letter* 127 (To Principia) 5.
9. On patristic Eve–Magdalene typology: Augustine of Hippo, *De diversis quaestionibus 83*, q. 73; Ambrose of Milan, *Expositio Lucam* 10.150–60; John Chrysostom, *In Joannem* Hom. 86; Gregory the Great, *Homilies* 25 and 33. For a synthetic modern treatment, see S. Haskins, *Mary Magdalen* (New York, 1993).
10. John 20:1, 2, 8, 13, 15, 16.
11. John 20:17.
12. Gregory the Great, Homily 33 (on Luke 7:36–50).
13. Matthew 27:55–56; Mark 15:40–41.
14. A. G. Brock, *Mary Magdalene, the First Apostle* (Cambridge, MA, 2003); B. E. Reid, *Choosing the Better Part? Women in the Gospel of Luke* (Collegeville, MN, 1996).
15. Luke 8:1–3.
16. Reid, *Choosing the Better Part?* (cf. n14).
17. Luke 8:2.
18. Plato, *Symposium* 202d–e; on Middle Platonic daimonology, J. Dillon, *The Middle Platonists* (Ithaca, NY, 1977).
19. Colossians 4:14; see also Irenaeus, *Against Heresies* 3.14.1, trans. A. Roberts and J. Donaldson, *Ante-Nicene Fathers*, vol. 1 (1885; repr. Peabody, MA, 1994), 437–38.
20. Hippolytus of Rome, *Commentary on the Song of Songs* 24–26.
21. Dillon, *The Middle Platonists* (cf. n18).
22. S. Parkhouse, *Eschatology and the Saviour* (Cambridge, 2019).
23. Gregory the Great, Homily 33 (cf. n12 for full citation).
24. Gregory the Great, *Moralia in Job*, Book XXXI, CCSL 143A.
25. Evagrius Ponticus, *Praktikos* 6.
26. Augustine of Hippo, *De civitate Dei* 14.
27. T. Ilan, *Lexicon of Jewish Names in Late Antiquity, Part I*, TSAJ 91 (Tübingen, 2002).
28. T. Ilan, *Lexicon*, (cf. n27); on the historical Mariamne and her murder by Herod, see Josephus, *Antiquities of the Jews* 15.7.
29. A. J. Maas, "The Name of Mary," in *The Catholic Encyclopedia*, vol. 15 (New York, 1912).
30. M. Starbird, *The Woman with the Alabaster Jar* (Santa Fe, NM, 1993), esp. ch. 3.
31. E. Schrader and J. E. Taylor, "The Meaning of 'Magdalene,'" *Journal of Biblical Literature* 140, no. 4 (2021): 751–73.
32. M. Eliade, *The Sacred and the Profane*, trans. W. R. Trask (New York, 1959), 36–47.
33. Irenaeus, *Against Heresies* 3.11.8 (the four-pillared Gospel).
34. Matthew 26:6–13; Mark 14:3–9.
35. Luke 7:36–50.
36. John 12:1–8.

37. Hippolytus of Rome, *Commentary on the Song of Songs* §25, trans. Y. W. Smith (cf. n20).
38. S. Haskins, *Mary Magdalen*, chs. 3–4 (cf. n9 for full citation).
39. Gregory the Great, Homily 33 (cf. n12 for full citation).
40. R. A. Houston, *Literacy in Early Modern Europe*, 2nd ed. (London, 2002).
41. B. D. Ehrman, *Misquoting Jesus* (San Francisco, 2005).
42. Eusebius, *Ecclesiastical History*, LCL 153 and 265 (Cambridge, MA, 1926–32). The *Ecclesiastical History* also survives through earlier Syriac and Latin translations that preserve portions of the text —the Syriac is early fifth-century; Rufinus's Latin is c. 402–403.
43. L. H. Feldman, "On the Authenticity of the *Testimonium Flavianum* Attributed to Josephus," in *New Perspectives on Jewish-Christian Relations* (Leiden, 2012), 11–30.
44. Ehrman, *Misquoting Jesus*, (cf. n41). Covers both the Pericope Adulterae (John 7:53–8:11), absent from the earliest manuscripts, and the longer ending of Mark (16:9–20).
45. Papyrus 52 (the John Rylands fragment, John 18) and Papyrus 66 (Bodmer II; c. 200–250). L. W. Hurtado, *The Earliest Christian Artifacts* (Grand Rapids, MI, 2006).
46. E. Schrader, "Was Martha of Bethany Added to the Fourth Gospel in the Second Century?," *Harvard Theological Review* 110, no. 3 (2017): 360–92.
47. Tertullian, *Adversus Praxean* 23.
48. John Chrysostom, *Homiliae in Joannem* 62.1 (PG 59, 341–344); cited in Schrader, HTR 2017, 384–86.
49. Egeria, *Itinerarium* 29.4–5, trans. J. Wilkinson, *Egeria's Travels*, 3rd ed. (Warminster, 1999). For Schrader's framing of Egeria within the Martha argument, see her Westar Institute lecture *Was Martha of Bethany Added to the Gospel of John?* and her conversation with D. Butler Bass, *Elizabeth Schrader on Preaching John 11* (The Cottage, March 20, 2023).
50. Schrader, HTR 2017, 371–73 (Figures 7 and 8).
51. R. Bultmann, *Das Evangelium des Johannes*, 10th ed. (Göttingen, 1941), 309; cited in Schrader, HTR 2017, 380 n. 64.
52. 1 Corinthians 15:44.
53. K. L. King, *The Gospel of Mary of Magdala* (Santa Rosa, CA, 2003).
54. W. Assad, eyewitness to the Zeitoun apparition (1968–69) and father-in-law of author A. Assad, personal communications with the author, over many years.
55. S. L. Zimdars-Swartz, *Encountering Mary* (Princeton, 1991), chs. 1–2.
56. A. Heo, "The Virgin Made Visible," *Comparative Studies in Society and History* 54, no. 2 (2012): 361–91; P. Zaki, *Our Lord's Mother Visits Egypt in 1968 & 1969* (Cairo, 1977).

Chapter 5: Wells Cathedral

1. Revelation 5:5.
2. T. Bree, *The Cosmos in Stone* (Bath, 2023).
3. Bernard of Clairvaux, *De consideratione* 5.13.
4. A. Kateusz, *Mary and Early Christian Women* (Cham, 2019).
5. M. Starbird, *Mary Magdalene, Bride in Exile* (Rochester, VT, 2005), 127–30.
6. Congregation for Divine Worship and the Discipline of the Sacraments, decree *Apostolorum Apostola*, 3 June 2016 (published 10 June 2016).
7. E. Van Der Zee, *Wells Cathedral*, 2nd ed. (Wells, Somerset, UK, 2017), 122.

8. Revelation 22:16.
9. Exodus 22:18.
10. D. Wolkstein and S. N. Kramer, *Inanna, Queen of Heaven and Earth* (New York, 1983), 106, xvi.

Chapter 6: Wisdom & Her Serpent

1. 1 Kings 10:1; cf. 2 Chronicles 9:1.
2. 1 Kings 10:3, 10:7, 10:10.
3. Wisdom of Solomon 7:22–23.
4. J. B. Connelly, *Portrait of a Priestess* (Princeton, NJ, 2007).
5. B. Horayot 12a; b. Yoma 52b.
6. P. Fredriksen, *Ancient Christianities* (Princeton, NJ, 2024).
7. J. D. Crossan and J. L. Reed, *Excavating Jesus* (New York, 2001), ch. 1.
8. Numenius of Apamea, fragment preserved in Clement of Alexandria, *Stromateis* 1.22.150.4; Eusebius, *Praeparatio Evangelica* 11.10.14. On the wider Jewish/Greek synthesis at Alexandria, Fredriksen, *Ancient Christianities.*
9. S. B. Pomeroy, *Women in Hellenistic Egypt* (New York, 1984); S. Schiff, *Cleopatra* (New York, 2010).
10. Josephus, *Antiquities* 18.81–84; *Against Apion* 2.282; Juvenal, *Satires* 14.96–106; Tacitus, *Histories* 5.5; Epictetus, *Discourses* 2.9.20.
11. B. J. Brooten, *Women Leaders in the Ancient Synagogue* (Atlanta, 1982); T. Ilan, *Jewish Women in Greco-Roman Palestine* (Tübingen, 1995; reissue 1996); Fredriksen, *Ancient Christianities.*
12. B. Porten, *Archives from Elephantine* (Berkeley, 1968); R. S. Bagnall and R. Cribiore, *Women's Letters from Ancient Egypt, 300 BC–AD 800* (Ann Arbor, 2006).
13. Philo, *De specialibus legibus* 3.29.
14. R. S. Kraemer, *When Aseneth Met Joseph* (New York, 1998).
15. Josephus, *Antiquities* 13.62–73; *Jewish War* 7.420–432.
16. Hosea 11:1; Matthew 2:15.
17. Connelly, *Portrait of a Priestess*, esp. chs. 2–5 on the regional variation of Mediterranean female priesthoods.
18. On Enheduanna: B. De Shong Meador, *Inanna, Lady of Largest Heart* (Austin, 2000). On Minoan Crete: N. Marinatos, *Minoan Religion* (Columbia, 1993). On the priestess of Athena Polias: Connelly, *Portrait of a Priestess*, ch. 2. On the Artemision: L. R. LiDonnici, *The Epigraphical Evidence of the Festival of the Artemis Ephesia* (Atlanta, 1992).
19. M. Beard, "The Sexual Status of Vestal Virgins," *Journal of Roman Studies* 70 (1980): 12–27.
20. B. S. Lesko, *The Great Goddesses of Egypt* (Norman, 1999).
21. Hermetic *Asclepius* 24–26, in B. P. Copenhaver, trans., *Hermetica* (Cambridge, 1992).
22. L. Manniche, *Sacred Luxuries* (Ithaca, NY, 1999).
23. S. Cauville, *Dendara*, 3 vols. (Cairo, 1997–1998).
24. O. Goldwasser, "How the Alphabet Was Born from Hieroglyphs," *Biblical Archaeology Review* 36, no. 2 (March/April 2010): 40–53.
25. R. E. Witt, *Isis in the Ancient World* (Baltimore, 1971; reissue 1997); G. Pinch, *Egyptian Mythology* (Oxford, 2002).

26. Plutarch, *De Iside et Osiride* 12–19.
27. Mark 14:3.
28. T. N. D. Mettinger, *King and Messiah* (Lund, 1976).
29. J. J. Collins, *The Scepter and the Star*, 2nd ed. (Grand Rapids, MI, 2010).
30. L. W. Hurtado, *Lord Jesus Christ* (Grand Rapids, MI, 2003).
31. R. Bauckham, *The Testimony of the Beloved Disciple* (Grand Rapids, MI, 2007), on the sandwich-composition argument and Judas.
32. Luke 7:38; John 12:3.
33. John 13:16; on the verb *tithēsin ta himatia* echoing Jesus's laying down his life, R. E. Brown, *The Gospel According to John*, vol. 2 (Garden City, NY, 1970).
34. Luke 7:47.
35. Ilan, *Jewish Women in Greco-Roman Palestine*; on the *sotah* ritual, Numbers 5:18; on hair-uncovering as grounds for divorce, Mishnah Ketubot 7:6.
36. Bauckham, *The Testimony of the Beloved Disciple*, 184, 186, 188, arguing that the anointing scene typologically presents Jesus as the anointed Davidic king; 1 Samuel 16:1–13.
37. Manniche, *Sacred Luxuries*, 47–55, on the seven sacred oils of the Egyptian temples.
38. Mark 14:3 (*nardou pistikēs*); John 12:3 (*murou nardou pistikēs*); on the Indian-to-Mediterranean nard trade, L. Casson, *The Periplus Maris Erythraei* (Princeton, 1989), §§39, 48.
39. Plutarch, *De Iside et Osiride* 80.
40. P. Dioscorides, *De materia medica* 1.6–7, in L. Y. Beck, trans., *Pedanius Dioscorides of Anazarbus*, 3rd ed. (Hildesheim, 2017).
41. Song of Songs 1:12; 4:13–14.
42. Mishnah Yadayim 3:5; M. H. Pope, *Song of Songs* Anchor Bible 7C (Garden City, NY, 1977), 19–23.
43. H. N. Parker, "Women and Medicine," in *A Companion to Women in the Ancient World* (Malden, MA, 2012), 107–124.
44. Bernard of Clairvaux, *Sermones super Cantica Canticorum*, Sermon 2.
45. M. Baigent, R. Leigh, and H. Lincoln, *Holy Blood, Holy Grail* (London, 1982); M. Starbird, *The Woman with the Alabaster Jar* (Santa Fe, NM, 1993); D. Brown, *The Da Vinci Code* (New York, 2003).
46. Josephus, *Jewish War* 2.119–161.
47. John 20:13, 15; John 2:4; John 19:26.
48. Gospel of Philip 59:6–11 and 63:32–64:5, in M. Meyer, ed., *The Nag Hammadi Scriptures* (New York, 2007), 161–187. On *koinōnos* and Mary's relationship to Jesus: K. L. King, *The Gospel of Mary of Magdala* (Santa Rosa, CA, 2003).
49. K. L. King, "'Jesus Said to Them, "My Wife . . . "'" announced 18 September 2012 at the International Congress of Coptic Studies, Rome. On the forgery determination: A. Sabar, "The Unbelievable Tale of Jesus's Wife," *The Atlantic* (July/August 2016).
50. J. Schaberg, in D. Burstein and A. J. de Keijzer, eds., *Secrets of Mary Magdalene* (New York, 2006), 157.
51. M. Eliade, *Patterns in Comparative Religion*, trans. R. Sheed (London, 1958), ch. 7.
52. S. L. Budin, *The Myth of Sacred Prostitution in Antiquity* (Cambridge, 2008); Herodotus, *Histories* 1.199.

53. On the Eleusinian rites: W. Burkert, *Ancient Mystery Cults* (Cambridge, MA, 1987). On the Isis cult: S. A. Takács, *Isis and Sarapis in the Roman World* (Leiden, 1995). On the Bacchanalia: J.-M. Pailler, *Bacchanalia* (Rome, 1988).
54. Budin, *The Myth of Sacred Prostitution in Antiquity*, on the absence of evidence for sacred prostitution as institution rather than literary trope.
55. S. Schiff, *Cleopatra* (New York, 2010).
56. Pistis Sophia, Book 1, in C. Schmidt and V. MacDermot, eds., *Pistis Sophia*, Nag Hammadi Studies 9 (Leiden, 1978).
57. Dialogue of the Savior (NHC III,5) 139:11–13.
58. Acts of Philip, Act VIII §§94–95 and Martyrdom §126.
59. Gospel of Philip 59:6–11. On *koinōnos* in the New Testament: Philemon 17; Luke 5:10; Hebrews 10:33.
60. Gospel of Thomas, logion 114.
61. King, *Gospel of Mary of Magdala*, 145–156; P. Perkins, *The Gnostic Dialogue* (New York, 1980), 131–143.
62. Justin Martyr, *Dialogue with Trypho* 8; Clement of Alexandria, *Stromateis* I and VI. S. K. Stowers, "Does Pauline Christianity Resemble a Hellenistic Philosophy?," in *Paul Beyond the Judaism / Hellenism Divide* (Louisville, KY, 2001), 81–102; Acts 17:18–34.
63. D. Laertius, *Lives of Eminent Philosophers* 8.8; Plutarch, *Moralia* 437d–438d.
64. M. E. Waithe, ed., *A History of Women Philosophers*, vol. 1, *Ancient Women Philosophers, 600 B.C.–500 A.D.* (Dordrecht, 1987); on Aspasia, M. M. Henry, *Prisoner of History* (Oxford, 1995); on Diotima, Plato, *Symposium* 201d–212c; on Hipparchia, Diogenes Laertius 6.96–98; on Hypatia, M. Dzielska, *Hypatia of Alexandria*, trans. F. Lyra (Cambridge, MA, 1995).
65. J. E. Taylor, *Jewish Women Philosophers of First-Century Alexandria* (Oxford, 2003); Philo, *De vita contemplativa*.
66. M. Eliade, *Patterns in Comparative Religion*, trans. R. Sheed (London, 1958), §52 ("The Moon and the Serpent").
67. Euripides, *Medea*, line 285; cited in Schiff, *Cleopatra*.
68. Ovid, *Metamorphoses* 4.617–620; S. R. Wilk, *Medusa*.
69. Metternich Stela, Spell 5, Metropolitan Museum of Art, accession no. 50.85 (greywacke, c. 360–342 BCE). Translation in M. Bommas, "I Am Isis" in *Egypt and the Classical World* (Los Angeles, 2022), open access at getty.edu/publications/egypt-classical-world/03/.
70. Fredriksen, *Ancient Christianities*; T. S. de Bruyn, *Making Amulets Christian* (Oxford, 2017); J. Naveh and S. Shaked, *Amulets and Magic Bowls* (Jerusalem, 1985).
71. Wisdom of Solomon 7:26–27.

Chapter 7: The Fields of Somerset

1. Attributed to Isadora Duncan.
2. C. de Troyes, *Perceval, ou le Conte du Graal* (c. 1181–1190); Geoffrey of Monmouth, *Historia Regum Britanniae* (c. 1136); R. de Boron, *Joseph d'Arimathie* (c. 1191–1202). For a scholarly overview, R. Barber, *The Holy Grail* (London, 2004).

3. Gerald of Wales (Giraldus Cambrensis), *De principis instructione* (c. 1193); also *Speculum Ecclesiae*.
4. M. Watterson, *Mary Magdalene Revealed* (Carlsbad, CA, 2019), xiv. Watterson herself credits the phrase "farther up and further in" to C. S. Lewis, *The Chronicles of Narnia* (Watterson, *Mary Magdalene Revealed*, 63).

Chapter 8: The Beloved Disciple

1. John 13:21–23.
2. John 13:24, 26.
3. D. Brown, *The Da Vinci Code* (New York, 2003); L. Picknett and C. Prince, *The Templar Revelation* (London, 1997); M. Baigent, R. Leigh, and H. Lincoln, *Holy Blood, Holy Grail* (New York, 1982); M. Starbird, *The Woman with the Alabaster Jar* (Santa Fe, 1993).
4. E. McCurdy, *Leonardo da Vinci's Note-Books* (New York, 1908), 55 (MS E 43 r.).
5. Grandes Heures d'Anne de Bretagne, BnF MS Lat. 9474, f. 201v; É. Mâle, introduction to *Les Heures d'Anne de Bretagne*, *Verve*, vol. IV, nos. 14–15 (Paris, 1946).
6. R. Kysar, *John, the Maverick Gospel*, 3rd ed. (Louisville, 2007).
7. S. M. Schneiders, *Written That You May Believe*, rev. and exp. ed. (New York, 2003), 73.
8. P. F. Ellis, *The Genius of John* (Collegeville, MN, 1984); B. Barnhart, *The Good Wine* (New York, 1993); Schneiders, *WTYMB*, 29.
9. John 1:1, 4–5.
10. J. D. G. Dunn, *Christology in the Making*, 2nd ed. (London, 1989).
11. John 19:35; 21:24.
12. R. E. Brown, *The Community of the Beloved Disciple* (New York, 1979); Brown, *The Gospel According to John*, Anchor Bible 29 and 29A, 2 vols. (Garden City, NY, 1966–1970).
13. Irenaeus of Lyon, *Against Heresies* 3.1.1; 3.11.8.
14. Eusebius of Caesarea, *Ecclesiastical History*.
15. Papias of Hierapolis, *Expositions of the Sayings of the Lord* (fragmentary).
16. Justin Martyr, *Dialogue with Trypho* 81.4; 88; *First Apology* 61; C. E. Hill, *The Johannine Corpus in the Early Church*.
17. Theophilus of Antioch, *Ad Autolycum* 2.22; Polycrates of Ephesus, letter to Victor I of Rome (c. 190).
18. Muratorian Fragment, lines 9–16; B. M. Metzger, *The Canon of the New Testament* (Oxford, 1987).
19. Mark 5:37; Mark 9:2–8 par.; Mark 14:33 par.; Mark 3:17; Mark 10:35–45; Luke 9:51–56.
20. D. Trobisch, *The First Edition of the New Testament* (New York, 2000), 52–54.
21. John 21:25.
22. Trobisch, *First Edition*, 52–54 (note 20); R. Bultmann, *Das Evangelium des Johannes* (Göttingen, 1941); Brown, *Gospel of John* (note 12); R. Bauckham, *The Testimony of the Beloved Disciple* (Grand Rapids, MI, 2007); Bauckham, *Jesus and the Eyewitnesses*, 2nd ed. (Grand Rapids, MI, 2017); on Sinaiticus, B. M. Metzger, *A Textual Commentary on the Greek New Testament*, 2nd ed. (Stuttgart, 1994), 220.
23. Revelation 1:9.

24. Dionysius of Alexandria.
25. R. H. Charles, *A Critical and Exegetical Commentary on the Revelation of St. John*, 2 vols., International Critical Commentary (Edinburgh, 1920), R. E. Brown, *An Introduction to the New Testament* (New York, 1997); A. Y. Collins, *The Apocalypse* (Wilmington, DE, 1979); D. E. Aune, *Revelation*, 3 vols. (Dallas, 1997–1998); B. D. Ehrman, *The New Testament*, 7th ed. (New York, 2020).
26. Irenaeus, *Against Heresies* 3.16.5; 3.16.8.
27. R. E. Brown, *The Epistles of John* (Garden City, NY, 1982); Ehrman, *New Testament* (note 25).
28. John 1:35–40; Brown, *Gospel of John* (note 12); Brown, *Community* (note 12).
29. John 12:1–8; Brown, *Gospel of John* (note 12).
30. On *kolpos* at John 13:23 and its echo with John 1:18, Brown, *Gospel of John* (note 12).
31. John 13:34.
32. John 19:26–27.
33. John 20:1–10.
34. John 21:1–14.
35. John 14:15.
36. John 13:1–11.
37. John 13:36–38.
38. John 21:15–17.
39. John 21:18.
40. John 21:19.
41. Papyrus 66 (P66), c. 200 CE, Bibliotheca Bodmeriana, Cologny; Codex Vaticanus, mid-fourth century, Biblioteca Apostolica Vaticana, MS Vat. gr. 1209; Codex Sinaiticus, mid-fourth century, British Library, Add MS 43725.
42. John 21:20–22.
43. John 21:22–23.
44. Brown, *Community* (note 12), 31–34.
45. F. V. Filson, "Who Was the Beloved Disciple?," *Journal of Biblical Literature* 68, no. 2 (1949): 83–88; J. H. Charlesworth, *The Beloved Disciple* (Valley Forge, PA, 1995); M. W. G. Stibbe, *John as Storyteller* (Cambridge, 1994).
46. John 18:15–16; Brown, *Gospel of John* (note 12).
47. Schneiders, *WTYMB* (note 7), ch. 6 "Women in the Fourth Gospel" (93–114), esp. p. 99; "alter ego," p. 251.
48. E. Schrader, "Was Martha of Bethany Added to the Fourth Gospel in the Second Century?," *Harvard Theological Review* 110, no. 3 (2017): 360–392.
49. *Oxford English Dictionary*, 3rd ed., s.v. "maudlin"; Gregory the Great, Homily 33 (on Luke 7:36–50).
50. Gospel of Philip 59:6–11 (the three Marys); 63:32–64:9 (the kiss / "loved her more than all the disciples"); text and translation in B. Layton, *The Gnostic Scriptures* (New York, 1987); also in J. M. Robinson, ed., *The Nag Hammadi Library in English*, 3rd ed. (San Francisco, 1990); on Greek *koinōnos*, see Layton ad loc.
51. Gospel of Mary 10:1–6 (Peter's "Sister, we know that the Savior loved you more than all other women"); Pistis Sophia, ch. 17 ff. (the Mary–Peter contrast); K. L. King, *The Gospel of Mary of Magdala*.

52. R. K. Jusino, "Mary Magdalene," *Southern Cross Review*, no. 37 (1998); Schneiders, *WTYMB* (note 7), 233–254; King, *Gospel of Mary* (note 51); S. Parkhouse, *Eschatology and the Saviour* (Cambridge, 2019); E. A. de Boer, *The Gospel of Mary* (London, 2004).
53. C. Setzer, "Excellent Women," *Journal of Biblical Literature* 116, no. 2 (1997): 259–272, cited in Jusino (note 52).
54. Schneiders, *WTYMB* (note 7), 233–254 (on masculine *huios* at John 19:26).
55. Schneiders, *WTYMB* (note 7), 243.
56. Ibid., 250–254.
57. Brown, *Community* (note 12).
58. Schneiders, *WTYMB* (note 7), 42.
59. John 4:10–14, 26.
60. Irenaeus, *Against Heresies* 3.11.7; Tertullian, *De praescriptione haereticorum* 38.
61. Clement of Alexandria, *Stromateis* 4.9; Origen of Alexandria, *Commentary on the Gospel of John*; Heracleon.
62. Irenaeus, *Against Heresies* 1.8.5; 1 Timothy 6:20; full Greek title: *Ἔλεγχος καὶ ἀνατροπὴ τῆς ψευδωνύμου γνώσεως.*
63. Gospel of Philip 63:32–64:9; Layton (note 50).
64. B. W. Bacon, *The Gospel of the Hellenists* (New York, 1933); J. N. Sanders, *The Fourth Gospel in the Early Church* (Cambridge, 1943); E. C. Hoskyns, *The Fourth Gospel* (London, 1940); Hill, *Johannine Corpus* (note 16); A. D. DeConick, *Voices of the Mystics*, JSNTSup 157 (London, 2001).
65. Eusebius, *Hist. eccl.* 2.16.
66. Brown, *Epistles of John* (note 27); E. Pagels, *The Gnostic Gospels* (New York, 1979).
67. Schneiders, *WTYMB* (note 7), 245.
68. Ibid., 245.
69. Bauckham, *Testimony of the Beloved Disciple* (note 22); Bauckham, *Jesus and the Eyewitnesses* (note 22); Schneiders, *WTYMB* (note 7); Barnhart, *The Good Wine* (note 8).
70. Schneiders, *WTYMB* (note 7), 88.
71. R. Pernoud and M. Clin, *Joan of Arc*, trans. J. duQ. Adams (New York, 1998); L. J Taylor, *The Virgin Warrior* (New Haven, 2009).

Chapter 9: Basilica San Clemente

1. L. Byron, *Childe Harold's Pilgrimage*, Canto IV, stanza 145, in J. J. McGann, ed., *The Complete Poetical Works*, vol. 2 (Oxford, 1980). The lines descend from a Latin proverb reported by Bede of Anglo-Saxon pilgrims and quoted by E. Gibbon, *The Decline and Fall of the Roman Empire*, ch. 71.
2. N. Hawthorne, *The Marble Faun, or, The Romance of Monte Beni* (Boston, 1860), ch. 16, "A Moonlight Ramble."
3. J. E. B. Lloyd, "The Building History of the Medieval Church of S. Clemente in Rome," *Journal of the Society of Architectural Historians* 45, no. 3 (September 1986): 197–223.
4. Gregory the Great, Homily 33 (on Luke 7:36–50).
5. J. Osborne, "Early Medieval Painting in San Clemente, Rome," *Gesta* 20, no. 2 (1981): 299–310. On the 1857 Mullooly discovery, Basilica di San Clemente, "The Frescos of the Lower Basilica."

6. L. E. Boyle, O.P., *A Short Guide to St Clement's, Rome* (Rome, n.d.).
7. John 14:27: "Peace I leave with you; my peace I give you. I do not give to you as the world gives. Do not let your hearts be troubled and do not be afraid."
8. Ephesians 6:15: "and with your feet fitted with the readiness that comes from the gospel of peace."
9. C. P. Estés, *Women Who Run with the Wolves* (New York, 1992), 230–275; and *The Red Shoes: On Torment and the Recovery of Soul Life*, audiobook (Louisville, CO).

Chapter 10: Of Pinecones and Peacocks

1. A. M. Carruba, *La Lupa Capitolina* (Rome, 2006).
2. H. Belting, *Likeness and Presence*, trans. E. Jephcott (Chicago, 1994); on the 2018 Vatican Museums restoration of the Salus Populi Romani panel.
3. Irenaeus of Lyon, *Adversus Haereses* 3.1.1.
4. D. Trobisch, *On the Origin of Christian Scripture* (Minneapolis, 2023).
5. D. Trobisch, *The First Edition of the New Testament* (Oxford, 2000), and *On the Origin of Christian Scripture* (Minneapolis, 2023); M. Vinzent, *Marcion and the Dating of the Synoptic Gospels* (Leuven, 2014); N. E. Livesey, *The Letters of Paul in their Roman Literary Context* (Cambridge, 2024).
6. Josephus, *Antiquities of the Jews* 20.9.1 (the "James, the brother of Jesus" passage) and 18.3.3 (the Testimonium Flavianum); for the modern scholarly framing, P. Fredriksen, *When Christians Were Jews* (New Haven, 2018).
7. C. Bourgeault, *The Meaning of Mary Magdalene* (Boston, 2010), 35.
8. Romans 16:1–7, 16:12, and Philippians 4:2.
9. Pliny the Younger, *Epistles* 10.96; Origen, *Contra Celsum* 5.62.
10. J. K. Elliott, *The Apocryphal New Testament* (Oxford, 1993); F. Bovon, "Mary Magdalene in the *Acts of Philip*," in *Which Mary? Marys in Early Christian Tradition* (Atlanta, 2002); *The Life of Saint Nino*, trans. M. Wardrop (Oxford, 1900).
11. A. Kateusz, *Mary and Early Christian Women* (Cham, 2019).
12. E. Pagels, *The Gnostic Gospels* (New York, 1979), 91.
13. K. L. King, *The Gospel of Mary of Magdala* (Santa Rosa, CA, 2003).
14. A. Roberts, *Hathor Rising* (Rochester, VT, 1997).
15. P. Fredriksen, *Ancient Christianities* (Princeton, 2024), 5.
16. 1 Corinthians 14:34–35; on the disputed authenticity of the passage, G. Fee, *The First Epistle to the Corinthians*, rev. ed. (Grand Rapids, MI, 2014).
17. Tertullian, *De Virginibus Velandis* 9.1, and *De Cultu Feminarum* 1.1.
18. King, *Gospel of Mary of Magdala*.
19. Matthew 16:18; on the early manuscript witness, B. Metzger and B. Ehrman, *The Text of the New Testament*, 4th ed. (New York, 2005).
20. B. D. Ehrman, *Forged* (New York, 2011).
21. Eusebius of Caesarea, *Historia Ecclesiastica* 2.25.8, quoting Dionysius of Corinth.
22. A. G. Brock, *Mary Magdalene, The First Apostle* (Cambridge, MA, 2003).
23. Trobisch, *Origin of Christian Scripture*, 134–135.
24. Irenaeus, *Adversus Haereses* 3.3.2 (apostolic succession), 3.11.7 (Valentinian use of John), 3.11.8 (the fourfold gospel), 3.14.1 (Luke as Paul's companion). On the late attestation of Acts: R. Pervo, *Dating Acts* (Santa Rosa, CA, 2006).

25. R. H. Connolly, *Didascalia Apostolorum* (Oxford, 1929), ch. 15.
26. E. Duffy, *Saints and Sinners*, 4th ed. (New Haven, 2014).
27. For Canon 11 of the Council of Laodicea (363–364): H. R. Percival, ed., *The Seven Ecumenical Councils*, NPNF, ser. 2, vol. 14. For the persistence of women in eucharistic functions into ninth-century Gaul: G. Macy, *The Hidden History of Women's Ordination* (Oxford, 2008).
28. Pagels, *Gnostic Gospels*, 155.
29. K. G. Elkins, *Mary, Mother of Martyrs* (Indianapolis, 2018).
30. For Perpetua: D. Elliott, *The Bride of Christ Goes to Hell* (Philadelphia, 2012), Kindle p. 30. For Eulalia of Barcelona: Prudentius, *Peristephanon* 3 ("Hymn to the Martyr Eulalia"), trans. H. J. Thomson, LCL 387, vol. II (Cambridge, MA, 1953); Augustine of Hippo, *Sermon 313* (on the feast of Saint Eulalia).
31. Ambrose of Milan, *De Virginibus* 1.6; Jerome, *Letter 22 to Eustochium*, §20, in NPNF, ser. 2, vol. 6; Cyprian of Carthage, *De Habitu Virginum* 22.
32. Tertullian, *De Virginibus Velandis* 13; Cyprian of Carthage, *De Habitu Virginum*.
33. Elliott, *Bride of Christ Goes to Hell*.
34. J. Ramirez, *Femina* (New York, 2022), 42–44 (on Theodora). For Pulcheria, Macrina, and Olympias: Socrates Scholasticus, *Ecclesiastical History*; Sozomen, *Ecclesiastical History*; Gregory of Nyssa, *Life of Macrina*.
35. Ramirez, *Femina*, 36–45.
36. H. E. Mayer, "Studies in the History of Queen Melisende of Jerusalem," *Dumbarton Oaks Papers* 26 (1972): 93–182.
37. Ramirez, *Femina*, 169–218.
38. Elliott, *Bride of Christ Goes to Hell*. The quoted phrase "offered select women an unprecedented degree of freedom and privilege in the church" is Elliott's.
39. *The Book of Margery Kempe*, ed. L. Staley (Kalamazoo, MI, 1996), Book I, ch. 5. For Dorothea of Montau: Elliott, *Bride of Christ Goes to Hell*.
40. Ramirez, *Femina*, 311–312 (on Birgitta); Elliott, *Bride of Christ Goes to Hell*, Kindle pp. 215–217 (on Catherine of Siena).
41. M. Porete, *The Mirror of Simple Souls*, trans. E. L. Babinsky (New York, 1993); Elliott, *Bride of Christ Goes to Hell*, Kindle pp. 277–279.
42. P. F. Cholakian and R. C. Cholakian, *Marguerite de Navarre* (New York, 2006); M. Shell, ed., *Elizabeth's Glass* (Lincoln, NE, 1993).
43. J. Lefèvre d'Étaples, *De Maria Magdalena et triduo Christi disceptatio* (Paris, early 1518). On Lefèvre's argument and the debates that followed, see S. M. Porrer, ed. and trans., *Jacques Lefèvre d'Étaples and the Three Maries Debates* (Geneva, 2009).
44. S. O'Shea, *The Perfect Heresy* (New York, 2000); Ramirez, *Femina*, 222–233.
45. O'Shea, *Perfect Heresy*, 42.
46. The "Kill them all; the Lord knows those who are his" line is attributed to Arnaud Amalric in Caesarius of Heisterbach's *Dialogus Miraculorum* (early thirteenth century); on the disputed historicity of the attribution, O'Shea, *Perfect Heresy*.
47. O'Shea, *Perfect Heresy*, 42.
48. N. Cohn, *Europe's Inner Demons*, rev. ed. (Sussex, 1993), ch. 8.
49. B. Ehrenreich and D. English, *Witches, Midwives, and Nurses*, 2nd ed. (New York, 2010).
50. Ibid.

51. J. Chapa, ed., "5577. Christian Theological Text," in *The Oxyrhynchus Papyri*, vol. LXXXVII (London, 2023); S. Parkhouse, "'Therefore I Say, Mary,'" *Novum Testamentum* 66, no. 3 (2024): 382–401; E. Schrader Polczer, "'An Image of Eternal Incorruptible Light,'" *Journal of Early Christian Studies* 33, no. 1 (2025): 151–168; King, *Gospel of Mary of Magdala*; Matthew 3:11 and Luke 3:16.

Chapter 11: Santa Maria Maddalena

1. On the history of the church: Santa Maria Maddalena dei Battuti began as a fourteenth-century chapel of the Confraternita dei Disciplinati (first documented 1403), serving Abruzzese expatriates and *transumanza* shepherds in Rome. The Magdalene dedication followed the 1279 Saint-Maximin relic discovery in Provence. In 1586 Pope Sixtus V transferred the church to Camillo de Lellis and the newly recognized Camillians as their mother house; the rebuild was completed in 1699, and Giuseppe Sardi added the Rococo façade in 1735. The 1732 vault and apse cycle (notes 2 and 6) preceded Camillus's beatification (1742) and canonization (1746) by Benedict XIV. L. Mortari, *S. Maria Maddalena* (Rome, 1987).
2. M. Cerruti (1663–1749), *Stories of the Life of Saint Mary Magdalene*, fresco cycle, central vault of Santa Maria Maddalena in Campo Marzio, Rome, 1732.
3. M. Rocca (1671–1751), *Mary Magdalene Penitent (Mary Magdalene Adoring the Cross)*, high altarpiece, oil on canvas, Santa Maria Maddalena in Campo Marzio, 1698; with É. Parrocel (1696–1776), *Saint Camillus de Lellis Presented to the Holy Trinity by Saint Mary Magdalene*, dome fresco, 1739.
4. V. Garine, Magdalene fresco cycle, Monastère Orthodoxe Saint-Michel-du-Var (Var, Provence; French Orthodox community founded 1981), Byzantine style, 2002–2017.
5. K. McGowan, *The Boleyn Heresy* (independently published, c. 2022), prologue (Kindle pp. 9–23); with W. A. Sibly and M. D. Sibly, trans. and ed., *The History of the Albigensian Crusade* (Woodbridge, 1998).
6. A. Milani (Bologna 1675 – Rome 1749), *The Preaching of Christ*, apse fresco, Santa Maria Maddalena in Campo Marzio, 1732 (commissioned by Father Costantini, Camillian Provincial of Rome).
7. S. Parkhouse, *Eschatology and the Saviour* (Cambridge, 2019), 137–138, on the mountain as the setting for the Gospel of Mary.
8. Gospel of Mary 7:1.
9. "Ma Chi Fu Veramente Maria Maddalena?" Pamphlet from Santa Maria Maddalena, Rome. August 2025.
10. M. Angelou, *I Know Why the Caged Bird Sings* (New York, 1969); the title descends from P. L. Dunbar, "Sympathy," in *Lyrics of the Hearthside* (New York, 1899).

Chapter 12: The Miraculous Catch

1. E. J. Watts, *Hypatia* (Oxford, 2017).
2. A. Cameron, "Isidore of Miletus and Hypatia," *Greek, Roman, and Byzantine Studies* 31 (1990): 103–127.
3. Socrates Scholasticus, *Ecclesiastical History* 7.15.
4. On Mary the Jewess: Zosimos of Panopolis, *Authentic Memoirs*.

5. On John 21 authorship —later-redactor position: R. E. Brown, *The Gospel According to John (xiii–xxi)* (New York, 1970), 1077–82. Redacted-but-integral position: P. S. Minear, "The Original Functions of John 21," *Journal of Biblical Literature* 102, no. 1 (1983): 85–98. Original-composition-by-the-Beloved-Disciple position: S. M. Schneiders, *Written That You May Believe* (New York, 2003), esp. ch. 11; R. Bauckham, *The Testimony of the Beloved Disciple* (Grand Rapids, MI, 2007), 271–84.
6. John 21:1–14; John 15:13.
7. Aristotle, *Metaphysics* 1.5 (986a22–b8).
8. J. Assmann, *Death and Salvation in Ancient Egypt*, trans. D. Lorton (Ithaca, NY, 2005); with C. Zivie-Coche, "Imentet," in D. B. Redford, ed., *The Oxford Encyclopedia of Ancient Egypt*, vol. 2 (Oxford, 2001), 156–57.
9. John 6:1–15; John 6:35, 51, 53.
10. Luke 5:1–11.
11. D. Trobisch, *The First Edition of the New Testament* (Oxford, 2000); A. G. Brock, *Mary Magdalene, the First Apostle* (Cambridge, MA, 2003), esp. chs. 1–2.
12. J. de Voragine, *The Golden Legend*, trans. W. G. Ryan (Princeton, 2012), "Saint Mary Magdalene."
13. S. K. Heyob, *The Cult of Isis Among Women in the Greco-Roman World* (Leiden, 1975).
14. R. E. Brown, *The Gospel According to John (i–xii)* (New York, 1966), Appendix IV: "Egō Eimi —'I AM,'" 533–38.
15. D. Wolkstein and S. N. Kramer, *Inanna, Queen of Heaven and Earth* (New York, 1983), 106, xvi.
16. C. R. Koester, *Symbolism in the Fourth Gospel*, 2nd ed. (Minneapolis, 2003), ch. 9.
17. R. Bultmann, *The Gospel of John*, trans. G. R. Beasley-Murray, R. W. N. Hoare, and J. K. Riches (Philadelphia, 1971), 218–37 (on John 6:51c–58 as later ecclesiastical redaction); originally *Das Evangelium des Johannes*, Kritisch-exegetischer Kommentar über das Neue Testament 2, 10th ed. (Göttingen, 1941).
18. B. Barnhart, *The Good Wine* (Mahwah, NJ, 1993).
19. On Papyrus 75 as the earliest surviving witness to John 21:11 (late second / early third century), and on Papyrus 66's damage at this line: L. W. Hurtado, *The Earliest Christian Artifacts* (Grand Rapids, MI, 2006).
20. H. Crouzel, *Origen*, trans. A. S. Worrall (San Francisco, 1989); with Augustine of Hippo, *Tractatus in Evangelium Joannis* 122.8 (cf. endnote 23) for the 153 interpretation as later transmitted.
21. Porphyry, *Vita Pythagorae* 25.
22. Jerome, *Commentariorum in Hiezechielem* 14.47.
23. Augustine of Hippo, *Tractatus in Evangelium Joannis* 122.8.
24. Gregory the Great, *Homiliae in Evangelia*, Homily 24.
25. Plutarch, *De Iside et Osiride* 42 (Moralia 367E).
26. Genesis 7:11 and 8:4.
27. Plutarch, *De Iside et Osiride*, ch. 13 (Moralia 356C) for the Osiris murder on 17 Athyr; ch. 18 (Moralia 357F) for the fourteen scattered parts; in Plutarch, *Moralia*, vol. V.
28. M. Gimbutas, *The Living Goddesses* (Berkeley, 1999).

29. Archimedes, *Measurement of a Circle* (*Kuklou Metresis*), Proposition 3.
30. Euclid, *Elements*, Book I, Proposition 1, in T. L. Heath, *The Thirteen Books of Euclid's Elements*, 2nd ed., 3 vols. (Cambridge, 1925; repr. New York: Dover, 1956), 1:241–42.
31. M. A. Murray, *The Osireion at Abydos*, British School of Archaeology in Egypt 9 (London, 1904).
32. *Avatamsaka Sutra (Flower Garland Sutra)*, trans. T. Cleary, *The Flower Ornament Scripture* (Boston, 1993).
33. K. L. King, *The Gospel of Mary of Magdala* (Santa Rosa, CA, 2003), 13–18 (translation of the surviving Greek and Coptic text).
34. E. A. de Boer, *The Gospel of Mary* (London, 2004), chs. 3–5.
35. Proverbs 8:34.
36. R. E. Brown, *The Gospel According to John (xiii–xxi)* (New York, 1970), 1071–72 ad loc.
37. R. O. Faulkner, *A Concise Dictionary of Middle Egyptian* (Oxford, 1962), 21 s.v. *imnt*, for the lexical equivalence of *imnt* (right) and *imnt* (west) in Middle Egyptian. Cf. endnote 8 for the broader Egyptian-theology sources (Assmann, Zivie-Coche).
38. R. O. Faulkner, trans., *The Ancient Egyptian Book of the Dead* (Austin, 1990), 149–51 (Spell 153A: "Spell for escaping from the catcher of fish"; Spell 153B: "Spell for escaping from the trap-net"). The modern spell numbering goes back to K. R. Lepsius, *Das Todtenbuch der Ägypter nach dem hieroglyphischen Papyrus in Turin* (Leipzig, 1842).
39. A. D. DeConick, *Holy Misogyny* (New York, 2011); B. A. Pearson, *Gnosticism, Judaism, and Egyptian Christianity* (Minneapolis, 1990); E. A. de Boer, *The Gospel of Mary* (London, 2004) (cf. note 34); E. Hornung, *The Secret Lore of Egypt*, trans. D. Lorton (Ithaca, NY, 2001).
40. S. Parkhouse, *Eschatology and the Saviour* (Cambridge, 2019).
41. R. Bauckham, *The Testimony of the Beloved Disciple* (Grand Rapids, MI, 2007), 271–84.
42. M. Starbird, *The Woman with the Alabaster Jar* (Santa Fe, NM, 1993), 50–53.
43. M. Manilius, *Astronomica* 2.435ff and 4.701.
44. *Gospel of Thomas*, Logion 107, NHC II,2.
45. *Gospel of Truth* 31:35–32:17.
46. *Gospel of Thomas*, Logion 3, NHC II,2.

Conclusion: A Jar of Hope

1. Song of Songs 4:7; the Latin epigraph (*Tota pulchra es, amica mea, et macula non est in te*, Cant. 4:7), *Biblia Sacra Vulgata*.
2. Revelation 12:1.
3. Revelation 12:3 and 12:9.
4. *Biblia Sacra Vulgata*, Genesis 3:15 —*ipsa conteret caput tuum*.

SELECTED BIBLIOGRAPHY

Mary Magdalene

Apostolos-Cappadona, Diane, *Mary Magdalene: A Visual History* (Collegeville, MN: Liturgical Press, 2018).

Bourgeault, Cynthia, *The Meaning of Mary Magdalene: Discovering the Woman at the Heart of Christianity* (Boston: Shambhala, 2010).

Brock, Ann Graham, *Mary Magdalene, the First Apostle: The Struggle for Authority* (Cambridge, MA: Harvard University Press, 2003).

de Boer, Esther A., *The Gospel of Mary: Beyond a Gnostic and a Biblical Mary Magdalene* (London: T&T Clark, 2004).

de Boer, Esther A., *The Mary Magdalene Cover-Up: The Sources Behind the Myth* (London: T&T Clark, 2007).

Ehrman, Bart D., *Peter, Paul, and Mary Magdalene: The Followers of Jesus in History and Legend* (New York: Oxford University Press, 2006).

Haskins, Susan, *Mary Magdalen: Myth and Metaphor* (New York: Harcourt Brace, 1993).

Jansen, Katherine Ludwig, *The Making of the Magdalen: Preaching and Popular Devotion in the Later Middle Ages* (Princeton: Princeton University Press, 2000).

King, Karen L., *The Gospel of Mary of Magdala: Jesus and the First Woman Apostle* (Santa Rosa, CA: Polebridge Press, 2003).

Leloup, Jean-Yves, *The Gospel of Mary Magdalene*, trans. Joseph Rowe (Rochester, VT: Inner Traditions, 2002).

Leloup, Jean-Yves, *The Sacred Embrace of Jesus and Mary: The Sexual Mystery at the Heart of the Christian Tradition*, trans. Joseph Rowe (Rochester, VT: Inner Traditions, 2006).

Malvern, Marjorie M., *Venus in Sackcloth: The Magdalen's Origins and Metamorphoses* (Carbondale: Southern Illinois University Press, 1975).

McDonald, Jan, *Mary Magdalene: Lost Goddess, Lost Gospels* (Chieveley, UK: Capall Bann, 2007).

Parkhouse, Sarah, *Eschatology and the Saviour: The 'Gospel of Mary' among Early Christian Dialogue Gospels* (Cambridge: Cambridge University Press, 2019).

Schaberg, Jane, in Dan Burstein and Arne J. de Keijzer, eds., *Secrets of Mary Magdalene: The Untold Story of History's Most Misunderstood Woman* (New York: Weinstein Books, 2006).

Schaberg, Jane, *The Resurrection of Mary Magdalene: Legends, Apocrypha, and the Christian Testament* (New York: Continuum, 2002).

Schaberg, Jane, with Melanie Johnson-DeBaufre, *Mary Magdalene Understood* (New York: Continuum, 2006).

Starbird, Margaret, *Magdalene's Lost Legacy: Symbolic Numbers and the Sacred Union in Christianity* (Rochester, VT: Bear & Company, 2003).

Starbird, Margaret, *Mary Magdalene, Bride in Exile* (Rochester, VT: Bear & Company, 2005).

Starbird, Margaret, *The Tarot Trumps and the Holy Grail: Great Secrets of the Middle Ages* (Boulder, CO: Woven Word Press, 2000).

Starbird, Margaret, *The Woman with the Alabaster Jar: Mary Magdalene and the Holy Grail* (Santa Fe, NM: Bear & Co., 1993).

Tuckett, Christopher, ed. and trans., *The Gospel of Mary* (Oxford: Oxford University Press, 2007).

Watterson, Meggan, *Mary Magdalene Revealed: The First Apostle, Her Feminist Gospel & the Christianity We Haven't Tried Yet* (Carlsbad, CA: Hay House, 2019).

Women in Christianity

Clendenen, Avis, *Experiencing Hildegard: Jungian Perspectives* (Wilmette, IL: Chiron Publications, 2009).

Dirvin, Joseph I., *Saint Catherine Labouré of the Miraculous Medal* (New York: Farrar, Straus and Cudahy, 1959; repr. Rockford, IL: TAN Books, 1992).

Ehrenreich, Barbara, and Deirdre English, *Witches, Midwives, and Nurses: A History of Women Healers*, 2nd ed. (New York: The Feminist Press at CUNY, 2010).

Elkins, Kathleen Gallagher, *Mary, Mother of Martyrs: How Motherhood Became Self-Sacrifice in Early Christianity* (Indianapolis: FSR Books, 2018).

Elliott, Dyan, *The Bride of Christ Goes to Hell: Metaphor and Embodiment in the Lives of Pious Women, 200–1500* (Philadelphia: University of Pennsylvania Press, 2012).

Estés, Clarissa Pinkola, *Untie the Strong Woman: Blessed Mother's Immaculate Love for the Wild Soul* (Boulder, CO: Sounds True, 2011).

Frymer-Kensky, Tikva, *Reading the Women of the Bible* (New York: Schocken, 2002).

Kateusz, Ally, *Mary and Early Christian Women: Hidden Leadership* (Cham, Switzerland: Palgrave Macmillan, 2019).

Limberis, Vasiliki, *Divine Heiress: The Virgin Mary and the Creation of Christian Constantinople* (London: Routledge, 1994).

Meyers, Carol, *Discovering Eve: Ancient Israelite Women in Context* (New York: Oxford University Press, 1988).

Parker, Julie Faith, *Eve Isn't Evil: Feminist Readings of the Bible to Upend Our Assumptions* (Grand Rapids, MI: Eerdmans, 2023).

Reid, Barbara E., *Choosing the Better Part? Women in the Gospel of Luke* (Collegeville, MN: Liturgical Press, 1996).

Rising, Melinda J., *Put the Blame on Eve: What Women Must Overcome to Feel Worthy* (Burdett, NY: Larson Publications, 2018).

Schüssler Fiorenza, Elisabeth, *In Memory of Her: A Feminist Theological Reconstruction of Christian Origins* (New York: Crossroad, 1983).
Trible, Phyllis, *God and the Rhetoric of Sexuality* (Philadelphia: Fortress, 1978).

Christianity

Baigent, Michael, Richard Leigh, and Henry Lincoln, *Holy Blood, Holy Grail* (London: Jonathan Cape, 1982).
Baigent, Michael, *The Jesus Papers: Exposing the Greatest Cover-Up in History* (San Francisco: HarperSanFrancisco, 2006).
Barnhart, Bruno, *The Good Wine: Reading John from the Center* (Mahwah, NJ: Paulist Press, 1993).
Bauckham, Richard, *The Testimony of the Beloved Disciple: Narrative, History, and Theology in the Gospel of John* (Grand Rapids, MI: Baker Academic, 2007).
Bauman, Lynn C., Ward J. Bauman, and Cynthia Bourgeault, *The Luminous Gospels: Thomas, Mary Magdalene, and Philip* (Telephone, TX: Praxis, 2008).
Bree, Tom, *The Cosmos in Stone: Sacred Geometry of a Master Mason* (Bath: Squeeze Press, 2023).
Cavallo, Adolfo Salvatore, *The Unicorn Tapestries at The Metropolitan Museum of Art* (New York: The Metropolitan Museum of Art, 1998).
Crossan, John Dominic, and Jonathan L. Reed, *Excavating Jesus: Beneath the Stones, Behind the Texts*, rev. ed. (New York: HarperOne, 2001).
Crossan, John Dominic, *The Historical Jesus: The Life of a Mediterranean Jewish Peasant* (San Francisco: HarperSanFrancisco, 1991).
de Voragine, Jacobus, *The Golden Legend: Readings on the Saints*, trans. William Granger Ryan (Princeton, NJ: Princeton University Press, 2012).
DeConick, April D., *Holy Misogyny: Why the Sex and Gender Conflicts in the Early Church Still Matter* (New York: Continuum, 2011).
Douglas-Klotz, Neil, *Revelations of the Aramaic Jesus: The Hidden Teachings on Life and Death* (Charlottesville, VA: Hampton Roads, 2022).
Duffy, Eamon, *Saints and Sinners: A History of the Popes*, 4th ed. (New Haven: Yale University Press, 2014).
Dunn, James D. G., *Christology in the Making: A New Testament Inquiry into the Origins of the Doctrine of the Incarnation*, 2nd ed. (London: SCM Press, 1989).
Ehrman, Bart D., *Forged: Writing in the Name of God —Why the Bible's Authors Are Not Who We Think They Are* (New York: HarperOne, 2011).
Ellis, Peter F., *The Genius of John: A Composition-Critical Commentary on the Fourth Gospel* (Collegeville, MN: Liturgical Press, 1984).
Fredriksen, Paula, *Ancient Christianities: The First Five Hundred Years* (Princeton, NJ: Princeton University Press, 2024).
Freeman, Margaret B., *The Unicorn Tapestries* (New York: Metropolitan Museum of Art / E. P. Dutton, 1976).
Guy, John, and Julia Fox, *Hunting the Falcon: Henry VIII, Anne Boleyn, and the Marriage That Shook Europe* (New York: HarperCollins, 2023).

Heiser, Michael S., *The Unseen Realm: Recovering the Supernatural Worldview of the Bible* (Bellingham, WA: Lexham Press, 2015).
Issa, Islam, *Alexandria: The City That Changed the World* (New York: Pegasus Books, 2023).
Klinghardt, Matthias, *The Oldest Gospel and the Formation of the Canonical Gospels* (Leuven: Peeters, 2021).
Kysar, Robert, *John, the Maverick Gospel*, 3rd ed. (Louisville, KY: Westminster John Knox Press, 2007).
Lane Fox, Robin, *Pagans and Christians* (New York: Alfred A. Knopf, 1987).
Leloup, Jean-Yves, *The Gospel of Philip: Jesus, Mary Magdalene, and the Gnosis of Sacred Union*, trans. Joseph Rowe (Rochester, VT: Inner Traditions, 2004).
Leloup, Jean-Yves, *The Gospel of Thomas: The Gnostic Wisdom of Jesus*, trans. Joseph Rowe (Rochester, VT: Inner Traditions, 2005).
Lincoln, Henry, *Key to the Sacred Pattern: The Untold Story of Rennes-le-Château* (Moreton-in-Marsh, UK: Windrush Press, 1997).
Meyer, Marvin, ed. and trans., *The Nag Hammadi Scriptures: The Revised and Updated Translation of Sacred Gnostic Texts Complete in One Volume* (New York: HarperOne, 2007).
Moss, Candida, *The Myth of Persecution: How Early Christians Invented a Story of Martyrdom* (New York: HarperOne, 2013).
O'Shea, Stephen, *The Perfect Heresy: The Revolutionary Life and Death of the Medieval Cathars* (New York: Walker & Co., 2000).
Pagels, Elaine, *Revelations: Visions, Prophecy, and Politics in the Book of Revelation* (New York: Viking, 2012).
Pagels, Elaine, *The Gnostic Gospels* (New York: Random House, 1979).
Pagels, Elaine, *The Origin of Satan: How Christians Demonized Jews, Pagans, and Heretics* (New York: Random House, 1995).
Pearson, Birger A., *Gnosticism, Judaism, and Egyptian Christianity* (Minneapolis: Fortress, 1990).
Römer, Thomas, *The Invention of God*, trans. Raymond Geuss (Cambridge, MA: Harvard University Press, 2015).
Schneiders, Sandra M., *Written That You May Believe: Encountering Jesus in the Fourth Gospel*, rev. ed. (New York: Crossroad, 2003).
Schüssler Fiorenza, Elisabeth, *The Power of the Word: Scripture and the Rhetoric of Empire* (Minneapolis: Fortress, 2007).
Silva, Freddy, *The Divine Blueprint: Temples, Power Places, and the Global Plan to Shape the Human Soul* (Invisible Temple, 2012).
Smith, Andrew Phillip, *The Lost Teachings of the Cathars: Their Beliefs and Practices* (London: Watkins, 2015).
Smith, Mark S., *The Early History of God: Yahweh and the Other Deities in Ancient Israel*, 2nd ed. (Grand Rapids, MI: Eerdmans, 2002).
Taussig, Hal, ed., *A New New Testament: A Bible for the Twenty-First Century Combining Traditional and Newly Discovered Texts* (Boston: Houghton Mifflin Harcourt, 2013).
Trobisch, David, *On the Origin of Christian Scripture: The Evolution of the New Testament Canon in the Second Century* (Minneapolis: Fortress Press, 2023).

Trobisch, David, *The First Edition of the New Testament* (Oxford: Oxford University Press, 2000).

Weis, René, *The Yellow Cross: The Story of the Last Cathars' Rebellion Against the Inquisition, 1290–1329* (New York: Alfred A. Knopf, 2001).

Williamson, John, *The Oak King, the Holly King, and the Unicorn: The Myths and Symbolism of the Unicorn Tapestries* (New York: Harper & Row, 1986).

The Sacred Feminine & the Ancient World

Ackerman, Susan, *Women and the Religion of Ancient Israel* (New Haven: Yale University Press, 2022).

Armstrong, Karen, *Sacred Nature: Restoring Our Ancient Bond with the Natural World* (New York: Alfred A. Knopf, 2022).

Assmann, Jan, *The Mind of Egypt: History and Meaning in the Time of the Pharaohs*, trans. Andrew Jenkins (New York: Metropolitan Books, 2002).

Assmann, Jan, *The Search for God in Ancient Egypt*, trans. David Lorton (Ithaca, NY: Cornell University Press, 2001).

Barrera, José María, *Dendera, Temple of Time: The Celestial Wisdom of Ancient Egypt*, foreword by Bob Brier (Rochester, VT: Inner Traditions, 2024).

Budin, Stephanie Lynn, *The Myth of Sacred Prostitution in Antiquity* (Cambridge: Cambridge University Press, 2008).

Campbell, Joseph, *Goddesses: Mysteries of the Feminine Divine*, ed. Safron Rossi (Novato, CA: New World Library, 2013).

Campbell, Joseph, *The Masks of God*, 4 vols. (New York: Viking, 1959–1968).

Campbell, Joseph, *Thou Art That: Transforming Religious Metaphor* (Novato, CA: New World Library, 2001).

Connelly, Joan Breton, *Portrait of a Priestess: Women and Ritual in Ancient Greece* (Princeton, NJ: Princeton University Press, 2007).

Dzielska, Maria, *Hypatia of Alexandria*, trans. F. Lyra (Cambridge, MA: Harvard University Press, 1995).

Ehrenreich, Barbara, and Deirdre English, *For Her Own Good: Two Centuries of the Experts' Advice to Women*, rev. ed. (New York: Anchor Books, 2005).

Ehrenreich, Barbara, *Dancing in the Streets: A History of Collective Joy* (New York: Metropolitan Books, 2006).

Eliade, Mircea, *A History of Religious Ideas*, 3 vols. (Chicago: University of Chicago Press, 1978–1985).

Eliade, Mircea, *Patterns in Comparative Religion*, trans. Rosemary Sheed (London: Sheed & Ward, 1958).

Estés, Clarissa Pinkola, *Women Who Run with the Wolves: Myths and Stories of the Wild Woman Archetype* (New York: Ballantine Books, 1992).

Faulkner, Raymond O., trans., *The Ancient Egyptian Book of the Dead*, rev. ed., ed. Carol Andrews (Austin: University of Texas Press, 1990).

Gimbutas, Marija, *The Living Goddesses*, ed. Miriam Robbins Dexter (Berkeley: University of California Press, 1999).

Graves-Brown, Carolyn, *Dancing for Hathor: Women in Ancient Egypt* (London: Continuum, 2010).

Heyob, Sharon Kelly, *The Cult of Isis Among Women in the Greco-Roman World* (Leiden: Brill, 1975).
Hornung, Erik, *Conceptions of God in Ancient Egypt: The One and the Many*, trans. John Baines (Ithaca, NY: Cornell University Press, 1982).
James, Sharon L., and Sheila Dillon, eds., *A Companion to Women in the Ancient World* (Malden, MA: Wiley-Blackwell, 2012).
Javane, Faith, and Dusty Bunker, *Numerology and the Divine Triangle* (West Chester, PA: Whitford Press, 1979).
Lesko, Barbara S., *The Great Goddesses of Egypt* (Norman: University of Oklahoma Press, 1999).
Manniche, Lise, *Sacred Luxuries: Fragrance, Aromatherapy, and Cosmetics in Ancient Egypt* (Ithaca, NY: Cornell University Press, 1999).
Meador, Betty De Shong, *Inanna, Lady of Largest Heart: Poems of the Sumerian High Priestess Enheduanna* (Austin: University of Texas Press, 2000).
O'Donohue, John, *Anam Cara: A Book of Celtic Wisdom* (New York: Cliff Street Books, 1997).
Pinch, Geraldine, *Magic in Ancient Egypt* (Austin: University of Texas Press, 1994).
Pomeroy, Sarah B., *Women in Hellenistic Egypt: From Alexander to Cleopatra* (New York: Schocken Books, 1984).
Ramirez, Janina, *Femina: A New History of the Middle Ages, Through the Women Written Out of It* (New York: Hanover Square Press, 2022).
Roberts, Alison, *Hathor Rising: The Power of the Goddess in Ancient Egypt* (Rochester, VT: Inner Traditions, 1997).
Schiff, Stacy, *Cleopatra: A Life* (New York: Little, Brown, 2010).
Starbird, Margaret, *Goddess in the Gospels: Reclaiming the Sacred Feminine* (Rochester, VT: Bear & Company, 1998).
Stone, Merlin, *When God Was a Woman* (New York: Harcourt Brace Jovanovich, 1976).
Watts, Edward J., *Hypatia: The Life and Legend of an Ancient Philosopher* (Oxford: Oxford University Press, 2017).
Wolkstein, Diane, and Samuel Noah Kramer, *Inanna, Queen of Heaven and Earth: Her Stories and Hymns from Sumer* (New York: Harper & Row, 1983).
Wolkstein, Diane, *The First Love Stories: From Isis and Osiris to Tristan and Iseult* (New York: HarperCollins, 1991).

Fiction

Brown, Dan, *The Da Vinci Code* (New York: Doubleday, 2003).
Hoffman, Alice, *The Dovekeepers* (New York: Scribner, 2011).
McGowan, Kathleen, *The Boleyn Heresy: Part One—The Time Will Come* (independently published, c. 2022).
McGowan, Kathleen, *The Expected One* (New York: Touchstone, 2006).

ABOUT THE AUTHORS

Alicia Assad is the mother of five children and lives with her husband in Bedford, New York. *Fishing on the Right Side of the Boat* is her first book. Her writing on resilience and motherhood has appeared in online publications, and she is the editor of *A Book of Love*. She holds a Master of Applied Positive Psychology from the University of Pennsylvania and a Bachelor of Science in Arts Administration, with a minor in Dance, from Wagner College.

Kelly Ingraham is the mother of four children and lives with her husband in Lyme, Connecticut. *Fishing on the Right Side of the Boat* is her first book. Her writing on spirituality and the history of religion has appeared online and on podcasts. She holds a Bachelor of Arts in History and Literature from Harvard University.

*

Fishing on the Right Side of the Boat was written, edited, and published by Alicia and Kelly under their imprint, La Suvera Press. La Suvera can be read two ways: as *souveraine*—sovereign—and as the *suvera*, the Tuscan cork oak, which survives being stripped of its bark and grows it back, season after season. The name honors feminine sovereignty, reclaimed through the power of stories. Read and follow Alicia and Kelly's work at themagdalenethread.com.

Printed in Dunstable, United Kingdom

86920375R00241